How to Read Chinese Poetry Workbook

How to Read Chinese Poetry Workbook

Jie Cui and Zong-qi Cai

Columbia University Press   New York

Columbia University Press

Publishers Since 1893

New York   Chichester, West Sussex

cup.columbia.edu

The Library of Congress has catalogued Zong-qi Cai, *How to Read Chinese Poetry: A Guided Anthology* as follows:

How to read Chinese poetry: a guided anthology / edited by Zong-qi Cai.

p. cm.

Chinese and English.

Includes bibliographical references and index.

ISBN 978-0-231-13940-3 (cloth : alk. paper)

ISBN 978-0-231-13941-0 (paper : alk. paper)

ISBN 978-0-231-51188-9 (electronic)

1. Chinese poetry—History and criticism. 2. Chinese poetry—Translations into English. I. Cai, Zong-qi. II. Title.

PL2308.H65 2007

895.1'1009—dc22

2007023263

Jie Cui and Zong-qi Cai, *How to Read Chinese Poetry Workbook*:

ISBN 978-0-231-15658-5 (paper : alk. paper)

ISBN 978-0-231-52722-4 (electronic)

目 录

Table of Contents

序 Preface   xi

符号与缩写 Symbols and Abbreviations   xv

第一单元 爱情：君子情思 Love: The Voice of Men

P01 《诗经 • 国风 • 关雎》" Guan, Guan," Cry the Ospreys (anon.)   1

P02 刘禹锡《杨柳枝》Willow Branch (Liu Yuxi)   5

P03 李商隐《无题 • 相见时难别亦难》Untitled (Li Shangyin)   6

P04 《南歌子》其一 To the Tune "Southern Tune," No. 1 (anon.)   9

练习 Exercises   10

第二单元 爱情：闺妇情语 Love: The Voice of Women

P05 《南歌子》其二 To the Tune "Southern Tune," No. 2 (anon.)   12

P06 汉乐府《有所思》There Is One I Love (anon.)   13

P07 白居易《长相思》Prolonged Longing (Bai Juyi)   16

P08 李清照《一剪梅》To the Tune "A Twig of Plum Blossom" (Li Qingzhao)   18

P09 徐在思《沉醉东风 • 春情》To the Tune "Deeply Drunk in the East Wind"

      Spring Passions (Xu Zaisi)   20

练习 Exercises   22

第三单元 田园 Fields and Gardens

P10 陶潜《归园田居》其一 Returning to Live on the Farm, No. 1 (Tao Qian) 24

P11 陶潜《饮酒》其五 On Drinking Wine, No. 5 (Tao Qian)   27

P12 孟浩然《过故人庄 》Visiting My Old Friend's Farmstead (Meng Haoran)   28

P13 王安石《书湖阴先生壁》Written on Master Huyin's Wall, No. 1 (Wang Anshi) 30

练习 Exercises   31

第四单元 游览 Landscape: Excursions

P14 谢朓《游东田诗》An Outing to the Eastern Field (Xie Tiao) 33

P15 王维《终南山》Zhongnan Mountain (Wang Wei) 34

P16 辛弃疾《西江月·夜行黄沙道中》To the Tune "West River Moon": An Evening Journey on the Path to Huangsha (Xin Qiji) 36

P17 陆游《游山西村》An Outing to Villages West of the Mountains (Lu You) 38

练习 Exercises 40

第五单元 山水大观 Landscape: Grand Scenes

P18 崔颢《黄鹤楼》The Yellow Crane Tower (Cui Hao) 42

P19 李白《望庐山瀑布水》Watching the Waterfall of Mount Lu (Li Bai) 44

P20 杜甫《绝句四首·三》Four Quatrains, No. 3 (Du Fu) 45

P21 李贺《梦天》Dreaming Heaven (Li He) 46

P22 杜牧《江南春绝句》A Quatrain on the Spring South of the Yangtze (Du Mu) 48

练习 Exercises 49

第六单元 山水禅境 Landscape: Chan (Zen) Vision

P23 常建《题破山寺后禅院》Written for the Meditation Lodge (Chang Jian) 51

P24 王维《过香积寺》Visiting the Xiangji Temple (Wang Wei) 52

P25 王维《鹿柴》The Deer Fence (Wang Wei) 54

P26 王维《竹里馆》The Lodge in the Bamboo Grove (Wang Wei) 55

P27 王维《鸟鸣涧》Calling-Bird Brook (Wang Wei) 56

练习 Exercises 57

第七单元 山水速写 Landscape: Random Sketches

P28 孟浩然《春晓》The Dawn of a Spring Day (Meng Haoran) 59

P29 李白《独坐敬亭山》Sitting Alone in the Jingting Mountain (Li Bai) 60

P30 柳宗元《江雪》River Snow (Liu Zongyuan) 61

P31 苏轼《饮湖上，初晴后雨二首，其一》Drinking on the Lake, No. 1 (Su Shi) 62

P32 杨万里《小池》A Small Pond (Yang Wanli) 64

P33 白朴《天净沙·秋》To the Tune of "Sky-Clear Sand": Autumn (Bai Pu) 65

练习　Exercises　66

第八单元　山水理趣 Landscape: A Source of Wisdom

P34　王之涣《登鹳雀楼》Climbing Crane Tower (Wang Zhihuan)　68

P35　李白《早发白帝城》Departing Baidi in the Morning (Li Bai)　69

P36　苏轼《题西林壁》Written on the Wall of the West Wood Temple (Su Shi)　70

P37　朱熹《观书有感二首》其一 Two Poems Written After Reading, No. 1 (Zhu Xi)　72

练习　Exercises　73

第九单元　送别 Parting

P38　《古诗十九首》其一 Nineteen Old Poems, No. 1 (anon.)　75

P39　王维《渭城曲》A Weicheng Tune (Wang Wei)　77

P40　李白《黄鹤楼送孟浩然之广陵》Sending off Meng Haoran (Li Bai)　79

P41　李白《赠汪伦》To Wang Lun (Li Bai)　80

P42　孟郊《游子吟》Song of a Traveling Son (Meng Jiao)　81

练习　Exercises　82

第十单元　羁旅 Sojourns of the Wandering Men

P43　孟浩然《宿建德江》An Overnight Stay by the Jiande River (Meng Haoran)　84

P44　杜甫《江汉》The Jiang and Han Rivers (Du Fu)　85

P45　张继《枫桥夜泊》Nightly Mooring at the Maple Bridge (Zhang Ji)　87

P46　温庭筠《商山早行》Early Morning Journey in the Shang Mountains (Wen Tingyun)　88

P47　马致远《天净沙·秋思》To the Tune "Sky-Clear Sand": Autumn Thoughts (Ma Zhiyuan)　90

练习　Exercises　91

第十一单元　边塞与战争 Frontiers and Wars

P48　王之涣《凉州词》Songs of Liangzhou, No. 1 (Wang Zhihuan)　93

P49　王昌龄《从军行》Following the Army (Wang Changling)　94

P50　王昌龄《出塞》Setting Out for the Frontiers (Wang Changling)　96

P51　王翰《凉州词二首》其一 Two Songs of Liangzhou, No. 1 (Wang Han)　98

P52 杜甫《闻官军收河南河北》Upon Hearing of the Recapture of Henan and Hebei by the Government Army (Du Fu) 99

P53 文天祥《过零丁洋》Crossing the Sea of Loneliness (Wen Tianxiang) 102

练习 Exercises 104

第十二单元 思乡 Homesickness

P54 贺知章《回乡偶书》Random Notes Upon Returning to My Hometown (He Zhizhang) 106

P55 王维《九月九日忆山东兄弟》On the Double Ninth Festival: Thinking of My Brothers in Shangdong (Wang Wei) 107

P56 王维《杂诗》其二 Miscellaneous Poems, No. 2 (Wang Wei) 109

P57 李白《静夜思》Quiet Night Thoughts (Li Bai) 110

P58 贾岛《渡桑乾》Crossing the Sanggan River (Jia Dao) 111

P59 李商隐《夜雨寄北》Night Rain: A Poem Sent to the North (Li Shangyin) 112

练习 Exercises 113

第十三单元 闺怨 Plaints of Young Women (I)

P60 《古诗十九首》其二 Nineteen Old Poems, No. 2 (anon.) 115

P61 金昌绪《春怨》Spring Lament (Jin Changxu) 117

P62 李商隐《无题·飒飒东风细雨来》Untitled (Li Shangyin) 118

P63 温庭筠《更漏子》To the Tune "On the Water Clock at Night" (Wen Tingyun) 120

P64 温庭筠《菩萨蛮》To the Tune "Buddha-Like Barbarian" (Wen Tingyun) 122

练习 Exercises 124

第十四单元 闺怨 Plaints of Young Women (II)

P65 韦庄《谒金门》To the Tune "Audience at Golden Gate" (Wei Zhuang) 126

P66 李煜《乌夜啼》To the Tune "Crows Call at Night" (Li Yu) 127

P67 欧阳修《蝶恋花》To the Tune "Butterflies Lingering Over Flowers" (Ouyang Xiu) 129

P68 李清照《武陵春》Spring at Wuling (Li Qingzhao) 131

练习 Exercises 132

第十五单元 宫怨 Plaints of Palace Ladies

P69 谢朓《玉阶怨》 Jade Stairs Resentment (Xie Tiao)   134

P70 李白《玉阶怨》 Lament of the Jade Stairs (Li Bai)   135

P71 王昌龄《长信秋词》其三 Songs of the Autumn of the Abiding Faith Hall, No. 3 (Wang Changling)   136

P72 杜牧《秋夕》 Autumn Evening (Du Mu)   137

P73 李商隐《嫦娥》 Chang' e (Li Shangyin)   138

练习 Exercises   139

第十六单元 咏物 Depiction of Things: Sensuous, Allegorical, and Personified

P74 王融《咏池上梨花诗》 In Praise of Pear Blossoms on the Pond (Wang Rong)   141

P75 李商隐《锦瑟》 Brocade Zither (Li Shangyin)   142

P76 林逋《山园小梅》其一 Small Plum Tree in a Garden in the Hills, No. 1 (Lin Bu)   144

P77 王安石《梅花》 Plum Blossom (Wang Anshi)   146

P78 苏轼《海棠》 Crabapple (Su Shi)   147

P79 陆游《梅花绝句》 A Quatrain on Plum Blossoms (Lu You)   148

练习 Exercises   150

第十七单元 咏史: 名人 Meditation on History: Famous People

P80 杜甫《咏怀古迹》其三 Meditation on Ancient Ruins, No. 3 (Du Fu)   151

P81 杜甫《八阵图》 The Diagram of Eight Formations (Du Fu)   153

P82 李商隐《隋宫》 Sui Palace (Li Shangyin)   155

P83 苏轼《念奴娇·赤壁怀古》 To the Tune "The Charm of Niannu": Meditation on the Past at Red Cliff (Su Shi)   157

P84 辛弃疾《南乡子·登京口北固亭有怀》 To the Tune of "South Village": Meditation on the Past on the Beigu Pavilion (Xin Qiji)   160

练习 Exercises   162

第十八单元 咏史: 王朝兴衰 Meditation on History: Rise and Fall of Dynasties

P85 杜甫《秋兴》其八 Autumn Meditations, No. 8 (Du Fu)   164

P86 刘禹锡《乌衣巷》 Black Clothes Alley (Liu Yuxi)   166

P87 杜牧《赤壁》Red Cliff (Du Mu)   167

P88 章碣《焚书坑》The Book-Burning Pits (Zhang Jie)   169

P89 张养浩《山坡羊•潼关怀古》To the Tune "Sheep on Mountain Slope":
Meditation on the Past at Tong Pass (Zhang Yanghao)   171

练习 Exercises   172

第十九单元 咏怀：感物而发 Reflection: In Response to Scenes and Events

P90 陈子昂《登幽州台歌》A Song on Ascending Youzhou Terrace (Chen Zi'ang)   174

P91 杜甫《春望》Spring Scene (Du Fu)   175

P92 杜甫《曲江》其二 The Qu River, No. 2 (Du Fu)   176

P93 杜甫《登高》Climbing High (Du Fu)   178

P94 杜甫《倦夜》A Weary Night (Du Fu)   180

P95 李贺《秋来》The Advent of Autumn (Li He)   181

练习 Exercises   184

第二十单元 咏怀：往事回忆 Reflection: Remembering Things Past

P96 杜牧《遣怀》Dispelling Sorrow (Du Mu)   185

P97 李煜《虞美人》To the Tune "Beautiful Lady Yu" (Li Yu)   186

P98 晏殊《浣溪沙》To the Tune "Sand in Silk-Washing Stream" (Yan Shu)   188

P99 苏轼《江城子•十年生死两茫茫》To the Tune "River City" (Su Shi)   189

P100 陆游《钗头凤》To the Tune "Phoenix Hairpin" (Lu You)   191

练习 Exercises   194

文学议题列表 List of Literary Issues Discussed   195

入声字列表 List of Entering-Tone Characters, with Phonetic Transcriptions   199

所用字列表 Character List   201

练习答案 Answer Key to Unit Exercises   211

Preface

We would like to dedicate this book to the enthusiastic readers of *How to Read Chinese Poetry: A Guided Anthology,* edited by Zong-qi Cai (Columbia, 2008; hereafter *HTRCP*). To them we are greatly indebted for the original conception of this book and for their continual feedback and encouragement.

In the fall of 2009, Philip Merrill, a professional writer working in the recording industry and an aficionado of Chinese poetry and language, sent a kind thank-you note to the editor of *HTRCP* in which he expressed his hope for a special workbook for learners of Chinese at advanced beginning or higher levels. When his suggestion was passed on to the Press, it won quick approval. So we embarked upon a new adventure: to produce a book that integrates the learning of Chinese language and poetry in ways not previously attempted in the English-speaking world.

In preparing this book, we have retained and improved on various popular features of *HTRCP,* and have introduced a number of new features aimed at enhancing language training and literary comprehension.

Each of the 100 selected poems (as well as the accompanying prose translations) is presented in simplified characters. The use of simplified Chinese characters is an imperfect but practical choice. No one doubts that, for historical and aesthetic reasons, classical Chinese poems are best presented in traditional, unsimplified Chinese. However, in a book primarily for learners of Chinese, demographic and pedagogical considerations outweigh other concerns. Simplified characters are now used in China by hundreds of millions in teaching and studying classical Chinese poetry, and have been adopted in most Chinese language textbooks. Given this, we cannot but follow the general practice. But to mitigate an imperfect choice, we have also provided unsimplified characters for all the simplified characters explained in the vocabulary notes.

The presentation of each poem and its prose translation is followed by copious vocabulary notes. A total of 634 characters and 397 compounds from the poems are explained in the vocabulary notes, with 427 modern Chinese equivalents (including 378 compounds) given in tandem. A large number of sample sentences are included to illustrate the idiomatic usage of these modern Chinese characters and compounds. A complete list of characters is provided at the end of the book, which contains extensive cross-references between classical and modern Chinese usage, between characters and compounds, and between multiple meanings of the same character.

There is one exercise unit for every five units of poetry, which provides extensive drills on modern Chinese words, phrases, and syntax. The drills both enhance readers' ability to read classical Chinese and test their understanding of the poems studied. An answer key can be found in the end matter.

Each of the 100 poems is given tone-marked romanization, accompanied by sound recording for the poem as well as its prose translation. Sound recording can be accessed and downloaded free of charge at **cup.columbia.edu/static/cai-sound-files-wkbk**. All the entering-tone characters used in the recent-style poetry and lyric songs are clearly marked, with their phonetic transcriptions given in the end matter. Also clearly marked is the use of rhymes. Different markers are used to distinguish between the level-tone rhyme and the oblique-tone rhyme and to differentiate multiple rhymes used in a single poem.

To turn rigorous language learning into a pleasurable literary experience, we have taken pains to provide as much literary aid as possible. The comprehension and appreciation of the poems is aided by notes on their historical and cultural contexts and by comments and questions about their unique artistic features, with extensive references to more in-depth discussion in *HTRCP*. All famous, oft-quoted poetic lines are accentuated by shading and should be learnt by heart.

We hope that readers will not only learn to appreciate the beauty of individual poems but also gain a broad view of the entire Chinese poetic tradition. For this reason, we have selected 100 of the best-known, oft-recited classical Chinese poems. These poems are representative of the major poetic genres developed from their inception through the Yuan Dynasty, and are organized into twenty units around the most popular themes in classical Chinese poetry. A list of literary issues discussed amplifies the cohesiveness of the selected poems as a whole. A thorough study of the poems in conjunction with *HTRCP* should illuminate the complex contours of the generic, thematic, and formal evolution of classical Chinese poetry.

Thanks to the incorporation of the features mentioned above, the book has grown beyond a normal workbook and has in effect become a thematic guided anthology of classical Chinese poetry for learners of Chinese. Fifty-six of the 100 poems are newly selected, translated, and commented on. While the book can stand alone, using it together with *HTRCP* allows for their optimal mutual enhancement.

Having benefited so much from the *HTRCP* readers both inside and outside academia, we wish to engage the readers of this book in an even more dynamic fashion. Facebook makes it possible for us to communicate with all interested readers simultaneously and interactively. We encourage all interested readers to visit **facebook.com/HowtoReadChinesePoetryZongqiCai** and work together to form an active community of Chinese poetry lovers. We shall do our best to foster and maintain an informative dialogue on all matters related to this book, *HTRCP,* and the learning of Chinese poetry and poetic language in general.

Finally, we would like to thank Jennifer Crewe, associate director and editorial director of Columbia University Press, for her enthusiastic support of this project. Our thanks to Anne McCoy and Michael Simon of Columbia University Press for their editorial guidance; to Philip Merrill, again, for his meticulous copy-editing of the entire manuscript; to E Li and Qinghai Liu for helping to proofread the manuscript; and to Majia Bell Samei, Paula Varsano, and Wendy Swartz for writing or checking vocabulary notes and comments on the poems translated by them.

Zong-qi Cai

Symbols and Abbreviations

	Oblique tone in a prosody table
—	Level tone in a prosody table
Δ	End rhythm in level tone
▲	End rhythm in oblique tone
Δ^a, Δ^b, ▲^{a}, ▲^{b}	In a poem that employs more than one rhyme, the first rhyme is indicated as Δ^a or ▲^{a}, the second rhyme as Δ^b or ▲^{b}, the third rhyme as Δ^c or ▲^{c}, and so on.
P01	Poem 01 in this book
👉	A marker of reference or cross-reference
月.	A black dot beneath a character indicates that it is pronounced in the entering tone (characterized by an unaspirated p, t, or k ending) in Middle Chinese. All entering-tone characters in recent-style *shi* poems and *ci* poems have been so identified. The reconstructed pronunciations of these characters are given in "Phonetic Transcriptions of Entering-Tone Characters" at the end of this workbook.
也，归来	A wavy underline is applied to a modern Chinese word, given as a gloss to a classical Chinese word and/or used in the modern Chinese translation.
窈 窕 淑 女 君 子 好 逑	Shading is applied to all famous and oft-quoted poetic lines.

MdnC	Modern Chinese
HTRCP	Zong-qi Cai, ed., *How to Read Chinese Poetry: A Guide Book*. New York: Columbia University Press, 2008.

How to Read Chinese Poetry Workbook

1

爱情：君子情思

Love: The Voice of Men

guān jū
关 雎
shī jīng guó fēng
《诗经 • 国风》[1]

"Guan, Guan," Cry the Ospreys

(The first of the airs of the *Book of Poetry*)

guān	*guān*	*jū*	*jiū*	
关	关[2]	雎	鸠△[a 3]	"Guan, guan," cry the ospreys
zài	*hé*	*zhī*	*zhōu*	
在	河	之[4]	洲△[a 5]	On the islet in the river.
yǎo	*tiǎo*	*shū*	*nǚ*	
窈	窕[6]	淑[7]	女	Graceful is this fair maiden,
jūn	*zǐ*	*hǎo*	*qiú*	
君	子[8]	好	逑△[a 9]	A fine bride for a gentleman.

cēn	*cī*	*xìng*	*cài*	
参	差[10]	荇	菜[11]	Thick and thin grows the water mallow,
zuǒ	*yòu*	*liú*	*zhī*	
左	右	流△[a 12]	之[13]	Left and right one gets it in the flow.
yǎo	*tiǎo*	*shū*	*nǚ*	
窈	窕	淑	女	Graceful is this fair maiden,
wù	*mèi*	*qiú*	*zhī*	
寤[14]	寐[15]	求△[16]	之	Awake or asleep, I am seeking her.

qiú	*zhī*	*bù*	*dé*	
求	之	不	得▲[b 17]	Seeking though I was, I could not possess her,
wù	*mèi*	*sī*	*fú*	
寤	寐	思[18]	服▲[b 19]	Awake or asleep I was longing for her.
yōu	*zāi*	*yōu*	*zāi*	
悠	哉[20]	悠	哉	Alas, longing and forlorn
zhǎn	*zhuǎn*	*fǎn*	*cè*	
辗	转[21]	反	侧▲[b 22]	I tossed and turned in bed.

cēn	*cī*	*xìng*	*cài*	
参	差	荇	菜	Thick and thin grows the water mallow,
zuǒ	*yòu*	*cǎi*	*zhī*	
左	右	采△c 23	之	Left and right one plucks it.
yǎo	*tiǎo*	*shū*	*nǚ*	
窈	窕	淑	女	Graceful is the fair maiden,
qín	*sè*	*yǒu*	*zhī*	
琴24	瑟25	友△c 26	之	With zither and zithern I will befriend her.

cēn	*cī*	*xìng*	*cài*	
参	差	荇	菜	Thick and thin grows the water mallow,
zuǒ	*yòu*	*mào*	*zhī*	
左	右	芼△d 27	之	Left and right one gathers it.
yǎo	*tiǎo*	*shū*	*nǚ*	
窈	窕	淑	女	Graceful is this fair maiden,
zhōng	*gǔ*	*lè*	*zhī*	
钟28	鼓29	乐▲d 30	之	With bells and drums I will gladden her.

[四言诗 tetrasyllabic verse]

(Tr. Zong-qi Cai)

字词释义 Vocabulary Notes

1. 《诗经》 (詩經) or the *Book of Poetry* (hereafter the *Poetry*) is the fountainhead of Chinese poetry as well as one of the Five Classics (*Wǔ jīng* 五经) in the Confucian tradition. This collection consists of 305 earliest extant poems, divided into three parts: *fēng* 风 (airs) or *guó fēng* 国风 (airs of the states), *yǎ* 雅 (odes), and *sòng* 颂 (hymns). "'Guan Guan,' Cry the Ospreys" (《关雎》) is the first poem of the *Poetry* and this title is composed of two characters from the poem's first line. Other poems in the *Poetry* are also entitled with one or more characters from the first line.

2. 关关 (關關) onomatopoeic reduplicative.　　3. 雎鸠 (鳩) n. osprey.

4. 之 auxiliary particle. MdnC: 的 (*de*). See note 13 for a different meaning of this character.

5. 洲 n. an islet in a river.

6. 窈窕 a rhyming reduplicative, used here (as well as in MdnC) to convey impression of a woman's gracefulness.

7. 淑 adj. kind and gentle, fair. 淑女 a fair maiden.

8. 君子 n. gentleman.　　9. 逑 n. spouse. MdnC: 配偶 (*pèi ǒu*) [formal].

10. 参差 an alliterative reduplicative, used here (as well as in MdnC) to convey the perception of something irregular, uneven. 👉参差不齐 uneven, not uniform.

11. 荇菜 n. water mallow.

12. 流 v. to flow. Here it means "to pick in the flow." MdnC: 摘 (*zhāi*). 👉我给你摘个苹果 I will pick an apple for you.

13. 之 pron. It refers to the fair maiden mentioned in the third line. MdnC: 她 (*tā*).

14. 寤　v. to wake up. MdnC: 睡醒 (*shuì xǐng*). 👉他睡醒了 He woke up.
15. 寐　v. to be asleep. MdnC: 睡着 (*shuì zháo*). 👉他睡着了 He is asleep.
16. 求　v. to seek. MdnC: 追求 (*zhuī qiú*). 👉他在追求一个女孩 He is chasing a girl.
17. 得　v. to get. MdnC: 得到 (*dé dào*). 👉他终于得到了这份工作 He finally got this job.
18. 思　used here as an auxiliary particle with no meaning.
19. 服　v. to long for, miss. MdnC: 思念 (*sī niàn*). 👉他思念着家人 He longs for his family.
20. 悠　adv. longing for. 哉 auxiliary particle, no meaning.
21. 辗转 (輾轉)　v. to pass through many hands or places. Here it means "to toss about (in bed)."
22. 反侧 (側)　v. to toss and turn, turn one's body from side to side. 👉他辗转反侧，不能成眠 He is tossing in bed and unable to fall asleep.
23. 采　v. to pick, pluck. 👉姑娘们正在采苹果 The girls are picking apples.
24. 琴　n. a seven-stringed plucked instrument in ancient China.
25. 瑟　n. a twenty-five-stringed plucked instrument in ancient China. See also P75 note 1.
26. 友　n. friend, used here as a verb, meaning "to befriend". MdnC: 亲近 (*qīn jìn*). 👉大家都愿意亲近她 Everyone wants to befriend her.
27. 芼　v. to pick. MdnC: 摘 (*zhāi*). Cf. 流 in note 12 and 采 in note 23.　28. 钟 (鐘)　n. bell.
29. 鼓　n. drum. See also P17 note 10.
30. 乐 (樂 *lè*)　adj. happy, used here as a verb, meaning "to please." MdnC: 取悦 (*qǔ yuè*), to please (often in a derogatory sense). 👉他试图取悦他的老板 He tried to please his boss.

现代文翻译 Modern Chinese Translation

关关鸣叫的雎鸠，在河中间的[4]小洲上。温柔美丽的姑娘，是君子的好配偶。[9]

参差不齐[10]的荇菜，摘[12]了左边摘右边。温柔美丽的姑娘，无论(我)睡醒[14]或睡着[15]时，都想追求[16]她。

(我)追求她却无法得到[17]她，无论(我)醒着或睡着，都思念[19]着她。想念着，想念着，(我)辗转反侧，[22]不能入睡。

参差不齐的荇菜，采[23]了左边采右边。温柔美丽的姑娘，(我)弹琴鼓瑟来亲近[26]她。

参差不齐的荇菜，摘了左边摘右边。温柔美丽的姑娘，(我)敲钟击鼓来取悦[30]她。

评论与提问 Comments and Questions

The *Book of Poetry* is a Confucian canonical work studied more extensively than any other text, probably with the exception of the *Book of Changes* (*Yì jīng* 易经). Of the 305 poems in this collection, this first poem is discussed more extensively than any other poem. It has been re-interpreted incessantly right up to our time. In premodern times, it was read almost solely as a political and moral allegory. The beautiful woman in the poem was identified by some as an ideal mate (and, allegorically, a worthy talent) being sought for King Wen 文王 (1152?–1056? B.C.E), the founder of the Zhou Dynasty. This poem was lauded as a testament to the great moral influence of King Wen.

In modern times, however, the *Poetry* is mostly read and appreciated as a literary work. Freed of the allegorical baggage, we could easily see this first poem for what it most likely was when first composed: a simple love poem by a man. It is the only tetrasyllabic poem (*sì yán shī* 四言诗) in this workbook. Tetrasyllabic verse is representative of the *Poetry*, as more than 90 percent of 6,595 lines in the *Poetry* are tetrasyllabic. After the Han, however, tetrasyllabic verse lost its appeal as a vehicle of lyrical expression and became a niche subgenre of hymns and eulogies. ☞ *HTRCP*, pp. 4–5 for an account of major Chinese poetic genres and subgenres.

This poem features some of the most important formal strategies extensively employed in the "Airs of the States" and frequently used in later poetry: affective image, reduplicatives, topic+comment sentence, topic+comment stanza, and incremental repetition.

1. Affective image is called *xing* 兴 (興 *xīng*) in Chinese. If used as a verb, *xing* means "to evoke" or "to bring forth." Indeed, an affective image usually occurs at the beginning of a stanza, evoking a sustained emotional response from the speaker: an emotive perception of the image itself, followed by emotive statements about the circumstances of his or her life. Can you identify the affective images used in this poem?

2. A reduplicative, called *lianmianzi* 连绵字 (*lián mián zǐ*) in Chinese, refers to a compound (also called "binome") that is derived from a complete or partial reduplication of the phonetic quality of one character. 关关 on line 1 is a complete reduplicative and probably onomatopoeic. 窈窕 on line 3 and 参差 on line 5 are partial reduplicatives. For further distinction, 窈窕) may be called a rhyming reduplicative because of its reduplication of the vowel; 参差 an alliterative reduplicative because of its reduplication of the initial consonant. It is important to note that most of the reduplicatives used in the *Poetry* do not have a fixed conceptual meaning and are primarily sound registers of emotional response to things being observed.

3. "Topic+comment" is a term used by scholars of the Chinese language to describe the structure of Chinese sentences that do not display a subject-predicate relationship. "Topic" refers to an object, a scene, or an event being observed; and "comment" an implied observer's response (usually emotive) to the topic. Topic and comment are not spatio-temporally or causally linked as subject and predicate are. In the *Poetry*, an affective image usually occurs together with an emotionally charged reduplicative. Considering the absence of clear spatio-temporal and causal linkage between the two, this combination of an affective image and a reduplicative obviously constitutes a topic+comment sentence. Could you identify the topic+comment sentences in this poem? ☞ *HTRCP*, pp. 380–382 for a discussion of "topic+comment" vs. "subject + predicate" syntax.

4. Topic+comment stanza may be seen as topic+comment sentence writ large. In this poem, all stanzas except the third strike us as topic+comment stanzas: two lines of nature depiction (topic) are juxtaposed with two lines of emotive statements (comment). Apparently, the principle of juxtaposition (of spatio-temporally and logically unrelated parts) operates on the higher level of stanzaic organization as well as the syntactic level.

    The inherent relationship between topic+comment sentence and topic+comment stanza is aptly reflected in the use of the term *xing* 兴. This term was first applied only to a single affective image (usually found in the first sentence of a stanza, as just noted), but later broadened to denote a bipartite, juxtapostional stanzaic organization. Thanks to its evocative function at both syntactic and stanzaic operation, *xing* is much praised as the most poetical of the three modes of presentation in the *Poetry* and exerts a great influence on later poetry. ☞ *HTRCP*, pp. 13–14 for a discussion of the three modes of presentation.

5. The organization of the entire poem seems a stacking up of five self-contained stanzas. Given the regular recurrence of words, phrases, and syntax in these stanzas, the poem may be seen as a series of repetition of the same oral formula, with different degrees of variation. "Incremental repetition," a term of English poetry criticism, readily lends itself to describing such a pattern of interstanzaic progression. Compared to their counterpart in English and Scottish ballads, however, incremental repetition is used in the *Poetry* less for advancing a narrative than revealing a speaker's complex mental process. Identify the incremental repetitions and discuss how they reveal a steady intensification of the speaker's yearning for his ideal mate. ☞ *HTRCP*, pp. 18–20 for a dramatic example of incremental repetition.

P02

yáng liǔ zhī
杨 柳 枝[1]

[táng] liú yǔ xī
[唐] 刘 禹 锡[2]

Willow Branch

[Tang Dyn.] Liu Yuxi

qīng jiāng yì qū liǔ qiān tiáo
清 江 一 曲[3] 柳[4] 千 条△

The Qing River meanders through thousands of willow branches,

èr shí tī qián jiù bǎn qiáo
二 十 梯[5] 前 旧 板 桥△[6]

Before the twenty steps is the same old plank bridge.

céng yǔ měi rén qiáo shàng bié
曾 与 美 人 桥 上 别

Once I said farewell to my beauty,

hèn wú xiāo xī dào jīn zhāo
恨 无 消 息 到 今 朝△

Regrettably, there has been no news from her to this day.

(Tr. Li E)

[七言律绝 heptasyllabic regulated quatrain, tonal pattern Ia, see *HTRCP*, p. 171]

字词释义 Vocabulary Notes

1. 杨柳枝 "Willow Branch," a poem rewritten from the famous Tang poet Bai Juyi's 白居易 "Road of Plank Bridge" ("Bǎnqiáo lù" 板桥路). Bai's poem is a six-line ancient-style poem. Liu Yuxi cut two lines off and used flashbacks and this re-write was highly praised by the Ming scholars Yang Shen 杨慎 (1488–1559) and Hu Yingling 胡应麟 (1551–1602). See Bai Juyi's biographic note in P07 note 2.

2. 刘禹锡 (劉禹錫) (style 字, Mèngdé 梦得, 772–842), a mid-Tang poet. He often expressed his deep understanding of human life and history in succinct and fresh poetic language, and thus was highly praised as the "hero-poet" (*shīháo* 诗豪) by Bai Juyi. He is also known for his imitation of the Southern folksongs, such as "Bamboo Sprig" ("Zhúzhī cí" 竹枝词).

3. 曲   adj. curved, used here to mean the curved part of the river. MdnC: 曲折 (*qū zhé*). ☞河道 很曲折 The river has a winding course. See also P24 note 13.

4. 柳   n. willow tree. Willow trees are often planted on the sides of river banks in ancient China. Its pronunciation "*liǔ*" is very similar to 留's (*liú*, meaning "to ask somebody to stay."). Thus, people often break off one branch of willow and give it to the one who is going to leave. This tradition started during the Han and became very popular in the Tang. Therefore, 柳 often appears in poems to suggest a reluctant feeling to part with friends and family members, or strong homesickness.

5. 梯   n. ladder, steps. MdnC: 台阶 (*tái jiē*).   6. 板桥 (橋) n. plank bridge. See also P46 note 7.

现代文翻译 Modern Chinese Translation

清澈的江水曲折³地流着，两岸的柳枝处处可见。二十个台阶⁵前那旧板桥上， （我）曾经和一位美丽的姑娘分别。可惜到现在还没有她的消息。

评论与提问 Comments and Questions

1. This poem is a heptasyllabic regulated quatrain. ☞ *HTRCP,* pp. 199–200, 212–223 for a description of the structural, prosodic, and aesthetic features of the quatrain form.

2. Compare the treatment of the sorrow of separation in P07 and this poem. Think about a contrast between prolonged longing and a sad moment of remembrance. Is the quatrain form particularly conducive to an expression of the latter kind of feeling? If so, why?

P03

	wú	*tí*					Untitled
	无	题¹					

[*táng*] *lǐ shāng yǐn*
[唐] 李 商 隐²   [Tang Dyn.] Li Shangyin

xiāng	*jiàn*	*shí*	*nán*	*bié*	*yì*	*nán*
相	见	时³	难⁴	别	亦⁵	难△

It is hard to meet,
      and parting is just as hard.

dōng	*fēng*	*wú*	*lì*	*bǎi*	*huā*	*cán*
东	风	无	力⁶	百	花	残△⁷

The east wind is listless,
      hundreds of flowers' withered.

chūn	*cán*[8]	*dào*	*sǐ*	*sī*[9]	*fāng*[10]	*jìn*[11]
春	蚕	到	死	丝	方	尽

Not until its death does a spring silkworm
          stop spinning its threads;

là	*jù*[12]	*chéng*	*huī*[13]	*lèi*	*shǐ*[14]	*gān*△
蜡	炬	成	灰	泪	始	干

Only when a candle's wick is burned to ashes
          do its tears dry up.

xiǎo[15]	*jìng*	*dàn*[16]	*chóu*[17]	*yún*	*bìn*[18]	*gǎi*[19]
晓	镜	但	愁	云	鬓	改

Looking at the mirror at dawn, she would fear
          a change in her cloud-like temples;

yè	*yín*[20]	*yīng*	*jué*	*yuè*	*guāng*	*hán*△
夜	吟	应	觉	月	光	寒

Chanting a poem at night, she would feel
          the moonbeams' coldness.

péng	*shān*[21]	*cǐ*	*qù*	*wú*	*duō*	*lù*
蓬	山	此	去	无	多	路

Peng Mount, from here
          not much distance is left,

qīng	*niǎo*[22]	*yīn*	*qín*[23]	*wèi*	*tàn*	*kān*△[24]
青	鸟	殷	勤	为	探	看

Blue Birds, be diligent,
          spy out the route for me.
          (Tr. Zong-qi Cai)

[七言律诗 heptasyllabic regulated verse, tonal pattern IIa, see *HTRCP*, p. 172]

字词释义 Vocabulary Notes

1. 无题 (無題) "Untitled." The poet was apparently reluctant to give a title to his poem.
2. 李商隐 (隐) (style 字, Yìshān 义山; literary name 号, Yùxī shēng 玉谿生, 813–858), a great late Tang poet. He is famous for his poems on history and love. He is also known for his dense and allusive poetic language. He and another late Tang poet Du Mu 杜牧 are often mentioned together as "younger Li-Du" (*xiǎo* Lǐ Dù 小李杜) as opposed to "older Li [Bai]-Du [Fu]". See Du Mu's biographic note in P22 note 2.
3. 时 (時) n. chance. MdnC: 时机 (*shí jī*). 👉他错过了时机 He lost a chance. See P27 note 5 for a different meaning of the word.
4. 难 (難) adj. difficult. There are two 难's in the first line. The first 难 refers to the difficulty in getting a chance to meet each other (*nán dé* 难得). The second 难 refers to the difficulty in saying goodbye (*nán shě nán fēn* 难舍难分).
5. 亦 adv. also, too. MdnC: 也 (*yě*). 👉他也来了 He came, too.
6. 无 (無) 力 v. to lack strength, feel weak. Here it means (that the wind) "dropped."
7. 残 (殘) adj. ruined, withered. MdnC: 凋谢 (*diāo xiè*). 👉花都凋谢了 The flowers all withered away. See also P08 note 4, P33 note 4, and P63 note 11.
8. 蚕 (蠶) n. silkworm.   9. 丝 (絲) n. silk. See also P62 note 12.
10. 方 adv. not until. MdnC: 才 (*cái*). 👉今天的会下午四点才开始 Today's meeting will not begin until 4 p.m. See also P07 note 12. See P10 note 13 and P31 note 4 for different meanings of the word.
11. 尽 (盡) v. to exhaust. 👉他尽了全力 He exerted himself to the utmost. See also P34 note 5, P39 note 9, P40 note 11, and P68 note 6.

12. 蜡 (蠟) 炬 n. candle. MdnC: 蜡烛 (*là zhú*).   13. 灰 n. ash.   14. 始 adv. not until.

15. 晓 (曉) n. dawn. MdnC: 拂晓 (*fú xiǎo*) [formal]. See also P28 note 1, P73 note 6, P75 note 8, and P79 note 4.

16. 但 adv. only. MdnC: 只(*zhǐ*). 👈我只担心你 I only worry about you. See P50 note 7 for a different meaning of the word.

17. 愁 v. to worry. MdnC: 担忧 (*dān yōu*). 👈不要为我担忧 Don't worry about me. See P07 note 8 for a different meaning of the word.

18. 鬓 (鬢) n. hair on the temples. See also P54 note 5, P63 note 10, P93 note 15, and P99 note 11. 云鬓 hair as thick and beautiful as clouds.

19. 改 v. to change. MdnC: 改变 (*gǎi biàn*). 👈他改变了主意 He changed his mind.

20. 吟 v. to chant, recite. MdnC: 吟唱 (*yín chàng*). 👈他反复吟唱着这首歌 He is chanting this song again and again. See also P42 note 2, P76 note 16, and P85 note 25.

21. 蓬山 or 蓬莱山, Penglai Mount, one of the three legendary mountains inhabited by immortals. See P21 note 12 for the note on the three legendary mountains (*sān shān* 三山).

22. 青鸟 (鳥) blue birds, who deliver mails for Queen Mother of the West (Xīwángmǔ 西王母) in the ancient legends.

23. 殷勤 adv. solicitously. 👈感谢你们的殷勤接待 Thanks for your solicitous hospitality.

24. 探看 (*kān*) v. to look over. MdnC: 查看 (*chá kàn*). 👈他在查看帐目 He is checking the accounts.

25. 弱 (*ruò*) adj. weak.   26. 燃烧 (*rán shāo*) v. to burn.

现代文翻译 Modern Chinese Translation

    相见的时机³很难得,⁴离别时更是难舍难分。⁴（晚春的时候,）东风转弱,²⁵百花都凋谢⁷了。春蚕直到死时,才将丝吐尽。¹¹蜡烛¹²要燃烧²⁶成灰时,蜡烛的眼泪才会流干。

    拂晓¹⁵时起来,看到镜中的自己,只¹⁶担心¹⁷美丽的鬓发改变¹⁹(颜色)。夜晚,（无法入睡,）独自吟唱,²⁰会感到月光寒冷。从这里去蓬山,没多少路。希望有青鸟能为我殷勤²³地查看²⁴消息。

评论与提问 Comments and Questions

1. This poem is a heptasyllabic regulated verse. 👈 *HTRCP*, pp. 161–200, 212–223 for a discussion of semantic, syntactic, structural, prosodic rules of regulated verse in general; and pp. 181–183 for further comments on the tonal patterning of heptasyllabic regulated verse.

2. The second couplet is one of the best-known metaphorical statements on love in Chinese poetry. Images are considered metaphorical when they occur as correlatives to an abstract idea rather than part of a literal description. Besides the images of a silkworm and a candle in the second couplet, what images can be taken to be metaphorical?

P04

nán gē zǐ   qí yī
南 歌 子[1] 其 一

To the Tune "Southern Tune," No. 1

xié   yìn   zhū   lián   lì
斜   隐[2] 珠[3] 帘[4] 立

Standing leaning at the beaded curtain,

qíng   shì   gòng   shéi   qīn
情   事[5] 共[6] 谁   亲△[7]

With whom have you been sharing your heart?

fēn   míng   miàn   shàng   zhǐ   hén   xīn
分   明[8] 面[9] 上   指[10] 痕[11] 新△

The new scratches on your face are plain as day.

luó   dài   tóng   xīn   shéi   wǎn
罗[12] 带[13] 同   心[14] 谁   绾[15]

Who tied the love knot in your silk sash?

shèn   rén   tà   pò   qún
甚[16] 人   踏[17] 破   裙△

And who's torn the hem of your skirt?

chán   bìn   yīn   hé   luàn
蝉   鬓[18] 因   何   乱

Why are your cicada locks in disarray?

jīn   chāi   wèi   shèn   fēn
金   钗[19] 为   甚   分△

And your hairpin—why is it broken?

hóng   zhuāng   chuí   lèi   yì   hé   jūn
红   妆[20] 垂[21] 泪   忆[22] 何   君△

For whom these tear streaks in your rouge?

fēn   míng   diàn   qián   shí   shuō
分   明   殿[23] 前   实   说

Tell me straight, here before the hall.

mò   chén   yín
莫[24] 沉   吟△[25]

Don't hem and haw.

[小令 short lyric song]

(Tr. Maija Bell Samei, *HTRCP*, p. 249)

字词释义 Vocabulary Notes

1. 南歌子 "Southern Tune," title of a tune.
2. 隐 (隐 *yìn*) v. to lean. MdnC: 靠 (*kào*).   3. 珠 n. pearl, bead.
4. 帘 (簾) n. curtain.   5. 情事 n. an affair.   6. 共 conj. and. MdnC: 和 (*hé*).
7. 亲 (親) adj. close. MdnC: 亲密 (*qīn mì*). 👉他们关系很亲密 Their relationship is pretty close.
8. 分明 adv. clearly, plainly. 👉这分明是不对的. This is clearly not right.
9. 面 n. face. MdnC: 脸 (*liǎn*).   10. 指 n. finger. MdnC: 手指 (*shǒu zhǐ*).
11. 痕 n. mark. MdnC: 痕迹 (*hén jì*). 👉地上有车轮的痕迹 There are wheel tracks on the ground.
12. 罗 (羅) n. a kind of silk gauze. See P10 note 20 for a different meaning of the word.
13. 带 n. sash.   14. 同心 with one heart. Here it refers to a love knot (*tóng xīn jié* 同心结).

15. 绾（綰） v. to tie. MdnC: 系 (*jì*). 👉他系了个同心结 He tied a love knot.

16. 甚 pron. what. MdnC: 什么 (*shénme*). 👉他说了什么 What did he say?

17. 踏 v. to step on, stamp. 👉春天他要去踏青 He will go for a walk in the country in spring. See also P41 note 4.

18. 蝉鬓（蟬鬢） one of the female hairstyles in ancient China. For this hairstyle, the hair on the temples is as thin as a cicada's wings.

19. 钗（釵） n. hairpin worn for adornment by women in the past. It consists of two strands and therefore 分钗 comes to mean the separation of a couple.

20. 妆（妝） makeup. See also P60 note 8 and P99 note 15. 红妆 refers to his wife. See also P78 note 10.

21. 垂 v. to hang down. 👉他垂手站着 He stands with hands at his sides. See also P82 note 14.

22. 忆（憶） v. to recall, miss. MdnC: 思念 (*sī niàn*). See also P55 note 2.   23. 殿 n. hall, palace.

24. 莫 v. don't. MdnC: 不要 (*bú yào*). See also P17 note 2 and P51 note 10. See P100 note 16 for a different meaning of the word.

25. 沉吟 v. to mutter to oneself, unable to make up one's mind.

26. 吞吞吐吐 (*tūntūn tǔtǔ*) v. to hesitate in speech, hem and haw.

现代文翻译 Modern Chinese Translation

　　(丈夫回来，看到妻子) 斜靠²在珠帘旁站着，(顿时起了疑心，问)，你和⁶谁有了亲密⁷关系？你脸⁹上的手指¹⁰痕迹¹¹分明⁸是新的！谁在你的丝带上系¹⁵了同心结？¹⁴什么人踏¹⁷破了你的裙子？

　　你的发鬓为什么乱了？金钗为什么分了？你流着眼泪思念²²的是谁？在房前给我说清楚，不许吞吞吐吐²⁶的！

评论与提问 Comment and Question

This poem and the next poem (P05) are taken from the collection of anonymous poems discovered in the Dunhuang Caves (Dūnhuáng shíkū 敦煌石窟) in the early 20th century. This pair of poems constitutes the dramatic exchange of a jealous husband's interrogation and his quick-witted wife's repartee. 👉*HTRCP*, pp. 249–251. What words and phrases add to the colloquial flavor of both poems?

练习 EXERCISES

一 填空 Fill in blanks

A. 诗词填字: 难 乱 灰 淑 晓 残 曲 参 尽 条 流 甚 吟 亲 梯 友 差 干 寒 隐

1. ＿＿ ＿＿荇菜，左右＿＿之。   2. 春蚕到死丝方＿＿，蜡炬成＿＿泪始＿＿。

3. 窈窕＿＿＿女，琴瑟＿＿＿之。　　4. 清江一＿＿柳千＿＿，二十＿＿前旧板桥。

5. 蝉鬓因何＿＿＿，金钗为＿＿＿分。　6. ＿＿镜但愁云鬓改，夜＿＿应觉月光＿＿。

7. 斜＿＿＿珠帘立，情事共谁＿＿＿。　8. 相见时＿＿＿别亦＿＿＿，东风无力百花＿＿＿。

B. 现代文填词：思念 时机 亲近 痕迹 殷勤 曲折 担忧 吟唱

1. 他反复＿＿＿ ＿＿＿这首歌。　 2. 大家都愿意＿＿＿ ＿＿＿她。　 3. 不要＿＿＿ ＿＿＿我的身体。

4. 黄河的河道很＿＿＿ ＿＿＿。　 5. 他受到了＿＿＿ ＿＿＿接待。　 6. 他＿＿＿ ＿＿＿着家人。

7. 他错过了最好的＿＿＿ ＿＿＿。　 8. 地上有车轮的＿＿＿ ＿＿＿。

二 形近字辨析 Distinguish easily confused characters

1. 分明面上指＿＿＿新　a. 恨　b. 痕　c. 狠　　2. ＿＿＿江一曲柳千条　a. 清　b. 情　c. 晴

3. ＿＿＿镜但愁云鬓改　a. 晓　b. 绕　c. 饶　　4. 青鸟殷勤为＿＿＿看　a. 探　b. 琛　c. 深

5. 红妆＿＿＿泪对何君　a. 重　b. 垂　c. 捶　　6. 悠＿＿＿悠＿＿＿　　　a. 载　b. 栽　c. 哉

三 连句 Match the first part with the second

1. 窈窕淑女( )　2. 蓬山此去无多路( )　3. 曾与美人桥上别( )　4. 红妆垂泪忆何君( )

5. 春蚕到死丝方尽( )　6. 悠哉悠哉( )　7. 分明面上指痕新( )　8. 清江一曲柳千条( )

a. 恨无消息到今朝　 b. 蜡炬成灰泪始干　 c. 辗转反侧　　　　 d. 二十梯前旧板桥

e. 罗带同心谁绾　　 f. 君子好逑　　 g. 青鸟殷勤为探看　 h. 分明殿前实说

四 句读 Punctuate and translate the following excerpts from three or more poems

参差荇菜左右采之窈窕淑女琴瑟友之参差荇菜左右芼之窈窕淑女钟鼓乐之春蚕到死丝方尽蜡炬成灰泪始干曾与美人桥上别恨无消息到今朝蝉鬓因何乱金钗为甚分红妆垂泪忆何君分明殿前实说莫沉吟

五 听写 Dictation

1. ＿＿＿ ＿＿＿ ＿＿＿ ＿＿＿ ＿＿＿，在 ＿＿＿ ＿＿＿ ＿＿＿。＿＿＿ ＿＿＿ ＿＿＿女，＿＿＿ ＿＿＿好＿＿＿。

2. ＿＿＿ ＿＿＿ ＿＿＿ ＿＿＿丝 ＿＿＿ ＿＿＿，＿＿＿ ＿＿＿ ＿＿＿ ＿＿＿ ＿＿＿ ＿＿＿干。

3. ＿＿＿ ＿＿＿ ＿＿＿ ＿＿＿ ＿＿＿条，二十 ＿＿＿ ＿＿＿ ＿＿＿ ＿＿＿。

4. ＿＿＿ ＿＿＿ ＿＿＿上 ＿＿＿ ＿＿＿，＿＿＿ ＿＿＿同心 ＿＿＿ ＿＿＿。

5. ＿＿＿之不得，＿＿＿ ＿＿＿思＿＿＿。＿＿＿ ＿＿＿ ＿＿＿ ＿＿＿，＿＿＿ ＿＿＿ ＿＿＿ ＿＿＿。

2

爱情：闺妇情语

Love: The Voice of Women

P05

<table>
<tr><td>nán</td><td>gē</td><td>zǐ</td><td>qí</td><td>èr</td></tr>
<tr><td>南</td><td>歌</td><td>子¹</td><td>其</td><td>二</td></tr>
</table>

To the Tune "Southern Tune," No. 2

zì	cóng	jūn	qù	hòu		
自	从	君	去	后		

Since you went away

wú	xīn	liàn	bié	rén		
无	心	恋	别	人		

I've no heart to love another.

mèng	zhōng	miàn	shàng	zhǐ	hén	xīn
梦	中	面	上	指	痕	新△

New scratches on my face appeared in my dreams.

luó	dài	tóng	xīn	zì	wǎn	
罗	带	同	心	自	绾	

I tied the love knot in my own silk sash.

bèi	mán	ér	tà	pò	qún	
被	蛮²	儿³	踏	破	裙△	

It was the child who stepped on my hem.

chán	bìn	zhū	lián	luàn		
蝉	鬓	朱⁴	帘	乱		

The beaded curtain mussed my cicada locks

jīn	chāi	jiù	gǔ	fēn		
金	钗	旧	股⁵	分△		

The hairpin broke along an old crack.

hóng	zhuāng	chuí	lèi	kū	láng	jūn
红	妆	垂	泪	哭	郎	君△⁶

These streaks in my makeup are from crying for you.

qiè	shì	nán	shān	sōng	bó	
妾⁷	是	南	山	松	柏⁸	

I'm like the cypresses on South Mountain—

wú	xīn	liàn	bié	rén		
无	心	恋	别	人△		

I've no heart to love another.

[小令 short lyric song]

(Tr. Maija Bell Samei, *HTRCP*, p. 250)

字词释义 Vocabulary Notes

1. 南歌子 "Southern Tune," title of a tune. See P04 note 1.
2. 蛮 adj. reckless, unreasoning. MdnC: 莽撞 (*mǎng zhuàng*). 📖他很莽撞 He is very impetuous.

3. 儿 (兒) n. child. MdnC: 小孩儿 (*xiǎo háir*).

4. 朱 adj. red. It is used here in the sense of 珠 (*zhū*), meaning "bead."   5. 股 n. strand.

6. 郎君 n. (my) darling, used by a woman for her husband or lover in ancient China.

7. 妾 n. concubine; a humble first-person pronoun used, as here, by a woman. See also P61 note 5.

8. 松柏 n. pine and cypress. In the *Analects*, Confucius says, "It is only when winter comes that it becomes apparent that pine and cypress are the last to shed their greenery" (岁寒，然后知松柏之后凋也 *suì hán, rán hòu zhī sōng bó zhī hòu diāo yě*). Pine and cypress are thus used together to symbolize a person's noble constancy of character.

9. 划 (*huá*) v. to scratch.

10. 坚贞 (*jiān zhēn*) adj. faithful and constant.

现代文翻译 Modern Chinese Translation

(妻子回答说)自从您离开后，我无心爱上别人 。脸上的指痕是睡梦中划⁹的。丝带上的同心结是自己系的。裙子是莽撞²的小孩儿³给踏破的。

发鬓被珠帘弄乱了；金钗旧了，两股分开了，我留着眼泪是在思念你啊！我象南山的松柏一样坚贞，¹⁰根本无心爱上别人！

评论与提问 Comment and Question

Read the two poems together and comment on how cleverly the wife turns the tables on her accusatory husband. ☞*HTRCP*, pp. 249−251 for an analysis of the two poems.

P06

yǒu suǒ sī
有 所 思¹

There Is One I Love

yǒu	*suǒ*	*sī*		
有	所²	思		

There is one I love

nǎi	*zài*	*dà*	*hǎi*	*nán*
乃³	在	大	海	南△ᵃ

He is south of the great sea.

hé	*yòng*	*wèn*	*wèi*	*jūn*
何	用⁴	问⁵	遗⁶	君

Why should I send you anything!

shuāng	*zhū*	*dài*	*mào*	*zān*
双	珠	玳	瑁⁷	簪△ᵃ ⁸

As for your tortoiseshell hairpin with twin pearls,

yòng	*yù*	*shào*	*liáo*	*zhī*
用	玉	绍	缭△ᵇ ⁹	之

I braided it with jade.

wén	*jūn*	*yǒu*	*tā*	*xīn*		Yet when I heard that you have another love,
闻	君	有	它	心		

lā	*zá*	*cuī*	*shāo*	*zhī*		I shattered it, smashed and burned it,
拉[10]	杂[11]	摧[12]	烧△[b]	之		

cuī	*shāo*	*zhī*		Smashed and burned it.
摧	烧△[b]	之		

dāng	*fēng*	*yáng*	*qí*	*huī*		Facing the wind I scattered its ashes.
当[13]	风	扬[14]	其	灰△[c]		

cóng	*jīn*	*yǐ*	*wǎng*		From this day on
从	今	以	往		

wù	*fù*	*xiāng*	*sī*		I will absolutely love you no more.
勿[15]	复	相	思△		

xiāng	*sī*	*yǔ*	*jūn*	*jué*		My love for you is severed.
相	思	与	君	绝[16]		

jī	*míng*	*gǒu*	*fèi*		Cocks crow, dogs bark,
鸡[17]	鸣[18]	狗	吠△[c] [19]		

xiōng	*sǎo*	*dāng*	*zhī*	*zhī*		My brother and sister-in-law will know.
兄	嫂	当[20]	知△[d]	之		

fēi	*hū*	*xī*		Alas! Alas!
妃	呼	狶△[d] [21]		

qiū	*fēng*	*sù*	*sù*	*chén*	*fēng*	*sī*		The autumn wind soughs, and a sparrow hawk shrieks,
秋	风	肃	肃[22]	晨	风[23]	飔△[d] [24]		

dōng	*fāng*	*xū*	*yú*	*gāo*	*zhī*	*zhī*		Soon in the east dawn will be breaking and it will be known.
东	方	须	臾[25]	高[26]	知△[d]	之		

[乐府 Music Bureau verse]

(Tr. Jui-lung Su, *HTRCP*, p. 93)

字词释义 Vocabulary Notes

1. 有所思 There is one I love, a famous Han dynasty *yuefu* song classified under "Lyrics for Drum and Pipe Songs" (*gǔchuī qǔcí* 鼓吹曲辞) in Guo Maoqian's 郭茂倩 (1041–1099) *Collection of Yuefu poetry* (*Yuèfǔ shījí* 乐府诗集).

2. 所 auxiliary particle. 所 + verb is a structure similar to an object clause in English like "what+subject+verb", "the one (which, whom) +subject+verb", etc. For instance, 所思 means "the one whom I miss."

3. 乃 v. to be. MdnC: 是 (*shì*).

4. 何用 or "何以," why. MdnC: 为什么 (*wèi shén me*).

5. 问 v. to ask. Here it means "to send one's respect to someone." MdnC: 问候 (*wèn hòu*). ☞请 代我问候他 Please send my respect to him for me.

6. 遗 (*wèi*) v. to offer as a gift. MdnC: 赠送 (*zèng sòng*). 👉他赠送了一个花篮 He presented a basket of flowers as a gift.

7. 玳瑁 n. hawksbill turtle. Its shell is used as adornment.

8. 簪 n. hairpin. 玳瑁簪 refers to hairpin with the tortoiseshell adornment.

9. 绍缭 (紹繚) v. to twine, bind. MdnC: 缠绕 (*chán rào*). 👉树上缠绕着藤. There is wisteria twining round the tree.

10. 拉 v. to pull. Here it means to break off. MdnC: 折断 (*zhé duàn*). 👉他把树枝折断了 He broke off a branch.

11. 杂 (雜) adj. miscellaneous. Here it means "smashed." 拉杂 together means "to break (the hairpin) into very small pieces"(*zhé suì* 折碎).

12. 摧 v. to break. MdnC: 毁坏 (*huǐ huài*). 👉不要毁坏桌椅 Don't damage the tables and chairs.

13. 当 (當) prep. facing, to sb's face. 👉请当着大家的面说清楚. Please make it clear in the presesence of everyone. See note 20 for a different meaning of the word.

14. 扬 (揚) v. to throw up and scatter sth. 👉不要把土扬起来！ Don't scatter the dirt!

15. 勿 adv. don't. 👉请勿吸烟 Please do not smoke! See also P38 note 21.

16. 绝 (絕) v. to cut off, sever. MdnC: 断绝 (*duàn jué*). 👉他要跟家人断绝关系 He wants to sever all the ties with his family. See P30 note 2 for a different meaning of the word.

17. "鸡鸣"句 an allusion to "Cock Crow" ("Jī míng" 鸡鸣) in *The Book of Poetry*. The story tells that "a young woman begs her lover to keep quiet during their tryst so that the dogs will not bark." Here, it refers to the sweet time that the girl and her lover were together. (Su; *HTRCP*, p. 94).

18. 鸣 (鳴) v. (bird, animals, or insects) to cry. MdnC: 叫 (*jiào*).

19. 吠 v. to bark. MdnC: 叫 (*jiào*).

20. 当 (當) adv. should, ought to. MdnC: 应当 (*yīng dāng*). 👉我们应当互相帮助 We should help each other. See note 13 for a different meaning of the word.

21. 妃呼豨 auxiliary particle, a sigh.

22. 肃肃 the sound of wind.

23. 晨风 (風) n. bird name.

24. 飑 (颸) v. used here for "思." This word means "(a bird) shrieks to woo."

25. 须臾 adv. moment, instant. MdnC: 很快 (*hěn kuài*).

26. 高 adj. tall, used here in the sense of "皓" (*hào*), meaning "to become bright."

27. 幽会 (*yōu huì*) n. a secret meeting of lovers.

现代文翻译 Modern Chinese Translation

　　我思念的人，在大海的南边。(你问我)为什么⁴要送你礼物问候⁵你？ (因为你曾送我)双珠的玳瑁簪！ (我特意)用玉缠绕⁹这支簪！

　　听说你有了别的爱人，(我气愤得)把这支簪折碎¹¹ 毁坏¹² 然后烧掉！迎着风，我把这支簪烧成的灰扬¹⁴起来！从今以后，不再思念你。我的思念从此不再有你！

(当初)我们幽会[27]的事情，我的哥哥和嫂子<u>应当</u>[20]是知道的。唉！秋风吹着，晨风鸟鸣叫着，天<u>很快</u>[25]就亮了，就会知道该怎么样了！

评论与提问 Comments and Questions

1. This poem is a Music Bureau poem (*yuèfǔ* 乐府). When poets of later generations wrote poems in the *yuefu* style, they often used the original *yuefu* titles. "There Is One I Love" is one of those frequently used titles. The traditional image of women in Chinese poetry is usually someone longing for love or waiting for her lover to return, such as the speaker in P05. However, this poem presents a different kind of female figure who reveals her anger, determination, and confusion after her lover has jilted her. Compare this poem with P05, paying special attention to their different personae and styles. ☞ *HTRCP*, pp. 84–85 and pp. 93–95 for an introduction to *yuefu* poetry and for an analysis of this poem.

2. This poem is written with uneven lines ranging from trisyllabic, tetrasyllabic, pentasyllabic to heptasyllabic lines. A rhetorical device, anadiplosis, called *liánzhū* 连珠 in Chinese, is also used, for example, "摧烧之" appears twice to link up lines 7 and 8, as does "相思" to link up lines 11–12. Do the variation in line length and the use of *lianzhu* facilitate the expression of strong emotions by the speaker?

P07

cháng xiāng sī
长 相 思[1]

Prolonged Longing

[*táng*] *bái jū yì*
[唐] 白 居 易[2]

[Tang Dyn.] Bai Juyi

biàn shuǐ liú
汴 水[3] 流△

The Bian River flows,

sì shuǐ liú
泗 水[4] 流△

The Si River flows,

liú dào guā zhōu gǔ dù tóu
流 到 瓜 洲[5] 古 渡 头△[6]

Reaching the Gourd Isle, and its ferry of old.

wú shān diǎn diǎn chóu
吴 山[7] 点 点 愁△[8]

Wu Mountains afar: dots and dots of sorrow.

sī yōu yōu
思 悠 悠△[9]

My longing, long and forlorn,

hèn yōu yōu
恨[10] 悠 悠△

My regret, long and prolonged,

hèn dào guī shí fāng shǐ xiū
恨 到 归[11] 时 方[12] 始 休△[13]

Until he returns, shall go on and on.

yuè　míng　rén　yǐ　lóu
月　明　人　倚^14　楼△

The moon shines upon the tower
I'm leaning on.

[小令 short lyric song]

(Tr. Zong-qi Cai)

字词释义 Vocabulary Notes

1. 长 (長) 相思　"Prolonged Longing," title of a tune.

2. 白居易　(style 字, Lètiān 乐天; literary name 号, Xiāngshān jūshì 香山居士, 772–846) is a famous mid-Tang poet. He is known for his "New *yuefu*" (*xīn yuèfǔ* 新乐府), namely narrative poems on corruption and injustice he witnessed.　He also wrote in a variety of styles, including the two famous long poems "The Mandolin Ballad" ("Pípa xíng" 琵琶行) and "Song of Lasting Sorrow" ("Chánghèn gē" 长恨歌).

3. 汴水　Bian river, eastern part of the Tongji Canal (Tōngjì qú 通济渠) in the Sui Dynasty. It originates in present-day Kaifeng 开封, Henan province. Bian River flows southeast to Si county 泗县, Anhui province where Bian River and Si River meet and then flow to Huai River (Huái hé 淮河).

4. 泗水　Si river, a major branch of Huai River, originates in present-day Shandong province.

5. 瓜洲　a famous ancient ferry on the northern bank of the Yangtze River. It is in present-day Yangzhou 扬州, Jiangsu province.

6. 渡头 (頭)　n. ferry. MdnC: 渡口 (*dù kǒu*).

7. 吴 (吳) 山　the Wu mountain, in present-day Zhejiang province. Here it refers to mountains south of the Yangtze River.

8. 愁　n. sorrow. Here it refers to the sorrow of separation (*lí chóu* 离愁). See also P03 note 17.

9. 悠悠　adv. long. See also P01 note 20, P18 note 6, P84 note 10, and P90 note 5.

10. 恨　v. to hate, to resent. MdnC: 怨恨 (*yuàn hèn*) n. resentment. See P81 note 8 for a different meaning of the word.

11. 归 (歸)　v. to go back to, return. MdnC: 归来 (*guī lái*) [formal]. 👉他刚从海外归来 He just return from overseas. See also P42 note 9, P44 note 4, and P58 note 6.

12. 方　adv. not until. See also P03 note 10. 方始 also means "not until."

13. 休　v. to stop. MdnC: 停止 (*tíng zhǐ*). 👉所有的活动都停止了 All activities have stopped. See also P68 note 8 and P84 note 16.

14. 倚　v. to lean on. MdnC: 靠 (*kào*). 👉他靠在窗边 He leans on the window.

现代文翻译 Modern Chinese Translation

　　汴水流啊，　泗水流啊，流到瓜州古老的渡口^6那里，远处的吴山点点，如同离愁。^8
　　思念很深长，但心中也充满了怨恨。^10 这怨恨要到(他)归来^11的时候才会停止。^13 月明的时候，人靠^14在楼上(思念着远方的人)。

评论与提问 Comments and Questions

1. "Prelonged Longing" 长相思 is not the poem's thematic title, but its tune title. All lyric songs, long or short, are composed and often sung to a given tune and therefore always carry a tune title, with or without a thematic subtitle. Each tune prescribes the number of lines, the number of characters in each line, as well as the tonal pattern of the entire poem. ☞ *HTRCP*, pp. 245–249, 262–264 for a discussion of the formal features of lyric songs.

2. Read the comments on topic+comment stanza given in P01, and determine if the two stanzas of this poem can be seen as topic+comment ones.

3. Given an obvious break between natural description and emotive statements, would you go one step further and describe the structure of the entire poem in terms of topic and comment?

P08

yì jiǎn méi
一 剪 梅[1]

[sòng] lǐ qīng zhào
[宋] 李清照[2]

To the Tune "A Twig of Plum Blossom"

[Song Dyn.] Li Qingzhao

hóng ǒu xiāng cán yù diàn qiū
红 藕[3] 香 残[4] 玉 簟[5] 秋△

The fragrance of the red lotus lingers and the jade-like bamboo mat spreads the air of autumn.

qīng jiě luó cháng
轻 解 罗 裳[6]

Gently, I take off my silk skirt.

dú shàng lán zhōu
独[7] 上 兰 舟△[8]

Alone, I board a magnolia boat.

yún zhōng shuí jì jǐn shū lái
云 中 谁 寄[9] 锦 书[10] 来

Through the clouds who's sent a love letter?

yàn zì huí shí
雁 字[11] 回 时

The wild geese're returning, arrayed like a character when

yuè mǎn xī lóu
月 满 西 楼△

the moonlight fills the western pavilion.

huā zì piāo líng shuǐ zì liú
花 自 飘 零[12] 水 自 流△

All by themselves, the flowers fade and fall, and the water flows on.

yì zhǒng xiāng sī
一 种 相 思

One type of love-sickness;

liǎng	*chù*	*xián*	*chóu*	
两	处	闲	愁△¹³	two places of idled sadness.

cǐ	*qíng*	*wú*	*jì*	*kě*	*xiāo*	*chú*	
此	情	无	计¹⁴	可	消	除¹⁵	This love-sickness, there is no way to eliminate it:

cái	*xià*	*méi*	*tóu*	
才	下	眉¹⁶	头	Just get it down the brows.

què	*shàng*	*xīn*	*tóu*	
却¹⁷	上	心	头△	It comes up back again to my heart.

[小令 short lyric song]   (Tr. Li E)

字词释义 Vocabulary Notes

1. 一剪梅　"A Twig of Plum Blossom," title of a tune.

2. 李清照　(literary name 号, Yì'ān jūshì 易安居士, 1084–1151) a renowned female Song poet, who has been regarded as a representative of the "delicate and restrained" school (*wǎnyuēpài* 婉约派). She is also one of the earliest theorists of the Song *ci*. In "A Critique of the Song lyric" ("Cílùn" 词论), she advocates a careful distinction between the *ci* 词 and the *shi* 诗.

3. 藕　n. lotus root. Here it refers to lotus (*hé huā* 荷花).

4. 残　adj. withered. See P03 note 7.

5. 簟　n. bamboo mat. MdnC: 竹席 (*zhú xí*).

6. 裳　n. skirt. MdnC: 裙(*qún*). See also P52 note 9.

7. 独 (獨)　adv. alone. MdnC: 独自 (*dú zì*). 👉他独自完成了任务 He completed the mission by himself. See also P26 note 3.

8. 兰 (蘭) 舟　magnolia boat, a literary name for a boat, usually used in poetry.

9. 寄　v. to send, post, mail. 👉我去寄信 I am going to mail a letter. See also P59 note 1 and P65 note 8.

10. 锦书 (錦書) or 锦字书　an embroidered letter. According to "The Biographies of Famous Women" ("Liènǚzhuàn" 列女传) in *The History of the Jin Dynasty* (*Jìn shū* 晋书), Dou Tao 窦滔 in the Former Qin State (351−394) garrisoned the frontier and could not go home for a long time. His wife Miss Su 苏氏 missed him very much. Then she wove a silk brocade with a palindrome poem and sent it to his husband to show how much she missed him, 锦书 is thus used to refer to love letters, especially between husband and wife. See also P100 note 14.

11. 雁字　literally "a character formed by wild geese." A flock of wild geese usually fly in an array that resembles Chinese character "一" or "人".

12. 飘零　v. (of flower and leaves) to fade and fall.

13. 闲 (閒) 愁　n. unknown anxiety. Here it refers to yearning between wife and husband.

14. 计 (計)　n. a way to solve something. MdnC: 办法 (*bàn fǎ*). 👉我找到了一个办法 I found a way. See also P65 note 5.

15. 消除　v. to dissipate, remove.

16. 眉　n. eyebrow. 眉头 means brow.

17. 却 (卻) conj. but, yet. Here it means "again" (yòu 又). See also P59 note 8 and P70 note 5. For a different meaning of the word, see P52 note 10.

18. 精致 (jīng zhì) adj. fine, delicate, exquisite.   19. 凋落 (diāo luò) v. to wither and fall.

20. 紧锁 (jǐn suǒ) v. to knit (one's brow)   21. 舒展 (shū zhǎn) v. to extend, smooth out.

现代文翻译 Modern Chinese Translation

红荷花³的香气渐渐淡了。秋天到了，在精致¹⁸的竹席⁵(上休息有些凉了)。轻轻解开丝裙，⁶独自⁷上船。谁寄来了书信？ 一群大雁飞回, (我正在)月光照满的西楼上(盼望着呢！)

花儿总要凋落,²⁰ 水总在流。 相思之情，我和他虽分处两地，却是一样的！这相思没有办法¹⁴可以消除¹⁵掉，(紧锁²⁰的)眉头(才刚舒展²¹开)，心头又¹⁷开始思念！

评论与提问 Comments and Questions

1. This poem exhibits a theme and structure commonly seen in short lyric songs. It consists of four tripling semantic units in two stanzas. For major themes of short song lyrics, ☞ *HTRCP*, p. 260.

2. Identify the autumnal images in this poem. How are they utilized by the poet to express her emotions? In P01, we talked about the "affective image" 兴 (xīng), and can you find the use of 兴 in this song lyric? In lines 8 & 9, "一种相思，两处闲愁", what does "两处" refer to?

P09

shuāng diào   chén zuì dōng fēng chūn qíng
【双调¹】沉 醉 东 风² 春 情³

[yuán] xú zài sī
[元] 徐 再 思⁴

To the Tune "Deeply Drunk in the East Wind" [*Shuangdiao* key]: Spring Passions

[Yuan Dyn.] Xu Zaisi

yí	*zì*	*duō*	*cái*	*jiān*	*kuò*		
一	自⁵	多	才⁶	间	阔 ▲ᵃ⁷		

Ever since I was apart from this versatile man,

jǐ	*shí*	*pàn*	*dé*	*chéng*	*hé*
几	时	盼	得	成	合 ₋ᵇ⁸

I have been wondering and expecting when I can be reunited with him.

jīn	*rì*	*gè*	*měng*	*jiàn*	*tā*		*mén*	*qián* *guò*
今	日	个⁹	猛¹⁰	见	他	、	门	前 过 ▲ᵃ

Today, I suddenly saw him, passing by my house.

dài	*huàn*	*zhe*	*pà*	*rén*	*qiáo*	*kē*
待¹¹	唤	着	怕	人	瞧	科 ₋ᵇ¹²

I wanted to call him, yet I was afraid to be seen by others.

wǒ	*zhè*	*lǐ*	*gāo*	*chàng*	*dāng*	*shí*	*shuǐ*	*diào*	*gē*	
我	这	里	高	唱	当	时	水	调	歌△b 13	Here I sing the popular tune of "Prelude to the River Tune" loudly.

yào	*shí*	*dé*	*shēng*	*yīn*	*shì*	*wǒ*	
要	识	得	声	音	是	我▲a	Please recognize my voice!

[小令 solo song poem]

(Tr. Li E)

字词释义 Vocabulary Notes

1. 双调 (雙調) *Shuangdiao* key, one of the *Gongdiao* keys (*gōng diào* 宫调). *Gongdiao* keys of *qu* 曲 came from palace music in the Sui and the Tang Dynasties. According to the Yuan scholar Yannan Zhi' an's 燕南芝庵 "Talk on Singing" ("Chàng lùn" 唱论), seventeen *Gongdiao* keys were used in *qu* genre. Each *Gongdiao* keys has its own basic key and distinguished style.

2. 沉醉东风 (東風) "Deeply Drunk in the East Wind," title of a tune.

3. 春情 title of the song, meaning "spring passions" or romantic passions.

4. 徐再思 (style 字, Dékě 德可; literary name 号, Tiánzhāi 甜斋, fl. 14th century), a *qu* poet in the Yuan Dynasty. He called himself "Sweet diet" (甜斋) since he loved sweet food. His contemporary Guan Yuanshi 贯云石, another famous *qu* poet in the Yuan, called himself "Sour diet" (Suānzhāi 酸斋). Therefore, their works were mentioned together as "sour and sweet *yuefu* poems" (*suāntián yuèfǔ* 酸甜乐府) in the Yuan.

5. 一自 prep. since, from. MdnC: 自从 (*zì cóng*).

6. 多才 adj. versatile, gifted in many ways. Here it refers to the versatile man the girl loves.

7. 间阔 (間闊) v. to be apart for a long time.

8. 合 adj. whole. 成合 means "to become reunited." MdnC: 团聚 (*tuán jù*). ☞一家人终于团聚了 The whole family were eventually reunited. See P12 note 7 and P76 note 13 for different meanings of the word.

9. 个 (個) a colloquial auxiliary word, often used after "yesterday," "today," or "tomorrow."

10. 猛 adv. suddenly, abruptly [informal]. ☞他猛地往前一蹦 He suddenly jumped forward.

11. 待 v. to wait. Here it is a special usage in dramas, novels, and dialects in premodern China, meaning "to want to" (*yào* 要).

12. 科 n. term in the Yuan drama, referring to the facial expression and action on the stage. Here it is used to emphasize the action of "staring at sth" (瞧).

13. 水调 (調) 歌 or 水调歌头, "Prelude to the River Tune," title of a tune.

14. 多才多艺 (*duō cái duō yì*) versatile, gifted in many ways.

现代文翻译 Modern Chinese Translation

自从5跟多才多艺14的他分别之后，什么时候(我)才能盼到和他团聚8啊！今天猛10地见到他从我家门前经过，想要11叫他，却又怕人瞧见。于是我在这里 高声唱着当时流行的《水调歌头》，（他听到）要认得唱歌的声音是我的呀！

评论与提问Comments and Questions

1. This is a solo song poem (*xiǎolìng* 小令) of the *sǎnqǔ* 散曲 poetry. Like a short lyric song (also called *xiǎolìng* 小令) of the *cí* 词 poetry, it is short and concise and is required to follow a specific tune pattern. However, compared to a short lyric song, a solo song poem usually contains more colloquial expressions, often vulgar ones, follows a stricter metrical pattern, and more freely employs "padding words" (*chènzì* 衬字). ☞ *HTRCP*, pp. 329–333 for an introduction to *sanqu*.

2. This poem vividly depicts a quick-witted woman's psychological response when she catches sight of her lover passing by her place. Pay attention to the colloquial style of this poem and compare it with P05 and P06: how does it differ from them in wording and emotional intensity?

练习 EXERCISES

一 填空 Fill in blanks

A. 诗词填字：妆 流 雁 瞧 摧 垂 解 股 待 休 独 零 乱 满 飘 兰 归 唤 闻

1. 轻＿＿罗裳，＿＿上＿＿舟。　　　2. 花自＿＿＿＿水自＿＿。
3. 红＿＿＿＿泪哭郎君。　　　4. ＿＿字回时，月＿＿西楼。
5. ＿＿＿＿着怕人＿＿科。　　　6. 恨到＿＿时方始＿＿。
7. ＿＿君有它心，拉杂＿＿烧之。　　　8. 蝉鬓朱帘＿＿，金钗旧＿＿分。

B. 现代文填词：团聚 停止 断绝 归来 毁坏 办法 问候 缠绕 莽撞 赠送

1. 他做事很＿＿＿＿。　　　2. 他刚从海外＿＿＿＿。
3. 请代我＿＿＿＿他。　　　4. 一家人终于＿＿＿＿了。
5. 所有的活动都＿＿＿＿了。　　　6. 树上＿＿＿＿着藤萝。
7. 不要＿＿＿＿桌椅。　　　8. 他和家人＿＿＿＿了关系。
9. 他＿＿＿＿了一个花篮。　　　10. 我们要找到解决问题的＿＿＿＿。

二 形近字辨析 Distinguish easily confused characters

1. 花自＿＿零水自流　a. 漂　b. 瓢　c. 飘　　　2. 几时＿＿得成合　a. 盼　b. 份　c. 吩
3. 待唤着怕人＿＿科　a. 樵　b. 瞧　c. 焦　　　4. 红＿＿垂泪裸郎君　a. 状　b. 妆　c. 壮
5. 此＿＿无计可消除　a. 清　b. 情　c. 请　　　6. 妾是南山松＿＿　a. 伯　b. 泊　c. 柏
7. 云中谁寄＿＿书来　a. 锦　b. 绵　c. 棉　　　8. 当风＿＿其灰　a. 杨　b. 扬　c. 汤

三 连句 Match the first part with the second

1. 从今以往( )　　2. 才下眉头( )　　3. 轻解罗裳( )　　4. 一自多才间阔( )
5. 雁字回时( )　　6. 闻君有它心( )　　7. 蝉鬓朱帘乱( )　　8. 一种相思( )
9. 自从君去后( )　　10. 鸡鸣狗吠( )

a. 无心恋别人 b. 拉杂摧烧之 c. 却上心头 d. 金钗旧股分
e. 勿复相思   f. 独上兰舟   g. 月满西楼 h. 兄嫂当知之
i. 几时盼得成合 j. 两处闲愁

四 句读 Punctuate and translate the following passage

花自飘零水自流一种相思两处闲愁自从君去后无心恋别人梦中面上指痕
新罗带同心自绾被蛮儿踏破裙今日个猛见他门前过待唤着怕人瞧科我这
里高唱当时水调歌要识得声音是我闻君有它心拉杂摧烧之摧烧之当风扬
其灰从今以往勿复相思相思与君绝

五 听写 Dictation

1. 云中 ___ ___ ___ ___ 来，___ ___ ___ 时, ___ ___ 西 ___。
2. ___ ___ ___ ___ ___ 风 ___，___ ___ ___ ___ ___ ___ ___ 之。
3. ___ ___ ___ 哭 ___ ___，___ 是南山 ___ ___，无心 ___ ___ 人。
4. ___ ___ 有 ___ ___，___ ___ ___ ___ 之。
5. 一 ___ ___ ___ ___ ___，几 ___ ___ ___ ___ ___ ___。

3

田 园 诗

Fields and Gardens

P10

guī yuán tián jū qí yī
归 园 田 居 其 一

[dōng jìn]   táo qián
[东晋] 陶 潜[1]

Returning to Live on the Farm, No. 1

[Jin Dyn.] Tao Qian

shào 少	*wú* 无	*shì* 适[2]	*sú* 俗[3]	*yùn* 韵[4]	Since youth out of tune with the vulgar world,
xìng 性	*běn* 本	*ài* 爱	*qiū* 丘	*shān* 山 △	My nature instinctively loves hills and mountains.
wù 误[5]	*luò* 落	*chén* 尘	*wǎng* 网[6]	*zhōng* 中	By mishap I fell into the dusty net,
yí 一	*qù* 去	*sān* 三	*shí* 十	*nián* 年 △[7]	Once gone, thirteen years went by.
jī 羁[8]	*niǎo* 鸟	*liàn* 恋	*jiù* 旧	*lín* 林	The caged bird longs for its grove of old,
chí 池	*yú* 鱼	*sī* 思	*gù* 故	*yuān* 渊 △[9]	The pond's fish thinks of its former depths.
kāi 开	*huāng* 荒[10]	*nán* 南	*yě* 野	*jì* 际[11]	Clearing land at the edge of the southern wilds,
shǒu 守	*zhuō* 拙[12]	*guī* 归	*yuán* 园	*tián* 田 △	Guarding simplicity, I returned to my farm.
fāng 方[13]	*zhái* 宅	*shí* 十	*yú* 余	*mǔ* 亩	The homestead amounts to ten-odd *mou*,
cǎo 草	*wū* 屋	*bā* 八	*jiǔ* 九	*jiān* 间 △	With a thatched hut of eight or nine bays.
yú 榆[14]	*liǔ* 柳[15]	*yìn* 荫[16]	*hòu* 后	*yán* 檐[17]	Elms and willows shade the rear eaves,
táo 桃[18]	*lǐ* 李[19]	*luó* 罗[20]	*táng* 堂[21]	*qián* 前 △	Peach and plum line up in front of the hall.
ài 暧	*ài* 暧[22]	*yuǎn* 远	*rén* 人	*cūn* 村	In a haze lie the distant villages,

yī 依	*yī* 依 23	*xū* 墟	*lǐ* 里 24	*yān* 烟 △25
gǒu 狗	*fèi* 吠	*shēn* 深	*xiàng* 巷 26	*zhōng* 中
jī 鸡	*míng* 鸣	*sāng* 桑 27	*shù* 树	*diān* 巅 △28

Indistinct is the smoke above the houses.

A dog barks somewhere in the deep alley,

A cock crows from atop the mulberry tree.

hù 户 29	*tíng* 庭 30	*wú* 无	*chén* 尘	*zá* 杂
xū 虚	*shì* 室	*yǒu* 有	*yú* 余	*xián* 闲 △
jiǔ 久	*zài* 在	*fán* 樊 31	*lóng* 笼	*lǐ* 里
fù 复	*dé* 得	*fǎn* 返	*zì* 自	*rán* 然 △

My home is unsoiled by worldly dust,

Within empty rooms I have peace to spare.

For long I have lived within a cage,

And now I may return to nature.

[五言古诗 pentasyllabic ancient-style verse]

(Tr. Wendy Swartz, *HTRCP*, pp.122–123)

字词释义 Vocabulary Notes

1. 陶潜 (style 字, Yuānmíng 渊明, 365? – 427) a renowned Eastern Jin poet who developed farmstead poetry or literally "poetry of fields and gardens" (*tiányuán shī* 田园诗).

2. 适 (適) v. to adapt to something. MdnC: 适应 (*shì yìng*). 👉他很适应新环境 He is well adapted to the new environment .

3. 俗 adj. mundane, mundaneness. MdnC: 世俗 (*shì sú*). 👉你不用在意这些世俗之见 You don't have to heed these mundane views.

4. 韵 (韻) n. rhyme, used figuratively here to mean one's nature. MdnC: 个性 (*gè xìng*). 👉他的个性很强 He has a strong personality.

5. 误 (誤) n. mistake. MdnC: 错误 (*cuò wù*). 👉他犯了个错误 He made a mistake.

6. 尘网 n. dusty net, used figuratively to mean the bondage of officialdom.

7. 三十年 Modern scholars have emended the text to read "thirteen years" (*shísān nián* 十三年) based on the widely accepted belief that Tao entered officialdom in 393 and retired in 405.

8. 羁 (羈) v. to trammel, to bridle. 羁鸟 a caged bird.

9. 渊 (淵) n. deep pool.

10. 荒 n. wasteland. MdnC: 荒地 (*huāng dì*).

11. 际 (際) n. border. See also P40 note13.

12. 拙 adj. clumsy, awkward. MdnC: 朴拙 (*pǔ zhuō*). 👉他人很朴拙 He is simple and sincere.

13. 方 n. rectangle. See P03 note 10 and P31 note 4 for different meanings of the word. 方宅 refers to homestead.

14. 榆 n. elm.

15. 柳 n. willow. See P02 note 4.

16. 荫 (蔭 *yìn*) v. to shade. MdnC: 遮蔽 (*zhē bì*). 👉树林遮蔽了视线 The woods block my view.

17. 檐 (簷) n. eaves. MdnC: 屋檐 (*wū yán*). See also P13 note 5.

18. 桃　n. peach.　　　　　　　　　19. 李　n. plum.

20. 罗 (羅)　v. to line up. MdnC: 罗列 (*luó liè*) [formal]. 👉房屋罗列在山上 The houses line up on the hillside. See P04 note 12 for a different meaning of the word.

21. 堂　n. the main room of a house. See also P86 note 7.

22. 暧暧 (暧)　adv. indistinct, hidden from the view. See also P14 notes 11.

23. 依依　adv. softly, gently.

24. 墟里　n. village. MdnC: 村落 (*cūn luò*) [formal].

25. 烟　n. smoke. Here it refers to smoke from kitchen chimneys (*chuī yān* 炊烟).

26. 巷　n. alley.　　　　　　　　　27. 桑　n. mulberry.

28. 巅 (巔)　n. mountain peak.

29. 户　n. door.

30. 庭　n. front yard. MdnC: 庭院 (*tíng yuàn*).　See also P94 note 5.

31. 樊　n. fence. 樊笼 means a cage.

32. 迎合 (*yíng hé*)　v. to cater to.

33. 官场 (*guān chǎng*)　n. the world of officialdom.

34. 开垦 (*kāi kěn*)　v. to clear land.

35. 依稀 (*yī xī*)　adv. vaguely.

36. 烦杂 (*fán zá*)　adj. diverse and miscellaneous.

现代文翻译 Modern Chinese Translation

　　年轻时(我)就没有迎合³²世俗³的个性,⁴天性原本喜欢山川。错误⁵地进入了官场,³³一去就是十三年。⁷笼中的鸟儿仍想着住过的树林,池中的鱼儿忘不了游过的水潭。在南边的田野开垦³⁴荒地,¹⁰有着朴拙¹²本性的我回到田原。家里有十多亩地,八九间茅草屋。房后榆树和柳树成荫,房前罗列²⁰着桃树和李树。远处的山村依稀³⁵可见；村中的炊烟²⁵轻柔地飘起。狗在巷中叫着,鸡在桑树顶叫着。家里没有世俗烦杂³⁶的事情干扰,空空的房间中有的是悠闲的生活。留在笼子一样的官场里太久了,现在终于可以重新回到自然了。

评论与提问 Comments and Questions

1. Is the poet depicting what he actually sees, what he imagines, or both? Consequently, is the poem a realistic description of the poet's farmstead or a projection of his agrarian utopia? 👉 *HTRCP*, pp. 122–124 and formulate your own view.

2. "A dog barks somewhere in the deep alley/A crock crows from atop the mulberry trees" is an allusive couplet. What famous philosophical text does it allude to? 👉 *HTRCP*, p. 123.

3. This poem is an ancient-style pentasyllabic poem. What does "pentasyllabic" refer to? What does "ancient-style" (*gǔtǐ* 古体) mean as opposed to "recent-style" (*jìntǐ* 近体)? 👉 *HTRCP*, pp. 103–104, 161–162.

4. Can you identify the distinctive semantic rhythm and rhyming scheme of a pentasyllabic poem like this one? 👉 *HTRCP*, p. 103–104.

P11

yǐn jiǔ qí wǔ
饮 酒 其 五
[*dōng jìn*] *táo qián*
[东晋] 陶 潜¹

On Drinking Wine, No. 5

[Jin Dyn.] Tao Qian

jié	*lú*	*zài*	*rén*	*jìng*
结²	庐³	在	人	境⁴
ér	*wú*	*chē*	*mǎ*	*xuān*
而	无	车	马	喧△⁵
wèn	*jūn*	*hé*	*néng*	*ěr*
问	君	何	能	尔⁶
xīn	*yuǎn*	*dì*	*zì*	*piān*
心	远	地	自	偏△⁷
cǎi	*jú*	*dōng*	*lí*	*xià*
采	菊⁸	东	篱⁹	下
yōu	*rán*	*jiàn*	*nán*	*shān*
悠	然¹⁰	见	南	山△
shān	*qì*	*rì*	*xī*	*jiā*
山	气	日	夕¹¹	佳
fēi	*niǎo*	*xiāng*	*yǔ*	*huán*
飞	鸟	相	与¹²	还△
cǐ	*zhōng*	*yǒu*	*zhēn*	*yì*
此	中	有	真	意
yù	*biàn*	*yǐ*	*wàng*	*yán*
欲	辨¹³	已	忘	言△

[五言古诗pentasyllabic ancient-style verse]

I built my hut in the midst of men,

Yet hear no clamor of horse and carriage.

You ask how it can be like this?

With the mind detached, place becomes remote.

Plucking chrysanthemums by the eastern hedge,

From afar I catch sight of the southern mountain.

The mountain air becomes lovely at sunset,

As flying birds return together in flocks.

In these things there is true meaning,

I'd like to explain, but have forgotten the words.

(Tr. Wendy Swartz, *HTRCP*, p. 125)

字词释义 Vocabulary Notes

1. See the biographic note in P10 note 1.
2. 结 (結) v. to build. MdnC: 建 (*jiàn*). 🗣房子建得很坚固 The house is very solidly built.
3. 庐 (廬) n. house. MdnC: 房屋 (*fáng wū*).
4. 境 n. place, area.
5. 喧 adj. noisy. MdnC: 喧闹 (*xuān nào*).
6. 尔 (爾) adv. like this. MdnC: 这样 (*zhè yàng*).
7. 偏 adj. slanting toward one side, remote. MdnC: 偏僻 (*piān pì*) remote. 🗣这里太偏僻了 Here is too remote. See P63 note 5 for a different meaning of the word.
8. 菊 n. chrysanthemums. MdnC: 菊花 (*jú huā*).

9. 篱 (籬) n. fence. MdnC: 篱笆 (*lí bā*).
10. 悠然 adv. far away.
11. 日夕 n. sunset. MdnC: 黄昏 (*huáng hūn*).
12. 相与 (與) adv. together. MdnC: 结伴 (*jié bàn*). ☞他们会结伴前来 They will come together.
13. 辨 v. to distinguish. MdnC: 辨析 (*biàn xī*) [formal]. ☞请辨析一下这两个词的意思 Please distinguish the meanings of these two words.

现代文翻译 Modern Chinese Translation

　　把房子建²在人多的地方，却听不到车马的喧闹⁵声。请问您怎么能够做到这样⁶呢？这是因为心远离了（官场），住的地方自然也就偏僻⁷了。在东边的篱笆⁹下采菊花，⁸一抬头，看到远处的南山。山上的云气黄昏¹¹时特别美好，成群的飞鸟结伴¹²而还。这里有着人生的真义，想辨析¹³出来，却忘了怎么用语言来表达。

评论与提问 Comment and Question

This poem is well known for its masterful description of the detached mind. How would you relate the landscape depiction (lines 5−8) to the preceding statements about the mind? Can you name a possible philosophical source for the poet's remarks on meaning and words? ☞ *HTRCP*, pp. 125−126.

P12

guò gù rén zhuāng
过¹ 故 人² 庄

[*táng*] *mèng hào rán*
[唐] 孟 浩 然³

Visiting My Old Friend's Farmstead

[Tang Dyn.] Meng Haoran

gù	*rén*	*jù*	*jī*	*shǔ*	
故	人	具⁴	鸡	黍⁵	My old friend prepared rice and chicken dishes,
yāo	*wǒ*	*zhì*	*tián*	*jiā*	
邀⁶	我	至	田	家△	And invited me to his farm cottage.
lǜ	*shù*	*cūn*	*biān*	*hé*	
绿.	树	村	边	合.⁷	Green trees encircled the village along its edge,
qīng	*shān*	*guō*	*wài*	*xié*	
青	山	郭.⁸	外	斜△	Blue mountains slant away beyond the walls.
kāi	*xuān*	*miàn*	*chǎng*	*pǔ*	
开	轩⁹	面	场¹⁰	圃¹¹	Windows open, we faced the threshing ground and garden plots,

bǎ	*jiǔ*	*huà*	*sāng*	*má*	
把¹²	酒	话	桑	麻△¹³	Wine in hand, we chatted about mulberry and hemp crops

dài	*dào*	*chóng*	*yáng*	*rì*	
待	到	重	阳¹⁴	日	"When the Double Ninth Day comes,

hái	*lái*	*jiù*	*jú*	*huā*	
还	来	就¹⁵	菊	花△	I will come again to enjoy the chrysanthemums."

(Tr. Zong-qi Cai)

[五言律诗 pentasyllabic regulated verse,
tonal pattern II, see *HTRCP*, p. 171]

字词释义 Vocabulary Notes

1. 过 (過) v. to visit. MdnC: 拜访 *(bài fǎng)* [formal]. 👉今天我专程去拜访了一位作家
   Today I made a special trip to call on a writer. See also P24 note 1.
2. 故人 n. old friend. See also P39 note 11 and P40 note 5.
3. 孟浩然 (689–740), a famous landscape poet in the Tang Dynasty. He and Wang Wei 王维,
   another famous landscape poet in the Tang, are often mentioned together as Wang-Meng
   (王孟). See Wang Wei's biographic note in P15 note 2.
4. 具 v. to prepare. MdnC: 准备 *(zhǔn bèi)*. 👉他正在为会议准备文件 He is preparing
   documents for a meeting.
5. 黍 n. brown rice.
6. 邀 v. to invite. MdnC: 邀请 *(yāo qǐng)*.
7. 合 v. to surround. MdnC: 环绕 *(huán rào)*. 👉院子四周环绕着绿树 The yard is surrounded
   by trees. See also P15 note 6. See P09 note 8 and P76 note 13 for different meanings of the
   word.
8. 郭 n. the outer wall of a city. See also P14 note 17 and P22 note 5.
9. 轩 (軒)   n. window. MdnC: 窗户 *(chuāng hù)*. See also P99 note13.
10. 场 (場)   n. ground. Here it refers to a threshing ground *(dǎ gǔ chǎng* 打谷场).
11. 圃 n. garden. Here it denotes a vegetable plot *(cài yuán* 菜园).
12. 把 v. to hold. MdnC: 握住 *(wò zhù)*. 👉握住我的手 Hold my hand. See also P65 note 12.
13. 麻 n. hemp. 桑麻 is used together to stand for agricultural work *(nóng shì* 农事) here.
14. 重阳 (陽)   the Double Ninth Festival (9th day of the 9th month in Chinese lunar calendar),   a
    traditional Chinese holiday. On this holiday, people often climb a mountain *(dēng gāo* 登高),
    drink chrysanthemums wine *(júhuā jiǔ* 菊花酒), and wear the plant of cornus officinalis *(zhū
    yú* 茱萸). See also P55 note 1.
15. 就 v. to draw near. MdnC: 靠近 *(kào jìn)*. 👉船正靠近码头 The ship is nearing the dock.
16. 伸展 *(shēn zhǎn)* v. to stretch.
17. 畅谈 *(chàng tán)* v. to talk freely.
18. 欣赏 *(xīn shǎng)* v. to appreciate, enjoy.

现代文翻译 Modern Chinese Translation

老朋友准备[4]好饭菜，邀请[6]我到他家里作客。村子外面绿树环绕，[7]四周的青山伸展[16]着。打开窗户，[9]面对打谷场[10]和菜园，[11]和朋友一边喝酒，一边畅谈[17]农事。[13] 等到重阳节的那一天，我还要来老朋友家喝酒欣赏[18]菊花。

评论与提问 Comments and Questions

1. This poem tells of the poet's pleasant trip to his friend's home on a farm. What details has he included in the poem and how has he organized them?

2. This poem is a pentasyllabic regulated poem composed of four couplets. Has the poet followed the standard four-stage progression of a regulated poem? To what effect? ☞ *HTRCP,* pp. 165–169 for the comments on the four-stage progression (*qǐ* 起, *chéng* 承, *zhuǎn* 转, *hé* 合) of a regulated poem.

P13

shū	*hú*	*yīn*	*xiān*	*shēng*	*bì*	*qí yī*
书	湖	阴	先	生[1]	壁[2]	其一

Written on Master Huyin's Wall, No. 1

[*běi sòng*]	*wáng*	*ān*	*shí*
[北宋]	王	安	石[3]

[Song Dyn.] Wang Anshi

máo	*yán*	*cháng*	*săo*	*jìng*	*wú*	*tái*
茅[4]	檐[5]	长	扫	净	无	苔△[6]

The entry beneath thatch-roof eaves,
often swept, is clean and free of moss.

huā	*mù*	*chéng*	*qí*	*shŏu*	*zì*	*zāi*
花	木	成	畦[7]	手	自	栽△[8]

Flowering trees grow neatly in rows,
he planted them with his own hands.

yì	*shuǐ*	*hù*	*tián*	*jiāng*	*lù*	*rào*
一	水	护[9]	田	将[10]	绿	绕[11]

A single river guards the fields,
encircling them in a band of emerald,

liǎng	*shān*	*pái*	*tà*	*sòng*	*qīng*	*lái*
两	山	排[12]	闼[13]	送	青	来△

Two mountains shove open the
doorway, sending their green inside.
(Tr. Ronald Egan, *HTRCP,* p. 315)

[七言律绝 heptasyllabic regulated quatrain,
tonal pattern Ia, see *HTRCP,* p. 171]

字词释义 Vocabulary Notes

1. 湖阴 (陰) 先生　杨德逢 (fl. 1080) Wang Anshi's neighbor.　2. 壁 n. wall. See also P36 note 3.

3. 王安石 (style 字, Jièfǔ 介甫; literary name 号, Bànshān 半山 1021–1086), a politician and famous poet in the Northern Song Dynasty. Wang Anshi is one of the "Eight Masters of the Tang and Song" (唐宋八大家 *Táng Sòng bādàjià*).

4. 茅 (茆) n. thatch. See also P16 note 10 and P46 note 5.

5. 檐 (簷) n. eaves. See also P10 note 17.

6. 苔 n. moss. MdnC: 青苔 (*qīng tái*). See also P25 note 4.

7. 畦 n. rectangular pieces of land in a field, separated by ridges.

8. 栽 v. to plant. MdnC: 种 (*zhòng*).

9. 护 v. to guard. MdnC: 保护 (*bǎo hù*).

10. 将 (將) v. to carry. MdnC: 携带 (*xié dài*). 📖国际航班每人可携带 40 磅的行李 Each passenger can carry up to 40 lbs of luggage for international flights.

11. 绕 (繞) v. to circle. MdnC: 围绕 (*wéi rào*). 📖月亮围绕着地球转动 The moon revolves round the earth.

12. 排 v. to move, push. MdnC: 推开 (*tuī kāi*). 📖请把门推开 Please push the door open.

13. 闼 (闥) n. door. MdnC: 门 (*mén*).

现代文翻译 Modern Chinese Translation

　　茅屋常常清扫，干净得连青苔[6]都没有。花和树木排成一块块方形的田地，这都是主人亲手种[8]的。院子外面，一条小河好像要保护[9]着农田，把绿色的田地围绕[11]起来。两面的青山好象是推开[12]的大门[13]一样，把青翠的山色送到面前来。

评论与提问 Comments and Questions

1. If the parts of speech of one line matches neatly with those of the following line, the two lines are called a parallel couplet (*duì jù* 对句). In a tonally regulated quatrain, the use of a parallel couplet is not mandatory but quite common. Has this poem employed any parallel couplet?

2. This poem, written by the poet to compliment his neighbor's well-kept farmstead, is deceptively simple. Two phrases in lines 3–4 are actually drawn from Han dynasty historical writings to add one more layer of communication between the poet and his friend—an allusion exercise less-informed readers will likely miss. 📖 *HTRCP*, pp. 315–317.

练习 EXERCISES

一 填空 Fill in blanks

A. 诗词填字: 适 渊 韵 意 郭 结 畦 羁 辨 暧 喧 邀 忘 恋 合 斜 栽 具 思 丘 墟 庐

1. 故人____鸡黍，____我至田家。　　2. 花木成____手自____。

3. 少无____俗____，性本爱____山。　　4. _____远人村，依依____里烟。

5. 此中有真____，欲____已____言。　　6. 绿树村边____，青山____外____。

7. ____ ____在人境，而无车马____。　　8. ____鸟____旧林，池鱼____故____。

B. 现代文填词：结伴 世俗 携带 拜访 准备 辨析 握住 建

1. 请____ ____我的手。　　　　　2. 他要去____ ____一位诗人。
3. 他们会____ ____而来。　　　　4. 请____ ____这两个字的意思。
5. 这个房子____得很坚固。　　　 6. 你不用在意这些____ ____观念。
7. 他在____ ____文件。　　　　　8. 坐飞机每人可____ ____20公斤的行李。

二 形近字辨析 Distinguish easily confused characters

1. 结庐在人____　　　 a. 镜　b. 竟　c. 境　　2. 欲____已忘言　　a. 辨　b. 辩　c. 辫
3. ____树村边合　　　 a. 绿　b. 缘　c. 录　　4. 户____无尘杂　　a. 廷　b. 庭　c. 挺
5. 一水护田将绿____　 a. 饶　b. 晓　c. 绕　　6. ____到重阳日　　a. 侍　b. 待　c. 寺
7. 花木称畦手自____　 a. 载　b. 栽　c. 哉　　8. 守拙归____田　　a. 园　b. 圆　c. 因

三 连句 Match the first part with the second

1. 开轩面场圃( )　　2. 户庭无尘杂( )　　3. 结庐在人境( )　　4. 开荒南野际( )
5. 暧暧远人村( )　　6. 问君何能尔( )　　7. 采菊东篱下( )　　8. 待到重阳日( )

a. 心远地自偏　　　 b. 还来就菊花　　　 c. 悠然见南山　　　 d. 依依墟里烟
e. 虚室有余闲　　　 f. 把酒话桑麻　　　 g. 而无车马喧　　　 h. 守拙归园田

四 句读 Punctuate and translate the following passage

茅檐长扫净无苔花木成畦手自栽一水护田将绿绕两山排闼送青来采菊东篱下悠然见南山山气日夕佳飞鸟相与还此中有真意欲辨已忘言方宅十余亩草屋八九间榆柳荫后檐桃李罗堂前暧暧远人村依依墟里烟狗吠深巷中鸡鸣桑树巅户庭无尘杂虚室有余闲

五 听写 Dictation

1. ____ ____恋 ____ ____, ____ ____ ____故____。
2. ____ ____ ____ ____ 下, ____ ____ ____南 山。
3. ____ ____村 ____ ____,青 山____ ____ ____。
4. ____ 水 ____ ____ ____ ____ ____, 两 山____ ____ ____ ____。
5. ____ ____面 ____ ____ , ____ ____ ____桑 麻。
6. ____ ____ ____后 ____, ____ ____ ____ ____前。
7. 山 ____ ____ ____ ____, ____ ____ ____ ____。

4

游　览

Landscape: Excursions

yóu dōng tián shī
游 东 田[1] 诗
[nán cháo] xiè tiào
[南朝] 谢 朓[2]

An Outing to the Eastern Field

[Southern Dyn.] Xie Tiao

qī	*qī*	*kŭ*	*wú*	*cōng*	
戚	戚[3]	苦	无	悰[4]	Despondent, suffering from lack of cheer,
xié	*shŏu*	*gòng*	*xíng*	*lè*	
携[5]	手	共	行	乐 ▲	We go out for pleasure, hand in hand.
xún	*yún*	*zhì*	*lěi*	*xiè*	
寻	云	陟[6]	累[7]	榭[8]	Seeking clouds, we ascend a tiered kiosk;
suí	*shān*	*wàng*	*jūn*	*gé*	
随	山	望	菌[9]	阁 ▲[10]	Following the hills, we gaze at the mushroom-like pavilions.
yuăn	*shù*	*ài*	*qiān*	*qiān*	
远	树	暧[11]	仟	仟[12]	Distant trees are hazy in their luxuriance;
shēng	*yān*	*fēn*	*mò*	*mò*	
生	烟[13]	纷[14]	漠	漠 ▲[15]	A mist rises, spreading in billows.
yú	*xì*	*xīn*	*hé*	*dòng*	
鱼	戏	新	荷[16]	动	Where fish sport, new lotuses stir;
niăo	*sàn*	*yú*	*huā*	*luò*	
鸟	散	余	花	落 ▲	As birds scatter, remaining flowers fall.
bú	*duì*	*fāng*	*chūn*	*jiŭ*	
不	对	芳	春	酒	If not facing the fragrant spring ale,
huán	*wàng*	*qīng*	*shān*	*guō*	
还	望	青	山	郭 ▲[17]	We shall gaze at villages in the blue hills instead.

[五言古诗 pentasyllabic ancient-style verse]

(Tr. Xiaofei Tian, *HTRCP,* p. 142)

字词释义 Vocabulary Notes

1. 东 (東) 田　name of a luxury villa at the foot of Zhong Mountain, which belonged to Crown Prince Wenhui 文惠 (458–493) of the Southern Qi.

2. 谢 (謝) 朓 (style 字, Xuánhuī 玄晖, 464–499), a famous landscape poet in the Southern Qi. He was mentioned together with another famous landscape poet Xiè Língyùn 谢灵运 (385–433) as "the elder Xie and the younger Xie" (dà xiǎo xiè 大小谢).

3. 戚戚 adv. despondently. MdnC: 悲伤 (bēi shāng). 👉心中的悲伤难以言表 The sorrow inside could not be expressed in words.

4. 惊 n. happiness. MdnC: 欢乐 (huān lè). 👉公园里到处都是欢乐的人群 Happy crowds are everywhere in the park.

5. 携 (攜) v. to take sb. by hand. 👉让我们携手共进 Let us join hands and advance together.

6. 陟 v. to ascend. MdnC: 登 (dēng). 👉他登上了峰顶 He reached the summit.

7. 累 adj. one on top of another, overlapping. MdnC: 重叠 (chóng dié). 👉两条曲线重叠在一起 Two curves overlap.

8. 榭 n. pavilion.

9. 菌 n. mushroom. MdnC: 蘑菇 (mó gu).

10. 阁 (閣) n. pavilion (usu. two-storied). See also P100 note 12.

11. 暧 (曖) adj. indistinct, hidden from the view. See also P10 note 22.

12. 仟仟 adv. luxuriantly. MdnC: 茂盛 (mào shèng). 👉草长得很茂盛 The grass grows luxuriantly.

13. 生烟 (煙) n. mist. MdnC: 烟气 (yān qì).

14. 纷 (紛) adj. numerous and various.

15. 漠漠 adj. misty, foggy.

16. 荷 n. lotus.

17. 郭 n. See P12 note 8.

18. 密集 (mì jí) adj. crowded.

19. 葱郁 (cōng yù) adj. verdant [formal].

20. 纷乱 (fēn luàn) adj. numerous and disorderly [formal].

21. 迷离 (mí lí) adj. blurred, misted [formal].

22. 嬉戏 (xī xì) v. to play [formal].

现代文翻译 Modern Chinese Translation

心中悲伤³苦闷，没有欢乐，⁴于是我们一同去寻找快乐。寻着云彩，我们登⁶上了重叠⁷的台榭；沿着山势，我们观望着密集 ¹⁸的楼阁。远处的树木葱郁 ¹⁹茂盛，¹² 烟气¹³纷乱²⁰迷离。²¹鱼儿在水中嬉戏，²² 碰到了新生的荷叶。鸟儿飞走了，树枝上的花朵也散落下来。这个时候，既然不能饮酒，就来看看青山吧。

评论与提问 Comment and Question

Xie Tiao is well-known for his meticulous attention to parallel phrasing (duì zhàng 对仗) and tonal variation. Would you consider this poem something of a prototype of pentasyllabic regulated poetry? You will find an answer to this question after you have read the comments on this poem and on the syntactic, structural, and tonal rules of regulated poetry in *HTRCP*, pp. 142–143, 162–173.

P15

zhōng nán shān
终 南 山¹

Zhongnan Mountain

[*táng*] *wáng wéi*
[唐] 王 维[2]   [Tang Dyn.] Wang Wei

tài	*yǐ*	*jìn*	*tiān*	*dū*	
太	乙[3]	近	天	都[4]	Taiyi Peak approaches heaven's capital,
lián	*shān*	*dào*	*hǎi*	*yú*	
连	山	到	海	隅△[5]	The rolling mountains extend to the edge of the sea.
bái	*yún*	*huí*	*wàng*	*hé*	
白	云	回	望	合[6]	White clouds, when I look back, converge,
qīng	*ǎi*	*rù*	*kàn*	*wú*	
青	霭[7]	入[8]	看	无△	The greenish haze, once I walk in to see it, disappears.
fēn	*yě*	*zhōng*	*fēng*	*biàn*	
分	野[9]	中	峰	变	The divided regions, when seen from the middle peak, change,
yīn	*qíng*	*zhòng*	*hè*	*shū*	
阴[10]	晴[11]	众	壑[12]	殊△[13]	Shaded or in the sun, the myriad valleys look different.
yù	*tóu*	*rén*	*chù*	*sù*	
欲	投[14]	人	处	宿[15]	To find a dwelling of man for the night,
gé	*shuǐ*	*wèn*	*qiáo*	*fū*	
隔	水	问	樵	夫△[16]	Across the brook I called to a woodcutter.

[五言律诗 pentasyllabic regulated verse,
tonal pattern Ia, see *HTRCP*, p. 172]

(Tr. Zong-qi Cai)

字词释义 Vocabulary Notes

1. 终 (終) 南山   name of a mountain south of Chang'an or togday's Xi'an 西安, Shaanxi.
2. 王维 (維)   (style 字, Mójié 摩诘, 701–761), a great High Tang poet and artist. He is known as "Buddha-poet" (*shīfó* 诗佛) for the perfect fusion of art and Buddhist vision in his works.
3. 太乙   another name of 终南山.
4. 天都   heaven capital, used figuratively to denote the Tang capital Chang'an 长安。
5. 隅   n. border. See also P94 note 6. 海隅 means "sea coast" (*hǎi biān* 海边).
6. 合   v. to close. See also P12 note 7.
7. 霭 (靄)   n. mist, haze. MdnC: 雾气 (*wù qì*).
8. 入   v. to enter. MdnC: 接近 (*jiē jìn*). 📖他慢慢地接近树上的小鸟 He is slowly walking close to the small bird on the tree.
9. 分野   according to astronomy in ancient China, the positions of twelve stars in the heaven, called divided stars(*fēn xīng* 分星), are correlated with twelve states on earth, called divided regions (*fēn yě* 分野).
10. 阴 (陰)   adj. shaded, overcast. See P85 note 7 for a different meaning of the word.

11. 晴   adj. fine, sunny. See also P18 note 7.

12. 壑   n. valley. See also P80 note 4.

13. 殊   adj. different. MdnC: 悬殊 (*xuán shū*) [formal]. ☞这两个篮球队实力相差很悬殊 There is a huge gap in actual strength between these two basketball teams.

14. 投   v. to go to, join. MdnC: 投宿 (*tóu sù*) [formal] to find overnight lodgings. ☞今晚，他要找个人家投宿 He wants to find lodgings in someone's home tonight.

15. 宿   v. to lodge for the night, stay overnight. See also P43 note 1 and P94 note 11.

16. 樵夫   n. woodcutter.   17. 雄伟 (*xióng wěi*) adj. grand [formal].

18. 弥漫 (*mí màn*) v. to fill the air.   19. 蒙蒙 (*méng méng*) adj. drizzly, misty.

现代文翻译 Modern Chinese Translation

终南山高大雄伟，[17] 接近天都。 山脉相连，直到海边。[5] 白云弥漫，[18] 回头望，已看不见来时的路。青色的雾气[7]蒙蒙，[19] 接近[8]细看，却并不存在。以中峰为分界。 阴天晴天，山中景象变化悬殊。[13] 天晚了，想找个人家投宿，[14] 我只好隔着水，询问樵夫。[16]

评论与提问 Comment and Question

Wang Wei's poetry is admired for its exceptional pictorial appeal and its *chan* (Zen) vision (*chánjìng* 禅境). Can you find these two features in this poem? ☞*HTRCP*, pp.177–179.

P16

xī jiāng yuè yè xíng huáng shā dào zhōng
西 江 月[1] 夜 行 黄 沙[2] 道 中

[nán sòng] xīn qì jí
[南宋] 辛 弃 疾[3]

To the Tune "West River Moon": An Evening Journey on the Path to Huangsha

[Song Dyn.] Xin Qiji

míng yuè bié zhī jīng què
明   月   别   枝[4]   惊   鹊[5]

Bright moon, slanted branches, startled magpies;

qīng fēng bàn yè míng chán
清   风   半   夜   鸣   蝉△[6]

Pure breeze, midnight, and singing cicada.

dào huā xiāng lǐ shuō fēng nián
稻[7]   花   香   里   说   丰[8]   年△

In the thick of the fragrance of rice flowers, I listen to the talk of a year of bumper harvest—

tīng qǔ wā shēng yí piàn
听   取   蛙[9]   声   一   片▲

frogs croaking in chorus.

qī	*bā*	*gè*	*xīng*	*tiān*	*wài*	
七	八	个	星	天	外	Seven or eight stars—far away in the sky

liǎng	*sān*	*diǎn*	*yǔ*	*shān*	*qián*	
两	三	点	雨	山	前△	Two or three rain drops—in front of the mountain.

jiù	*shí*	*máo*	*diàn*	*shè*	*lín*	*biān*	
旧	时	茅[10]	店	社[11]	林	边△	The old thatch store, nestled in the woods by the temple,

lù	*zhuǎn*	*xī*	*qiáo*	*hū*	*xiàn*	
路	转[12]	溪[13]	桥	忽	见▲[14]	the path turning, the brook bridge crossed, suddenly appears.

[小令 short lyric song]   (Tr. Zong-qi Cai)

字词释义 Vocabulary Notes

1. 西江月 "West River Moon," title of a tune.
2. 黄沙 or 黄沙岭, place name. It is in present-day Raoxi 饶西, Jiangxi province.
3. 辛弃疾 (style 字, Yòu'ān 幼安; literary name 号, Jiàxuān Jūshì 稼轩居士, 1140–1207), a famous Southern Song *ci* poet who has been regarded as representative of the school of "heroic abandon" (*háofàngpài* 豪放派).
4. 枝 n. branches. 别枝 slanted branches.
5. 鹊 (鵲) n. magpie. MdnC: 喜鹊 (*xǐ què*).
6. 蝉 (蟬) n. cicada.   7. 稻 n. rice. See also P85 note 9.
8. 丰 (豐) adj. abundant. MdnC: 丰收 (*fēng shōu*) bumper harvest. 今年水果又丰收了 There is a bumper harvest of fruits this year.
9. 蛙 n. frog. MdnC: 青蛙 (*qīng wā*).
10. 茅 n. thatch. See also P13 note 4.
11. 社 n. a temple to house and sacrifice a village deity. MdnC: 土地庙 (*tǔ dì miào*). See also P17 note11.
12. 转 (轉 *zhuǎn*) v. to turn. MdnC: 转弯 (*zhuǎn wān*). 银行一转弯儿就是 The bank is just round the corner. See also P78 note 7.
13. 溪 n. brook. MdnC: 小溪 (*xiǎo xī*).
14. 见 v. to see, used here as a loan word for "现"(*xiàn*: to appear). See also P92 note 11.
15. 诉说 (*sù shuō*) v. to tell [formal].

现代文翻译 Modern Chinese Translation

　　明月升起，惊动了树枝上的喜鹊。[5] 轻柔的夜风吹过，传来蝉的叫声。稻花的香气弥漫着，似乎诉说[15]着今年是个丰收[8]年。停下脚步，会听到一片片青蛙[9]的叫声。

　　天空上有七八个星星，山前落了两三滴雨。以前社林边的茅屋小店，在转过小溪[13]桥之后，突然出现在眼前。

评论与提问 Comments and Questions

1. This poem is a feast of the senses. Lines 1–2 blend sights with sounds—sudden cries of magpies and the singing of cicadas. Lines 3–4 enliven the sense of smell with that of hearing—the rustle of rice plants and the croaking of frogs. Lines 5–6 again bring another sharp contrast of grand and small images. The last two lines usher in a rapid succession of images seen on the move, culminating in a surprise discovery. With this extraordinary symphony of sense impressions, what kind of feelings has the poet conveyed?

2. This short *ci* 词 poem employs many hexasyllabic lines (*liùyán jù* 六言句) that are seldom used in the *shi* 诗 poetry. A hexasyllabic line does not have a fixed prosodic rhythm like 2+3 in a pentasyllabic line or 2+2+3/4+3 in a heptasyllabic line. Consequently, the pauses of a hexasyllabic line are almost solely determined by its semantic rhythms, that is, its sense.

3. In hexasyllabic lines, there are five major semantic rhythms: a) 2+2+2; b) 3+3; c) 4+2; d) 1+5; e) 2+4. Which of these rhythms are used in this poem? How does this variation of rhythms contribute to the aesthetic effect of this poem? ☞For discussion of semantic rhythms, look up "Semantic Rhythm" in the Thematic Table of Contents of *HTRCP*, p. xvii.

P17

yóu	*shān*	*xī*	*cūn*			
游	山	西	村			

An Outing to Villages West of the Mountains

[nán sòng]	*lù*	*yóu*
[南宋]	陆	游[1]

[Southern Song Dyn.] Lu You

mò	*xiào*	*nóng*	*jiā*	*là*	*jiǔ*	*hún*
莫[2]	笑	农	家	腊[3]	酒	浑△[4]

Don't laugh at the peasant's winter wine for being murky,

fēng	*nián*	*liú*	*kè*	*zú*	*jī*	*tún*
丰	年	留	客	足	鸡	豚△[5]

In abundant years there are enough chickens and pigs to entertain a guest.

shān	*chóng*	*shuǐ*	*fù*	*yí*	*wú*	*lù*
山	重[6]	水	复[7]	疑[8]	无	路

The mountains are chaotic, the river doubles back and forth, as if there's no way through,

liǔ	*àn*	*huā*	*míng*	*yòu*	*yì*	*cūn*
柳	暗	花	明	又	一	村△

Dark green are the willows, bright the blossoms, as one more village comes into view.

xiāo	*gǔ*	*zhuī*	*suí*	*chūn*	*shè*	*jìn*
箫[9]	鼓[10]	追	随	春	社[11]	近

Groups of pipe players and drummers follow each other, Spring Festival must be approaching,

yī	*guān*	*jiǎn*	*pǔ*	*gǔ*	*fēng*	*cún*
衣	冠¹²	简	朴¹³	古	风	存△

Simple and rustic are the villagers' caps and clothes, preserving the flavor of ancient times.

cóng	*jīn*	*ruò*	*xǔ*	*xián*	*chéng*	*yuè*
从	今	若¹⁴	许¹⁵	闲	乘¹⁶	月

If you allow me to visit when I have leisure, taking advantage of a full moon,

zhǔ	*zhàng*	*wú*	*shí*	*yè*	*kòu*	*mén*
拄¹⁷	仗¹⁸	无	时¹⁹	夜	扣²⁰	门△

I'll lean on my staff and knock on your door whenever I can.

(Tr. Ronald Egan, *HTRCP*, p. 320)

[七言律诗 heptasyllabic regulated verse, tonal pattern IIa. See *HTRCP*, p. 172.]

字词释义 Vocabulary Notes

1. 陆游 (陸遊) (style 字, Wùguān 务观; literary name 号, Fàng wēng 放翁, 1125–1210), a famous Southern Song poet who left behind more than 9000 poems. He and You Mao 尤袤 (1127–1202), Yang Wanli 杨万里 (1127–1206), and Fan Chengda 范成大 (1126–1193) are known as the "Four Great Poets of the Regeneration Period" (*zhōngxīng sìdà shīrén* 中兴四大诗人) in the Southern Song. See Yang Wanli's biographic note in P32 note 1.

2. 莫 v. don't. See P04 note 24.

3. 腊 (臘) n. the twelfth month of the lunar year. MdnC: 腊月 (*là yuè*).

4. 浑 (渾) adj. murky. MdnC: 浑浊 (*hún zhuó*). ☞ 湖水很浑浊 The lake water is pretty murky. See P91 note 9 for a different meaning of the word.

5. 豚 n. pig, used here in the sense of meat.

6. 重 n. layers. MdnC: 重叠 (*chóng dié*). See also P35 note 9 and P67 note 7. See P38 note 1 for a different meaning of the word.

7. 复 (複) adj. again. MdnC: 重复 (*chóng fù*). ☞ 请避免不必要的重复 Please avoid unnecessary repetitions.

8. 疑 v. to doubt. MdnC: 怀疑 (*huái yí*). ☞ 请不要怀疑别人的诚意 Please don't doubt other people's sincerity. See also P19 note 9 and P57 note 2.

9. 箫 (簫) n. a vertical bamboo flute.

10. 鼓 n. drum. See also P01 note 29.

11. 社 n. date for sacrifice to a village deity. 春社 is an ancient sacrifice to pray for a great harvest which usually happens before spring plowing. See also P16 note 11.

12. 冠 (*guān*) n. hat. MdnC: 帽 (*mào*).   13. 朴 adj. rustic.

14. 若 conj. if. MdnC: 如果 (*rú guǒ*).

15. 许 (許) v. to allow. MdnC: 允许 (*yǔn xǔ*). ☞ 请允许我代表全校师生感谢你们 Please allow me to thank you on behalf of the teachers and students of our school. See also P67 note 3 for a different meaning of the word.

16. 乘 v. to take advantage of sth. MdnC: 趁 (*chèn*). ☞ 趁这个机会我讲几句 I want to take this chance to say a few words. See P18 note 4 for a different meaning of the word.

17. 拄　v. to lean on (a walking stick).
18. 杖　n. walking stick. MdnC: 拐杖 (*guǎi zhàng*).
19. 无时 (無時)　adv. any time. MdnC: 随时 (*suí shí*). ☞有问题随时找我 Tell me when you have any problem.
20. 扣　v. to knock at sth. MdnC: 敲 (*qiāo*). 21. 酿 (*niàng*)　v. to brew (wine).
22. 美味 (*měi wèi*)　n. delicious food.
23. 款待 (*kuǎn dài*)　v. to entertain (with food and beverages).
24. 茂密 (*mào mì*)　adj. (of tree) dense. 25. 明艳 (*míng yàn*)　adj. bright and beautiful.

现代文翻译 Modern Chinese Translation

不要笑话农家腊月³酿²¹的酒浑浊,⁴ 丰收之年，农家有足够的美味²²来款待²³客人。面对重重叠叠⁶的群山流水，正当我怀疑⁸无路可走时，忽然看见柳树茂密²⁴花朵明艳,²⁵ 又一座村庄出现了。吹着箫，打着鼓，大家结队庆 祝，春社已经临近。穿戴着简朴的衣帽,¹² 古风俗依然留存。从今以后，如果 ¹⁴允许¹⁵我趁¹⁶着美丽的月色闲游，我就拄着拐杖,¹⁸ 随时¹⁹来敲开农家的大门。

评论与提问 Comment and Question

This poem is similar, in theme, structure, style, and even mood, to P12 "Visiting My Old Friend's Farmstead" by Meng Haoran. However, this poem is a heptasyllabic regulated poem while P12 is a pentasyllabic one. With the addition of two extra characters per line, what more has Lu You accomplished than Meng Haoran? For comments on this poem, ☞ *HTRCP*, pp. 320–322.

练习 EXERCISES

一 填空 Fill in blanks

A. 诗词填字： 浑 累 乘 暖 扣 菌 蛙 溪 漠 隔 郭 留 投 茅 陟 对 稻

1. ＿＿花香里说丰年，听取＿＿声一片。 2. 寻云＿＿ ＿＿榭，随山望＿＿阁。
3. 旧时 ＿＿店社林边，路转＿＿桥忽见。 4. 欲＿＿人处宿，＿＿水问樵夫。
5. 莫笑农家腊酒＿＿， 丰年＿＿客足鸡豚。 6. 不＿＿春芳酒，还望青山＿＿。
7. 从今若许闲＿＿月,挂杖无时夜＿＿门。 8. 远树＿＿仟仟，生烟纷＿＿ ＿＿。

B. 现代文填词： 允许 丰收 投宿 浑浊 悲伤 随时 重叠 悬殊

1. 有问题＿＿ ＿＿向我报告。 2. 心中的＿＿ ＿＿难以言表。
3. 请＿＿ ＿＿我代表学校向你表示感谢。 4. 今年是个＿＿ ＿＿年。
5. 今晚，他要找个人家＿＿ ＿＿。 6. 两条曲线＿＿ ＿＿在一起。
7. 河水很＿＿ ＿＿。 8. 两队实力相差＿＿ ＿＿。

二 形近字辨析 Distinguish easily confused characters

1. 远树____仟仟　　a. 暖　b. 缓　c. 暧　　2. 分野中____变　a. 峰　b. 锋　c. 缝
3. ____鼓追随春社近　a. 萧　b. 箫　c. 肃　　4. 连山到海____　a. 偶　b. 隅　c. 遇
5. 莫笑农家____酒浑　a. 腊　b. 蜡　c. 借　　6. 戚戚苦无____　a. 综　b. 踪　c. 惊
7. ____三点____山前　a.雨　b. 而　c. 两　　8. 生烟____漠漠　a. 吩　b. 纷　c. 份

三 连句 Match the first part with the second

1. 太乙近天都( )　　2. 不对芳春酒( )　　3. 寻云陟累榭( )　　　4.七八个星天外( )
5. 鱼戏新荷动( )　　6. 白云回望合( )　　7. 山重水复疑无路( )　8. 萧鼓追随春社近( )
9. 旧时茅店社林边( )　　　10. 明月别枝惊鹊( )

a. 柳暗花明又一村　b. 路转溪桥忽见　c. 两三点雨山前　d. 随山望菌阁　　e. 青蔼入看无
f. 衣冠简朴古风存　g. 鸟散余花落　　h. 清风半夜鸣蝉　i. 还望青山郭　　j. 连山到海隅

四 句读 Punctuate and translate the following passage

明月别枝惊鹊清风半夜鸣蝉稻花香里说丰年听取蛙声一片萧鼓追随春社
近衣冠简朴古风存从今若许闲乘月拄杖无时夜叩门远树暧仟阡生烟纷漠
漠鱼戏新荷动鸟散余花落

五 听写 Dictation

1. ____ ____ ____ ____ ____ 无 路，____ ____ ____ ____ 又 一 村。
2. ____ ____ 近 ____ ____，____ ____ 到 ____ ____。
3. ____ 云 ____ ____，____ ____ ____ 无。
4. 鱼 ____ ____ ____，____ ____ ____ 花 ____。
5. 明 月 ____ ____ ____，____ ____ 半 夜 ____ ____。
6. ____ ____ ____ ____ 春 社 ____，衣 ____ ____ ____ 古 风 ____。

5

山 水 大 观

Landscape: Grand Scenes

P18

huáng	*hè*	*lóu*				
黄	鹤	楼[1]				

[*táng*]	*cuī*	*hào*
[唐]	崔	颢[2]

The Yellow Crane Tower

[Tang Dyn.] Cui Hao

xī	*rén*	*yǐ*	*chéng*	*huáng*	*hè*	*qù*
昔[3]	人	已	乘[4]	黄	鹤	去

The men of old rode
　　　　　the yellow crane away,

cǐ	*dì*	*kōng*	*yú*	*huáng*	*hè*	*lóu*
此	地	空	余	黄	鹤	楼△

This place is left with
　　　　　only the Yellow Crane Tower.

huáng	*hè*	*yí*	*qù*	*bú*	*fù*	*fǎn*
黄	鹤	一	去	不	复	返

Once gone, the yellow crane
　　　　　will never return,

bái	*yún*	*qiān*	*zǎi*	*kōng*	*yōu*	*yōu*
白	云	千	载[5]	空	悠	悠△[6]

O'er a thousand years, white clouds
　　　　　float alone and aimless.

qíng	*chuān*	*lì*	*lì*	*hàn*	*yáng*	*shù*
晴[7]	川[8]	历	历[9]	汉	阳[10]	树

Gleams and glitters the river in the sun
　　　　　—the trees of Hanyang;

fāng	*cǎo*	*qī*	*qī*	*yīng*	*wǔ*	*zhōu*
芳	草	萋	萋[11]	鹦	鹉	洲△[12]

Thickly, thickly grow the fragrant grass
　　　　　—the Parrots Isle.

rì	*mù*	*xiāng*	*guān*	*hé*	*chù*	*shì*
日	暮[13]	乡	关[14]	何	处	是

In this sundown, my hometown
　　　　　where to find?

jiāng	*shàng*	*yān*	*bō*	*shǐ*	*rén*	*chóu*
江	上	烟	波	使	人	愁△

Over the river, the waves of mist
　　　　　fill my heart with melancholy.
　　　　　　　　(Tr. Zong-qi Cai)

[七言律诗 heptasyllabic regulated verse, tonal pattern I, imperfect, see *HTRCP,* p. 170]

字词释义 Vocabulary Notes

1. 黄鹤楼 (黃鶴樓) The Yellow Crane Tower, built on the Yellow Crane Hill (Huánghè shān 黄鹤山) in present-day Wuhan 武汉, Hubei province. *According to Records of Qi Xie (Qí Xié zhì*

齐谐志), the ancient immortal Zi'an 子安 once passed by this tower riding a yellow crane. *Records of the Peace World* (*Tài píng huán yǔ jì* 太平寰宇记) tells of a man named Fei Wenwei 费文伟 riding a crane here and becoming an immortal. 昔人 in the first poetic line refers to these immortals. See also P40 note 1.

2. 崔颢 (顥) (704?–754) a Tang poet. 3. 昔 n. the past. See also P60 note 11 and P85 note 22.

4. 乘 v. to ride. ☞ 他要乘公共汽车去火车站 He will go to the train station by bus. See also P41 note 3. See P17 note 16 for a different meaning of the word.

5. 载 (載 *zǎi*) n. year. See also P80 note 19. See P68 note 14 for a different meaning of the word.

6. 悠悠 adv. leisurely. See also P07 note 9.   7. 晴 adj. fine, sunny. See also P15 note 11.

8. 川 n. river [formal]. ☞ 名山大川 famous mountains and big rivers. See also P19 note 8.

9. 历历 (歷歷) adv. clearly [formal]. ☞ 往事历历在目 The past events come clearly into view.

10. 汉阳 (漢陽) a town in Wuhan, Hubei province.   11. 萋萋 adv. luxuriantly.

12. 鹦鹉洲 (鸚鵡洲) The Parrot Islet, now in the Yangtze River of the Wuhan area. According to *History of the Later Han* (*Hòu Hàn shū* 后汉书), when Huang She 黄射, the first son of Huang Zu 黄祖(prefect of Jiangxia 江夏, a county in the Later Han) once had a banquet here, a parrot was offered as a gift by a guest. Mi Heng 祢衡 thus made a poem entitled "*Fu* on the Parrot" ("Yīngwǔ fù" 鹦鹉赋). This place was therefore named 鹦鹉洲.

13. 暮 n. dusk, evening. MdnC: 傍晚 (*bàng wǎn*). See also P24 note 11, P43 note 6, and P82 note 15. See P67 note 14 for a different meaning of the word.

14. 乡关 (鄉關) n. hometown.   15. 晴朗 (*qíng lǎng*) adj. sunny.   16. 清晰 (*qīng xī*) adj. clear.

现代文翻译 Modern Chinese Translation

传说中的仙人早已乘⁴着黄鹤离开了，这里只留下了空空的黄鹤楼。飞走的黄鹤不再回来，只有悠悠的白云千年⁵依旧。晴朗¹⁵的天空下，江边绿树清晰¹⁶可见；鹦鹉洲上的芳草也茂密浓郁。傍晚¹³时分，(望向远方) 何处才是我的故乡？面对江上的阵阵烟雾，心里感到愁苦。

评论与提问 Comment and Question

The Yellow Crane Tower is a very famous historical site that has attracted numerous poets to inscribe their poems on its walls. None of these poems is more famous than this poem by Cui Hao. The legend has it that Li Bai was so awestruck by this poem that he decided not to write a poem of his own to compete with it. This poem has been lavishly praised for its skillful contrast of past and present (lines 1–4), its creative use of an imperfect parallel couplet (lines 3–4), his successive use of three reduplicatives (lines 4–6), its juxtaposition of broad scenes and close-ups (lines 5–6), and its climatic melancholic reflection. All these impressive qualities seem to have resulted from Cui's bold adoption of the unadorned ancient style in a regulated verse.

Some traditional Chinese critics went so far as to call this poem the greatest heptasyllabic regulated verse ever written. Would you agree or disagree with this assessment? Read other heptasyllabic regulated verses in this workbook and give your answer.

P19

wàng lú shān pù bù shuǐ
望 庐 山¹瀑²布水

[táng] lǐ bái
[唐] 李 白³

Watching the Waterfall of Mount Lu

[Tang Dyn.] Li Bai

rì	*zhào*	*xiāng*	*lú*	*shēng*	*zǐ*	*yān*
日	照	香	炉⁴	生	紫⁵	烟△

The sun lights up the Incense Burner,
    sending off a veil of purple smoke,

yáo	*kàn*	*pù*	*bù*	*guà*	*qián*	*chuān*
遥⁶	看	瀑	布	挂⁷	前	川△⁸

Look afar: a waterfall or a river
    hanging down over there.

fēi	*liú*	*zhí*	*xià*	*sān*	*qiān*	*chǐ*
飞	流	直	下	三	千	尺

A raging torrent cascades
    down three thousand feet,

yí	*shì*	*yín*	*hé*	*luò*	*jiǔ*	*tiān*
疑⁹	是	银	河¹⁰	落	九	天△¹¹

Or is the Milky Way falling
    through the nine heavens?
    (Tr. Zong-qi Cai)

[七言律绝 heptasyllabic regulated quatrain, tonal pattern II, see *HTRCP,* p. 171]

字词释义 Vocabulary Notes

1. 庐 (盧) 山 Lu Mountain, in present-day Jiujiang 九江, Jiangxi province.   2. 瀑布 n. waterfall.

3. 李白 (style 字, Tàibái 太白; literary name 号, Qīnglián jūshì 青莲居士, 701–762) He is known
    as the "immortal-poet" (*shīxiān* 诗仙) for his quest of immortality in the Daoist vein and for
    his extraordinary power of imagination. He and Du Fu 杜甫 (712–770) are considered the
    two greatest poets of China. See Du Fu's biographic note in P20 note 1.

4. 香炉 (爐) incense burner. 香炉 here indicates Xianglu Peak 香炉峰 which is in the
    northwest of Mount Lu.

5. 紫 adj. purple.

6. 遥 adj. distant, remote. MdnC: 遥远 (*yáo yuǎn*). 👉路途很遥远 There is a long way to go.
    See also P55 note 9, P77 note 3, and P83 note 15.

7. 挂 v. to hang. 👉请把地图挂在墙上 Please hang the map up on the wall.

8. 川 n. river. See also P18 note 8. Here it refers to the waterfall.

9. 疑 v. to doubt. See also P17 note 8.

10. 银 (銀) 河 the Milky Way or literally "Silver River."

11. 九天 the highest part of heaven. It means "extremely high" here. According to ancient legend,
    there are nine levels in the heaven, also called *jiǔchóngtiān* 九重天 or *jiǔxiāo* 九霄.

12. 生发 (*shēng fā*) v. to arise; to grow.

13. 奔流 (*bēn liú*) v. to flow at great speed, pour [formal].

现代文翻译 Modern Chinese Translation

太阳照着香炉峰，紫色的烟雾生发[12]出来。从远处看，瀑布就像是挂[7]在山前的大河。水从三千尺的高处奔流[13]而下，不禁让人怀疑是银河从天上流下来了吗？

评论与提问 Comment and Question

The poet entertains us with an exhilearting experience of movement by changing the distance and position from which we view the famous waterfall of Mount Lu. First, he leads us to view it from a long distance. Against the backdrop of the haze-veiled peak, it appears as something immobile, hanging out there like a scroll. Then, he abruptly shatters this illusion of immobility by bringing us right down below the waterfall. Looking up at the waterfall gushing down from a height of three thousand feet, one just wonders if the Milky Way is falling through the nine heavens! Isn't it pleasurable to follow such abrupt shifts and turns in Li Bai's flight of imagination?

P20

jué jù sì shǒu sān
绝句四首 三
[táng] dù fǔ
[唐] 杜 甫[1]

Four Quatrains, No. 3

[Tang Dyn.] Du Fu

liǎng	*gè*	*huáng*	*lí*	*míng*	*cuì*	*liǔ*
两	个	黄	鹂[2]	鸣	翠[3]	柳

Two yellow orioles
          sing in the lushly green willow,

yì	*háng*	*bái*	*lù*	*shàng*	*qīng*	*tiān*
一	行	白	鹭[4]	上	青	天△

One line of white egrets
          fly into the blue sky.

chuāng	*hán*	*xī*	*lǐng*	*qiān*	*qiū*	*xuě*
窗	含[5]	西	岭[6]	千	秋	雪

The windows frame in the West Mountain,
          with its snow of a thousand years.

mén	*bó*	*dōng*	*wú*	*wàn*	*lǐ*	*chuán*
门	泊[7]	东	吴[8]	万	里	船△

Outdoors is moored an Eastern Wu boat
          from ten thousand leagues away.
          (Tr. Zong-qi Cai)

[七言律绝 heptasyllabic regulated quatrain, tonal pattern II, see *HTRCP,* p. 171]

字词释义 Vocabulary Notes

1. 杜甫 (style 字, Zǐměi 子美; literary name 号, Shàolíng yělǎo *少陵野老*，712–770). He is known as the "sage-poet" (*shīshèng* 诗圣) for his Confucian vision of the universe and the self. He is also praised as "historian-poet" (*shīshǐ* 诗史) for his realistic depiction of common people's suffering from famine and wars. He and Li Bai 李白 the "immortal-poet" (诗圣) are considered the two greatest poets of China. See Li Bai's biographic note in P19 note 3.
2. 鹂 (鸝) n. oriole. 3. 翠 adj. emerald green. See also P63 note 8 and P85 note 18.

4. 鹭 (鷺) n. egret. 5. 含 v. to keep in mouth. 👉她含了块糖 She kept a candy in her mouth.

6. 西岭 West Mountain, also 西岭雪山, in present-day Chengdu 成都, Sichuan province.

7. 泊 v. to berth, moor. MdnC: 停泊 (*tíng bó*). 👉港口停泊着几艘船 Several ships are berthed in the harbor. See also P43 note 4.

8. 东吴 (東吳) Eastern Wu (222–265), one of the state in the Three Kingdoms period. Here it refers to the large area in the east of present-day Jiangsu and Zhejiang provinces.

9. 化 (*huà*) v. to melt, dissolve.   10. 积雪 (*jī xuě*) n. accumulated snow.

现代文翻译 Modern Chinese Translation

两只黄鹂在绿色的柳树上叫着，一行白鹭飞上蓝蓝 的天空。窗外，西山雪岭上满是千年不化⁹的积雪，¹⁰ 门外(河中)停泊⁷着从万里之外的东吴开来的船。

评论与提问 Comment and Question

Interestingly, the construction of a quatrain has been conceived by some Chinese critics in terms of cutting off two couplets from a regulated verse in four different ways. First, if the opening and closing couplets of a regulated verse are taken out, we have a quatrain entirely made up of parallel couplets, like this poem. Second, if the first and second couplets are taken out, we have a quatrain that begins with a parallel couplet but ends with a non-parallel couplet, like P27, P29, P31, P34 and other poems. Third, if the two middle parallel couplets are taken out, we have a quatrain solely composed of non-parallel couplets, like P19, P22, P25, P26, P28, P30, P35–37 and many other poems. Fourth, if the third and fourth couplets are taken out, we have a quatrain that begins with a non-parallel couplet but ends with a parallel couplet, like P13, P43. Given this, the common English translation of *jueju* 绝句 as "cut-off verse" seems right to the point.

As reflected in this workbook, the third category of quatrains (the one without any parallel couplet) is the most frequently used, while the first category (the one solely made up of parallel couplets) is used the least. As a rule, parallel couplets are most often used for the purpose of description. In this poem Du Fu seeks to describe what he sees, probably from inside a house, in four different directions. By using two parallel couplets, has he enhanced or diminished the impact of his description? Give your answer and explain why.

P21

	mèng	*tiān*				
	梦	天				

Dreaming Heaven

[*táng*] *lǐ* *hè*
[唐] 李 贺¹

[Tang Dyn.] Li He

lǎo	*tù*	*hán*	*chán*	*qì*	*tiān*	*sè*
老	兔	寒	蟾²	泣³	天	色
yún	*lóu*	*bàn*	*kāi*	*bì*	*xié*	*bái*
云	楼	半	开	壁	斜	白 ▲ᵃ

Old hare and cold toad weep sky's sheen;

a cloud-enfurled tower half opens: on the walls slants whiteness.

yù	*lún*[4]	*yà*[5]	*lù*[6]	*shī*	*tuán*[7]	*guāng*
玉	轮	轧	露	湿	团	光

The jade wheel presses dew: wet balls of light;

luán[8]	*pèi*[9]	*xiāng*	*féng*	*guì*[10]	*xiāng*	*mò* ▲a[11]
鸾	珮	相	逢	桂	香	陌

Simurgh bells and pendants meet on cassia-scented lanes

huáng	*chén*	*qīng*	*shuǐ*	*sān*	*shān*[12]	*xià*
黄	尘	清	水	三	山	下

Yellow dust, clear water, beneath the Immortal mountains,

gēng[13]	*biàn*	*qiān*	*nián*	*rú*	*zǒu*	*mǎ* ▲b[14]
更	变	千	年	如	走	马

change in turn, a thousand years like a horse that gallops by.

yáo	*wàng*	*qí*	*zhōu*[15]	*jiǔ*	*diǎn*	*yān*[16]
遥	望	齐	州	九	点	烟

Gaze far-off on the middle continent, those nine spots of smoke:

yì	*hóng*[17]	*hǎi*	*shuǐ*	*bēi*	*zhōng*	*xiè* ▲b[18]
一	泓	海	水	杯	中	泻

a single stream of ocean water poured into a cup.

(Tr. Robert Ashmore, *HTRCP*, p. 188)

[古诗 ancient-style verse]

字词释义 Vocabulary Notes

1. 李贺 (style 字, Chángjí 长吉, 790–816), a great mid-Tang poet. He is well known as "ghost-poet" (*shīguǐ* 诗鬼) for his marvelous and often morbid imagination and for his depiction of fantastic lands. He excelled in ancient-style poems but did not write any regulated verse.

2. 蟾　n. toad. MdnC: 蟾蜍 (*chán chú*).　Hare and toad are two animals in the Moon Palace according to ancient legend and are used here as metonymies for the moon.

3. 泣　v. to weep. MdnC: 哭泣 (*kū qì*). 👉请不要再哭泣了 Please don't cry any more.

4. 轮 (輪)　n. wheel. 玉轮 refers to the moon here.

5. 轧 (軋)　v. to roll, run over. 👉他被车轧伤了 He was run over and injured by a car.

6. 露 (*lù*)　n. dew. See also P94 note 7. See P32 note 6 for a different meaning of the word.

7. 团　a ball or yarn (of wool, cotton, etc.).

8. 鸾 (鸞)　n. a mystical bird related to the phoenix.

9. 珮　n. jade ornament. See also P80 note 17. 鸾珮 is a metonym for fairy maidens in the Moon Palace.

10. 桂　n. cassia tree. 11. 陌 n. a path between fields (running east and west). MdnC: 小路 (*xiǎo lù*).

12. 三山　three legendary mountains inhabited by immortals. They are Penglai (蓬莱), Fangzhang (方丈), and Yingzhou (瀛州) mountains, respectively. See also P03 note 20.

13. 更 (*gēng*)　v. to change, replace. MdnC: 更新 (*gēng xīn*). 👉他们要更新设备 They want to replace old equipments with new ones. See P63 note 15 for a different meaning of the word.

14. 走马 (馬)　v. to trot along on horseback. 👉走马观花 "look at flowers while riding on horseback", an idiom meaning "to gain a superficial understanding through cursory observation."

15. 齐 (齊) 州　or 中州, "Qi Region" or "Middle Region," an ancient name for China.

16. 九点烟 (點煙) According to the *Book of Documents* (*Shàng shū* 尚书), there are nine states in China. Here the poet imagines that the nine states look like nine dots of smoke when seen from the moon.

17. 泓 n. a deep pool (of water).

18. 泻 (瀉) v. to pour out. 👉长江一泻千里 The Yangtze River rushes down for a thousand *li*.

19. 裂开 (*liè kāi*) v. to split open.   20. 缝 (*fèng*) n. chink, crack.

21. 轮廓 (*lún kuò*) n. outline.   22. 打湿 (*dǎ shī*) v. to make sth. wet.   23. 飘 (*piāo*) v. to float.

24. 烟尘 (*yān chén*) n. smoke and dust.   25. 打翻 (*dǎ fān*) v. to knock over.

现代文翻译 Modern Chinese Translation

　　(夜里下着雨，像是) 月宫中的玉兔和蟾蜍[2]在哭泣，[3]天色都阴暗了。雨停了，云层裂开，[19]像是高高的楼。月光从云缝[20]中透过来，云块显出白色的轮廓，[21]好像是月光斜照在墙壁上一样。玉环一般的月亮轧[5]过空气中的水珠，发出的一团月光被打湿[22]了。

　　(我进入月宫，)在桂花飘[23]香的小路上，遇到了一群仙女。(回望)大地，流水和仙山，世上的一切迅速地更新[13]变化着。看看九州就如同九点烟尘[24]一样小，而大海也就像一杯水打翻[25]了流出来那么大。

评论与提问 Comments and Questions

1. This poem is a heptasyllabic ancient-style verse. In writing an ancient-style poem, a poet has more freedom in the use of languages, rhythm, poetic device than he does when writing a regulated verse. 👉 *HTRCP*, p. 226 for a brief introduction to the ancient-style *shi* poetry of the Tang dynasty. Can you discern in this ancient-style poem some stylistic features that are seldom seen in in a heptasyllabic regulated verse?

2. What images are associated with the moon or moonlight in the first four lines of this poem? How does the poet use these images to create a fantastic world? 👉 *HTRCP* pp.188–189 for a detailed analysis of this poem.

P22

jiāng nán chūn jué jù
江 南[1] 春 绝 句

[táng] dù mù
[唐] 杜 牧[2]

A Quatrain on the Spring South of the
Yangtze

[Tang Dyn.] Du Mu

qiān	*lǐ*	*yīng*	*tí*	*lǜ*	*yìng*	*hóng*
千	里	莺[3]	啼	绿	映[4]	红

Orioles sing through miles and miles
　　of green land dotted with red,

shuǐ	*cūn*	*shān*	*guō*	*jiǔ*	*qí*	*fēng*
水	村	山	郭[5]	酒	旗[6]	风△

In villages by water, on walls along the hills,
　　wine-shop banners flutter in the wind.

nán	*cháo*[7]	*sì*	*bǎi*	*bā*	*shí*	*sì*
南	朝	四	百	八	十	寺

Of the four hundred and eighty temples,
　　　built in the Southern Dynasties,

duō	*shǎo*	*lóu*	*tái*	*yān*	*yǔ*	*zhōng*△
多	少	楼	台	烟	雨	中△

How many of their towers and terraces
　　　are shrouded in mist and rain?
　　　　　　　　　　　　(Tr. Zong-qi Cai)

[七言律绝 heptasyllabic regulated quatrain, tonal pattern IIa, see *HTRCP,* p. 171]

字词释义 Vocabulary Notes

1. 江南　the area south of the Yangtze River.
2. 杜牧　(style 字, Mùzhī 牧之; literary name 号, Fánchuān jūshì 樊川居士，803–852) is called as "younger Du" (*xiǎo Dù* 小杜) in order to be distinguished from Du Fu.
3. 莺 (鶯)　n. oriole.
4. 映　v. to reflect, set sth. off. MdnC: 映衬 (*yìng chèn*). 👍红花绿树相互映衬 Red flowers and green trees set each other off beautifully. See also P64 note 17 and P74 note 8.
5. 郭　n. the outer wall of a city. See also P12 note 8.
6. 旗　n. flag. 酒旗 a flag hanging outside a wine shop as a sign.
7. 南朝　the Southern Dynasties (420–589), including Song, Qi, Liang, and Chen dynasties. Plenty of temples were built in the Southern Dynasties.
8. 辽阔 (*liáo kuò*)　adj. vast, extensive.　　9. 若隐若现 (*ruò yǐn ruò xiàn*)　to appear indistinctly.

现代文翻译 Modern Chinese Translation

　　辽阔[8]的江南，到处都能听到鸟儿的鸣叫，看到绿叶映衬[4]的红花。水边的村庄，山边的城郭，酒旗在春风中飘荡。南朝时建造的一座座寺庙，如今都在烟雨之中若隐若现。[9]

评论与提问 Comment and Question

This poem may make you think of landscape paintings by French impressionist Claude Monet. How does the poet convey his sensuous feel of the spring in the medium of language? Observe how deftly the poet interweaves a panorama and close-ups, aural and visual images, and the seen and the unseen scenes.

练习　EXERCISES

一 填空 Fill in Blanks

A. 诗词填字：挂 载 含 更 飞 鸣 壁 啼 旗 陌 疑 寒 暮 逢 走 川 映 是 翠 遥 返 泊 泣 落

1. 黄鹤一去不复____，白云千____空悠悠。　　2. 两个黄鹂____ ____柳。

3. 千里莺____绿____红，水村山郭酒____风。　　4. ____变千年如____马。

5. 老兔____蟾____天色，云楼半开____斜白。　　6. ____看瀑布____前____。

7. ____流直下三千尺，____是银河____九天。　　8. 鸾珮相____桂香____。

9. 窗____西岭千秋雪，门____东吴万里船。　　10. 日____乡关何处____。

B. 现代文填词：映衬 轧 更新 载 停泊 泻 遥远 历历

1. 他们正准备____ ____设备。　　2. 港口里____ ____了几艘船。　　3. 往事____ ____在目。

4. 红花绿叶相互____ ____。　　5. 此去路途____ ____。　　6. 他被车____伤了。

7. 黄河一____千里。　　8. 他要去个一年半____才能回来。

二 形近字辨析 Distinguish easily confused characters

1. ____川历历汉阳树　a. 晴　b. 睛　c. 清　　2. 千里莺啼绿____红　a. 泱　b. 央　c. 映

3. 门____东吴万里船　a. 伯　b. 泊　c. 柏　　4. 窗含西____千秋雪　a. 领　b. 岭　c. 冷

5. 白云千____空悠悠　a. 载　b. 栽　c. 哉　　6. 鸾珮相逢桂香____　a. 佰　b. 百　c. 陌

7. 云楼半开____斜白　a. 壁　b. 璧　c. 碧　　8. ____看瀑布挂前川　a. 摇　b. 谣　c. 遥

三 连句 Match the first part with the second

1. 窗含西岭千秋雪( )　2. 千里莺啼绿映红( )　3. 飞流直下三千尺( )

4. 晴川历历汉阳树( )　5. 黄尘清水三山下( )　6. 日暮乡关何处是( )

7. 玉轮轧露湿团光( )　8. 两个黄鹂鸣翠柳( )

a. 一行白鹭上青天　b. 鸾珮相逢桂香陌　c. 水村山郭酒旗风　d. 江上烟波使人愁

e. 芳草萋萋鹦鹉洲　f. 更变千年如走马　g. 门泊东吴万里船　h. 疑是银河落九天

四 句读 Punctuate and translate the following passage

昔人已乘黄鹤去此地空余黄鹤楼飞流直下三千尺疑是银河落九天两个黄鹂鸣翠柳一行白鹭上青天黄尘清水三山下更变千年如走马

五 听写 Dictation

1. ____ ____ ____ ____ ____ ____ ____树，芳____ ____ ____ ____ ____ ____ ____。

2. ____ ____ ____ ____ ____ ____ ____雪，门____ ____ ____ ____ ____ ____ ____。

3. ____ ____ ____蟾____ ____ ____，____ ____ ____ ____ ____ ____ ____白。

4. ____ ____ ____ ____ ____三____ ____ ____，____ ____ ____ ____ ____ ____天。

5. ____ ____ ____ ____ ____ ____ ____红，____ ____ ____ ____ ____ ____风。

6

山 水 禅 境

Landscape: Chan (Zen) Vision

tí pò shān sì hòu chán fáng
题 破 山 寺¹ 后 禅² 房

[táng] cháng jiàn
[唐] 常 建³

Written for the Meditation Lodge
Behind the Broken Mountain Temple

[Tang Dyn.] Chang Jian

qīng	*chén*	*rù*	*gǔ*	*sì*
清	晨	入	古	寺

In the morning I walk into the ancient temple,

chū	*rì*	*zhào*	*gāo*	*lín*
初⁴	日	照	高	林△

The morning sun shines upon the tall trees.

zhú	*jìng*	*tōng*	*yōu*	*chù*
竹⁵	径⁶	通	幽⁷	处

The bamboo path leads to a reclusive site,

chán	*fáng*	*huā*	*mù*	*shēn*
禅	房	花	木	深△

The meditation lodge nestles deep in trees and flowers.

shān	*guāng*	*yuè*	*niǎo*	*xìng*
山	光	悦⁸	鸟	性

The mountain light delights the spirit of birds,

tán	*yǐng*	*kòng*	*rén*	*xīn*
潭⁹	影¹⁰	空¹¹	人	心△

The pond's reflection empties the mind of man.

wàn	*lài*	*cǐ*	*jù*	*jì*
万	籁¹²	此	俱	寂

All sounds have ceased at this moment,

dàn	*yú*	*zhōng*	*qìng*	*yīn*
但	余	钟	磬¹³	音△

But the echoes of metal and stone bells linger on.

(Tr. Zong-qi Cai)

[五言律诗 pentasyllabic regulated verse, tonal pattern II, imperfect, see *HTRCP,* p. 171]

字词释义 Vocabulary Notes

1. 破山寺   Broken Mountain Temple, in present-day Jiangsu province.
2. 禅 (禪)   The word "meditation" (*chán*禪) is the Chinese translation of the Sanskrit term "dhyāna." After Buddhism was introduced to China, the Chan practice gave rise to the

Meditation School (*chán zōng* 禅宗), a distinctly Chinese sect of Buddhism. The impact of Chan Buddhism on Chinese literature, art, and culture is immeasurable. Chan Buddhism was introduced into Japan in the twelfth century and has profoundly influenced Japanese culture ever since. "Zen" is the Japanese pronunciation of Chan and better known in the west.

3. 常建 (708–765) a Tang poet, famous for his landscape poems.

4. 初 adj. beginning. 初日 means the morning sun.   5. 竹 n. bamboo.

6. 径 n. path. MdnC: 小路 (*xiǎo lù*). See also P24 note 5, P30 note 3, and P98 note 4.

7. 幽 adj. deep and remote. MdnC: 幽深 (*yōu shēn*). See also P26 note 4 and P99 note 12.

8. 悦 v. to please. MdnC: 取悦 (*qǔ yuè*).

9. 潭 n. deep pool. See also P24 note 12.

10. 影 n. reflection. MdnC: 倒影 (*dào yǐng*). ☞水中的倒影清晰可见 The inverted reflection is pretty clear in the water.

11. 空 (*kòng*) v. to empty. MdnC: 涤荡 (*dí dàng*) to cleanse.

12. 籁 (籟) n. sound from holes (e.g., musical pipe). 万籁 means "sounds of all kinds."

13. 磬 n. inverted stone bell (a percussion instrument).   14. 照耀 (*zhào yào*) v. to shine.

15. 高耸 (*gāo sǒng*) adj. towering.   16. 回荡 (*huí dàng*) v. to resound.

现代文翻译 Modern Chinese Translation

清晨，(我)走进古老的寺院，看到太阳正照耀[14]着高耸[15]的树林。竹林里一条小路[6]通向幽深[7]的地方，在那花草树木的深处，是寺院的禅房。山中的阳光，让鸟儿感到快乐。潭中的倒影[10]涤荡[11]着人心。这时，万籁寂静，只有钟磬声在山林中回荡。[16]

评论与提问 Comment and Question

Chan vision may be understood as the moments of heightened perception or consciousness, in which boundaries between being and non-being, the phenomenal and the noumenal, reality and illusion cease to exist. A Chan poet seeks to evoke this transformed mental state through a masterful play of appearance and hiddenness, silence and sounds. Does this poem entail any deliberate play of elusive images? If so, describe its effect on your state of mind. ☞Compare this poem with "Zhongnan Mountain" (P15), a similar regulated verse of Chan vision by Wang Wei, discussed in *HTRCP*, pp. 177–179. You may also compare it with the following regulated verse by Wang Wei.

P24

guò xiāng jī sì
过[1] 香 积 寺[2]

[táng] wáng wéi
[唐] 王 维[3]

Visiting the Xiangji Temple

[Tang Dyn.] Wang Wei

bù	*zhī*	*xiāng*	*jī*	*sì*	
不	知	香	积	寺	Where is the Xiangji Temple?

shù	*lǐ*	*rù*	*yún*	*fēng*	
数	里	入	云	峰△⁴	Many a mile into a cloud-veiled peak.

gǔ	*mù*	*wú*	*rén*	*jìng*	
古	木	无	人	径⁵	The old forest knows no path of man,

shēn	*shān*	*hé*	*chù*	*zhōng*	
深	山	何	处	钟△	But deep in the mountain, from where come the sounds of a bell?

quán	*shēng*	*yè*	*wēi*	*shí*	
泉⁶	声	咽⁷	危⁸	石	A babbling spring makes precipitous rocks sob,

rì	*sè*	*lěng*	*qīng*	*sōng*	
日	色	冷⁹	青	松△	The feeble sunlight adds coldness to the green pines.

bó	*mù*	*kōng*	*tán*	*qū*	
薄¹⁰	暮¹¹	空	潭¹²	曲¹³	Evening approaching, by an empty pond's bend

ān	*chán*	*zhì*	*dú*	*lóng*	
安	禅¹⁴	制¹⁵	毒	龙△¹⁶	I sit in meditation to subdue the venomous dragon.

[五言律诗 pentasyllabic regulated verse, tonal pattern II, see *HTRCP*, p. 171]

(Tr. Zong-qi Cai)

字词释义 Vocabulary Notes

1. 过 (過) v. See P12 note 1.   2. 香积寺 a temple in present-day Xi'an 西安 in Shaanxi province.
3. See the biographic note in P15 note 2.
4. 峰 n. mountain peak. MdnC: 山峰 (*shān fēng*). ☞山峰高耸入云 The mountain peak reaches to the sky. See also P36 note 7.
5. 径 n. path. See also P23 note 6.
6. 泉 n. spring. MdnC: 泉水 (*quán shuǐ*).
7. 咽 v. to choke with sobs. MdnC: 哽咽 (*gěng yè*). ☞说到去世的父亲，他的声音哽咽了 His voice was choked with sobs when he talked about his deceased father.
8. 危 adj. dangerous, precipitous. MdnC: 陡 (*dǒu*). ☞这座山很陡 This hill is very steep.
9. 冷 adj. cold, used here as a verb, meaning "to make something cold."
10. 薄 v. to approach, near [formal]. ☞日薄西山 The sun is setting behind the western mountains. See P63 note 9 for a different meaning of the word.
11. 暮 n. dusk. See also P18 note 13.
12. 潭 n. deep pool. See also P23 note 9.
13. 曲 adj. curved. See also P02 note 3. Here it is used as a noun, meaning "a bend."
14. 安禅 v. to sit in meditation (*jìng zuò rù dìng* 静坐入定). [Buddhist term]

15. 制　v. to control. MdnC: 控制 (*kòng zhì*). ☞他控制了局面 He had the situation under control.
16. 毒龙　n. venomous dragon, a Buddhist metaphor for craving. MdnC: 欲念 (*yù niàn*) [formal].
17. 陡峭 (*dǒu qiào*)　adj. precipitous [formal].

现代文翻译 Modern Chinese Translation

　　不知香积寺在哪里，进山几里之后，就登 上了高耸入云的山峰 。[4] 古老浓密的树林下，没有人可走的小路。深山中哪里传来了钟声。泉水流过陡峭[17]的岩石，似哭泣哽咽。[7]松林浓密，阳光无法照入，让人感到清冷。快要傍晚了， (我) 在水潭边静坐入定,[14] 心中的欲念[16]终被控制。[15]

评论与提问 Comment and Question

Sentence inversion is a syntactical maneuver frequently used in a pentasyllabic regulated verse, especially in its parallel couplets. Lines 5 and 6 each effect an inversion of the second half of the line. If not inverted, the two lines read: 泉声危石咽 Amidst the babbles of a spring, precipitous rocks sob, /日色青松冷 (In feeble) sunlight, the green pines become cold. When the two verbs (咽, 冷) are moved up to the third-character position, a "chain reaction" happens: first, the two verbs change from intransitive to transitive; second, the subjects (危石, 青松) now become objects; and third, the truncated adverbial phrases (泉声[中], 日色[里]) now become the subjects. Is this syntactical maneuvering conducive to enhancing the poem's aesthetic effect? If so, explain why. ☞ *HTRCP*, pp. 386–387 for an analysis of similar syntactical maneuvering in Xie Lingyun's famous line "池塘生春草，园柳变鸣禽".

P25

			lù	*zhài*
			鹿	柴[1]

The Deer Fence

[*táng*] *wáng wéi*
[唐] 王 维[2]

[Tang Dyn.] Wang Wei

kōng	*shān*	*bú*	*jiàn*	*rén*
空	山	不	见	人
dàn	*wén*	*rén*	*yǔ*	*xiǎng*
但	闻	人	语	响▲
fǎn	*yǐng*	*rù*	*shēn*	*lín*
反	景[3]	入	深	林
fù	*zhào*	*qīng*	*tái*	*shàng*
复	照	青	苔[4]	上▲

On the empty mountain, no one is seen

But the sound of voices is heard

Returning: light enters the deep forest

Again: it shines on the green moss

[五言古绝 pentasyllabic ancient-style quatrain]

(Tr. Charles Egan, *HTRCP*, p. 207)

字词释义 Vocabulary Notes

1. 柴 (*chái*) n. firewood. MdnC: 柴火 (*cháihuo*). Here it is pronounced as *zhài*, meaning "fence." 鹿柴 means "deer fence."
2. See the biographic note in P15 note 2.
3. 景 n. shadow, used here in the sense of "影 (*yǐng*)" and should be pronounced as such. 反景 means "returning sunlight."
4. 苔 n. moss. See also P13 note 6.
5. 夕阳 (*xī yáng*) n. the setting sun.
6. 余晖 (*yú huī*) n. lingering sunshine [formal].

现代文翻译 Modern Chinese Translation

空山中不见人影，只听见说话声。夕阳⁵的余晖⁶照进幽深的树林，又照在青苔上。

评论与提问 Comment and Question

The ideal poetic form for capturing Chan, a flash of religious enlightenment, should be one that is brief and intense like the enlightenment itself. So it is not surprising that almost all famous Chan poems are composed in pentasyllabic rather than heptasyllabic lines. Similarly, the finest of the pentasyllabic Chan poems are mostly quatrains instead of the longer *lüshi* poems. For instance, this and the next two poems by Wang Wei are generally considered the best of his Chan poems. Compare these three quatrains with P23 and P24 and observe how they have halved the poem length by dispensing with the narrative frame and discursive statements. Comment on the effect of this radical reduction of length. ☞ *HTRCP,* pp. 207–210 for comments on this poem and P27.

P26

zhú lǐ guǎn
竹 里 馆¹
[*táng*] *wáng wéi*
[唐] 王 维²

The Lodge in the Bamboo Grove

[Tang Dyn.] Wang Wei

dú	*zuò*	*yōu*	*huáng*	*lǐ*
独³	坐	幽⁴	篁⁵	里
tán	*qín*	*fù*	*cháng*	*xiào*
弹	琴	复	长	啸 ▲⁶
shēn	*lín*	*rén*	*bù*	*zhī*
深	林	人	不	知
míng	*yuè*	*lái*	*xiāng*	*zhào*
明	月	来	相	照 ▲

Alone I sit deep in the bamboo grove,

Plucking the lute and whistling along.

In the deep woods: no one knows,

The bright moon comes to shine upon me.

[五言古绝 pentasyllabic ancient-style quatrain]

(Tr. Zong-qi Cai)

字词释义 Vocabulary Notes

1. 馆 (館)　n. house.
2. See the biographic note in P15 note 2.
3. 独 (獨)　adv. alone. See alsoP08 note 7.
4. 幽　adj. deep and remote. See also P23 note 7.
5. 篁　n. bamboo grove.
6. 啸 (嘯)　v. to whistle. MdnC: 呼啸 (*hū xiào*) [formal]. 👉火车呼啸而过 The train whizzed past. See also P93 note 4.

现代文翻译 Modern Chinese Translation

独自坐在幽深的竹林里，一边弹着琴一边长啸。 幽深的树林中，无人知道，只有明月照下来。

评论与提问 Comment and Question

Compare the play of light and darkness, sounds and silence, absence and presence in this and the preceding poem.

P27

niǎo	*míng*	*jiàn*		
鸟	鸣	涧[1]		

[*táng*] *wáng wéi*
[唐] 王 维[2]

Calling-Bird Brook

[Tang Dyn.] Wang Wei

rén	*xián*	*guì*	*huā*	*luò*
人	闲[3]	桂	花[4]	落.
yè	*jìng*	*chūn*	*shān*	*kōng*
夜	静	春	山	空△
yuè	*chū*	*jīng*	*shān*	*niǎo*
月.	出.	惊	山	鸟
shí	*míng*	*chūn*	*jiàn*	*zhōng*
时[5]	鸣	春	涧	中△

Man quiet: sweet osmanthus falls

Night tranquil: the spring mountain empties

The rising moon startles mountain birds

Which call awhile in the spring stream
    (Tr. Charles Egan, *HTRCP,* p. 209)

[五言律绝 pentasyllabic regulated quatrain, tonal pattern II (imperfect), see *HTRCP*, p. 170]

字词释义 Vocabulary Notes

1. 涧 (澗)　n. brook.
2. See the biographic note in P15 note 2.
3. 闲 (閒)　adj. quiet. MdnC: 安静 (*ān jìng*). 👉请保持安静 Please keep quiet. See P29 note 5 for a different meaning of the word.

4. 桂花 n. sweet osmanthus. It blossoms in September and October—roughly the eighth month in the Chinese Lunar calendar. This eighth month is thus called Gui Month (*guì yuè* 桂月) and is when the Mid-Autumn Festival (*zhōng qiū jié* 中秋节) is celebrated, an occasion for appreciating the bright moon and sweet osmanthus. In poems and legends, the moon and sweet osmanthus are often associated with each other.

5. 时 (時) adv. often. MdnC: 不时 (*bù shí*). ☞他不时来看她 He often comes to see her. See P03 note 3 for a different meaning of the word.

6. 寂静 (*jì jìng*) adj. quiet.

现代文翻译 Modern Chinese Translation

　　深山中，桂花飘落着。寂静⁶的夜晚，春天的山谷空空荡荡。月亮出来了，月光惊动了山中的小鸟。鸟叫的声音，不时⁵回荡在山涧之中。

评论与提问 Comment and Question

The first three lines are each composed of two subject+predicate sentences—one in the bisyllabic segment and the other in the trisyllabic one. In each line, the progression from one subject+predicate to another does not merely indicate a temporal sequence but also implies a causal relationship between the two acts of perception. Does the recognition of this causal relationship entail a flight of imagination?

练习 EXERCISES

一 填空 Fill in blanks

A. 诗词填字: 幽 深 涧 制 咽 照 惊 曲 悦 响 冷 径 潭 钟 空 危 鸣 闻 薄

1. 山光＿＿鸟性，＿＿影＿＿人心。　　2. 泉声 ＿＿ ＿＿石 ，日色＿＿青松。

3. 月出＿＿山鸟，时＿＿春＿＿中。　　4. 古木无人＿＿ ，＿＿山何处＿＿。

5. 竹＿＿ 通＿＿处，禅房花木＿＿。　　6. ＿＿山不见人，但＿＿人语＿＿。

7. ＿＿林人不知，明月来相 ＿＿。　　8. ＿＿暮空＿＿ ＿＿，安禅＿＿毒龙。

B. 现代文填词: 倒影 控制 山峰 哽咽 呼啸 不时 安静

1. 火车＿＿ ＿＿ 而过。　　　　　　2. ＿＿ ＿＿高耸入云。

3. 他已经＿＿ ＿＿ 了局面。　　　　4. 他＿＿ ＿＿来看看她。

5. 请保持＿＿ 。　　　　　　　　　6. 水中的＿＿ ＿＿清晰可见。

7. 说到去世的母亲时，他＿＿ ＿＿了。

二 形近字辨析 Distinguish easily confused characters

1. 夜____春山空　　a. 净　b. 静　c. 晴　　2. 人____桂花落　　a. 间　b. 闲　c. 闭
3. 清晨____古寺　　a. 入　b. 人　c. 八　　4. 深山何处____　　a. 仲　b. 种　c. 钟
5. 月出____山鸟　　a. 惊　b. 凉　c. 晾　　6. 山光____鸟性　　a. 税　b. 悦　c. 说
7. 万____此俱寂　　a. 赖　b. 籁　c. 懒　　8. ____房花木深　　a. 禅　b. 蝉　c. 单

三 连句 Match the first part with the second

1. 反景入深林( )　　2. 泉声咽危石( )　　3. 人闲桂花落( )　　4. 古木无人径( )
5. 万籁此俱寂( )　　6. 独坐幽篁里( )　　7. 清晨入古寺( )　　8. 不知香积寺( )
9. 竹径通幽处( )　　10. 深林人不知( )

a. 夜静春山空　　　b. 但余钟磬音　　　c. 弹琴复长啸　　　d. 日色冷青松
e. 禅房花木深　　　f. 明月来相照　　　g. 初日照高林　　　h. 复照青苔上
i. 数里入云峰　　　j. 深山何处钟

四 句读 Punctuate and translate the following excerpts from three or more poems

不知香积寺数里入云峰古木无人径深山何处钟竹径通幽处禅房花木深万
籁此俱寂但余钟磬音空山不见人但闻人语响月出惊山鸟时鸣春涧中

五 听写 Dictation

1. ____ ____ ____ ____ 石，日 ____ ____ ____ ____ 。
2. ____ ____ ____ ____ 处，____ ____ 花 ____ ____ 。
3. ____ 出 ____ ____ ____ ，____ ____ ____ ____ 中。
4. ____ ____ 入 ____ ____ ，____ ____ ____ ____ 上 。
5. 山____ ____ ____ ____ ，____ ____ ____ 人 ____ 。
6. ____ ____ ____ ____ 里，____ ____ ____ 长 ____ 。

7

山水速写

Landscape: Random Sketches

P28

chūn xiǎo
春 晓[1]

[táng] mèng hào rán
[唐] 孟 浩 然[2]

The Dawn of a Spring Day

[Tang Dyn.] Meng Haoran

chūn	*mián*	*bù*	*jué*	*xiǎo*
春	眠[3]	不	觉[4]	晓 ▲
chù	*chù*	*wén*	*tí*	*niǎo*
处	处	闻	啼	鸟 ▲
yè	*lái*	*fēng*	*yǔ*	*shēng*
夜	来	风	雨	声
huā	*luò*	*zhī*	*duō*	*shǎo*
花	落	知	多	少 ▲

[五言古绝 pentasyllabic ancient-style quatrain]

Lost in springtime slumber, I wasn't aware of the dawn,

Everywhere now I hear birds chirping.

All through the night: the howling of wind and rain,

Flowers, how many of them have fallen?

(Tr. Zong-qi Cai)

字词释义 Vocabulary Notes

1. 晓 (曉) n. dawn. See also P03 note 15.   2. 孟浩然. See the biographic note in P12 note 3.
3. 眠 n. sleep. MdnC: 睡觉 (shuì jiào). See also P45 note 7.
4. 觉 (覺 jué) v. to become aware of, sense. MdnC: 察觉 (chá jué). 👉他察觉这里有问题 He sensed something was wrong here. See P65 note 11 for a different meaning of the word.

现代文翻译 Modern Chinese Translation

春天睡得很好，都没有察觉[4]到天亮了，只听到处处都是鸟儿的叫声。夜里传来了风吹雨打的声音，不知道院子里的花落了多少啊！

评论与提问 Comment and Question

If a child in a Chinese-speaking family is asked to recite some Chinese poems, he or she most likely will be taught this poem as well as Li Bai's "Quiet Night Thought" (P57). Why does this poem have so much appeal for contemporary Chinese readers, old and young? To begin with, let us think about its language. Read the poem line by line, and you will see that this eighth-century poet uses a colloquial language quite close to today's—hence only two words need explanation! If read in isolation, each line is nothing but a casual statement. What is the magic that turns four casual statements into a great poem? This magic is part music and part spatiotemporal maneuvering. Tightly knit together by a dense rhyme, the two couplets present contrasting images of sound, sight, time, and place so compellingly that the reader vicariously re-lives the poet's sudden, delightful moment of perception and imagination.

P29

dú   zuò   jìng   tíng   shān
独 坐 敬 亭 山¹

Sitting Alone in the Jingting Mountain

[táng]   lǐ   bái
[唐] 李 白²

[Tang Dyn.] Li Bai

zhòng   niǎo   gāo   fēi   jìn
众 鸟 高 飞 尽³

Flocks of birds flew high and disappeared,

gū   yún   dú   qù   xián
孤⁴ 云 独 去 闲△⁵

The lone cloud went by itself to rest.

xiāng   kàn   liǎng   bú   yàn
相 看 两 不 厌⁶

Looking at each other, neither of us gets bored—

wéi   yǒu   jìng   tíng   shān
唯⁷ 有 敬 亭 山△

in front of me, only the Jingting mountain.

[五言律绝 pentasyllabic regulated quatrain, tonal pattern I, see *HTRCP*, p. 170]

(Tr. Zong-qi Cai)

字词释义 Vocabulary Notes

1. 敬亭山 Jingting Mountain, in present-day Xuanzhou 宣州, Anhui province.
2. See the biographic note in P19 note 3.
3. 尽 (盡) adv. completely, to the limits of sth. Cf. 绝 in P30 note 2.
4. 孤 adj. solitary, isolated, alone. MdnC: 孤单 (*gū dān*). 她总是孤孤单单一个人 She is always alone. See also P40 note 8, P44 note 9, and P48 note 4.
5. 闲 (閒) adv. leisurely. MdnC: 悠闲 (*yōu xián*). See P27 note 3 for a different meaning of the word.
6. 厌 (厭) v. to be satisfied. MdnC: 满足 (*mǎn zú*). 他非常满足于现状 He is very satisfied with his current situation.
7. 唯 adv. only, merely. MdnC: 只 (*zhǐ*). See also P40 note 12. Cf. 惟 in P99 note 17.

现代文翻译 Modern Chinese Translation

　　鸟儿都飞走了，孤独的白云也悠闲⁵地飘走了。(我坐在这里与敬亭山互相望着，)也只有我跟敬亭山，怎么看对方都看不够啊！

评论与提问 Comment and Question

Each line of this quatrain depicts a particular stage of a sustained contemplative process: watching the myriad birds fly away and feeling the quietude and loneliness (line 1), watching the lone cloud (after the noisy birds are gone) go away and a deepening of the felt quietude and loneliness (line 2), entering a state of reverie and looking at the mountain as a dear companion (line 3), and awakening from the reverie to realize that the dear companion is merely the Jingting Mountain (line 4). Does the development of these four lines represent a condensed version of the four-stage progression (*qǐ* 起, *chéng* 承, *zhuǎn* 转, *hé* 合) of couplets in regulated verse? ☞ "Visiting My Old Friend's Farmstead" (P12) and *HTRCP,* pp. 165–169 for a discussion of the four-stage progression.

P30

jiāng xuě
江 雪
.

[táng] liǔ zōng yuán
[唐] 柳 宗 元[1]

River Snow

[Tang Dyn.] Liu Zongyuan

qiān	*shān*	*niǎo*	*fēi*	*jué*
千	山	鸟	飞	绝[2]
wàn	*jìng*	*rén*	*zōng*	*miè*
万	径[3]	人	踪[4]	灭 ▲[5]
gū	*zhōu*	*suō*	*lì*	*wēng*
孤	舟	蓑[6]	笠[7]	翁[8]
dú	*diào*	*hán*	*jiāng*	*xuě*
独	钓[9]	寒	江	雪 ▲

[五言古绝 pentasyllabic ancient-style quatrain]

One thounsand mountains: all birds have flown
　　away;

Ten thousand paths: all traces of man are gone.

A lone boat, a straw hat and cape, an old man

Alone fishing the river snow.

(Tr. Zong-qi Cai)

字词释义 Vocabulary Notes

1. 柳宗元 (style 字，Zǐhòu 子厚, 773–819), a famous poet and writer in the mid-Tang Dynasty. Liu Zongyuan is one of the "Eight Masters of the Tang and Song Prose" (唐宋八大家 *Táng Sòng bādàjiā*).

2. 绝 (絕)　adv. to the limits of sth. Cf. 尽 in P29 note 3. See P06 note 16 for a different meaning of the word.

3. 径　n. path. See also P23 note 6.

4. 踪　n. footprint, track, trace. MdnC: 踪迹 (*zōng jì*). 👉这里没有熊的踪迹 There are no footprints of a bear here. Cf. 迹 in P46 note 6.

5. 灭 (滅)　v. (of a light, fire, etc.) to go out. See also P64 note 6. Here it means "to disappear."

6. 蓑　n. a rain cape made of straw or bamboo leaves.

7. 笠　n. a large bamboo or straw hat. MdnC: 斗笠 (*dǒu lì*).　　8. 翁　n. old man.

9. 钓 (釣)　v. to fish with a hook and line; to angle. 👉他在钓鱼 He is now angling.

10. 艘 (*sōu*)　measure word for boats.　　　　11. 覆盖 (*fù gài*)　v. to cover.

12. 垂钓 (*chuí diào*)　v. to angle.

现代文翻译 Modern Chinese Translation

　　千座大山中，鸟儿都飞走了；万条小路上，人的踪迹⁴都不见了。一艘¹⁰孤单的小船上，一位老人穿着蓑衣，带着斗笠，⁷独自在大雪覆盖¹¹的寒冷江面上垂钓¹²着。

评论与提问 Comment and Question

This is one of the most memorable character sketches done in the quatrain form. Through his carefully chosen images, what has the poet told us about the life of the fisherman?

P31

yǐn hú shàng, chū qíng hòu yǔ èr shǒu, qí yī
饮¹湖上，初晴后雨二首，其一

Drinking on the Lake, First in Sunshine and
Then in Rain, No. 1

[běi sòng] sū shì
[北宋] 苏轼²

[Northern Song Dyn.] Su Shi

shuǐ	*guāng*	*liàn*	*yàn*	*qíng*	*fāng*	*hǎo*
水	光	潋	滟³	晴	方⁴	好

The lake glistens with ripples
　　so beautiful in sunshine,

shān	*sè*	*kōng*	*méng*	*yǔ*	*yì*	*qí*
山	色	空	濛⁵	雨	亦	奇△

The hills are veiled in mist and are
　　just as spectacular in rain.

yù	*bǎ*	*xī*	*hú*	*bǐ*	*xī*	*zǐ*
欲	把	西	湖⁶	比	西	子⁷

If one wishes to liken the West Lake
　　to the Beauty Shi of the West,

dàn	*zhuāng*	*nóng*	*mǒ*	*zǒng*	*xiāng*	*yí*
淡	妆	浓	抹⁸	总	相	宜△⁹

Whether heavily or lightly made up,
　　she always looks just perfect.
　　　　　　　(Tr. Zong-qi Cai)

[七言律绝 heptasyllabic regulated quatrain, tonal pattern I, see *HTRCP*, p. 170]

字词释义 Vocabulary Notes

1. 饮 (飲) v. to drink. Here it refers to drinking wine.
2. 苏轼 (蘇軾) (style 字, Zǐzhān 子瞻; literary name 号, Dōngpō jūshì 东坡居士 1037–1101), a great poet and writer of the Song Dynasty. He is known for his great achievements in a variety of fields, including poetry, prose, aesthetic theory, painting, calligraphy, and so on. He is also regarded as the leader of the school of "heroic abandon" (háofàngpài 豪放派) in *ci* poetry.
3. 潋滟 (瀲灩) adj. (of water) waving, ripples.
4. 方 adv. just. MdnC: 正 (zhèng). See P03 note 10 and P10 note 13 for different meanings of the word.
5. 空濛 or 空蒙 adj. hazy, misty. See also P78 note 6.
6. 西湖 West Lake, in present-day Hangzhou 杭州, Zhejiang province. It is also called Xizi Lake (xī zǐ hú 西子湖) after this poem.
7. 西子 or 西施, original name Shi Yiguang 施夷光, a famous woman of the Yue state (in present-day Zhejiang province) during the Spring and Autumn Period (770–476 B.C.E.). She is the first of the "Four Beautiful Women" (sìdà měirén 四大美人) in ancient China.
8. 抹 v. to apply, put on. Here it means "to put on make-up." 淡妆浓抹 means light make-up and heavy make-up.
9. 宜 adj. suitable, right. MdnC: 适合 (shì hé). 👉这套书很适合孩子读 This series of books is suitable for children. See also P82 note 18.
10. 荡漾 (dàng yàng) v. to ripple, wave.

现代文翻译 Modern Chinese Translation

晴天的西湖，水波荡漾，¹⁰ 风景正⁴好。雨中的西湖，群山细雨蒙蒙，也很奇妙。要是把西湖比成美人西施，无论是淡妆还是浓妆的，都很适合。⁹

评论与提问 Comment and Question

Blending abstract comments with concrete natural depiction is a prominent tendency in Song *shi* poetry in general and in Su Shi's poetry in particular. This poem presents an intricate web of abstract statements: first two comments on the appearance of the West Lake under two different weather conditions (晴方好, 雨亦奇), and then a recapitulation and amplification of these two comments in the second couplet.

Why are we delighted, not bored, by all these abstract comments? This has much to do with the way Su integrates them with the imagistic part of the poem. The first two comments are made in response to the concrete scenes fondly observed; the last comment (总相宜) is made in response to a novel comparison of natural beauty to human beauty. Would you take the first two lines each as a topic+comment line? 👉 "'Guan, Guan,' Cry the Ospreys" (P01) and *HTRCP,* pp. 380–392 for discussions on topic +comment constructions.

P32

xiǎo chí
小 池

[nán sòng] yáng wàn lǐ
[南宋] 杨 万 里[1]

A Small Pond

[Southern Song Dyn.] Yang Wanli

quán	*yǎn*	*wú*	*shēng*	*xī*	*xì*	*liú*
泉	眼[2]	无	声	惜[3]	细	流△

The spring oozes soundlessly,
treasuring its slender flow,

shù	*yīn*	*zhào*	*shuǐ*	*ài*	*qíng*	*róu*
树	阴	照	水	爱	晴	柔△[4]

Trees cast their shade upon water,
enchanted by its pleasant sheen.

xiǎo	*hé*	*cái*	*lù*	*jiān*	*jiān*	*jiǎo*
小	荷[5]	才	露[6]	尖	尖	角[7]

The young lotus has just shown
its pointed buds,

zǎo	*yǒu*	*qīng*	*tíng*	*lì*	*shàng*	*tóu*
早	有	蜻	蜓[8]	立	上	头△

There're already dragonflies
perching on them..
(Tr. Zong-qi Cai)

[七言律绝 heptasyllabic regulated quatrain, tonal pattern IIa, see *HTRCP*, p. 171]

字词释义 Vocabulary Notes

1. 杨万里 (楊萬里) (style 字，Tíngxiù 廷秀; literary name 号, Chéngzhāi 诚斋, 1127–1206), a famous poet in the Southern Song Dynasty. He, You Mao 尤袤(1127–1202), Fan Chengda 范成大 (1126–1193), and Lu You 陆游 are known as the "Four Great Poets of the Regeneration Period" (*zhōngxīng sìdà shīrén* 中兴四大诗人). See Lu You's biographic note in P17 note 1.

2. 泉眼 n. the hole of a spring.

3. 惜 v. to cherish, care for tenderly. MdnC: 爱惜 (*ài xī*). 👉请爱惜生命 Please cherish lives!

4. 柔 adj. soft, gentle, mild. MdnC: 柔和 (*róu hé*). 👉这里的光线很柔和 The light here is soft.

5. 小荷 tender lotus.

6. 露 (*lù*) v. to show. See P21 note 6 for a different meaning of the word.

7. 角 n. horn. Here it refers to the top part of lotus bud (*hé bāo* 荷苞).

8. 蜻蜓 n. dragonfly.   9. 悄无声息 (*qiāo wú shēng xī*) adj. very quiet.

10. 涓涓 (*juān juān*) adv. trickling sluggishly [formal].

现代文翻译 Modern Chinese Translation

　　泉水从泉眼悄无声息[8]地流出，似乎是因为爱惜这涓涓[9]细流；池边的树荫照映在水中，好像是因为喜欢这晴朗柔和[4]的风光。荷苞[7]才刚刚把尖尖的顶端露出水面，蜻蜓就已经落在了上头。

评论与提问 Comment and Question

Like the preceding poem, this poem begins with two topic+comment lines. The comments (惜细流、爱晴柔), however, are of different kind. Instead of expressing the poet's own emotional response, they tell of the imagined feelings of the natural objects being observed. Have you heard of the English literary term "pathetic fallacy"? It refers to a presentation of inanimate objects as if they had human feelings, thought, or sensations. If you know of any examples of pathetic fallacy in English or American poetry, how would you compare them with these two lines? Is there any subtle difference between the English pathetic fallacy and its Chinese counterpart?

P33

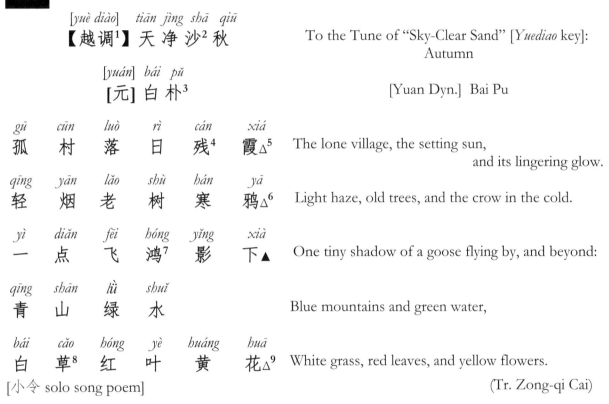

[yuè diào] tiān jìng shā qiū
【越调¹】天净沙² 秋

[yuán] bái pǔ
[元] 白朴³

To the Tune of "Sky-Clear Sand" [*Yuediao* key]:
Autumn

[Yuan Dyn.] Bai Pu

gū   cūn   luò   rì   cán   xiá
孤   村   落   日   残⁴   霞△⁵

The lone village, the setting sun,
and its lingering glow.

qīng   yān   lǎo   shù   hán   yā
轻   烟   老   树   寒   鸦△⁶

Light haze, old trees, and the crow in the cold.

yì   diǎn   fēi   hóng   yǐng   xià
一   点   飞   鸿⁷   影   下▲

One tiny shadow of a goose flying by, and beyond:

qīng   shān   lǜ   shuǐ
青   山   绿   水

Blue mountains and green water,

bái   cǎo   hóng   yè   huáng   huā
白   草⁸   红   叶   黄   花△⁹

White grass, red leaves, and yellow flowers.

[小令 solo song poem]

(Tr. Zong-qi Cai)

字词释义 Vocabulary Notes

1. 越调 (越調) *Yuediao* key, one of the *Gongdiao* keys (*gōng diào* 宫调) used in traditional Chinese music. See also P47. See P09 note 1 on 宫调.

2. 天净 (淨) 沙 "Sky-Clear Sand," tune of a solo song poem (*xiǎo lìng* 小令).

3. 白朴 (style 字, Rénfǔ 仁甫; literary name 号, Lángǔ xiānsheng 兰谷先生，1226–?), a famous *qu* poet and playwright in the Yuan. He, Guan Hanqin 关汉卿 (1220?–1307?), Ma Zhiyuan 马致远, and Zheng Guanzu 郑光祖(?) are known as the "Four Great Writers of the Yuan *qu*" (*Yuánqǔ sìdàjiā* 元曲四大家). See Ma Zhiyuan's biographic note in P47 note 3.

4. 残 (殘) adj. remaining, remnant, incomplete. See also P03 note 7.
5. 霞 n. rosy clouds. See also P82 note 5. 残霞 refers to the lingering glow of sunset.
6. 鸦 (鴉) n. crow. 寒鸦 indicates crows in the cold weather of late fall.
7. 鸿 (鴻) n. swan goose. MdnC: 大雁 (*dàyàn*).
8. 白草 n. white grass, a grass that grows in northwest China according to Yan Shigu 颜师古's (581−645) note on the "Biography of the Western Regions" ("Xīyù zhuàn"西域传) in the *History of the Han Dynasty (Hàn shū* 汉书).
9. 黄花 n. yellow flower. Here it refers to chrysanthemum (*jú huā* 菊花), which blossoms in fall.
10. 枫树 (*fēng shù*) n. maple.

现代文翻译 Modern Chinese Translation

　　傍晚时分，太阳渐渐落下，天边的晚霞也即将散去。　远远有座村庄，炊烟轻轻地吹着，乌鸦站在枯老的树上。忽然，一只大雁⁷飞过，顺着它的身影望去，　远处是一片青山绿水，近处到处都是白草，火红的枫树¹⁰叶和金黄色的菊花！⁹

评论与提问 Comments and Questions

1. This poem and Xu Zaisi's "Spring Passions" (P09) represent the polar opposites of Yuan *sǎnqǔ* 散曲 or song poems. While Xu's poem exhibits the *sanqu's* original quality (*běnsè* 本色) marked by an unabashed use of vulgar speech of lowly urban classes, this poem exemplifies an attempt by Yuan literati poets to elevate a new genre of vulgar origin into a vehicle of refined poetic expression. Cleansed of any colloquialism, vulgar or otherwise, the poem is practically a continuum of descriptive binomes or compounds most commonly used in earlier poetry. How does this piling up of descriptive binomes engender a brooding melancholy and afford a sensuous feel of an early autumn?

2. Compare this poem with P47—Ma Zhiyuan's "Autumn Thought"—composed to the same tune of "Sky-Clear Sand."

练习 EXERCISES

一 填空 Fill in blanks

A. 诗词填字: 钓 晓 濛 翁 鸿 潋 阴 轻 绝 流 啼 众 柔 径 惜 孤 眠 灭 潋 残 闲 空 影 眼

1. ＿＿ 舟蓑笠＿＿，独＿＿寒江雪。 2. 水光＿＿ ＿＿晴方好。
3. 春＿＿ 不觉＿＿，处处闻＿＿鸟。 4. 山色＿＿ ＿＿雨亦奇。
5. ＿＿ 鸟高飞尽，＿＿云独去＿＿。 6. 泉＿＿无声＿＿细＿＿。
7. ＿＿村落日＿＿霞，＿＿烟老树寒鸦。 8. 树＿＿照水爱晴＿＿。
9. 千山鸟飞＿＿，万＿＿人踪＿＿。 10. 一点飞＿＿ ＿＿下。

B. 现代文填词: 柔和 满足 察觉 孤单 适合 爱惜 踪迹 悠闲

1. 她总是____ ____ 一个人。　　　　2. 请____ ____ 生命。

3. 他过得很____ ____ 。　　　　　　4. 他____ ____这里有问题。

5. 这里没有熊的____ ____。　　　　6. 光线很____ ____。

7. 这本书很____ ____孩子读。　　　　8. 他很____ ____于现状。

二 形近字辨析 Distinguish easily confused characters

1. 泉眼无声____细流　 a. 昔　b. 惜　c. 蜡　　2. 轻烟老树寒____　 a. 鸦　b. 鸭　c. 鸿

3. 早有____蜓立上头　 a. 蜻　b. 晴　c. 睛　　4. 万径人____灭　　 a. 惊　b. 踪　c. 综

5. 山色空____雨亦奇　 a. 朦　b. 漾　c. 濛　　6. ____有敬亭山　　 a. 唯　b. 维　c. 惟

7. 淡妆____抹总相宜　 a. 浓　b. 脓　c. 侬　　8. ____云独去闲　　 a. 狐　b. 瓜　c. 孤

三 连句 Match the first part with the second

1. 众鸟高飞尽( )　　 2. 水光潋滟晴方好( )　　 3. 青山绿水( )　　 4. 小荷才露尖尖角 ( )

5. 夜来风雨声( )　　 6. 欲把西湖比西子( )　　 7. 千山鸟飞绝( ) 8. 孤村落日残霞( )

9. 春眠不觉晓( )　　 10. 泉眼无声惜细流( )

a. 白草红叶黄花　　 b. 树阴照水爱晴柔　　 c. 孤云独去闲　　 d. 花落知多少

e. 万径人踪灭　　　 f. 山色空濛雨亦奇　　 g. 处处闻啼鸟　　 h. 早有蜻蜓立上头

i. 淡妆浓抹总相宜　 j. 轻烟老树寒鸦

四 句读 Punctuate and translate the following excerpts from three or more poems

众 鸟 高 飞 尽 孤 云 独 去 闲 一 点 飞 鸿 影 下 青 山 绿 水 白 草 红 叶 黄 花 孤 舟 蓑 笠 翁 独 钓 寒 江 雪 欲 把 西 湖 比 西 子 淡 妆 浓 抹 总 相 宜 夜 来 风 雨 声 花 落 知 多 少

五 听写 Dictation

1. ____ ____ ____ ____ ____ ____好，山 ____ ____ ____ ____ ____ 。

2. ____ ____ 不 ____ ____，处 处 ____ ____ ____ 。

3. ____ ____ 两 ____ ____，____ 有 ____ ____ ____ 。

4. ____ 山 ____ ____ ____，____ ____ 人 ____ ____ 。

5. 一 点 ____ ____ ____ 下，____ 山 ____ 水，____ ____ ____ ____ ____ 。

8

山 水 理 趣

Landscape: A Source of Wisdom

dēng guàn què lóu
登 鹤 雀 楼¹

Climbing Crane Tower

[*táng*] *wáng zhī huàn*
[唐] 王 之 涣²

[Tang Dyn.] Wang Zhihuan

bái rì yī shān jìn
白 日³ 依⁴ 山 尽⁵

White sun rests on mountains—and is gone

huáng hé rù hǎi liú
黄 河 入 海 流△

Yellow River enters sea—and flows on

yù qióng qiān lǐ mù
欲 穷⁶ 千 里 目⁷

If you want to see a further thousand miles:

gèng shàng yì céng lóu
更 上 一 层 楼△

Climb another story in the tower

(Tr. Charles Egan, *HTRCP*, p. 206)

[五言律绝 pentasyllabic regulated quatrain, tonal pattern I, see *HTRCP*, p. 170]

字词释义 Vocabulary Notes

1. 鹳雀楼 (鸛雀樓) The Crane Tower, in present-day Yongji County 永济县, Shanxi province.
2. 王之涣 (style 字, Jìlíng 季凌，688–742), a High Tang poet. Although he only left behind six poems, three of them are regarded as masterpieces for the ages, including "Climbing Crane Tower" and P48 "Song of Liangzhou" ("Liángzhōu cí" 凉州词).
3. 白日 n. sun. MdnC: 太阳 (*tài yang*). See also P38 note 15 and P52 note 15.
4. 依 v. to rely on, depend on. MdnC: 依傍 (*yī bàng*). 👉 他现在无所依傍 He cannot depend on anything now. See also P38 note 9.
5. 尽 (盡) v. to exhaust. See also P03 note 11.
6. 穷 (窮) v. to exhaustively explore. MdnC: 穷尽 (*qióng jìn*). 👉 为了事业，他穷尽了毕生的心血 He devoted all his energies to his work.
7. 目 n. eye. Here it refers to a view of landscape (*fēng jǐng* 风景).

现代文翻译 Modern Chinese Translation

太阳³依傍⁴着群山，缓缓落下。黄河向东流入大海。如要穷尽⁶这千里之内的风景，⁷需要再上一层楼。

评论与提问 Comment and Question

This poem is one of the best-known panoramic sketches in Chinese poetry. It engenders in us a feeling of the sublime as it stretches our perceptual capacity to the limit, and beyond. The first couplet presents us with four expansive images (the sun, mountains, the Yellow River, and the sea) within an intricate nexus of correspondence, contrast, and movement. Can you perceive any contrast in the categories of things observed, in color, and in movement? While these contrasts enhance one another and expand our field of vision, the second couplet guides our vision or imagination further beyond the horizons. Ponder the differences between the perceptual and discursive modes of presentation employed in the two couplets respectively.

P35

zǎo fā bái dì chéng
早 发 白 帝 城¹

[táng] lǐ bái
[唐] 李 白²

zhāo cí bái dì cǎi yún jiān
朝³ 辞⁴ 白 帝 彩 云⁵ 间△

qiān lǐ jiāng líng yí rì huán
千 里 江 陵⁶ 一 日 还△

liǎng àn yuán shēng tí bú zhù
两 岸 猿⁷ 声 啼 不 住⁸

qīng zhōu yǐ guò wàn chóng shān
轻 舟 已 过 万 重⁹ 山△

Departing Baidi in the Morning

[Tang Dyn.] Li Bai

In the morning I departed Baidi
　　　　shrouded in tinted clouds,

Jiang Ling— a thousand miles downstream—
　　　　I reached it in just a day.

On both banks of the Yangtze
　　　　the cries of gibbons had hardly faded out

When my light boat passed through
　　　　ten thousand tiers of mountains.
　　　　　　　　(Tr. Zong-qi Cai)

[七言律绝 heptasyllabic regulated quatrain, tonal pattern Ia, see *HTRCP,* p. 171]

字词释义 Vocabulary Notes

1. 白帝城 The White Emperor City, built on the White Emperor Mountain (*báidì shān* 白帝山), in present-day Chongqing.
2. See the biographic note in P19 note 3.
3. 朝 (*zhāo*) n. early morning. MdnC: 早晨 (*zǎo chén*). See also P39 note 4.

4. 辞 (辭) v. to take leave of; depart from. MdnC: 告别 (*gào bié*). 👉他告别了北京 He left Beijing. See also P40 note 6.

5. 彩云 (雲) rosy clouds.

6. 江陵 in present-day Jiangling County 江陵县, Hubei province. It is about one thousand and two hundred *li* away from 白帝城.

7. 猿 n. ape. MdnC: 猿猴 (*yuán hóu*) apes and monkeys. See also P93 note 3.

8. 住 v. to stop. MdnC: 停止 (*tíng zhǐ*). 👉鸟叫从没停止过 The birds' singing has never stopped. See also P68 note 4.

9. 重 (*chóng*) n. layers. See P17 note 6.

现代文翻译 Modern Chinese Translation

早晨³告别⁴了彩云环绕的白帝城，一天时间，就回到了千里之外的江陵。(一路上，)听到两岸上猿猴⁷的叫声从未停止，⁸而轻快的小船已经过了重重叠叠的群山。

评论与提问 Comment and Question

This poem depicts the flying speed of a boat ride down through the Three Gorges on the Yangtze. Speed is the measure of the rate of motion: distance traveled divided by the time of travel. Our common feeling of speed, however, is a visual experience impacted as well by the distance between the viewer and what is viewed. The closer the points of spatial reference are to us, the greater the speed we would feel, and vice versa.

These physical and psychological laws of speed are exploited to the full in this poem. The first couplet affords a general, if not dry and scientific, sense of speed in the first couplet. "千里", "一日" spell out the distance traveled and the time used, while "白帝" and "江陵" indicate a change of spatial markers. In the second couplet, Li Bai dramatically increases the velocity of the boat ride by reducing the time of travel to just seconds (when the sounds of gibbons still linger in the ear) and by stressing the lightness of the boat. The changing of spatial markers from a distant city to towering cliffs close by also serves to enhance our sense of speed.

Thanks to these ingenious spatial and temporal maneuvers, Li Bai has created an exhilarating sense of speed that could only be imagined in his time, a speed probably comparable to a rocket ride in our time. The second couplet is now often cited to express anticipation of smooth or "speedy" sailing after completing a difficult task.

P36

tí xī lín bì
题¹ 西 林² 壁³

[*běi sòng*] *sū shì*
[北宋] 苏 轼⁴

Written on the Wall of the West Wood Temple

[Nothern Song Dyn.] Su Shi

héng	*kàn*	*chéng*	*lǐng*	*cè*	*chéng*	*fēng*
横[5]	看	成	岭[6]	侧	成	峰△[7]

All broad ridges it is, if seen lengthwise,
　　all soaring peaks it becomes,
　　　　if seen sideways;

yuǎn	*jìn*	*gāo*	*dī*	*gè*	*bù*	*tóng*
远	近	高	低	各	不	同△

Viewed from afar and near, high and low,
　　it looks all different.

bù	*shí*	*lú*	*shān*	*zhēn*	*miàn*	*mù*
不	识	庐	山	真	面	目[8]

The true face of Mount Lu I cannot tell

zhǐ	*yuán*	*shēn*	*zài*	*cǐ*	*shān*	*zhōng*
只	缘[9]	身	在	此	山	中△

Only because I am in the midst of it.

(Tr. Zong-qi Cai)

[七言律绝 heptasyllabic regulated quatrain, tonal pattern Ia, see *HTRCP*, p. 171]

字词释义 Vocabulary Notes

1. 题 (題)　v. to inscribe.
2. 西林 (寺)　West Woods Temple in Mount Lu, Jiangxi province.
3. 壁　n. wall. See also P13 note 2.　　4. See the biographic note in P31 note 2.
5. 横 (*héng*)　adj. horizontal. 横看 means looking at Mount Lu from east or west since it runs from north to south.
6. 岭　n. ridge.　　　　　　7. 峰　n. mountain peak. See P24 note 4.
8. 面目　n. face, appearance (of things). 👉我们要还原事情的本来<u>面目</u> We need to reveal the thing in its true colors.
9. 缘 (緣)　conj. because. MdnC: 因为 (*yīn wèi*). See also P82 note 8.
10. 连绵 (*lián mián*)　adj. continuous, uninterrupted.

现代文翻译 Modern Chinese Translation

　　从东西向看庐山，山岭连绵。[10]从侧面看庐山，山峰耸立。从远处，近处，高处，低处看庐山，看到的也各不相同。看不清庐山本来的<u>面目</u>，[8]只<u>因为</u>[9]自己身在庐山啊！

评论与提问 Comment and Question

This poem depicts the poet's failed attempt to understand the true character of the famous Mount Lu by looking at it from inside. In the first couplet, Su does not use images to evoke a perceptual process as Wang Zhihuan does in P34. Instead, he just reports in discursive language the discoveries of his perceptual investigation. In the second couplet, he consciously draws out a broader truth about life—one cannot take stock of a situation objectively if one is too involved in it. In many ways, this poem strikes us as a poetic replication of the then prevalent Neo-Confucian pursuit of "investigating things and obtaining knowledge" (*gé wù zhì zhī* 格物致知). Can the same be said of his poem on the West Lake (P31)?

P37

guān shū yǒu gǎn　èr shǒu qí yī
观书有感[1] 二首其一

[nán sòng] zhū xī
[南宋] 朱熹[2]

bàn	*mǔ*	*fāng*	*táng*	*yí*	*jiàn*	*kāi*
半	亩[3]	方	塘[4]	一	鉴[5]	开△

The square pond of a tiny size
　　　　spreads out like a mirror

tiān	*guāng*	*yún*	*yǐng*	*gòng*	*pái*	*huái*
天	光	云	影	共	徘	徊△[6]

In which the sky's light and clouds' shadows
　　　　dance together to and fro.

wèn	*qú*	*nǎ*	*dé*	*qīng*	*rú*	*xǔ*
问	渠[7]	那	得[8]	清[9]	如	许[10]

I ask the pond, "how come you get
　　　　to be as clear as this?"

wèi	*yǒu*	*yuán*	*tóu*	*huó*	*shuǐ*	*lái*
为	有	源	头[11]	活	水[12]	来△

"Only because there's a source
　　　　of fresh water flowing in."
　　　　　　　　(Tr. Zong-qi Cai)

[七言律绝 heptasyllabic regulated quatrain, tonal pattern IIa, see *HTRCP,* p. 171]

Two Poems Written After Reading, No. 1

[Southern Song Dyn.]　Zhu Xi

字词释义 Vocabulary Notes

1. 感　v. to feel, sense. Here it is used as a noun, meaning "impression, thoughts." MdnC: 感想 (*gǎn xiǎng*). 请谈谈看完这部电影后的感想 Please tell us what you think of the movie.

2. 朱熹　(style 字, Yuánhuì 元晦; literary name 号, Huìān 晦庵, 1130–1200), a most influential Confucian scholar in the Song Dynasty. He is the leading figure of the school of Principal (*lǐ xué* 理学). He assigned special significance to the *Analects*, *The Mencius*, *The Great Learning*, *The Doctrine of the Mean*, namely the Four Books (*Sì shū* 四书), which served as the basis of civil examinations in the Ming and the Qing.

3. 亩　measure word. a unit of area (=0.0667 hectares).

4. 塘　n. pond. MdnC: 池塘 (*chí táng*). See also P46 note 16 and P62 note 6.

5. 鉴 (鑒)　n. ancient bronze mirror. MdnC: 镜子 (*jìng zi*).

6. 徘徊　v. to hang around, pace up and down. 他在街上徘徊了很久 he hung around on the street for a while. See also P98 note 5.

7. 渠　pron. he or it. In modern Chinese, this word is used mostly as a noun meaning "ditch," "canal," but its old usage as a pronoun (as used here) is retained in the Cantonese dialect.

8. 那得　or 哪得 how come.

9. 清　adj. clear. MdnC: 清澈 (*qīng chè*). See also P43 note 8.　　　　10. 如许　like this.

11. 源头 (頭)　n. fountainhead, source.

12. 活水　n. flowing water.

现代文翻译 Modern Chinese Translation

半亩大的方池塘⁴像一面镜子⁵一样展开了，天上的光亮和白云的影子都映入水塘，在水中徘徊。⁶你问池塘中的水怎么会这样清澈？⁹那是因为有活水不断从源头流过来。

评论与提问 Comment and Question

This poem records an act representative of the Neo-Confucian way of learning—"investigating things and obtaining knowledge" (*gé wù zhì zhī* 格物致知)—by the poet, the greatest Neo-Confucian thinker. The thing being investigated: a pond's clear reflections. The knowledge obtained: clear reflections are made possible by a continuous inflow of water and, by analogy, a clear understanding is made possible by continual learning. Of this poem and the preceding poem, which is more obviously metaphorical and less aesthetically appealing?

练习 EXERCISES

一 填空 Fill in blanks

A. 诗词填字：楼 峰 依 源 影 轻 目 岸 亩 岭 缘 还 穷 徊 尽 重 啼 识 鉴 流 辞 渠 徘

1. 不____庐山真面目，只____身在此山中。　2. ____舟已过万____山。
3. 朝____白帝彩云间，千里江陵一日____。　4. 天光云____共____ ____。
5. 欲____千里____，更上一层____。　6. 横看成____侧成____。
7. 问____那得清如许，为有____头活水来。　8. 两____猿声____不住。
9. 白日____山____，黄河入海____。　10. 半____方塘一____开。

B. 现代文填词：依傍 徘徊 面目 告别 停止 穷尽

1. 他为了事业____ ____了毕生的心血。　2. 鸟叫声一直都没有____ ____。
3. 我们要还原事情的本来____ ____。　4. 他____ ____了北京。
5. 他现在无所____ ____。　6. 他在街上____ ____了很久。

二 形近字辨析 Distinguish easily confused characters

1. 为有____头活水来　a. 原 b. 源 c. 愿　2. 更上一层____　　　a. 楼 b. 搂 c. 缕
3. 只____身在此山中　a. 缘 b. 掾 c. 绿　4. 半亩方塘一____开 a. 监 b. 鉴 c. 临
5. 朝辞白帝____云间　a. 采 b. 踩 c. 彩　6. 远近高____各不同 a. 低 b. 纸 c. 抵
7. 千里江____一日还　a. 凌 b. 陵 c. 棱　8. ____舟已过万重山 a. 经 b. 径 c. 轻

三 连句 Match the first part with the second

1. 欲穷千里目( )　2. 横看成岭侧成峰( )　3. 半亩方塘一鉴开( )　4. 两岸猿声啼不住( )

5. 白日依山尽( )　6. 不识庐山真面目( )　7. 朝辞白帝彩云间( )　8. 问渠那得清如许( )

a. 千里江陵一日还　b. 轻舟已过万重山　c. 黄河入海流　　d. 只缘身在此山中
e. 为有源头活水来　f. 远近高低各不同　g. 更上一层楼　　h. 天光云影共徘徊

四　句读 Punctuate and translate the following excerpts from three or more poems

朝辞白帝彩云间千里江陵一日还问渠那得清如许为有源头活水来欲穷千
里目更上一层楼不识庐山真面目只缘身在此山中

五　听写 Dictation

1. ＿＿＿ ＿＿＿ ＿＿＿ ＿＿＿ ＿＿＿ ＿＿＿间，千＿＿＿ ＿＿＿ ＿＿＿ ＿＿＿ ＿＿＿ ＿＿＿。
2. ＿＿＿ ＿＿＿成＿＿＿ ＿＿＿ ＿＿＿ ＿＿＿，＿＿＿ ＿＿＿ ＿＿＿ ＿＿＿各 ＿＿＿ ＿＿＿。
3. ＿＿＿ ＿＿＿ ＿＿＿山 ＿＿＿，＿＿＿河 ＿＿＿ ＿＿＿ ＿＿＿。
4. ＿＿＿ ＿＿＿千 ＿＿＿ ＿＿＿，更＿＿＿ ＿＿＿ ＿＿＿ ＿＿＿。
5. 两＿＿＿ ＿＿＿ ＿＿＿ ＿＿＿ ＿＿＿ ＿＿＿，＿＿＿ ＿＿＿已＿＿＿ ＿＿＿ ＿＿＿ ＿＿＿。
6. 半＿＿＿ ＿＿＿ ＿＿＿ ＿＿＿ ＿＿＿ ＿＿＿，＿＿＿ ＿＿＿ ＿＿＿ ＿＿＿共 ＿＿＿ ＿＿＿。

9

送 别

Parting

gǔ shī shí jiǔ shǒu qí yī
古 诗 十 九 首 其 一

Nineteen Old Poems, No. 1
Anonymous

xíng	*xíng*	*chóng*	*xíng*	*xíng*	
行	行	重¹	行	行	On and on, again on and on [you go],
yǔ	*jūn*	*shēng*	*bié*	*lí*	
与	君	生²	别	离△ᵃ	I cannot but live apart from you.
xiāng	*qù*	*wàn*	*yú*	*lǐ*	
相	去³	万	余	里△ᵃ	The distance has grown ten thousand *li* and more,
gè	*zài*	*tiān*	*yì*	*yá*	
各	在	天	一	涯△ᵇ⁴	We are now at opposite ends of the sky.
dào	*lù*	*zǔ*	*qiě*	*cháng*	
道	路	阻⁵	且⁶	长△ᵇ	The road is rugged and long,
huì	*miàn*	*ān*	*kě*	*zhī*	
会	面	安⁷	可	知△ᶜ	How can I know when we shall meet again?
hú	*mǎ*	*yī*	*běi*	*fēng*	
胡⁸	马	依⁹	北	风	The Tartar horse leans into the north wind,
yuè	*niǎo*	*cháo*	*nán*	*zhī*	
越¹⁰	鸟	巢¹¹	南	枝△ᶜ	The Yue bird nests among southern branches.
xiāng	*qù*	*rì*	*yǐ*	*yuǎn*	
相	去	日	已	远▲ᵈ	Day by day our parting seems more remote,
yī	*dài*	*rì*	*yǐ*	*huǎn*	
衣	带	日	已	缓▲ᵈ¹²	Day by day robe and belt grow looser.
fú	*yún*	*bì*	*bái*	*rì*	
浮¹³	云	蔽¹⁴	白	日¹⁵	Drifting clouds hide the white sun,
yóu	*zǐ*	*bú*	*gù*	*fǎn*	
游	子¹⁶	不	顾¹⁷	反▲ᵈ¹⁸	The wanderer does not care to return.
sī	*jūn*	*lìng*	*rén*	*lǎo*	
思	君	令	人	老	Thinking of you makes me old,
suì	*yuè*	*hū*	*yǐ*	*wǎn*	
岁	月	忽	已	晚▲ᵈ¹⁹	Years and months are suddenly gone.

qì	*juān*[20]	*wù*[21]	*fù*	*dào*[22]	
弃	捐	勿	复	道	Forget all this—I will say no more about it,

nǔ	*lì*	*jiā*	*cān*	*fàn*	
努	力	加	餐	饭 ▲[d]	But try my utmost to eat my meals.

[五言古诗 pentasyllabic ancient-style verse]   (Tr. Zong-qi Cai, *HTRCP*, p. 105)

字词释义 Vocabulary Notes

1. 重 (*chóng*) adv. again. See P17 note 6 for a different meaning of the word.

2. 生 v. to give birth to somebody, used here as an adverb, meaning "while still alive." MdnC: 活生生 (*huó shēng shēng*).

3. 去 v. to be apart from. MdnC: 距离 (*jù lí*). ☞两地间的距离有五十里 The distance between the two places is 50 *li*. See P80 note 9 for a different meaning of the word.

4. 涯 n. shore, the edge of a vast expanse of water. See also P47 note 8.

5. 阻 v. to hinder, block; used here as an adjective, meaning difficult and dangerous. MdnC: 艰险 (*jiān xiǎn*). ☞这条路充满艰险 This road is full of obstacles and dangers.

6. 且 conj. and. MdnC: 而且 (*ér qiě*). ☞这个房子很大，而且很新 This house is big, and new.

7. 安 adj. quiet, calm, used here as a question word, meaning "how."

8. 胡 it refers to the ethnic groups in the north and west of ancient China. See also P50 note 11 and P80 note 21.

9. 依 v. to lean on, depend on. MdnC: 依恋 (*yī liàn*) to be reluctant to leave, to be attached to sth. ☞我深深依恋着我的故乡 I am deeply attached to my hometown. See also P34 note 4.

10. 越 it refers to ancient people of southern China, originally those along the eastern coastline of present-day Zhejiang province.

11. 巢 n. nest, used here as a verb, meaning "to nest" (*zhù cháo* 筑巢).

12. 缓 (緩) adj. slow, unhurried. Here it means "loose." MdnC: 松 (*sōng*) [informal]. ☞鞋带松了 The shoestring has come loose.

13. 浮 v. to float. MdnC: 飘浮 (*piāo fú*). ☞湖上飘浮着一些叶子 Some leaves are floating on the lake.

14. 蔽 v. to cover, shelter, hide. MdnC: 遮蔽 (*zhē bì*).   15. 白日 n. sun. See also P34 note 3.

16. 游子 n. man traveling or residing in a place far away from home. See also P42 note 1.

17. 顾 (顧) v. to take into consideration. MdnC: 考虑 (*kǎo lǜ*). ☞让我考虑一下 Let me think it over. See P99 note 16 for a different meaning of the word.

18. 反 n. back, used here in the sense of "返 (*fǎn*)," meaning "to return."

19. 晚 adj. late. Here it means "to be gone."

20. 捐 v. to abandon, relinquish; contribute. 弃捐 here means "to abandon what I want to say."

21. 勿 adv. don't. See also P06 note 15.

22. 道 v. to talk about. See also P63 note 16. MdnC: 说 (*shuō*).

23. 保重 (*bǎo zhòng*) v. to take care.

现代文翻译 Modern Chinese Translation

(你)走啊走啊，不停的走啊，就这样我与你被活生生²地分开了。从此你我的距离³如此遥远，你在天那边，我在天这边。路途艰险⁵漫长。想见一面要到什么时候呢？ 胡地的马依恋⁹北风。越地的鸟也在南面的树枝上筑巢。¹¹ 一天天过去了，我们的距离似乎更远了，(思念你让我变瘦，) 衣带越来越松。¹² 飘浮¹³的白云遮蔽¹⁴了太阳，远在他乡的游子不考虑¹⁷回来。因为想你，我都变老了。忽然才发现，岁月都过去了。 (心里还有很多话)不再说²²了，还是努力多吃点饭，好好保重²³自己！

评论与提问 Comments and Questions

1. "Nineteen Old Poems" is the earliest extant group of pentasyllabic poems, first collected in Xiao Tong 萧统's (501–531) *Anthology of Refined Literature* (*Wén xuǎn* 文选). Most modern scholars believe that most of the nineteen poems were composed toward the end of the later Han by an anonymous group of disenchanted literati. This poetical collection is often hailed as a fountainhead of Chinese lyricism and given a prominent place in the history of Chinese poetry. ☞ *HTRCP*, pp.103–116 for a detailed study of this poetic collection.

2. Can you discern a distinctive rhythm (a pattern of fixed and variable pauses) in this and other pentasyllabic poems discussed earlier? ☞ *HTRCP*, pp.103–105.

3. Can you perceive two opposite kinds of human time—time felt as painfully slow and time felt as dishearteningly fast—in this poem? If so, describe their aesthetic effects. ☞ *HTRCP*, pp. 105–106.

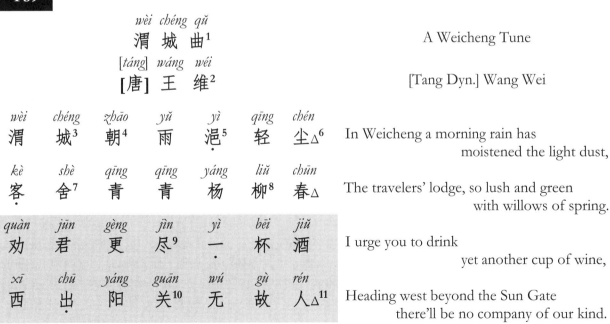

P39

wèi chéng qǔ
渭 城 曲¹

[*táng*] *wáng wéi*
[唐] 王 维²

wèi	*chéng*	*zhāo*	*yǔ*	*yì*	*qīng*	*chén*
渭	城³	朝⁴	雨	浥⁵	轻	尘△⁶
kè	*shè*	*qīng*	*qīng*	*yáng*	*liǔ*	*chūn*
客	舍⁷	青	青	杨	柳⁸	春△
quàn	*jūn*	*gèng*	*jìn*	*yì*	*bēi*	*jiǔ*
劝	君	更	尽⁹	一	杯	酒
xī	*chū*	*yáng*	*guān*	*wú*	*gù*	*rén*
西	出	阳	关¹⁰	无	故	人△¹¹

A Weicheng Tune

[Tang Dyn.] Wang Wei

In Weicheng a morning rain has
      moistened the light dust,

The travelers' lodge, so lush and green
      with willows of spring.

I urge you to drink
      yet another cup of wine,

Heading west beyond the Sun Gate
      there'll be no company of our kind.
      (Tr. Zong-qi Cai)

[七言律绝 heptasyllabic regulated quatrain, tonal pattern Ia (imperfect), see *HTRCP,* p. 171]

字词释义 Vocabulary Notes

1. 渭城曲 "A Weicheng Song," also called 阳关 (*Yáng guān*), title of a *yuefu* song. This poem is also named "See off Yuan Er on His Journey to Anxi" ("sòng yuán'èr shǐ ān xī" 送元二使安西).
2. See the biographic note in P15 note 2.
3. 渭城　in present-day Xianyang 咸阳, Shaanxi province.
4. 朝 (*zhāo*)　n.　morning.　See also P35 note 3.
5. 浥　v. to moisten. MdnC: 湿润 (*shī rùn*). ☞与朋友告别时我的眼睛湿润了 My eyes were moist with tears while saying good-bye to friends.
6. 尘　n.　dirt, dust. MdnC: 尘土 (*chén tǔ*). ☞街上尘土飞扬 The dust was blowing in the streets. See also P68 note 5.
7. 舍 (*shè*)　n.　house, shed.　客舍 means "traveler's lodge"(*lǚ guǎn* 旅馆). See also P58 note 3.
8. 杨 (楊) 柳　n. poplar and willow. Here it refers to willows only. See P02 note 4 on 柳.
9. 尽 (盡)　v. to exhaust. See also P03 note 11.
10. 阳关 (陽關)　the Sun Gate, in the present-day southwest area of Dunhuang 敦煌, Gansu province. It was first established as a frontier defense post by the Emperor Wu (Hàn Wǔdì 汉武帝 r. 140–87 B.C.E.) in the Han Dynasty. The Sun Gate and the Jade Gate (*Yùmén guān* 玉门关) were the two most important passes leading to the Silk Road (*Sīchóu zhīlù* 丝绸之路) before the Song dynasty. See Jade Gate in P48 note 10.
11. 故人　n. old friend. See also P12 note 2.

现代文翻译 Modern Chinese Translation

　　渭城的早晨，一阵小雨让轻轻飘起的尘土[6]变得湿润。[5] 旅馆[7]四周是青青的杨柳，显示着春天的来临。劝您再喝干一杯酒吧，向西出了阳关，就再也没有老朋友了。

评论与提问 Comment and Question

This poem is one of the most famous poems on parting. Typically, a poem on parting usually bemoans an imminent separation of a wandering man from his friend(s), his lover or courtesan, but rarely his wife. The separation between husband and wife is a theme reserved largely for poems of the wandering man (*yóu zǐ* 游子) and of the abandoned woman. The moods of a poem on parting are usually melancholic rather than cheerful.

　　The Sun Gate is a well-known landmark that bestrides the two polar worlds in the traditional Chinese consciousness: a land of peace, prosperity, and sophisticated culture in the east and a land of wars, poverty, and barbarism in the west. So, a journey through this gate toward the west occasions a parting of the most sorrowful kind. How does the poet convey the particular poignancy of this parting? You may think about the powerful effects of the turn engineered by the third line: an abrupt shift from quiet observation to direct speech; from a drowsy springtime morning to a countdown to the departure (enough time only for taking another drink); and from a warm, cozy lodge to a barren, friendless land.

P40

huáng hè lóu sòng mèng hào rán zhī guǎng líng
黄 鹤 楼¹ 送 孟 浩 然² 之 广 陵³

[táng] lǐ bái
[唐] 李 白⁴

Sending off Meng Haoran to Guangling at the Yellow Crane Tower

[Tang Dyn.] Li Bai

gù	*rén*	*xī*	*cí*	*huáng*	*hè*	*lóu*
故	人⁵	西	辞⁶	黄	鹤	楼△

An old friend leaves the west at Yellow Crane Tower

yān	*huā*	*sān*	*yuè*	*xià*	*yáng*	*zhōu*
烟	花⁷	三	月	下	扬	州△

And in flower mists of the third month descends to Yangzhou

gū	*fān*	*yuǎn*	*yǐng*	*bì*	*kōng*	*jìn*
孤⁸	帆⁹	远	影	碧¹⁰	空	尽¹¹

The far shadow of a lone sail is lost in the azure sky

wéi	*jiàn*	*cháng*	*jiāng*	*tiān*	*jì*	*liú*
唯¹²	见	长	江	天	际¹³	流△

I see only the Yangtze River, flowing to the edge of heaven
            (Tr. Charles Egan, *HTRCP*, p. 216)

[七言律绝 heptasyllabic regulated quatrain, tonal pattern IIa (Imperfect), see *HTRCP*, p. 171]

字词释义 Vocabulary Notes

1. 黄鹤楼 The Yellow Crane Tower, see P18 note 1.   2. See the biographic note in P12 note 3.

3. 广 (廣) 陵 or 扬(揚)州 present-day Yangzhou, Jiangsu province. It was first called Guangling in the Warring States Period (475–221 B.C.E.), and was changed to Yangzhou in the Sui Dynasty. This persisted until the Tang Emperor Xuan (Táng Xuánzōng 唐玄宗 r. 712–756) renamed it Guangling. Yangzhou was used through the Ming and the Qing. Therefore, Guangling and Yangzhou in this poem are two names for the same place.

4. See the biographic note in P19 note 3.   5. 故人 n. old friend. See also P12 note 2.

6. 辞 (辭) v. to take leave of; depart from. See P35 note 4.

7. 烟 (煙) 花 n. flowers in the mist. Here it refers to the beautiful spring scenes.

8. 孤 adj. solitary, isolated, alone. See also P29 note 4.

9. 帆 n. sail. Here it refers to the boat. See also P82 note 10.

10. 碧 adj. bluish green, blue. MdnC: 碧蓝 (*bì lán*) dark blue. 📖碧蓝的大海一望无际 The blue sea stretches to the horizon. See also P65 note 16 and P85 note 13.

11. 尽 (盡) v. to exhaust. See also P03 note 11.   12. 唯 adv. only. See also P29 note 7.

13. 际 (際) n. border. See also P10 note 11. 天际 means "the edge of the sky" (*tiān biān* 天边).

现代文翻译 Modern Chinese Translation

　　老朋友在黄鹤楼(与我)告别，在鲜花盛开的三月顺流而下前往扬州。 他的小船远远地消失在蓝天的尽头，(我)只看见长江水流向天边！¹³

评论与提问 Comment and Question

There is a marked contrast between the delightful spring scene suggested by the second line and the melancholic sight of a boat disappearing beyond the horizon in the second couplet. Does this contrast detract from or contribute to the poignancy of this parting? *HTRCP*, pp. 216 for an analysis of this poem.

P41

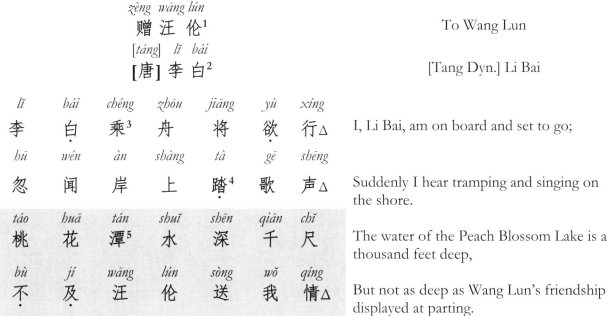

zèng wāng lún

赠 汪 伦¹

[*táng*] *lǐ bái*

[唐] 李 白²

To Wang Lun

[Tang Dyn.] Li Bai

lǐ	*bái*	*chéng*	*zhōu*	*jiāng*	*yù*	*xíng*
李	白	乘³	舟	将	欲	行△

I, Li Bai, am on board and set to go;

hū	*wén*	*àn*	*shàng*	*tà*	*gē*	*shēng*
忽	闻	岸	上	踏⁴	歌	声△

Suddenly I hear tramping and singing on the shore.

táo	*huā*	*tán*	*shuǐ*	*shēn*	*qiān*	*chǐ*
桃	花	潭⁵	水	深	千	尺

The water of the Peach Blossom Lake is a thousand feet deep,

bù	*jí*	*wāng*	*lún*	*sòng*	*wǒ*	*qíng*
不	及	汪	伦	送	我	情△

But not as deep as Wang Lun's friendship displayed at parting.

(Tr. Yin-ching Chen)

[七言律绝 heptasyllabic regulated quatrain, tonal pattern IIa, see *HTRCP*, p. 171]

字词释义 Vocabulary Notes

1. 汪伦 (倫)   Li Bai's friend who lived in Jingxian 泾县, in present-day Anhui province.
2. See the biographic note in P19 note 3.   3. 乘 v. to ride. See also P18 note 4.
4. 踏 v. to step on, stamp. See P04 note 17. Here it refers to beating time by stamping one's feet.
5. 桃花潭   Peach Blossom Lake, in present-day Jingxian 泾县, Anhui province.
6. 节拍 (*jié pāi*)   n. [music] beat, time.
7. 情谊 (*qíng yì*)   n. friendly feelings, friendly sentiments.

现代文翻译 Modern Chinese Translation

李白(我)乘上小船刚要离开，忽然听到岸上传来歌声：有人正一边踏地打着节拍,⁶ 一边唱歌(给我送行)。桃花潭水即使有千尺深，也比不上汪伦送我这份情谊⁷深!

评论与提问 Comment and Question

Compare this poem with the preceding poem by the same poet. How differently does the poet treat the theme of parting in these two poems?

P42

yóu zǐ yín
游子¹ 吟²

[táng] mèng jiāo
[唐] 孟 郊³

Song of a Traveling Son

[Tang Dyn.] Meng Jiao

cí	*mǔ*	*shǒu*	*zhōng*	*xiàn*	
慈⁴	母	手	中	线⁵	The thread in a loving mother's hand
yóu	*zǐ*	*shēn*	*shàng*	*yī*	
游	子	身	上	衣 △	was sewn into the clothes for her traveling son.
lín	*xíng*	*mì*	*mì*	*féng*	
临⁶	行	密	密	缝⁷	When the son was about to leave, she set the stitches firm and tight
yì	*kǒng*	*chí*	*chí*	*guī*	
意	恐⁸	迟	迟	归△⁹	for fear that he might return late.
shuí	*yán*	*cùn*	*cǎo*	*xīn*	
谁	言	寸	草¹⁰	心	Who would claim that the heart of an inch-long piece of grass
bào	*dé*	*sān*	*chūn*	*huī*	
报¹¹	得	三	春¹²	晖△¹³	could ever repay the spring sunshine?

[五言古诗 pentasyllabic ancient-style verse]

(Tr. Yin-ching Chen)

字词释义 Vocabulary Notes

1. 游子 n. man traveling or residing in a place far away from home. See also P38 note 16.
2. 吟 v. to chant, recite, used here as an indicator of a song type. See also P03 note 20.
3. 孟郊 (style 字, Dōngyě 东野, 751–814), a famous mid-Tang poet. His poems are famous for their unpolished style, which was criticized as being "cold" (*jiāo hán* 郊寒) by the great Song poet Su Shi 苏轼. He and Jia Dao 贾岛, a late-Tang poet, are regarded as the two representatives of "tirelessly chanting" (*kǔ yín* 苦吟) poets. See Jia Dao's biographic note in P58 note 2.
4. 慈 adj. kind, loving. MdnC: 慈祥 (*cí xiáng*). 他经常想起那位慈祥的老人 He often thinks about that kind old man.
5. 线 (線) n. thread. 6. 临(臨) prep. on the point of, just before. 临行 means "before leaving."
7. 缝 (縫) v. to stitch, sew. See also P69 note 7.
8. 恐 v. to dread, fear. MdnC: 担心 (*dān xīn*) to worry. 家人很担心她的健康 Her family worries about her health. See also P68 note 12 and P78 note 9.

9. 归 (歸) v. to go back to, return. See also P07 note 11.

10. 寸草 inch-long grass, used as a metaphor for children. 寸草心 refers to children's love for their parents.

11. 报 v. to repay. MdnC: 报答 (*bào dá*) to requite, repay. ☞要怎么才能报答他为我们做的一切呢 What can we do to repay him for all he has done for us?

12. 三春 three months in the spring. According to the Chinese lunar calendar, the first month of spring is called Meng Spring (*mèngchūn* 孟春), the second Zhong Spring (*zhòngchūn* 仲春), and the third Ji Spring (*jìchūn* 季春).

13. 晖 (暉) n. sunshine, sunlight. 三春晖 means "sunshine of the three months of spring." Here it refers to a mother's love.

现代文翻译 Modern Chinese Translation

　　慈祥⁴的母亲手中拿着线，为即将远行的孩子缝⁷衣服。临行前认真仔细的缝着，心中担心⁸孩子很晚才回来。谁能够明白，一寸长的小草，怎样才能报答¹¹春天给它的阳光呢！(子女怎样才能报答母亲深厚的爱呢！)

评论与提问 Comment and Question

This poem exhibits a distinct topic+comment structure: the first two couplets make up the topic and the third couplet the comment. The topic is the scene of a mother making clothes for her traveling son right before his departure. We have, first, a "static" close-up: the thread in the mother's hand and her son's clothes, and then a quickened process of stitching driven by her fear of her son's late return. This scene reveals different dimensions of the mother's love: an inseparable bond with her son as suggested by the sewn thread, her heartwarming love as tangibly felt while wearing the clothes, and her perpetual yearning for her son's return as embodied by her firm and dense needlework.

　　The comment ushers in the emotional response to this scene by an implied observer (be he the son, a poetic speaker, or the poet himself). The emotional response comes in the form of a rhetorical question, made unforgettable by a touching analogy: a son cannot requite his mother's love just as an inch-long blade of grass cannot requite the life-giving sunshine. This analogy has undoubtedly made the poem the best-known piece on a mother's love and helped inculcate the Confucian virtue of filial piety in the hearts of generation after generation. Can you discern some important differences in form between this 6-line, ancient-style poem and a regulated verse?

练习 EXERCISES

一 填空 Fill in blanks

A. 诗词填字: 辞 浥 碧 踏 烟 言 涯 巢 尽 蔽 报 乘 春 顾 帆 晖 去 依

1. 渭城朝雨＿＿轻尘，客舍青青杨柳＿＿。　2. 胡马＿＿北风，越鸟＿＿南枝。

3. 李白＿＿舟将欲行，忽闻岸上＿＿歌声。　4. 孤＿＿远影＿＿空＿＿。

5. 谁____寸草心，____得三春____。　　　6. 相____万余里，各在天一____。
7. 故人西____黄鹤楼，____花三月下扬州。　8. 浮云____白日，游子不____反。

B. 现代文填词：依恋 艰险 飘浮 尘土 碧蓝 慈祥 报答 距离
1. 怎么____ ____他为我们做的一切呢？　　2. 湖面上____ ____着一些树叶。
3. 我总是想起那位____ ____的老人。　　　4. 街上____ ____飞扬。
5. 这条路充满____ ____。　　　　　　　　6. 两地间的____ ____只有五十里。
7. ____ ____的大海一望无际。　　　　　　8. 我深深地____ ____着我的故乡。

二 形近字辨析 Distinguish easily confused characters

1. 客舍青青____柳春　a. 扬　b. 杨　c. 汤　　2. 临行密密____　　a. 缝　b. 逢　c. 篷
3. ____花潭水深千尺　a. 桃　b. 挑　c. 佻　　4. 衣带日已____　　a. 暖　b. 缓　c. 暖
5. 孤帆远影____空尽　a. 壁　b. 碧　c. 璧　　6. 报得三春____　　a. 辉　b. 挥　c. 晖

三 连句 Match the first part with the second

1. 慈母手中线( )　2. 桃花潭水深千尺( )　3. 劝君更尽一杯酒( )　4. 孤帆远影碧空尽( )
5. 道路阻且长( )　6. 渭城朝雨浥轻尘( )　7. 故人西辞黄鹤楼( )　8. 思君令人老( )

a. 唯见长江天际流　b. 客舍青青杨柳春　c. 会面安可知　　d. 不及汪伦送我情
e. 岁月忽已晚　　　f. 西出阳关无故人　g. 游子身上衣　　h. 烟花三月下扬州

四 句读 Punctuate and translate the following excerpts from three or more poems

行行重行行与君生别离相去万余里各在天一涯道路阻且长会面安可知临
行密密缝意恐迟迟归谁言寸草心报得三春晖李白乘舟将欲行忽闻岸上踏
歌声孤帆远影碧空尽唯见长江天际流

五 听写 Dictation

1. ___ ___ ___ ___ ___ 尘，___ ___ ___ ___ ___ 春。
2. ___ ___ ___ ___ 心，___ 得 ___ ___ ___。
3. ___ ___ ___ 北 ___，___ ___ ___ 南 ___。
4. ___ ___ ___ 道，___ ___ ___ 加 ___ ___。
5. ___ ___ ___ 尽，___ ___ 长江 ___ ___ ___。
6. 桃___ ___ ___ ___ ___ ___ ___，___ ___ ___ ___ ___ 我___。

10

羈 旅

Sojourns of the Wandering Men

P43

sù jiàn dé jiāng
宿¹ 建 德 江²

[*táng*] *mèng hào rán*
[唐] 孟 浩 然³

An Overnight Stay by the Jiande River

[Tang Dyn.] Meng Haoran

yí	*zhōu*	*bó*	*yān*	*zhǔ*
移	舟	泊⁴	烟	渚⁵

Moving the boat to moor at a misty isle,

rì	*mù*	*kè*	*chóu*	*xīn*
日	暮⁶	客	愁	新△

In the sunset I succumbed to sorrow anew.

yě	*kuàng*	*tiān*	*dī*	*shù*
野	旷⁷	天	低	树

So boundless the wilderness: the sky's pushing the trees lower;

jiāng	*qīng*	*yuè*	*jìn*	*rén*
江	清⁸	月	近	人△

So clear the river: the moon's approaching man.

(Tr. Zong-qi Cai)

[五言律绝 pentasyllabic regulated quatrain, tonal pattern II, see *HTRCP*, p. 170]

字词释义 Vocabulary Notes

1. 宿 v. to lodge for the night. See also P15 note 15.
2. 建德江 part of the Xin'an River (Xīn'ān jiāng 新安江), in present-day Jiande 建德, Zhejiang province.
3. See the biographic note on P12 note 3.   4. 泊 v. to berth, moor. See also P20 note 7.
5. 渚 n. small piece of land surrounded by water, islet [formal]. See also P93 note 6.
6. 暮 n. dusk, evening. See also P18 note 13.
7. 旷 (曠) adj. vast, spacious. MdnC: 空旷 (*kōng kuàng*). 房子后面是一片空旷的田野 The back side of the house has an uninterrupted stretch of countryside.
8. 清 adj. clear. See also P37 note 9.

现代文翻译 Modern Chinese Translation

把小船停泊在烟雾弥漫的江中空地边。太阳落山了，旅客有了新愁思。原野空旷，⁷天空看起来好像比近处的树还要低。江水清澈，水中的月亮似乎和人很近！

评论与提问 Comment and Question

This poem provides an excellent opportunity to test your mastery of characters, binomes, and syntax, and to deepen your understanding of Chinese poetic art.

   To begin with, try to identify the parts of speech of each of the 20 characters in the poem. It is not hard for you to see that all these characters are "content characters" (*shí zì* 实字) of three kinds: nouns, verbs, and adjectives. Neither "empty characters" (*xū zì* 虚字), namely, characters that perform syntactic functions but have no meaning in themselves, nor pronouns are used. In the highly condensed regulated poems, especially those in the descriptive style, empty words and pronouns are kept to a minimum or even totally dispensed with in order to maximize the imagistic impact of content characters. ☞ *HTRCP,* pp. 162–164.

   Most content characters can be used as an independent word or form with another character into a binome—a two-character compound or a two-character verbal phrase. This flexibility of word formation is consciously exploited by Chinese poets to allow for different readings of poetic lines and couplets. In the third line, for instance, the character 低 can be taken either as a stand-alone verb ("to lower, to push down") or an adjectival component ("low") in the compound "low trees." Consequently, the line lends itself to two different readings: 1) "wilderness is so expansive: the sky, and low trees," and 2) "Wilderness is so expansive: the sky seems to be lowering the trees."

   If the first reading traces a linear perceptual movement from one scene to another, the other reading presents an optical illusion: the trees become smaller than they actually are when viewed against the expansive wilderness and hence the illusion of the sky pushing the trees lower. Parse the fourth line and see if you can produce two different readings as well. Does a conflation of such different readings enhance the moods of melancholy and loneliness?

P44

jiāng   hàn
江¹ 汉²
[táng] dù fǔ
[唐] 杜 甫³

The Jiang and Han Rivers

[Tang Dyn.] Du Fu

jiāng	*hàn*	*sī*	*guī*	*kè*
江	汉	思	归⁴	客
qián	*kūn*	*yì*	*fǔ*	*rú*
乾	坤⁵	一	腐⁶	儒△⁷
piàn	*yún*	*tiān*	*gòng*	*yuǎn*
片	云	天	共	远
yǒng	*yè*	*yuè*	*tóng*	*gū*
永⁸	夜	月	同	孤△⁹

By the Jiang and Han rivers, a homeward traveler,

Between heaven and earth, one worthless scholar.

A lone cloud, and the sky (and I) join in being faraway,

A long night, and the moon (and I) share the loneliness.

luò	*rì*	*xīn*	*yóu*¹⁰	*zhuàng*¹¹	
落.	日.	心	犹¹⁰	壮¹¹	The setting sun—yet I remain ambitious at heart;
qiū	*fēng*	*bìng*	*yù*	*sū*_△¹²	
秋	风	病	欲.	苏_△¹²	The autumn wind—from illness I will recover.
gǔ	*lái*	*cún*	*lǎo*	*mǎ*¹³	
古.	来	存	老	马¹³	From antiquity old horses were kept,
bú	*bì*	*qǔ*	*cháng*	*tú*_△¹⁴	
不.	必.	取	长	途_△¹⁴	Not always for the sake of a long journey.

[五言律诗 pentasyllabic regulated verse, tonal pattern I, see *HTRCP*, p. 171]

(Tr. Zong-qi Cai)

字词释义 Vocabulary Notes

1. 江 or 长江, the Yangtze River. See also P83 note 5.

2. 汉 (漢) or 汉水, the Han River, one of the biggest branches of the Yangtze River, originates in present-day Shaanxi Province, and flows to the Yangtze River in present-day Wuhan 武汉, Hubei Province. This poem was written in the fall of 768, when Du Fu was in Gong'an 公安, Hubei province, which is located between the Yangtze River and the Han River.

3. See the biographic note in P20 note 1.

4. 归 (歸) v. to go back to, return. See also P07 note 11.

5. 乾坤 n. heaven and earth, the universe. According to "Explaining Trigrams" ("shuō guà" 说卦) in the *Book of Changes* (Yì 易), "乾 is heaven" (qián tiān yě 乾天也) and "坤 is earth" (kūn dì yě 坤地也).

6. 腐 adj. putrid. MdnC: 迂腐 (yū fǔ) pedantic [formal]. ☞这是很迂腐的见解 This is a very pedantic idea! See P82 note 12 for a different meaning of the word.

7. 儒 n. scholars or learned men (dúshū rén 读书人), Confucians, Confucianism.

8. 永 adj. eternal, forever, long. 永夜 means "a long night." (cháng yè 长夜).

9. 孤 adj. solitary, isolated, alone. See also P29 note 4.

10. 犹 (猶) adv. still. MdnC: 还 (hái). See also P71 note 11 and P97 note 11.

11. 壮 adj. strong; grand. MdnC: 壮志 (zhuàng zhì) great aspiration [formal].

12. 苏 (蘇) v. to revive, come to, used here meaning "to recover."

13. 老马 (馬) an old horse. Here is an allusion to "Miscellaneous Talks (I)" ("Shuōlín shàng"说林上) in *Han Fei Zi* (Hán fēi zǐ 韩非子). Guan Zhong 管仲 and Xi Peng 隰朋 followed Huan Emperor of Qi (齐桓公, ? –643 B.C.E.) to fight against the Guzhu State 孤竹. On their way back to Qi, they got lost. At that moment, Guan Zhong suggested that they take advantage of the intelligence of old horses. They unleashed the old horses, let them go ahead of the troops and then followed the horses. Eventually they found their way home.

14. 长 (長) 途 long distances. 不必取长途 means to say that people like Guan Zhong selected old horses, not for long-distance travel, but for their intelligence. Du Fu here compared himself to an old horse: old though he was, he still possessed intelligence and experience useful for his country.

15. 漂泊 (*piāo bó*)   v. to lead a wandering life, drift.
16. 好转 (*hǎo zhuǎn*)   v. to improve.
17. 智慧 (*zhì huì*)   n. wisdom, intelligence.
18. 跋涉 (*bá shè*)   v. to trudge, trek.

现代文翻译 Modern Chinese Translation

漂泊15在长江和汉水之间，我这思念故乡的游子，只是天地间一个迂腐6的读书人7罢了！(我就像)一片浮云飘荡在遥远的天空，只能和月亮一同孤独地度过漫漫长夜。我虽然老了，如同即将落山的太阳，但是我的心中仍有壮志。11秋风吹来，(我不觉寒冷，反而)感到我的病要好转。16自古以来养老马就是因为它有智慧，17而不必考虑它的体力，让他长途跋涉18啊！

评论与提问 Comment and Question

A salient feature of this poem is its use of topic+comment lines in all but the last two lines. In each of these six lines, the initial bisyllabic segment (a noun binome) presents a topic, a broad image observed by the poet, while the trisyllabic segment introduces a comment induced by the act of observation. ☞*HTRCP,* pp. 174–176, for a discussion on the aesthetic effect of this successive use of topic+comment lines.

P45

fēng qiáo yè bó
枫 桥1 夜 泊

[táng] zhāng jì
[唐] 张 继2

Nightly Mooring at the Maple Bridge

[Tang Dyn.] Zhang Ji

yuè	luò	wū	tí	shuāng	mǎn	tiān
月	落	乌3	啼	霜4	满	天△

The moon's setting, crows are croaking,
　　　under the sky all is frost,

jiāng	fēng	yú	huǒ	duì	chóu	mián
江	枫5	渔6	火	对	愁	眠△7

River maple, lights on fishing boats,
　　　and with sorrow I drifted into sleep.

gū	sū	chéng	wài	hán	shān	sì
姑	苏8	城	外	寒	山	寺9

Outside the Gusu city:
　　　the Cold Mountain Temple,

yè	bàn	zhōng	shēng	dào	kè	chuán
夜	半	钟	声	到	客	船△

At midnight its bell's struck:
　　　passenger boats are arriving.
　　　　　(Tr. Zong-qi Cai)

[七言律绝 heptasyllabic regulated quatrain, tonal pattern IIa, see *HTRCP*, p. 171]

字词释义 Vocabulary Notes

1. 枫桥 (楓橋)   The Maple Bridge, in present-day Suzhou 苏州, Jiangsu province.
2. 张继 (張繼)   (style 字, Yìsūn 懿孙 fl. 756), a mid-Tang poet. This poem earned him great fame.
3. 乌 (烏)   n. crow. MdnC: 乌鸦 (*wū yā*).
4. 霜   n. frost. See also P58 note 5 and P76 note 10.
5. 枫 (楓)   n. maple. MdnC: 枫树 (*fēng shù*).
6. 渔   n. fishing. 渔火 means "lights on fishing boats."
7. 眠   v. to sleep. MdnC: 入眠 (*rù mián*) [formal]. See also P28 note 3.
8. 姑苏 (蘇)   another name of present-day Suzhou, Jiangsu province. This name came from Gusu Mountain 姑苏山 in the Suzhou area.
9. 寒山寺   Cold Mountain Temple, near the Maple Bridge in present-day Suzhou, Jiangsu province. This temple was built during the Liang (502−557) of the Southern Dynasties (420−589) and became famous because of this poem.

现代文翻译 Modern Chinese Translation

月亮渐渐落下，偶尔传来几声乌鸦³叫，抬头望，空中似乎满是秋霜。(看看四周)江边的枫树，⁵渔船上的点点灯火，我独自伴着愁苦入眠。⁷只有半夜时分，姑苏城外寒山寺的钟声，不断地传到我的船上。

评论与提问 Comment and Question

It may be hard to believe that a poet, otherwise negligible, could earn himself eternal fame for nothing but a single quatrain. This is just the extraordinary luck Zhang Ji had with his "Nightly Mooring at the Maple Bridge." The poem is just as popular today as it was in Tang times. Yu Yue's 俞樾 (1821−1907) beautiful calligraphic writing of this poem, now mass-reproduced and sold in souvenir shops throughout China, has made this poem all the more famous. Of course, the fame of this poem depends ultimately on its own aesthetic appeal. In reading this poem, what delights you the most? Think about the interplay between light and darkness, quietude and sounds, between broad scenes and close-ups, and between nature and human activities. Another salient feature is its abundant use of sonorous vowels like "an," "ong" that makes the recitation particularly pleasurable.

P46

shāng shān zǎo xíng
商 山¹ 早 行   Early Morning Journey in the Shang Mountains

[*táng*] *wēng tíng yún*
[唐] 温 庭 筠²   [Tang Dyn.] Wen Tingyun

chén   qǐ   dòng   zhēng   duó
晨   起   动   征³   铎⁴   In the morning I woke up to
                                  the jingling of bells on horse carriages,

kè	xíng	bēi	gù	xiāng
客.	行	悲	故	乡△

Setting off on the road,
            I was saddened by homeward thoughts.

jī	shēng	máo	diàn	yuè
鸡	声	茅⁵	店	月.

Cock's crow, a thatched store, the moon,

rén	jì	bǎn	qiáo	shuāng
人	迹.⁶	板	桥⁷	霜△

man's footprints, a plank bridge, the frost.

hú	yè	luò	shān	lù
槲⁸	叶.	落.	山	路

The oak leaves rained on the mountain path,

zhǐ	huā	míng	yì	qiáng
枳⁹	花	明.¹⁰	驿¹¹	墙△

The *zhi* flowers brightened the walls of a post stop.

yīn	sī	dù	líng	mèng
因	思	杜	陵¹²	梦

I was lost in recalling my dream about Duling:

fú	yàn	mǎn	huí	táng
凫¹³	雁¹⁴	满	回¹⁵	塘△¹⁶

Wild ducks and geese're crowding the round pond.

[五言律诗 pentasyllabic regulated verse, tonal pattern I, see *HTRCP*, p. 171]

(Tr. Zong-qi Cai)

字词释义 Vocabulary Notes

1. 商山 or 楚山, Shang Mountain, in present-day Shangzhou 商州, Shaanxi province.
2. 温庭筠 (style 字, Fēiqīng 飞卿, 813?–870) a famous late-Tang poet. He "is usually credited with having adapted the popular form of the *ci* for a literati audience." (Samei; *HTRCP*, p. 251). He also has a reputation for his *shi* poetry and is often mentioned together with Li Shangyin 李商隐 as "Wen-Li" (温李). See Li Shangyin's biographic note in P03 note 2.
3. 征 (徵) v. to go on a journey. MdnC: 远行 (*yuǎn xíng*). See P50 note 6 for a different meaning of the word.
4. 铎 (鐸) n. bell. 征铎 the bells on the horses and carriages.
5. 茅 (茆) n. thatch. See also P13 note 4.
6. 迹 n. mark, trace. MdnC: 足迹 (*zú jì*) footprint, footmark. 📖雪地上的足迹是谁的呢 Whose footprints are those in the snow? Cf. 踪 in P30 note 4.
7. 板桥(橋) n. plank bridge. See also P02 note 6.
8. 槲 n. daimyo oak.   9. 枳 n. trifoliate orange.
10. 明 adj. bright, light, used here as a verb, meaning "brighten" (*zhào liàng* 照亮). See also P63 note 19.
11. 驿 (驛) n. post. MdnC: 驿站 (*yì zhàn*) post (where formerly couriers changed horses or rested).

12. 杜陵　in the southeast area of present-day Xi'an 西安, Shaanxi province. Wen Tingyun's family settled near Duling and he regarded Duling as his hometown, and once called himself "traveler from Duling" (*Dùlíng yóukè* 杜陵游客).

13. 凫 (鳬)　n. wild duck. MdnC: 野鸭 (*yě yā*).　　14. 雁　n. wild goose.

15. 回　adj. circular, winding.　　　　　　16. 塘　n. pond. See also P37 note 4.

17. 铃铛 (*líng dang*)　n. small bell.

现代文翻译 Modern Chinese Translation

　　早晨起来，听到旅店外车马的铃铛[17]声。要出门上路了，心中悲伤，一直思念着故乡。(虽然一早听到)鸡叫，(可站在)茅草店外，(看到)空中还挂着残月。走到板桥处，旅客的足迹[6]已踏乱了桥上刚结的霜。槲树的叶子落满了山路，枳树的白花照亮[10]了驿站[11]的墙壁。因为(我)还想着昨夜梦中的杜陵，(眼前似乎看到了)野鸭[13]和大雁在水塘里嬉戏游玩的情形。

评论与提问 Comment and Question

This poem is made up of a continuum of images seen by the poet on the move. By going through the images line by line, and couplet by couplet, can you perceive a continual change of time and space and thereby retrace the poet's journey? If you are a careful reader, you should be able to chart out his route as well as determine where and when it began—and ended. The second couplet is often cited as a consummate example of using noun-images alone to suggest a temporal process.

P47

[*yuè diào*]　*tiān jìng shā qiū sī*
【越调[1]】 天 净 沙[2] 秋 思

[*yuán*]　*mǎ zhì yuǎn*
[元] 马 致 远[3]

To the Tune "Sky-Clear Sand" [*Yuediao* key]: Autumn Thoughts

[Yuan Dyn.] Ma Zhiyuan

kū	*téng*	*lǎo*	*shù*	*hūn*	*yā*
枯[4]	藤[5]	老	树	昏[6]	鸦△
xiǎo	*qiáo*	*liú*	*shuǐ*	*rén*	*jiā*
小	桥	流	水	人	家△
gǔ	*dào*	*xī*	*fēng*	*shòu*	*mǎ*
古	道	西	风	瘦	马▲
xī	*yáng*	*xī*	*xià*		
夕	阳	西	下		
duàn	*cháng*	*rén*	*zài*	*tiān*	*yá*
断	肠[7]	人	在	天	涯△[8]

Withered vines, old trees, crows at dusk,

A small bridge, flowing water, people's homes,

An ancient road, the west wind, a lean horse.

The evening sun goes down in the west.

One heartbroken man at the end of the earth.

[小令 solo song poem]

(Tr. Xinda Lian, *HTRCP*, p. 334)

字词释义 Vocabulary Notes

1. 越调 (越調) See P33 note 1.   2. 天净 (淨) 沙   See P33 note 2.

3. 马致远 (馬致遠, 号, Dōnglí 东篱，1250?–1323?) a famous *qu* poet and playwright in the Yuan. He, Guan Hanqin 关汉卿 (1220?–1307?), Bai Pu 白朴, and Zheng Guanzu 郑光祖 (?) are known as the "Four Great Writers of the Yuan *qu*" (*Yuánqǔ sìdàjiā* 元曲四大家). See Bai Pu's biographic note in P33 note 3.

4. 枯   adj. withered. MdnC: 枯萎 (*kū wěi*). ☞叶子枯萎了 The leaves withered.

5. 藤   n. vine.   6. 昏   n. dusk. MdnC: 黄昏 (*huáng hūn*).

7. 肠 (腸)   n. intestines. See also P95 note 14. 断肠 means "heartbroken." 断肠人 indicates the traveler who misses his family very much.

8. 涯   n. shore. See also P38 note 4. 天涯 means "the edge of the world." See also P82 note 11.

9. 萧瑟 (*xiāo sè*) adj. rustle in the air.   10. 蹒跚 (*pán shān*) adv. (to walk) haltingly.

现代文翻译 Modern Chinese Translation

枯萎⁴的藤缠绕着老树， 树枝上落着黄昏⁶时回巢的乌鸦。小桥下，水流着，旁边有几户人家。 在古老的道路上，西风萧瑟，⁹我骑着一匹瘦马蹒跚¹⁰前行。太阳向西缓缓落下，悲伤的人还飘泊在天涯。

评论与提问 Comments and Questions

1. This poem by Ma Zhiyuan, or at least its first three lines, is probably inspired by the famous third couplet of the preceding poem by Wen Tingyun. Can you trace here a temporal process hidden behind the noun-images as you have done in Wen's poem? ☞ *HTRCP,* pp. 334–335, 395–396 for two analyses of this poem.

2. Wen and Ma's poems are composed in two different forms—regulated verse and short song poem. Which of the two forms is more conducive to a sustained "temporalization" of images?

3. Compare this poem also with Bai Pu's song poem composed to the same tune (P33). Is there a difference in the ways the two poets employ noun-images—and in the aesthetic effect produced?

练习 EXERCISES

一 填空 Fill in blanks

A. 诗词填字: 茅 永 壮 旷 晨 霜 乾 孤 征 昏 近 腐 苏 悲 共 眠 枯 流 思

1. 野 ＿＿＿ 天低树，江清月＿＿＿ 人。   2. 鸡声＿＿＿ 店月，人迹板桥 ＿＿＿。
3. 片云天＿＿＿ 远，＿＿＿ 夜月同＿＿＿。   4. 落日心犹＿＿＿，秋风病欲＿＿＿。
5. ＿＿＿ 藤老树＿＿＿ 鸦，小桥＿＿＿ 水人家。   6. 江汉＿＿＿ 归客，＿＿＿ 坤一＿＿＿ 儒。

7. 月落乌啼＿＿满天，江枫渔火对愁＿＿。 8. ＿＿起动＿＿铎，客行＿＿故乡。

B. 现代文填词：枯萎 空旷 迂腐 足迹

1. 这是很＿＿＿＿的见解。　　　　　2. 雪地上的＿＿＿＿是谁的？

3. 房子后面是＿＿＿＿的田野。　　　4. 树叶＿＿＿＿了。

二 形近字辨析 Distinguish easily confused characters

1. 落日心＿＿壮　　　a. 犹 b. 优 c. 忧　　2. 野＿＿天低树　　a. 矿 b. 广 c. 旷

3. 枳花明＿＿墙　　　a. 铎 b. 译 c. 驿　　4. 断＿＿人在天涯　　a. 场 b. 肠 c. 杨

5. 江枫渔火对愁＿＿　a. 民 b. 抿 c. 眠　　6. 人迹板桥＿＿　　a. 霜 b. 霞 c. 霖

7. 月落＿＿啼霜满天　a. 马 b. 乌 c. 鸟　　8. 乾坤一腐＿＿　　a. 濡 b. 需 c. 儒

三 连句 Match the first part with the second

1. 槲叶落山路( )　　2. 姑苏城外寒山寺( )　　3. 江汉思归客( )　　4. 古来存老马( )

5. 片云天共远 ( )　　6. 因思杜陵梦( )　　7. 野旷天低树( )　　8. 鸡声茅店月( )

9. 枯藤老树昏鸦( )　10. 移舟泊烟渚 ( )

a. 小桥流水人家　　　b. 乾坤一腐儒　　　　c. 永夜月同孤　　　d. 江清月近人

e. 人迹板桥霜　　　　f. 日暮客愁新　　　　g. 枳花明驿墙　　　　h. 夜半钟声到客船

i. 凫雁满回塘　　　　k. 不必取长途

四 句读 Punctuate and translate the following excerpts from three or more poems

移舟泊烟渚日暮客愁新古道西风瘦马夕阳西下断肠人在天涯月落乌啼霜满天江枫渔火对愁眠江汉思归客乾坤一腐儒片云天共远永夜月同孤槲叶落山路枳花明驿墙因思杜陵梦凫雁满回塘

五 听写 Dictation

1. ＿＿＿＿＿＿＿＿＿天，＿＿＿＿＿火＿＿＿＿。

2. ＿＿＿天＿＿＿，＿＿＿＿＿同＿＿。

3. ＿＿＿天＿＿＿，＿＿＿＿＿人。

4. ＿＿＿＿＿月，人＿＿＿＿＿。

5. ＿＿＿＿＿＿＿＿，＿＿＿西下，＿＿＿人在＿＿＿。

6. ＿＿日＿＿＿＿，＿＿风＿＿＿＿。

7. ＿＿＿＿＿，＿＿行＿＿＿。

11

边塞和战争

Frontiers and Wars

P48

liáng zhōu cí   qí yī
凉州¹ 词² 其一.

[táng] wáng zhī huàn
[唐] 王 之 涣³

Songs of Liangzhou, No. 1

[Tang Dyn.] Wang Zhihuan

huáng   hé   yuǎn   shàng   bái   yún   jiān
黄 河 远 上 白. 云 间△

Far up the Yellow River
    in the midst of white clouds:

yí   piàn   gū   chéng   wàn   rèn   shān
一. 片 孤⁴ 城 万 仞⁵ 山△

One stretch of a lone city
    against mountains of soaring height.

qiāng   dí   hé   xū   yuàn   yáng   liǔ
羌⁶ 笛⁷. 何 须 怨 杨 柳⁸

Why should the nomad flute
    lament with "Breaking Willow" tune?

chūn   fēng   bú   dù   yù   mén   guān
春 风 不. 度⁹ 玉. 门 关△¹⁰

Spring breeze can't pass
    through the Jade Gate Pass.
        (Tr. Zong-qi Cai)

[七言律绝 heptasyllabic regulated quatrain, tonal pattern Ia, see *HTRCP,* p. 171]

字词释义 Vocabulary Notes

1. 凉州　in present-day Wuwei county 武威县, Gansu Province.
2. 凉州词 (詞)　"Song of Liangzhou," title of a *yuefu* song, belonging to the *Gongdiao* key 宫调. It was originally a folk song of Liangzhou and was set to a tune in the *Gongdiao* key during the Kaiyuan Reign (713−741) of the Xuan Emperor of the Tang 唐玄宗.
3. See the biographic note in P34 note 2.　　　4. 孤　adj. isolated. See also P29 note 4.
5. 仞　an ancient measure of length. 万仞 means "extremely high."
6. 羌　an ethnic group living in the west of ancient China.
7. 笛　n. bamboo flute. 羌笛 refers to a musical instrument of the Qiang. See also P49 note 5.
8. 杨 (楊) 柳　n. poplar and willow. See also P39 note 8. Here it refers to the song "Breaking Willows" (*zhé yáng liǔ* 折杨柳).
9. 度　v. to cross, pass. MdnC: 过 (*guò*). See also P50 note 12 and P64 note 7.
10. 玉门关 (玉門關)　the Jade Gate, located northwest of Dunhuang 敦煌, Gansu province. Jade Gate and Sun Gate (*Yáng guān* 阳关) were the two most important western passes on the

way to the Silk Road (*Sīchóu zhīlù* 丝绸之路) before the Song Dynasty. See the Sun Gate in P39 note 10.

11. 矗立 (*chù lì*) v. to stand tall and upright [formal].   12. 抱怨 (*bào yuàn*) v. to complain.

现代文翻译 Modern Chinese Translation

黄河(奔流而去)远远地流到白云间，一座孤零零的城矗立[11]在高山上。羌笛何须吹出《折杨柳》(来抱怨[12]春天还没到来)！春风根本就吹不到玉门关啊！

评论与提问 Comments and Questions

1. From its start in antiquity, dynastic China was dogged by skirmishes and wars between the economically and culturally advanced China proper and the outlying regions inhabited by nomad tribes. It was not until the Tang, however, that frontiers emerged as an important subject of poetry and eventually gave rise to a new subgenre called "frontier poems" (*biān sài shī* 边塞诗).

   Many Chinese frontier poems carry anti-war overtones. Instead of glorifying military might and inciting jingoistic fervor, they dwell upon the sorrows of frontier wars: the barren and desolate landscape, the battlefield dead, long separation of soldiers from their wives, and pervasive homesickness. When the frontiers control was lost and nomad troops stormed into China proper, full-scale wars befell the homeland. The depiction of such "foreign" invasions introduced a new motif of lamentation: the loss of territory or even the country itself.

2. A great frontier poem distinguishes itself by its unique spatio-temporal maneuvering that renders otherwise well-worn motifs compellingly felt. Can you discern any remarkable act of spatio-temporal maneuvering in this poem? Think about the contrast, explicit or implicit, in space, in color, in points of view, as well as in time.

P49

cóng	*jūn*	*xíng*
从	军	行[1]

[*táng*] *wáng chāng líng*
[唐] 王昌龄[2]

Following the Army

[Tang Dyn.] Wang Changling

fēng	*huǒ*	*chéng*	*xī*	*bǎi*	*chǐ*	*lóu*
烽	火[3]	城	西	百	尺	楼△

Signal fires west of the wall, hundred-foot watchtowers

huáng	*hūn*	*dú*	*shàng*	*hǎi*	*fēng*	*qiū*
黄	昏	独	上	海[4]	风	秋△

Climbing alone at dusk—an autumn of desert wind

gèng	*chuī*	*qiāng*	*dí*	*guān*	*shān*	*yuè*
更	吹	羌	笛[5]	关	山	月[6]

What's more—"Mountain Pass Moon" plays on a nomad flute

wú	*nà*[7]	*jīn*	*guī*[8]	*wàn*	*lǐ*	*chóu*△
无	那	金	闺	万	里	愁

No way to reach the golden chamber, past ten thousand miles of sadness

[七言律绝 heptasyllabic regulated quatrain, tonal pattern IIa, see *HTRCP,* p. 171]

(Tr. Charles Egan, *HTRCP*, p. 213)

字词释义 Vocabulary Notes

1. 从军行 (從軍行) "Following the Army," title of a *yuefu* song, under "Lyrics for Accompanied Songs" (*xiànghè gēcí* 相和歌辞) in Guo Maoqian's 郭茂倩 (1041–1099) *Collection of Yuefu Poetry* (*Yuèfǔ shījí* 乐府诗集). The poems bearing this tune title normally depict the hard life of soldiers at the frontiers.

2. 王昌龄 (齡) (style 字, Shàobó 少伯, 698–ca.756), a High Tang poet. He is a High Tang master of the quatrain form, particularly well known for his frontier poems.

3. 烽火   n. beacon-fire, used to send a signal about an imminent enemy attack. See also P91 note 3. Here it refers to a beacon tower (*fēnghuǒ tái* 烽火台).

4. 海   n. ocean, sea. Here it indicates Qinghai Lake 青海湖. "海风" refers to the wind blowing from the Qinghai Lake.

5. 羌笛   musical instrument of the Qiang people. See P48 notes 6 and 7.

6. 关 (關) 山月   "Mountain Pass Moon," title of a *yuefu* song, under "Lyrics for Drum and Horn Songs" (*héngchuī qǔcí* 横吹曲辞) in Guo Maoqian's 郭茂倩 *Collection of Yuefu Poetry* (*Yuèfǔ shījí* 乐府诗集). Poems bearing this title mostly depict the sorrow of the separation between frontier soldiers and their wives at home.

7. 无 (無) 那   to have no choice; cannot help but. MdnC: 无奈 (*wú nài*). 👉出于无奈他只能同意 He had no choice but to agree.

8. 闺 (閨)   n. chamber, used here as a metonym for a soldier's wife.

现代文翻译 Modern Chinese Translation

城西边的烽火台[3]上，有百尺的高楼。黄昏时，(我)独自登上高楼，从青海湖[4]方向吹来阵阵秋风。 又听到远处传来《关山月》的笛声，(想着)万里之外，妻子心中愁苦，感到非常无奈。[7]

评论与提问 Comment and Question

The first couplet may be seen as a poetic version of what is depicted in this modern prose passage: 黄昏时候，（我）独自登上城西边的烽火台的百尺的高楼，从青海湖方向吹来阵秋风。 By comparing the couplet with this prose passage, you may perceive two typical moves made in composing a regulated quatrain.

The first is drastic condensation. Only a few imagistic content words remain: 黄昏…独上…城西…烽火…百尺楼…海…秋…风. For sure, classical Chinese prose is more condensed than modern Chinese prose, but not nearly as condensed as this cluster of words. The second move is inversion. "城西…烽火…百尺楼" becomes "烽火城西百尺楼" and "海…秋…风" becomes "海

风秋.” "烽火城西百尺楼," originally the object of the verb "上," is now repositioned to the very beginning and thus becomes a free-standing topic in the topic+comment sentence. A chain reaction follows: "海风秋," originally an adverbial clause, now becomes the new direct object of the verb "上." Similarly, the last line "无那金闺万里愁" may also be taken as an inverted version of "金闺无那万里愁" or even "金闺万里无那愁."

To conform to a fixed tonal pattern is apparently the immediate cause for all these syntactic inversions. But in the hands of a great poet, such inversions also produce a calculated effect of novelty or, to use modern critical parlance, "defamiliarization." Can you pinpoint the desired aesthetic effect of each of the inversions? ☞ *HTRCP,* p. 213 for a discussion of this poem.

P50

chū sài
出 塞[1]

[táng] wáng chāng líng
[唐] 王 昌 龄[2]

Setting Out for the Frontiers

[Tang Dyn.] Wang Changling

qín	*shí*	*míng*	*yuè*	*hàn*	*shí*	*guān*
秦[3]	时	明	月	汉[4]	时	关△[5]

wàn	*lǐ*	*cháng*	*zhēng*	*rén*	*wèi*	*huán*
万	里	长	征[6]	人	未	还△

This bright moon, still that of Qin times,
  these passes, still those of Han times,

From the thousand-mile expeditions:
  the troops are yet to return.

dàn	*shǐ*	*lóng*	*chéng*	*fēi*	*jiàng*	*zài*
但[7]	使	龙	城[8]	飞	将[9]	在

bú	*jiào*	*hú*	*mǎ*	*dù*	*yīn*	*shān*
不	教[10]	胡[11]	马	度[12]	阴	山△[13]

If the captor of the Dragon City—the
  Flying General—were still here,

He wouldn't have let the Hun cavalries
  Pass through the Yin Mountains!
      (Tr. Zong-qi Cai)

[七言律绝 heptasyllabic regulated quatrain, tonal pattern Ia, see *HTRCP,* p. 171]

字词释义 Vocabulary Notes

1. 塞 n. frontier, fortress, pass. 出塞 means "to set out for the frontiers."
2. See the biographic note in P49 note 2.
3. 秦 the Qin Dynasty (221−207 B.C.E.)
4. 汉 (漢) the Han Dynasty (206 B.C. E.− 220)
5. 关 (關) n. frontier pass.
6. 征 (徵) v. to go on an expedition. See also P51 note 12. 长征 means "long expedition." See P46 note 3 for a different meaning of the word.
7. 但 conj. as long as, provided. MdnC: 只要 (*zhǐ yào*). ☞只要努力，就会进步 Provided you work hard, you will surely make progress. See P03 note 16 for a different meaning of the word.

8. 龙 (龍)城   the Dragon City, the capital of Xiongnu 匈奴 during the Han Dynasty.

9. 将 (*jiàng*)   n. general. 飞将 refers to the famous general Li Guang 李广 (?−119 B.C. E.) in the Han Dynasty, who was called the "Flying General" (*fēi jiāngjūn* 飞将军) by the Xiongnu army. However, it was another Han general Wei Qing 卫青 (?−106 B.C. E.) who once captured the Dragon City of Xiongnu at that time.

10. 教 (*jiào*)   v. to teach. 不教 means "doesn't allow" (*bù yǔn xǔ* 不允许). See also P61 note 3.

11. 胡   See P38 note 8. 胡马 refers to nomad cavalries (*qí bīng* 骑兵).

12. 度   v. to cross, pass. See also P48 note 9.

13. 阴 (陰) 山   Yin Mountains, stretching more than 1200km across the Inner Mongolia Autonomous Region and the north of Hebei Province. The Yin Mountains were known as a stronghold of the Xiongnu invaders in the Han Dynasty.

14. 攻破 (*gōng pò*)   v. to make a breakthrough, capture.

现代文翻译 Modern Chinese Translation

明月和边关依然是秦汉时的明月和边关。可是士兵长征[6]万里，却没人能够回来。 要是当年攻破[14]龙城的飞将军还在，就不会允许[10]胡人的骑兵[11]过了阴山！

评论与提问 Comment and Question

What makes this piece a great frontier poem is its masterful intertwining of past and present. To evoke an overwhelming sense of melancholia is a common endeavor among the writers of frontier poetry. A frequently used strategy used for this end is a spatial one. The poet presents a boundless expanse of barren and hostile land, seen either from the east by those left behind by garrison soldiers (P48) or seen from the west by garrison soldiers longing to return home (P49). The viewing of this infinite space of desolation irresistibly engenders a profound sense of melancholia.

This poem, however, follows a different tack: that of temporal maneuvering. Instead of depicting a coherent scene, the poet introduces a few broad spatial markers as a springboard for temporal or historical imagination. The poem begins by linking, explicitly, the moon to the Qin and the mountain passes to the Han. By virtue of this linkage, the expedition troops mentioned in the next line become a broad general reference, which includes the Qin and Han expedition troops or their remains that are yet to return to their homeland.

This flight of temporal imagination introduces a few new elements otherwise absent in the poem: a reflection on China's perpetual curse of border wars and a subtle fear that many of today's garrison soldiers may never return like their Qin and Han brethren. The second couplet is an expression of a vain wish for an end to the frontier wars. This wish is couched in a subjunctive sentence, made up of an imagined condition (the Flying General would still be alive) and an imagined result (the nomad troops could not have invaded). This exercise of imagination is, again, a flight back to the historical past.

Through his temporal imagination, has the poet succeeded in evoking and amplifying a sense of melancholia without landscape depiction? Compare this poem with the previous two poems and give your answer.

P51

liáng zhōu cí   èr shǒu qí yī
凉州词[1]二首其一

[táng] wáng hàn
[唐] 王 翰[2]

Two Songs of Liangzhou, No. 1

[Tang Dyn.] Wang Han

pú	*táo*	*měi*	*jiǔ*	*yè*	*guāng*	*bēi*
葡	萄[3]	美	酒	夜	光	杯△[4]
yù	*yǐn*	*pí*	*pá*	*mǎ*	*shàng*	*cuī*
欲	饮	琵	琶[5]	马	上	催△[6]
zuì	*wò*	*shā*	*chǎng*	*jūn*	*mò*	*xiào*
醉[7]	卧[8]	沙	场[9]	君	莫[10]	笑[11]
gǔ	*lái*	*zhēng*	*zhàn*	*jǐ*	*rén*	*huí*
古	来	征[12]	战	几	人	回△

The fine grape wine,
      and a luminous cup—

I was about to drink it
      when *pipa* was strummed
      on horseback, urging me to hurry.

If I get drunk and lie on the battle ground
      I beg you not to laugh,

Since ancient times from each expedition
      how many made it back?
      (Tr. Zong-qi Cai)

[七言律绝 heptasyllabic regulated quatrain, tonal pattern Ia, see *HTRCP,* p. 171]

字词释义 Vocabulary Notes

1. 凉州词 (詞) "Song of Liangzhou," see P48 notes 1 and 2.

2. 王翰 (style 字, Zǐyǔ 子羽, 687? −726?), a famous High Tang poet known for his frontier poetry, especially this quatrain.

3. 葡萄 n. grape.

4. 夜光杯 n. luminous cup.

5. 琵琶 n. a plucked string instrument with a fretted fingerboard. Before it was introduced to the Han people, 琵琶 was mainly played on horseback by the nomadic peoples in the northwest of ancient China. See also P80 note 20.

6. 催 v. to urge, hurry. ☞你去催他一下 Go and hurry him up.

7. 醉 adj. drunk, tipsy. ☞他喝醉了 He is drunk. See also P92 note 5.

8. 卧 v. to lie. MdnC: 躺 (*tǎng*). ☞他躺在床上 He lay on the bed.

9. 沙场 (場) n. desert. Here it means "battlefield."

10. 莫 v. don't. See also P04 note 24.

11. 笑 v. to laugh. MdnC: 嘲笑 (*cháo xiào*) to laugh at. ☞不要嘲笑他 Don't laugh at him.

12. 征 (徵) n. to go on an expedition. See also P50 note 6. 征战 to go on a military expedition.

13. 斟 (*zhēn*) v. to pour (tea or wine) [formal].

现代文翻译 Modern Chinese Translation

(我)举起斟¹³满葡萄美酒的夜光杯刚要喝时，听到琵琶声从马上传来，催⁶我快喝。(如果我)喝醉⁷了，躺⁸在沙场上，请您不要嘲笑¹¹我！自古以来，征战的人有几个活着回来的！

评论与提问 Comment and Question

"See big within small" (*xiǎo zhōng jiàn dà* 小中见大) is an aesthetic ideal of the quatrain form. In the case of a character sketch done in the quatrain form, "small" refers to, not merely the size of a quatrain, but more importantly, an "insignificant" scene of a character's life chosen for depiction. As for "big," it refers to the whole life of the character, outer and inner, as revealed by that depicted moment.

This poem measures up to this aesthetic ideal most splendidly. Here we observe how a frontier soldier responds to an abrupt interruption of his hard-earned moment of wine-drinking. This depicted moment is undoubtedly "small" as compared with a "big" moment of heroic warriors charging against the enemy. Yet, it tells volumes about his outer and inner lives. The interruption of his wine-drinking underscores the degree of deprivation the soldiers are subjected to: even a brief moment of merriment is not spared in the midst of incessant calls to battle.

The soldier's words to his invisible audience leave us wondering about his complex inner life. Why doesn't he mind getting himself drunk before the battle? Is this an indication of his weariness, if not antipathy, toward the war? Is it a sign of an undiminished zest for life or a feeble resignation with the fate of death? Why does he urge us not to laugh at his being drunk in the battle field? Is this his painful admission of falling short of heroism or his thinly veiled dismissal of heroism as futile and meaningless? Is he a fearless, happy-go-lucky guy or is it that his manifested nonchalance belies a sensitive, melancholic soul?

By provoking all these questions, the poet has succeeded in creating an enigmatic sketch of a frontier soldier that fascinates the reader today as much as it did in Tang times.

P52

wén guān jūn shōu hé nán hé běi
闻 官 军¹ 收² 河 南 河 北³

Upon Hearing of the Recapture of Henan and Hebei by the Government Army

[táng] dù fǔ
[唐] 杜 甫⁴

[Tang Dyn.] Du Fu

jiàn	*wài*	*hū*	*chuán*	*shōu*	*jì*	*běi*
剑⁵	外	忽	传⁶	收	蓟⁷	北

Outside the Sword Gate suddenly came the word:
the northern Ji area was recaptured;

chū	*wén*	*tì*	*lèi*	*mǎn*	*yī*	*cháng*
初	闻	涕⁸	泪	满	衣	裳△⁹

Upon hearing this I was all tears—
on my clothes and everywhere.

què	kàn	qī	zǐ	chóu	hé	zài	
却[10]	看	妻	子[11]	愁	何	在	Turning around to see my wife and children where is their sorrow now?
màn	juǎn	shī	shū	xǐ	yù	kuáng	
漫[12]	卷[13]	诗	书	喜	欲	狂△[14]	Rolling up books mindlessly I've almost gone crazy with joy.
bái	rì	fàng	gē	xū	zòng	jiǔ	
白	日[15]	放[16]	歌	须	纵[17]	酒	Singing loudly on this bright day I must abandon myself to wine,
qīng	chūn	zuò	bàn	hǎo	huán	xiāng	
青	春[18]	作	伴[19]	好	还	乡△	With spring as our companion what a good time to return home!
jí	cóng	bā	xiá	chuān	wū	xiá	
即[20]	从	巴	峡[21]	穿[22]	巫	峡[23]	Pass the Ba Gorges we shall in no time and then go through the Wu Gorge,
biàn	xià	xiāng	yáng	xiàng	luò	yáng	
便	下	襄	阳[24]	向	洛	阳△[25]	Down to Xiangyang we shall go, and then head for Luoyang. (Tr. Zong-qi Cai)

[七言律诗 heptasyllabic regulated verse, tonal pattern II,
see *HTRCP*, p.171]

字词释义 Vocabulary Notes

1. 官军 (軍) n. government troops.

2. 收　v. to collect, receive. MdnC: 收复 (*shōu fù*) to recapture. 👉他们终于收复了失地 They finally recaptured the lost territory.

3. 河南河北　Henan province and Hebei province. This poem was written in the last year of the An Lushan Rebellion (*ānshǐ zhīluàn* 安史之乱, 755–763) during the Tang Dynasty. In the winter of 762, the Tang army won an important battle and recaptured Luoyang 洛阳 (in present-day Henan province), Zheng (present-day Zhengzhou 郑州, Henan province), and Bian (present-day Kaifeng 开封, Henan province). Many generals of the rebel army surrendered to the Tang government at the end of 762 and in the spring of 763.

4. See biographic note in P20 note 1.

5. 剑 (劍)　剑门关 the Sword Gate, in present-day Jiange County 剑阁县, Sichuan province. 剑外 refers to the area south of the Sword Gate in Sichuan.

6. 传 (傳 *chuán*)　v. to pass, spread. 👉消息很快传开了 The news spread very quickly. See also P65 note 6 and P92 note 15.

7. 蓟　蓟县 Ji County, belonging to Youzhou 幽州 (in the present-day Beijing area) during the Tang Dynasty.

8. 涕　n. tears. MdnC: 眼泪 (*yǎn lèi*). See also P90 note 7.

9. 裳　n. skirt. See also P08 note 6. 衣裳 means "clothes."

10. 却 (卻)　v. to turn one's head, turn round. MdnC: 回头 (*huí tóu*). See also P58 note 9. See also P08 note 17 for a different meaning of the word.

11. 子　n. children. MdnC: 孩子 (*háizi*). 妻子 means wife and children here.

12. 漫 adv. freely. MdnC: 随意 (*suí yì*). 👉他不能随意解雇工人 He cannot fire workers at will.

13. 卷 v. to roll up. 👉他卷起袖子开始干活儿 He rolled up his sleeves and began to work. See also P83 note 12.

14. 狂 adj. mad, crazy, wild, unrestrained. 👉他真是欣喜若狂 He is wild with joy.

15. 白日 n. white sun. Here it refers to daytime. See also P34 note 3.

16. 放 v. to release, set free. 放歌 means "to sing loudly" (*fàng shēng gē chàng* 放声歌唱).

17. 纵 (縱) v. to indulge, let loose, let oneself go. MdnC: 纵情 (*zòng qíng*) to one's heart's content. 👉我们要纵情歌唱 We will sing to our hearts' content.

18. 青春 n. youth, youthfulness. Here it means "spring" (*chūn tiān* 春天).

19. 伴 n. companion, partner. 作伴 means "to keep sb. company."

20. 即 adv. presently. MdnC: 立即 (*lì jí*) at once. 👉我立即出发 I will leave at once.

21. 巴峡 the Ba Gorges, made up of the Stone Cave Gorge 石洞峡, the Copper Gong Gorge 铜锣峡, and the Bright Moon Gorge 明月峡 to the east of present-day Chongqing.

22. 穿 v. to pass through, cross. 👉他穿过马路 He crossed a street. See also P92 note 9.

23. 巫峡 the Wu Gorge, one of the famous Three Gorges 三峡 of the Yangtze River. It starts from present-day Wu County 巫县, Sichuan province in the west and ends in Badong County 巴东县, Hubei province in the east.

24. 襄阳 (陽) Xiangyang City, in present-day Xiangfan 襄樊, Hubei province.

25. 洛阳 (陽) in present-day Luoyang, Henan province. Here the poet planed to go back to his hometown by ship from the west to the east. He would start from the eastern part of Sichuan province, cross Hubei province, and enter Henan province.

现代文翻译 Modern Chinese Translation

住在剑门关[5]外，忽然传[6]来官军收复[2]蓟北的消息。刚听到时开心的泪水沾满了我的衣服。回头[10]看，妻子和孩子[11]哪还有愁苦啊！我随意[12]地卷[13]起书本，欣喜若狂。[14]白天我要放声歌唱，[16]还要纵情[17]喝酒(来庆祝这个好消息。想着)春天[18]正好伴我返回故乡。(我)立即[20]就要出发，过了巴峡,再穿[22]过巫峡，然后经过襄阳转向洛阳。

评论与提问 Comment and Question

This poem offers a counterpoint to "Spring Scene" (P91), another regulated verse by Du Fu. "Spring Scene" is the example used in *HTRCP*, pp. 162–172 to explain the strict rules of regulated verse on semantic, syntactic, structural, and prosodic levels, and to show how Du Fu utilizes those strict rules as a means of deepening his self-reflection. In this poem, however, Du Fu makes bold to bend, if not violate outright, many of those rules as he seeks to adapt the *lüshi* 律诗 form to a literary endeavor for which it is ill suited: narration.

A steady forward movement is crucial to narration. There is little built in the *lüshi* form that propels forward movement, but much that impedes it. Regulated verse is a form developed essentially for description and reflection. In both description and reflection, temporal progression is often intentionally slowed to allow for a deep engagement with images, scenes, and thought by the reader. In fact, many *lüshi* practices and rules are intended to slow temporal progression—including a maximum use of imagistic content words, a dispensation of function words, the use of topic+comment lines and parallel couplets, and so on.

To build and maintain the momentum of forward movement in this regulated verse, Du Fu drastically alters those practices and rules. Consider the dearth of imagistic words and an abundance of function words. There is not a single topic+comment line (as compared with four in the next poem). All eight lines contain one or two subject+predicate constructions. In all cases of two subject+predicate constructions, there is a clear linear progression from one to the other. Also temporalized are the two parallel couplets, which now depict four consecutive actions: looking at…rolling up…singing and drinking…planning the return.

There is no longer the customary pairing of corresponding images in each parallel couplet, nor a standard turning at the third couplet. Du Fu's last move of temporalization is, ironically, to end his poem with a parallel couplet instead of a required non-parallel couplet. This ending parallel couplet is a special one known as "flowing-water couplet" (*liúshuǐ duì* 流水对). Instead of slowing forward movement like ordinary parallel couplets, this flowing water couplet actually quickens it through a rhythmic repetition of sequential adverbs (即，便) and directional verbs (从……穿；下……向).

Compare this poem with Wen Tingyun's "An Early Morning Journey in the Shang Mountains." Can you describe the differences between overt and covert narration shown in these two poems?

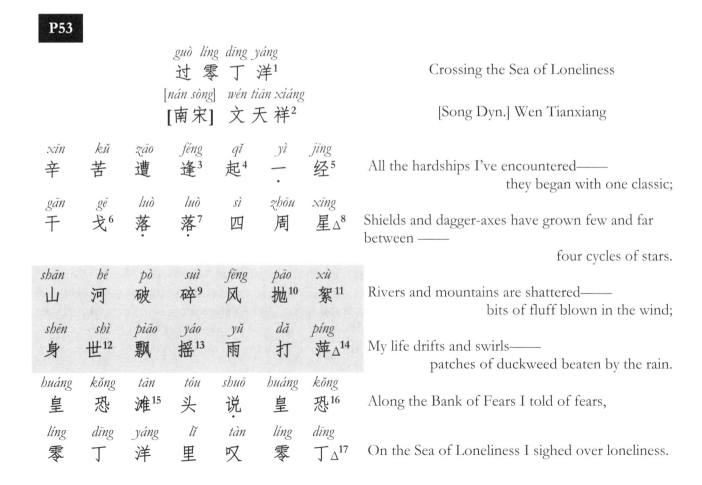

P53

guò líng dīng yáng
过 零 丁 洋[1]

[*nán sòng*] *wén tiān xiáng*
[南宋] 文 天 祥[2]

Crossing the Sea of Loneliness

[Song Dyn.] Wen Tianxiang

xīn kǔ zāo féng qǐ yì jīng
辛 苦 遭 逢[3] 起[4] 一 经[5]

All the hardships I've encountered——
　　they began with one classic;

gān gē luò luò sì zhōu xīng
干 戈[6] 落 落[7] 四 周 星△[8]

Shields and dagger-axes have grown few and far between ——
　　　　four cycles of stars.

shān hé pò suì fēng pāo xù
山 河 破 碎[9] 风 抛[10] 絮[11]

Rivers and mountains are shattered——
　　bits of fluff blown in the wind;

shēn shì piāo yáo yǔ dǎ píng
身 世[12] 飘 摇[13] 雨 打 萍△[14]

My life drifts and swirls——
　　patches of duckweed beaten by the rain.

huáng kǒng tān tóu shuō huáng kǒng
皇 恐 滩[15] 头 说 皇 恐[16]

Along the Bank of Fears I told of fears,

líng dīng yáng lǐ tàn líng dīng
零 丁 洋 里 叹 零 丁△[17]

On the Sea of Loneliness I sighed over loneliness.

rén	*shēng*	*zì*	*gǔ*	*shuí*	*wú*	*sǐ*	
人	生	自	古	谁	无	死	
liú	*qǔ*	*dān*	*xīn*	*zhào*	*hàn*	*qīng*	
留	取	丹[18]	心	照	汗	青△[19]	

Whose life, ever since antiquity, is without death?

Let my loyal heart shine on the bamboo tablets!

(Tr. Zong-qi Cai, *HTRCP*, p. 391)

[七言律诗 heptasyllabic regulated verse, tonal pattern IIa, see *HTRCP*, p. 172]

字词释义 Vocabulary Notes

1. 零丁洋 the Sea of Loneliness, in present-day Zhongshan 中山, Guangdong province. Wen Tianxiang was captured by the Mongol army in 1278 and he crossed the Sea of Loneliness when he was taken back to northern China as a prisoner the next year. Wen refused to surrender to the Yuan army and wrote this poem to show his loyalty to the Song. Soon after this poem was written, the Song army lost its last battle and the Southern Song fell.

2. 文天祥 (style 字, Lǚshàn 履善; literary name 号, Wénshān 文山, 1236−1283), a famous general in the Southern Song dynasty. He is a great national hero in Chinese history, known and loved for his unbending loyalty as powerfully expressed in this and other poems.

3. 遭逢 v. to meet with (hardship, misfortune). ☞他为遭逢不幸的朋友写了一首歌 He wrote a song for his friends who suffered misfortunes.

4. 起 v. to begin.

5. 经 (経) n. classics as a subject in civil service examinations. See P89 note 11 for a different meaning of the word.

6. 干戈 n. shield and dagger-ax, used as a metonym for battles. See also P94 note 12.

7. 落落 adj. few and scattered, few and far between. MdnC: 稀稀落落 (*xī xī luò luò*).

8. 周星 n. twelve years. A cycle of Age Star (*suì xīng* 岁星), twelve years, is called 周星. The poet was more than forty years old at that time. 四周星 here refers to Wen's age.

9. 破碎 adj. broken, destroyed. ☞国家已经支离破碎 The state has been broken into pieces.

10. 抛 v. to throw. ☞他抛出球 He threw a ball.   11. 絮 n. bits of fluff. MdnC: 柳絮 (*liǔ xù*).

12. 身世 n. one's life. ☞他的身世很凄惨 He had a miserable life.

13. 飘摇 (飄摇) v. to sway, shake, totter. ☞小树在风雨中飘摇 The small tree is buffeted by the wind and rain.

14. 萍 n. duckweed. MdnC: 浮萍 (*fú píng*). See also P74 note 7.

15. 皇恐滩 (灘) Bank of Fears, in present-day Wan'an County 万安县, Jiangxi province. In 1277, Wen Tianxiang's army was defeated by the Yuan army in Jiangxi province. Wen passed by the Bank of Fears when retreating with his army to Fujian province.

16. 皇恐 or 惶恐 adj. terrified, scared. ☞他非常惶恐不安 He is so terrified.

17. 零丁 or 伶仃 adj. alone and helpless. ☞他真是孤苦伶仃 He is alone and uncared for.

18. 丹 adj. red. 丹心 means "a loyal heart" (*zhōng xīn* 忠心).

19. 汗青 n. sweating green bamboo strips. To be used as writing tablets, bamboo strips were first dried (hence "sweating") over the fire. Here 汗青 means historical records (*shǐ cè* 史册).

20. 精通 (*jīng tōng*) v. to be proficient in, to master.

21. 进士 (*jìn shì*) n. a successful candidate in the imperial examinations after the Tang Dynasty.

现代文翻译 Modern Chinese Translation

　　(我)辛苦<u>遭逢</u>[3]了很多事情，全是(因为<u>精通</u>[20])一种经书(而考中<u>进士</u>[21]做了官)。(与元军作战到现在)战火已<u>稀稀落落</u>,[7]而我也四十多岁了。大好河山<u>支离破碎</u>,[9]如同被狂风吹卷的<u>柳絮</u>[11]一样。自己的<u>身世</u>[12]也如同被雨水打散的<u>浮萍</u>。[14]皇恐滩的失败让我至今感到<u>惶恐不安</u>,[16]在零丁洋上我只能叹息自己的<u>孤苦伶仃</u>。[17]自古以来，谁能不死呢？我只想留下我的<u>忠心</u>,[18]来照耀<u>史册</u>！[19]

评论与提问 Comment and Question

This poem exhibits a distinct topic+comment structure. The first half of the poem presents the wretched situations of the country and the poet himself, and the second half ushers in the poet's emotional response to these situations. The topic+comment principle operates on the syntactic level as well. The first half is composed of four successive topic+comment lines. In lines 2–4, an explicit depiction of human suffering (the first four characters) is juxtaposed with corresponding images of nature (the next three characters). Therefore, the rhythm of these lines is distinctly 4+3. ☞*HTRCP,* pp. 391–392 for a detailed discussion of this poem's syntactic and structural features.

练习　EXERCISES

一 填空 Fill in blanks

A. 诗词填字: 卧 汗 怨 吹 却 飘 照 破 纵 饮 关 摇 碎 度 征 闺 催 打 抛 放 卷 丹 须

1. 秦时明月汉时 ____，万里长____人未还。　2. 留取 ____心____ ____青。

3. 更____羌笛关山月，无那金____万里愁。　4. 白日____歌 ____ ____酒。

5. ____看妻子愁何在，漫____诗书喜欲狂。　6. 欲____琵琶马上____。

7. 羌笛何须____杨柳，春风不____玉门关。　8. 山河____ ____风____絮。

9. 醉____沙场君莫笑，古来____战几人回。　10. 身世____ ____雨____萍。

B. 现代文填词: 嘲笑 立即 飘摇 惶恐 无奈 身世 破碎 纵情 随意 遭逢

1. 国家已经支离____ ____了。　　　　　　2. 他的____ ____很凄惨。

3. 请不要____ ____我。　　　　　　　　　4. 你不可以____ ____解雇工人。

5. 我____ ____出发。　　　　　　　　　　6. 我们要 ____ ____歌唱。

7. 他____ ____之下，只好同意。　　　　　8. 小树在风雨中____ ____着。

9. 他为____ ____不幸的朋友写了首歌。　　10. 他非常____ ____不安。

二 形近字辨析 Distinguish easily confused characters

1. ____火城西白尺楼　a. 峰　b. 烽　c. 逢　　2. 即从巴____穿巫____　　a. 侠　b. 狭　c. 峡

3. ____卷诗书喜欲狂　a. 慢　b. 谩　c. 漫　　4. 白日放歌须____酒　　a. 从　b. 纵　c. 丛

5. 青春____伴好还乡　a. 作　b. 昨　c. 做　　6. 不____胡马度阴山　　　a. 叫　b. 教　c. 孝
7. 醉卧沙____君莫笑　a. 杨　b. 场　c. 扬　　8. 初闻____泪满衣裳　　　a. 涕　b. 梯　c. 剃

三　连句 Match the first part with the second

1. 皇恐滩头说皇恐( )　2. 但使龙城飞将在( )　3. 葡萄美酒夜光杯( )
4. 黄河远上白云间( )　5. 白日放歌须纵酒( )　6. 烽火城西百尺楼( )
7. 山河破碎风抛絮( )　8. 羌笛何须怨杨柳( )　9. 剑外忽传收蓟北( )

a. 欲饮琵琶马上催　b. 身世飘摇雨打萍　c. 黄昏独上海风秋　d. 不教胡马度阴山
e. 初闻涕泪满衣裳　f. 春风不度玉门关　g. 零丁洋里叹零丁　h. 一片孤城万仞山
i. 青春作伴好还乡

四　句读 Punctuate and translate the following passage

剑外忽传收蓟北初闻涕泪满衣裳却看妻子愁何在漫卷诗书喜欲狂皇恐滩
头说皇恐零丁洋里叹零丁人生自古谁无死留取丹心照汗青秦时明月汉时
关万里长征人未还醉卧沙场君莫笑古来征战几人回黄河远上白云间一片
孤城万仞山更吹羌笛关山月无那金闺万里愁

五　听写 Dictation

1. ____ 时 ____ ____ ____ 时 ____，____ ____ ____ ____ 人 ____ ____。
2. ____ ____ 何____ ____ ____ ____，____ ____ 不____ ____ ____ ____。
3. ____ ____ ____ 西 ____ ____ ____，____ ____ ____ ____ 风____。
4. ____ ____ ____ ____ ____ 笑，____ ____ ____ ____ ____ 人 ____。
5. ____ 看 ____ ____ ____ ____，____ ____ 书 ____ ____。
6. ____ 日 ____ ____ ____ ____，____ ____ ____ 好 ____ ____。
7. 人____ ____ ____ ____ ____，____ ____ 心____ ____。

12

思 乡

Homesickness

huí xiāng ǒu shū
回 乡 偶¹ 书

Random Notes Upon
Returning to My Hometown

[táng] hè zhī zhāng
[唐] 贺 知 章²

[Tang Dyn.] He Zhizhang

shào	*xiǎo*	*lí*	*jiā*	*lǎo*	*dà*	*huí*
少³	小	离	家	老	大	回△

I left home young and small
and returned old and big,

xiāng	*yīn*	*nán*	*gǎi*	*bìn*	*máo*	*cuī*
乡	音⁴	难	改	鬓⁵	毛	衰△⁶

My native accent is hardly changed,
but my hairs have gone grey.

ér	*tóng*	*xiāng*	*jiàn*	*bù*	*xiāng*	*shí*
儿	童	相	见	不	相	识

The children met me
but didn't know who I am,

xiào	*wèn*	*kè*	*cóng*	*hé*	*chù*	*lái*
笑	问	客	从	何	处	来△

They giggled and asked
"Where do you come from?"
(Tr. Zong-qi Cai)

[七言律绝 heptasyllabic regulated quatrain, tonal pattern IIa, see *HTRCP,* p. 171]

字词释义 Vocabulary Notes

1. 偶 adv. by chance, by accident. MdnC: 偶然 (*ǒu rán*). ☞他偶然遇见一位老朋友 He came across an old friend.

2. 贺 (賀) 知章 (style 字, Jìzhēn 季真, 659–744), a famous High Tang poet and calligrapher.

3. 少 (*shào*) adj. young. MdnC: 年轻 (*nián qīng*). ☞他很年轻 He is very young. See also P62 note 18.

4. 音 n. sound. MdnC: 口音 (*kǒu yīn*) accent. ☞他说话口音很重 He speaks with a strong accent.

5. 鬓 (鬢) n. hair on the temples. See also P03 note 18.

6. 衰 (*shuāi*) v. to decline. See also P95 note 4. Here it is pronounced as "*cuī*," meaning "scattered."

7. 斑白 (*bān bái*) adj. grizzled, grey.

现代文翻译 Modern Chinese Translation

　　我年少时离开家，年老了才回来。家乡的口音⁴没改，但两鬓已经斑白⁷了。小孩儿们看到我，都不认识我，笑着问，这位客人是从哪儿来的？

评论与提问 Comment and Question

Homesickness is an enduring subject in traditional Chinese poetry, one that belongs to men. In traditional China, it is men who left home in pursuit of their careers or got sent away on a military expedition. The author of a poem of homesickness is therefore almost always a man. In writing a poem of homesickness, the poet usually speaks in his own voice and identifies the object of his longing in the poem's title or the poem itself: his hometown or home village as a whole (P54, P56-58), his siblings (P55), or his wife (P59) —to use the the five poems in this unit as examples.

　　Homesickness is an unhappy state of mind, caused by a dislocation of space and further aggravated by an acutely felt sense of time. So, to make compellingly felt his homesickness, or a relief from it, a poet must handle space and time in an innovative fashion.

　　This poem begins with home returning, an end of a dislocation of space. So there seems little room for spatial maneuvering in this poem. Indeed, what is foregrounded here is the poet's reflections on his lived time. Upon entering his home village, he fell to pondering over what time has brought to him: a tiny village boy at the time of departure but now an old, big, and grey-haired man. This melancholic musing was interrupted for good by a casual encounter with jovial village boys who mistook him for a stranger. But this episode of misidentity is not all "comic relief," as it reveals a new dislocation of space: the poet is no longer accepted by all as belonging to the place he had long regarded as home.

　　With this deft handling of space and time, the poet conveys his complex emotional experience upon his return home. How would you describe the poet's feelings? Joyful or melancholic? Evenly joyful and melancholic? Or overwhelmingly joyful with a tinge of sadness?

P55

jiǔ yuè jiǔ rì   yì shān dōng xiōng dì
九月九日¹忆²山³东 兄弟

[táng] wáng wéi
[唐] 王 维⁴

On the Double Ninth Festival:
Thinking of My Brothers in Shandong

[Tang Dyn.] Wang Wei

dú	*zài*	*yì*	*xiāng*	*wéi*	*yì*	*kè*
独	在	异⁵	乡	为	异	客
měi	*féng*	*jiā*	*jié*	*bèi*	*sī*	*qīn*
每	逢⁶	佳⁷	节	倍⁸	思	亲△

Alone in the land of others
　　An outside visitor I am to them,

Whenever a festival arrives
　　I miss you folks all the more.

yáo	*zhī*	*xiōng*	*dì*	*dēng*	*gāo*	*chù*
遥⁹	知	兄	弟	登	高¹⁰	处

From afar I know you brothers
　　climbing up the mountains,

biàn *chā* *zhū* *yú* *shǎo* *yì* *rén*

遍¹¹ 插¹² 茱 萸¹³ 少 一 人ᐃ

The *zhuyu* plant is worn by all
except the one absent.
(Tr. Zong-qi Cai)

[七言律绝 heptasyllabic regulated quatrain, tonal pattern II, see *HTRCP,* p. 170]

字词释义 Vocabulary Notes

1. 九月九日　or 重阳　the Double Ninth Festival (9ᵗʰ day of the 9ᵗʰ month in the Chinese lunar calendar). See P12 note 14.

2. 忆 (憶)　v. to recall, reminisce. See also P04 note 22.

3. 山　n. mountain. Here it refers to Mount Hua 华山 in present-day Shaanxi province. 山东 refers to the area east of Mount Hua in present-day Shanxi province, where Wang Wei's hometown is.

4. See the biographic note in P15 note 2.

5. 异 (異)　adj. different. 异乡 means "other land"(*tā xiāng* 他乡). 异客 a visitor from other land.

6. 逢　v. to meet, come upon. ☞逢年过节他都会去看望自己的老师 He goes to see his teachers on New Year's Day or other festivals.

7. 佳　adj. fine, beautiful. 佳节 festival.

8. 倍　adv. doubly, ever more. MdnC: 更加 (*gèng jiā*).

9. 遥　adj. distant, remote. Here it refers to Chang'an which is far away from Wang Wei's hometown. See also P19 note 6.

10. 登高　to climb a mountain: a favorite activity for the Double Ninth Festival. See also P12 note 14.

11. 遍　adv. all over, throughout. ☞遍地都是黄花 The yellow flowers are all over the place.

12. 插　v. to stick in, insert. ☞他把手插在兜里 He put hands in his pockets.

13. 茱萸　n. cornus officinalis. 插茱萸 wearing a *zhuyu* plant was customary during the Double Ninth Festival. See also P12 note 14.

现代文翻译 Modern Chinese Translation

　　(我)独自在他乡⁵作客，每逢佳节，更加⁸思念亲人。(我)虽身在远方，却知道兄弟们今天会登上高处，身上都插¹²着茱萸，只少我一个。

评论与提问 Comment and Question

This poem, especially its first couplet, is still often cited in a homeward letter written during a holiday season. The first couplet gives a clear exposition of the two primary reasons for homesickness: a spatial dislocation (an unfamiliar land and being among unfamiliar people) and the passage of time (as measured by the advent of festivals). Next, the poet seeks to mitigate the separation by picturing how his brothers are celebrating the festival (line 3), but this imaginary reunion only ends up deepening his sense of loneliness (line 4). If this poem was to be shortened into a pentasyllabic quatrain, could Wang Wei still treat the theme in the same fashion? Study the next poem and find out what approaches he used in a pentasyllabic quatrain.

zá shī qí èr
杂 诗 其二
[táng] wáng wéi
[唐] 王 维¹

jūn	zì	gù	xiāng	lái
君	自	故	乡	来
yīng	zhī	gù	xiāng	shì
应	知	故	乡	事▲
lái	rì	qǐ	chuāng	qián
来	日·	绮²	窗	前
hán	méi	zhuó	huā	wèi
寒	梅³	著⁴·	花	未▲⁵

[五言古绝 pentasyllabic ancient quatrain]

Miscellaneous Poems, No. 2

[Tang Dyn.] Wang Wei

You've come from our hometown

And must know what's happening there

The day you left, by the patterned window

Was the cold plum tree in bloom?

(Tr. Charles Egan, *HTRCP*, p. 205)

字词释义 Vocabulary Notes

1. See the biographic note in P15 note 2.
2. 绮 (綺) adj. elegant, beautiful.
3. 梅 n. plum tree.
4. 著 (*zhù*) adj. marked, outstanding; here pronounced as "*zhuó*." 著花, to blossom (*kāi huā* 开花).
5. 未 adv. not yet. MdnC: 没有 (*méi yǒu*).

现代文翻译 Modern Chinese Translation

　　您从故乡来，应该知道故乡发生的事情。您来的那天，窗前的寒梅，开花⁴了没有？⁵

评论与提问 Comment and Question

A wandering person often gets homesick when recalling some "unimportant" details of his life in his hometown. This poem is a good example. It is rather surprising that the poet only asked whether the cold plum tree was in bloom when he met a friend from his hometown. It should be noted, however, that the cold plum is not just a tree, but a symbol of the poet's memories of his hometown and ultimately of his homesickness as well. Could you describe how differently Wang Wei approaches the same theme of homesickness in this and the previous poem?

P57

jìng yè sī
静 夜 思
[táng] lǐ bái
[唐] 李 白[1]

chuáng	*qián*	*míng*	*yuè*	*guāng*
床	前	明	月·	光△
yí	*shì*	*dì*	*shàng*	*shuāng*
疑[2]	是	地	上	霜△
jǔ	*tóu*	*wàng*	*míng*	*yuè*
举[3]	头	望	明	月·
dī	*tóu*	*sī*	*gù*	*xiāng*
低	头	思	故	乡△

[五言古绝 pentasyllabic ancient quatrain]

Quiet Night Thoughts

[Tang Dyn.]　Li Bai

Before my bed, the bright moonlight

I mistake it for frost on the ground

Raising my head, I stare at the bright moon;

Lowering my head, I think of home
(Tr. Charles Egan, *HTRCP*, p. 210)

字词释义 Vocabulary Notes

1. See the biographic note in P19 note 3.
2. 疑　v. to doubt. See also P17 note 8.
3. 举 (舉)　v. to raise, lift. 👉举起手来! Hands up!

现代文翻译 Modern Chinese Translation

　　明亮的月光照在床前，我还以为是地上的一层霜。抬起头来，看着天上的明月，低下头来，心中思念着故乡。

评论与提问 Comment and Question

This poem by Li Bai is arguably the most frequently recited of all Chinese poems. If a child living in or outside China is taught by his or her parents to recite Chinese poems, this poem is most likely the one to begin with. It has delighted all generations of Chinese readers, old and young, with its simple language, its musicality (thanks to the sonorous, "ang"-ending rhyme), and its poetic exaggeration. In real life, few of us could believe that one can mistake the moonlight for frost on the ground. But with a "willing suspension of disbelief" (John Keats' word), we can appreciate this exaggeration as expressive of the poet's severe homesickness. Can you think of any other reasons for the unrivaled popularity of this poem? 👉*HTRCP*, p. 210 for a discussion of this poem.

P58

dù sāng gān
渡 桑 乾¹

[*táng*] *jiǎ dǎo*
[唐] 贾 岛²

Crossing the Sanggan River

[Tang Dyn.] Jia Dao

kè	*shè*	*bīng*	*zhōu*	*yǐ*	*shí*	*shuāng*
客	舍³	并	州⁴	已	十	霜△⁵

My sojourn at Bingzhou
    has seen ten seasons of frost,

guī	*xīn*	*rì*	*yè*	*yì*	*xián*	*yáng*
归⁶	心	日	夜	忆	咸	阳△⁷

With a homesick heart day and night
    I fondly thought of Xianyang.

wú	*duān*	*gèng*	*dù*	*sāng*	*gān*	*shuǐ*
无	端⁸	更	渡	桑	乾	水

For no reason I further crossed
    the River of Sanggan,

què	*wàng*	*bīng*	*zhōu*	*shì*	*gù*	*xiāng*
却⁹	望	并	州	是	故	乡△

So now I behold Bingzhou
    as my hometown.
(Tr. Zong-qi Cai)

[七言律绝 heptasyllabic regulated quatrain, tonal pattern IIa, see *HTRCP,* p. 171]

字词释义 Vocabulary Notes

1. 桑乾 the Sanggan River. It originates in the north of Shanxi province and runs through Shanxi province, Hebei province, Beijing, and Tianjin before reaching the Bo Sea 渤海.

2. 贾岛 (style 字, Làngxiān 阆仙, 779−843), a late Tang poet. He and Meng Jiao 孟郊 are regarded as the representatives of "tirelessly chanting" (*kǔ yín* 苦吟) poets. See Meng Jiao's biographic note in P42 note 3. Some scholars argue that this poem should be attributed to Liu Zao 刘皂, a late Tang poet, entitled "Visiting Shuofang" ("Lǚ cì Shuòfāng" 旅次朔方).

3. 客舍 n. hotel. See also P39 note 7.

4. 并 (*bīng*) 州 Bing State, one of the nine states in ancient China according to *Zhou Rituals* (*Zhōu lǐ* 周礼) and "Records of Geography" ("Dìlǐ zhì" 地理志) in the *History of the Han* (*Hàn shū* 汉书). It includes the areas comprising present-day Baoding 保定 (in Hebei province), Taiyuan 太原 (in Shanxi province), and Datong 大同 (in Shanxi province). In the Tang dynasty, Bing State belonged to East River Way 河东道, and its government was located in present-day Taiyuan 太原, Shanxi province. The Sanggan River was in the north of the Bing State.

5. 霜 n. frost. See also P45 note 4. It used as a metonym for "a year." 十霜 means "ten years."

6. 归 (歸) v. to go back to. See also P07 note 11.

7. 咸阳 (陽) near the city of Xi'an 西安.

8. 无 (無) 端 adv. for no reason at all. MdnC: 无缘无故 (*wú yuán wú gù*). 📖你不可以无缘无故乱发脾气 You cannot lose your temper for no reason. See also P75 note 3.

9. 却 (卻) v. to turn one's head, turn round. See also P52 note 10.

现代文翻译 Modern Chinese Translation

(我)在并州已停留了十年，回家的心思特别强烈，日日夜夜都在思念着咸阳。当 (我)无缘无故[8]地过了桑乾河，回头望时，又觉得并州好像就是故乡了。

评论与提问 Comment and Question

This poem is a remarkable feat of spatial maneuvering. Each line introduces a new marker of space and, with it, a new revelation of the intensification of the poet's homesickness. The first line mentions Bingzhou as the place where the poet sojourned for ten long years. The second line identifies Xianyang as the poet's hometown, to which he imagined himself returning each day and night during the ten long years. Ironically, the poet's imagined linking of these two places only underscores his inability to surmount his physical separation from home. Just as we think that no more can be said of the poet's physical separation, the poet informs us of yet a new spatial dislocation of his: his transfer to an even more remote area on the other side of Sanggan River. To our further amazement, the poet engineers a startling reshuffling of space markers: Bingzhou now displacing Xianyang as the poet's hometown. This final act of spatial maneuvering bespeaks the worsening of the poet's homesickness to despair. In any poetic tradition you know, can you find, within four short lines, a more ingenious treatment of space?

P59

yè yǔ jì běi
夜 雨 寄[1] 北

[táng] lǐ shāng yǐn
[唐] 李 商 隐[2]

Night Rain: A Poem Sent to the North

[Tang Dyn.] Li Shangyin

jūn	wèn	guī	qī	wèi	yǒu	qī
君	问	归	期[3]	未	有	期△

You asked me the date of my return
　　but the date I do not yet know,

bā	shān	yè	yǔ	zhǎng	qiū	chí
巴	山[4]	夜	雨	涨[5]	秋	池△

Here a night rain in Ba Mountain
　　has sent the autumn ponds swelling.

hé	dāng	gòng	jiǎn	xī	chuāng	zhú
何	当	共	剪[6]	西	窗	烛[7]

When can we together trim
　　the candles by the western window

què	huà	bā	shān	yè	yǔ	shí
却[8]	话	巴	山	夜	雨	时△

And chat about this time of
　　night rain in Ba Mountain?
　　　　(Tr. Zong-qi Cai)

[七言律绝 heptasyllabic regulated quatrain, tonal pattern IIa, see *HTRCP*, p. 171]

字词释义 Vocabulary Notes

1. 寄　v. to send. See also P08 note 9. 寄北 means "to send a letter to family in the North."

2. See the biographic note in P03 note 2.

3. 期   n. a period of time, phase. MdnC: 日期 (*rì qī*) date. 👉他出发的日期定了吗 Has his departure date been fixed?

4. 巴山   or 大巴山   Ba Mountain, in present-day Nanjiang 南江, Sichuan province.

5. 涨 (漲)   v. (of water, price, etc.) to rise, go up. 👉河水又涨了 The river rose again.

6. 剪   v. to cut (with scissors). 👉她把头发剪短了 She cut her hair short. See also P66 note 6.

7. 烛 (燭)   n. (wax) candle. Here it refers to a candlewick (*zhú xīn* 烛芯).

8. 却 (卻)   adv. again. See also P08 note 17.

现代文翻译 Modern Chinese Translation

你问我回去的日期,³ 现在还没确定。今晚，巴山下着大雨，秋雨涨⁵满了池子。什么时候我才能与你一起剪⁶西窗边的烛芯,⁷ 跟你说说今夜巴山下雨时我对你的思念呢？

评论与提问 Comment and Question

This poem is a feat of temporal maneuvering as the previous poem (P58) is that of spatial maneuvering. Compared to a double shift of space markers in P58, this poem operates through a double journey in time. The first line spans from the recent past (when the addressee, probably the poet's wife living in his hometown, wrote him a letter) to an indefinite point in the future (the unknown time of the poet's return). Instead of explaining the deferment of his return, the poet writes about the night rain outside, probably as a symbol of his being stranded, in the third line.

If the first couplet represents a flight from the recent past to the future, the second couplet projects through a long question a reverse journey in time: from an indefinite point in the future (when the poet and his addressee "together trim the candles by the western window" at home) to the present moment of night rain (as recalled by them at the time of their future reunion). Through this act of temporal maneuvering, has the poet effectively revealed the state of his homesickness? How would you compare his homesickness with Jia Dao's (P58)?

练习 EXERCISES

一 填空 Fill in blanks

A. 诗词填字: 逢 插 识 异 低 疑 绮 涨 剪 霜 遥 问 床 倍 忆 著 举 话 归

1. 何当共＿＿＿西窗烛，却＿＿＿巴山夜雨时。 2. 独在＿＿＿乡为＿＿＿客。

3. 儿童相见不相＿＿＿，笑＿＿＿客从何处来。 4. 每＿＿＿佳节＿＿＿思亲。

5. 客舍并州已十＿＿＿，归心日夜＿＿＿咸阳。 6. ＿＿＿头望明月，＿＿＿头思故乡。

7. ＿＿＿知兄弟登高处，遍＿＿＿茱萸少一人。 8. 来日＿＿＿窗前，寒梅＿＿＿花未。

9. 君问＿＿＿期未有期，巴山夜雨＿＿＿秋池。 10. ＿＿＿前明月光，＿＿＿是地上霜。

B. 现代文填词: 遍 插 举 涨 剪 逢 偶然 口音

1. ＿＿＿ 年过节他都会去看老师。　　　2. 河水又＿＿＿起来了。

3. ＿＿＿ 地都是黄花。　　　4. 他把手＿＿＿在口袋里。

5. 有问题请＿＿＿ 手。　　　6. 她的头发＿＿＿得很短。

7. 他说话＿＿＿＿＿＿很重。　　　8. 他在路上＿＿＿＿＿＿遇到了一位老朋友。

二 形近字辨析 Distinguish easily confused characters

1. 何当共 ＿＿＿ 西窗烛　a. 煎　b. 前　c. 剪　　2. 君问归＿＿＿未有＿＿＿　a. 欺　b. 其　c. 期

3. 无端更＿＿＿桑乾水　a. 度　b. 镀　c. 渡　　4. 寒梅＿＿＿花未　a. 著　b. 者　c. 着

5. 巴山夜雨涨秋＿＿＿　a. 池　b. 他　c. 弛　　6. 每逢佳节＿＿＿思亲　a. 培　b. 倍　c. 陪

7. 来日＿＿＿窗前　a. 倚　b. 绮　c. 椅　　8. ＿＿＿插茱萸少一人　a. 遍　b. 编　c. 區

三 连句 Match the first part with the second

1. 床前明月光( )　　　2. 君自故乡来( )　　　3. 少小离家老大回( )　　　4. 何当共剪西窗烛( )

5. 举头望明月( )　　　6. 来日绮窗前( )　　　7. 无端更渡桑乾水( )　　　8. 独在异乡为异客( )

9. 君问归其未有期( )　10. 遥知兄弟登高处( )

a. 低头思故乡　　　b. 却望并州是故乡　　　c. 应知故乡事　　　d. 每逢佳节倍思亲

e. 寒梅著花未　　　f. 巴山夜雨涨秋池　　　g. 疑是地上霜　　　h. 遍插茱萸少一人

i. 却话巴山夜雨时　　　k. 乡音无改鬓毛衰

四 句读 Punctuate and translate the following passage

床 前 明 月 光 疑 是 地 上 霜 无 端 更 渡 桑 乾 水 却 望 并 州 是 故 乡 君 问 归 期 未 有 期 巴 山 夜 雨 涨 秋 池 遥 知 兄 弟 登 高 处 遍 插 茱 萸 少 一 人 君 自 故 乡 来 应 知 故 乡 事 儿 童 相 见 不 相 识 笑 问 客 从 何 处 来

五 听写 Dictation

1. ＿＿＿ 小 ＿＿＿＿＿＿＿＿＿＿＿＿，＿＿＿＿＿无 ＿＿＿＿＿＿＿＿＿。

2. 何 ＿＿＿＿＿＿＿＿＿＿＿＿，＿＿＿＿＿＿＿＿＿＿＿＿时。

3. ＿＿＿ 在＿＿＿＿＿＿＿＿＿＿，每＿＿＿＿＿＿＿＿＿＿＿。

4. ＿＿＿ 前＿＿＿＿＿＿，＿＿＿是 ＿＿＿上＿＿＿，＿＿＿头＿＿＿＿＿＿，
＿＿＿头＿＿＿＿＿。

5. ＿＿＿＿＿＿＿＿＿已 ＿＿＿＿＿，＿＿＿心＿＿＿＿＿＿＿＿。

6. ＿＿＿自＿＿＿＿＿，＿＿＿知＿＿＿。＿＿＿日＿＿＿＿＿前，＿＿＿＿＿
＿＿＿花＿＿＿。

13

闺 怨

Plaints of Young Women (I)

P60

gǔ shī shí jiǔ shǒu   qí èr
古 诗 十 九 首 其 二

Nineteen Old Poems, No. 2
Anonymous

qīng 青	*qīng* 青	*hé* 河	*pàn* 畔[1]	*cǎo* 草	Green, green	the grass by the river bank,
yù 郁	*yù* 郁[2]	*yuán* 园	*zhōng* 中	*liǔ* 柳 ▲	Lush, lush	the willow in the garden.
yíng 盈	*yíng* 盈[3]	*lóu* 楼	*shàng* 上	*nǚ* 女	Graceful, graceful	the woman in the tower,
jiǎo 皎	*jiǎo* 皎[4]	*dāng* 当	*chuāng* 窗	*yǒu* 牖 ▲[5]	Lustrous, lustrous	she stands by the window.
é 娥	*é* 娥[6]	*hóng* 红	*fěn* 粉[7]	*zhuāng* 妆[8]	Radiant, radiant	the touches of her rouge,
xiān 纤	*xiān* 纤[9]	*chū* 出	*sù* 素[10]	*shǒu* 手 ▲	Slender, slender	she stretches her hand.
xī 昔[11]	*wéi* 为	*chāng* 倡[12]	*jiā* 家	*nǚ* 女	Once she was a singing girl,
jīn 今	*wéi* 为	*dàng* 荡	*zǐ* 子[13]	*fù* 妇 ▲	Now the wife of a wanderer.
dàng 荡	*zǐ* 子	*xíng* 行	*bù* 不	*guī* 归	The wanderer is gone and does not return,
kōng 空	*chuáng* 床	*nán* 难	*dú* 独	*shǒu* 守 ▲[14]	The empty bed is hard for her to occupy alone.

(Tr. Zong-qi Cai)

[五言古诗 pentasyllabic ancient-style verse]

字词释义 Vocabulary Notes

1. 畔 n. side, bank. MdnC: 边 (*biān*).

2. 郁郁　adj.　lush, luxuriant. 👉山中的松树郁郁葱葱 The pines in the mountain are luxuriant.

3. 盈盈　adj.　in a good manner.　　　4. 皎皎　adj.　very clear and bright.

5. 牖　n.　window. MdnC: 窗户 (chuāng hu).　　6. 娥娥　adj.　(of a woman) beautiful, pretty.

7. 红 (紅) 粉　n.　make-up and face powder.　　8. 妆　n.　makeup. See also P04 note 20.

9. 纤纤 (纖纖)　adj.　thin, slender.　　　10. 素　adj.　white. See also P95 note 6.

11. 昔　n.　the past. See also P18 note 3.

12. 倡 (chāng)　n.　people who made a living by singing. 倡家女 singing girls (gē jì 歌伎).

13. 荡 (蕩) 子　n.　a wanderer who won't go home.

14. 守　v.　to keep, watch. 👉他在外面守了一夜 He kept watch outside for the whole night.

15. 优雅 (yōu yǎ)　adj.　elegant.　　　16. 纤细 (xiān xì)　adj.　slim.

17. 游荡 (yóu dàng)　v.　to wander.

现代文翻译 Modern Chinese Translation

河边[1]的草地青青翠翠，园中的柳树郁郁葱葱。[2] 楼上一位优雅[15]的女子站在窗前，美丽动人。她打扮得很漂亮，伸出纤细[16]白嫩的小手。她过去是歌伎，[12] 现在嫁给了一个总在外游荡[17]的人。 丈夫还没回来，她一个人守[14]着空床，很难忍受这份寂寞啊！

评论与提问 Comment and Question

If you compare this poem with the first poem of the *Book of Poetry* (P01), you shall see how topic+comment is drastically reconfigured in the new pentasyllabic *shi* poetry. On the syntactic level, we can observe a successive use of six topic+comment lines. In each of these lines, the last three characters are either a nominal or verbal phrase that introduces an observed image. For their part, the initial two characters are a reduplicative uttered as an emotive comment on the observed image.

The progression of these six lines reveals an observational process comparable to a cinematic shot zooming in from a broad scene to ever more minute details of observation. We move our gaze from river bank to the garden willow, the woman in the tower, her facing the window, her makeup, and her tender hands. The accompanying reduplicatives effectively turn this observational process into an emotionally charged one. Such a successive use of topic+comment lines is unseen in the *Book of Poetry*.

On the structural level, we can observe an evolution of topic+comment into an overarching structural principle. The first part of the poem introduces the topic (an abandoned woman being observed by the speaker, lines 1−6); the second half presents the speaker's empathetic comments on her miserable life (lines 7−10). This topic+comment structure features a descriptive-reflective mode of presentation. In the *Book of Poetry,* we may find such a topic+comment structure, or rather a prototype of it, only in a few poems. But in "Nineteen Old Poems," the earliest extant collection of pentasyllabic poetry, this topic+comment structure figures very prominently and is to become a prevalent structure in subsequent *shi* poetry, especially regulated verse. Is the four-stage division of a regulated verse just an elaboration of this structure?

P61

chūn yuàn
春　怨

[táng] jīn chāng xù
[唐] 金　昌　绪[1]

Spring Lament

[Tang Dyn.]   Jin Changxu

dǎ	*qǐ*	*huáng*	*yīng*	*ér*
打	起	黄	莺[2]	儿

Hit the yellow oriole

mò	*jiào*	*zhī*	*shàng*	*tí*
莫.	教[3]	枝	上	啼△

Don't let it sing on the branches

tí	*shí*	*jīng*	*qiè*	*mèng*
啼	时	惊[4]	妾[5]	梦.

When it sings, it breaks into my dreams

bù	*dé*	*dào*	*liáo*	*xī*
不	得	到	辽	西△[6]

And keeps me from Liaoxi!

(Tr. Charles Egan, *HTRCP,* p. 204)

[五言律绝 pentasyllabic regulated quatrain, tonal pattern Ia (imperfect), see *HTRCP*, p. 171]

字词释义 Vocabulary Notes

1. 金昌绪 (緒)　(fl. 713–742), a Tang poet.
2. 黄莺 (鶯)　n. yellow oriole.
3. 教 (*jiào*)　v. to allow. See also P50 note 10.
4. 惊 (驚)　v. to shock, surprise, alarm. MdnC: 惊醒(*jīng xǐng*) to awaken. ☞一声巨响把他从睡梦中惊醒 He was awakened by a terrible bang.
5. 妾　a humble first-person feminine pronoun. See also P05 note 7.
6. 辽 (遼) 西　West part of the Liao River 辽河, in the western part of present-day Liaoning province, where soldiers were sent to garrison the frontier in the Tang Dynasty.

现代文翻译 Modern Chinese Translation

　　把树上的黄莺打走，不要让它在树枝上叫。它的叫声把我从梦中惊醒[4]了，让我梦不到辽西！

评论与提问 Comment and Question

This poem is a colloquial-style pentasyllabic quatrain. It depicts the intense longing of a lonesome woman for her husband in the frontiers. What function(s) does the image of an oriole perform in the poem? ☞*HTRCP,* pp. 204–205, for a discussion of this poem.

P62

wú　　　　tí
无　　　题[1]

[*táng*]　*lǐ shāng yǐn*
[唐] 李 商 隐[2]

Untitled

[Tang Dyn.] Li Shangyin

sà	*sà*	*dōng*	*fēng*	*xì*	*yǔ*	*lái*
飒	飒[3]	东	风	细	雨[4]	来

Rustling, whistling, the east wind
and the fine rain come;

fú	*róng*	*táng*	*wài*	*yǒu*	*qīng*	*léi*
芙	蓉[5]	塘[6]	外	有	轻	雷△

beyond the lotus pool there is faint thunder.

jīn	*chán*	*niè*	*suǒ*	*shāo*	*xiāng*	*rù*
金	蟾[7]	啮[8]	锁[9]	烧	香	入

Gold toad gnaws the lock: burning incense, it enters;

yù	*hǔ*	*qiān*	*sī*	*jí*	*jǐng*	*huí*
玉	虎[10]	牵[11]	丝[12]	汲[13]	井	回△

jade tiger pulls silk cord: drawing well water, it turns.

jiǎ	*shì*	*kuī*	*lián*	*hán*	*yuàn*	*shào*
贾	氏[14]	窥[15]	廉[16]	韩	掾[17]	少[18]

Miss Jia peers in at the curtain: Secretary Han is young;

fú	*fēi*	*liú*	*zhěn*	*wèi*	*wáng*	*cái*
宓	妃[19]	留	枕[20]	魏	王	才△[21]

Empress Fu leaves behind a headrest: the prince of Wei is gifted.

chūn	*xīn*	*mò*	*gòng*	*huā*	*zhēng*	*fā*
春	心[22]	莫	共	花	争[23]	发[24]

Don't let your springtime heart vie with the flowers in blooming:

yī	*cùn*	*xiāng*	*sī*	*yī*	*cùn*	*huī*
一	寸	相	思	一	寸	灰△

an inch of love longing, an inch of ash.

[七言律诗 heptasyllabic regulated verse, tonal pattern IIa, see *HTRCP*, p. 172]

(Tr. Robert Ashmore, *HTRCP*, p. 193)

字词释义 Vocabulary Notes

1. 无题 (無題)　untitled. See P03 note 1.　　2. See the biographic note in P03 note 2.

3. 飒飒 (颯颯)　the sound of wind or rain. ☞秋风飒飒 The autumn wind is blowing briskly.

4. 细雨　n. drizzle. MdnC: 小雨 (*xiǎo yǔ*).

5. 芙蓉　n. lotus [formal]. MdnC: 荷花 (*hé huā*).　　6. 塘　n. pool, pond. See also P37 note 4.

7. 金蟾　n. golden toad. Here it means an incense burner (*xiāng lú* 香炉) with a toad-shaped knob.

8. 啮 (嚙)　v. to gnaw [formal]. MdnC: 咬 (*yǎo*). ☞他咬了一口苹果 He took a bite of an apple.

9. 锁 (鎖)　n. lock. Here it refers to the knob of an incense burner (*bí niǔ* 鼻纽). See P66 note 5 for a different meaning of the word.

10. 玉虎   n. tiger made of jade. Here it refers to the winch (*lùlu* 辘轳) which has a jade tiger as decoration.

11. 牵 (牽)   v. to lead along, pull. 👉他牵着马往前走 He led a horse and walked forward. See also P95 note 13.

12. 丝 (絲)   n. silk. See also P03 note 9. Here it refers to a large rope for a well (*jǐng suǒ* 井索).

13. 汲   v. to draw (water). 👉他正从井里汲水 He is drawing water from a well.

14. "贾氏"句   an allusion to *New Accounts of the Tales of the World* (*Shìshuō xīnyǔ* 世说新语). Han Shou 韩寿 was a young clerk working for the Jin Dynasty official Jia Chong 贾充. Jia Chong's daughter caught a glimpse of Han Shou through a window and began an affair with him. Later on, Jia Chong found out and let his daughter marry Han Shou. (Ashmore; *HTRCP*, p.194).

15. 窥 (窺)   v. to peep, spy. MdnC: 窥视 (*kuī shì*) [formal]. 👉一个可疑的人正向屋内窥视 A suspicious man is peeping into the house.

16. 廉   n. curtain, MdnC: 帘子 (*lián zi*).   17. 掾   n. a generic name for aides to officials.

18. 少 (*shào*)   adj. young. See also P54 note 3.

19. "宓妃"句   an allusion to the love story between the renowned poet Cao Zhi 曹植(192−232) and Empress Zhen 甄后, told by Li Shan 李善 (630−689) in his annotation on Cao Zhi's "*Fu* on the Luo River Goddess" ("Luòshén fù" 洛神赋) in *Anthology of Refined Literature* (*Wén xuǎn* 文选). Empress Zhen was the wife of Cao Zhi's brother, Cao Pi 曹丕 (187−226), Emperor Wen of the Wei dynasty. "Cao Zhi, the story has it, had unsuccessfully sought the hand of the future Empress Zhen before her betrothal to Cao Pi." Years later, after Empress Zhen was dead, Cao Pi happened to show Cao Zhi "an ornately inlaid headrest that belonged to Empress Zhen, Cao Zhi burst into tears on seeing this object." Cao Pi then gave him the headrest as a memento. (Ashmore; *HTRCP*, p.195).

20. 枕   n. headrest. See also P63 note 13. Here it refers to a "golden thread headrest" (*jīn lǚ zhěn* 金缕枕)

21. 才   n. gift, talent. MdnC: 才华 (*cái huá*). 👉他很有才华 He is very talented.

22. 春心   n. spring heart. Here it refers to the desire for beautiful love.

23. 争 (爭)   v. to contend, vie. 👉大家都争着发言 Everyone tried to have the floor before others.

24. 发 (發)   v. to develop. Here it means "to blossom." See P83 note 21 for a different meaning of the word.

25. 开启 (*kāi qǐ*)   v. to open. 26. 香料 (*xiāng liào*) n. perfume. 27. 装饰 (*zhuāng shì*) v. to decorate.

28. 状 (*zhuàng*)   n. shape   29. 向往 (*xiàng wǎng*)   v. to yearn for.

现代文翻译 Modern Chinese Translation

　　东风飒飒，³ 小雨⁴飘来，荷花⁵池外，有隐隐的雷声。开启²⁵金蟾咬⁸住的鼻纽，⁹放入香料，²⁶香炉⁷开始燃烧。用玉石装饰²⁷的虎状²⁸辘轳¹⁰牵¹¹着井索，¹² 汲¹³水出来后，辘轳井索回到原来的位置。 贾氏隔着帘子¹⁶窥视¹⁵着年轻的韩寿；宓妃死后，把金缕枕²⁰留给了有才华²¹的曹植。 (想着这些古老的爱情故事，却不得不提醒自己)， 向往²⁹爱情的心，不要和花争²³着开放，因为寸寸相思都会化成灰！

评论与提问 Comment and Question

Li Shangyin is a great poet best known for his innovative use of poetic allusions. If most other poets use allusions mainly for a specific rhetorical effect, he employs allusions for a broader end: to open up all possibilities of interpretation and entertain an elusive, enchanting play of meanings. In other words, his allusive art is marked by a conscious creation of ambiguity. How does he create rich ambiguities in his poems, especially his regulated verses? To most critics, those rich ambiguities simply stem from his dense stacking of allusions, both overt and covert. This is in many ways a mistaken or at least partially mistaken view. Allusions are not inherently ambiguous and a successive use of them does not automatically generate ambiguities. Only when allusions are arranged in an incoherent fashion do they generate the kind of rich ambiguities we see in Li's poems.

An investigation of poetic structure is therefore the key to understanding Li's allusive art. On the surface, this poem displays a topic+comment structure and operates in a typical descriptive-reflective mode. The first half of the poem depicts external scenes and the next half ushers in the speaker's emotive response to the scenes. Upon close scrutiny, however, we can easily see two significant ruptures in the inter-couplet organization.

The first rupture occurs between the first and second couplets. To continue the opening external description, this second couplet should present concrete images contiguously related to what is described in the opening couplet. If the toad-shape door knob is contiguous with the outdoor scene, the winch decorated with a jade tiger, presumably within a courtyard, is not. This leads many critics to take the depiction of the doorknob and the winch as metaphorical rather than literal: fragrant incense can penetrate a tightly closed door but a lover cannot; a winch can fetch water from a well however deep it is, but a lover cannot get close to the lady deep inside the house. This abrupt shift from literal to metaphorical description amounts to a break of the established "beginning-continuation" (*qǐchéng* 起承) relation between the first and second couplets. Only if we differ from the widely accepted view and assume the speaker to be a lady confined to her house (as we do here), can we perceive a coherent continuation of the initial literal description: a move from outdoors to what the lady sees in her courtyard. So, an ambiguity about the speaker's gender has arisen along with the undecidability between the literal and the metaphorical.

The second rupture occurs between the third and fourth couplets. Performing a turning (*zhuǎn* 转), the third couplet shifts from external depiction to a reflection about love—the immense gratification of its fulfillment (the story of Miss Jia) and the everlasting sorrow of its failure (the story of Empress Zhen). The pairing of these two opposite stories precludes the ending couplet from performing its expected function of conclusion or closure (*hé* 合). In many ways, this ending is no closure, but an opening—an unfolding of ambiguities about what leads to the speaker's lament about love. Does Jia's rare success makes her despair over her likely failure? Conversely, does the failure of Cao Zhi, Empress Zhen's suitor, harden her pessimistic expectation of failure? Or does her simultaneous allusion to Miss Jia and Empress Zhen reveal her intense, consuming anxiety over the future outcome of her pursuit of love? Ponder all these questions and formulate your own answers.

P63

gēng lòu zǐ
更 漏 子[1]

To the Tune "On the Water Clock at Night"

[*táng*] *wēng tíng yún*
[唐] 温 庭 筠²

[Tang Dyn.] Wen Tingyun

yù   lú   xiāng
玉 · 炉³ 香

Incense in the jade burner,

hóng   là   lèi
红 蜡⁴ 泪 · ▲ᵃ

Red wax tears

piān   zhào   huà   táng   qiū   sì
偏⁵ 照 画 堂⁶ 秋 思 ▲ᵃ⁷

Unbidden, reflect an autumn mood in the painted hall.

méi   cuì   bó
眉 翠⁸ 薄⁹·

Blackened brows fade,

bìn   yún   cán
鬓¹⁰ 云 残 △ᵇ¹¹

Cloud locks are tousled,

yè   cháng   qīn   zhěn   hán
夜 长 衾¹² 枕¹³ 寒 △ᵇ

The night is long, quilt and pillow cold.

wú   tóng   shù
梧 桐¹⁴ 树 ▲ᶜ

Wutong trees and

sān   gēng   yǔ
三 更¹⁵ 雨 ▲ᶜ

Third-watch rain are

bú   dào   lí   qíng   zhèng   kǔ
不 · 道¹⁶ 离 情 正 苦 ▲ᶜ

Unaware of separation throes.

yí   yè   yè
一 · 叶 · 叶 ·

Leaf after leaf,

yì   shēng   shēng
一 · 声 声 △ᵈ

Sound by sound

kōng   jiē   dī   dào   míng
空 阶¹⁷ 滴¹⁸ 到 明 △ᵈ¹⁹

Drips on the empty steps 'til dawn.

[小令 short lyric song]

(Tr. Maija Bell Samei, *HTRCP*, pp. 251−252)

字词释义 Vocabulary Notes

1. 更漏子 "On the Water Clock at Night," title of a tune.
2. See the biographic note in P46 note 2.
3. 炉 (爐) n. burner.   4. 蜡 n. (wax) candle.
5. 偏 adv. contrary to expectation. MdnC: 偏偏 (*piān piān*). 📖事情的发展偏偏跟他希望的相反 Things turned out just the opposite to what he hoped. See P11 note 7 for a different meaning of the word.
6. 画 (畫) 堂 n. painted hall. Here it indicates a beautiful room.   7. 思 (*sì*) n. mood.

8. 翠 adj. emerald green. See also P20 note 3. Here it refers to a beautiful black color (*cuì dài sè* 翠黛色) used as makeup to paint the eyebrows.

9. 薄 adj. weak, light. MdnC: 淡 (*dàn*). See also P96 note 12 and P100 note 6. 👉颜色变淡了 The color became lighter. See also P24 note 10 for a different meaning of the word.

10. 鬓 (鬢) n. hair on the temples. 鬓云 or 云鬓, see P03 note 18.

11. 残 (殘) adj. incomplete. Here it means "tousled." MdnC: 乱 (*luàn*). 👉她的头发乱了 Her hair is tousled. See also P03 note 7.

12. 衾 n. quilt. MdnC: 被子 (*bèizi*).   13. 枕 n. headrest. See also P62 note 20.

14. 梧桐 n. Chinese parasol tree. See also P66 note 4 and P85 note 14.

15. 更 (*gēng*) n. watch (one of the five two-hour periods into which the night was formerly divided). 三更, the third watch, is around the midnight. See P21 note 13 for a different meaning of the word.

16. 道 v. to speak. See also P38 note 22. Here it means "to give consideration to." MdnC: 在乎 (*zàihu*). 👉他不在乎个人安危，冲进火海救人 He didn't give a thought to his own safety and rushed into the fire to save people.

17. 阶 (階) n. stairs, steps. MdnC: 台阶 (*tái jiē*). See also P69 note 1.

18. 滴 v. to drip. 👉汗水直往下滴 Sweat kept dripping.

19. 明 adj. bright. See also P46 note 10. Here it refers to "dawn" (*tiān míng* 天明).

现代文翻译 Modern Chinese Translation

玉炉中点着香，蜡烛流着眼泪，这点烛光偏偏⁵照在美丽的房间内，引起她不尽的愁思。眉上画的翠黛色⁸淡⁹了，美丽的鬓发也乱¹¹了，夜很长，被子¹²和枕头却是冷的。

她正苦苦思念着离去的人，可是院子里的梧桐树和三更下起的雨却不在乎，¹⁶雨水滴在叶子上，落在台阶¹⁷上，声音一直持续到天明。¹⁹

评论与提问 Comments and Questions

1. This and the following two lyric songs (P64 and P65) are all from the literati *ci* anthology *Among the Flowers Collection* (*Huājiān jí* 花间集), which includes a large number of poems on the cloistered life of women. 👉*HTRCP*, p. 251 for a brief introduction to this anthology.

2. It is generally agreed that Wen Tingyun adapted the popular *ci* form for a literati audience. Compare this lyric and P64 with the anonymous folk lyrics from Dunhuang (P04 and P05) and describe in what aspects Wen developed the *ci* form to accommodate literati interest and taste. 👉*HTRCP*, pp. 251-253.

P64

pú   sà   mán
菩萨蛮¹

[táng] wēng tíng yún
[唐] 温庭筠²

To the Tune "Buddha-like Barbarian"

[Tang Dyn.] Wen Tingyun

xiǎo	*shān*[3]	*chóng*	*dié*[4]	*jīn*[5]	*míng*	*miè*
小	山	重	叠	金	明	灭 ▲a6

Layer on layer of little hills, golds shimmer and fade,

bìn	*yún*	*yù*	*dù*[7]	*xiāng*	*sāi*[8]	*xuě*
鬓	云	欲	度	香	腮	雪 ▲a9

Cloud locks hover over the fragrant snow of a cheek.

lǎn[10]	*qǐ*	*huà*	*é*[11]	*méi*
懒	起	画	蛾	眉△b

Lazily rising to paint on moth eyebrows,

nòng	*zhuāng*[12]	*shū*[13]	*xǐ*	*chí*
弄	妆	梳	洗	迟△b

Dallying with makeup and hair.

zhào	*huā*[14]	*qián*	*hòu*	*jìng*
照	花	前	后	镜 ▲c15

Blossoms are mirrored behind and before,

huā	*miàn*	*jiāo*	*xiāng*[16]	*yìng*
花	面	交	相	映 ▲c17

Flower faces reflect one another.

xīn	*tiè*[18]	*xiù*[19]	*luó*	*rú*
新	帖	绣	罗	襦△d20

Newly embroidered on a jacket of silk

shuāng	*shuāng*	*jīn*	*zhè*	*gū*
双	双	金	鹧	鸪△d21

Are pair after pair of golden partridges.

[小令 short lyric song]

(Tr. Maija Bell Samei, *HTRCP*, p. 253)

字词释义 Vocabulary Notes

1. 菩萨蛮 "Buddha-like Barbarian," title of a tune.   2. See the biographic note in P46 note 2.
3. 小山   little hills. Modern scholars have debated what 小山 means here. There are four possible explanations. First, 小山 could indicate a popular style of eyebrow in ancient China, namely 小山眉(*xiǎo shān méi*). Second, it may refer to a headrest (*shān zhěn* 山枕), which also appears in other *ci* poems of Wen's. Third, it may refer to a "screen" (*píng fēng* 屏风) in a bedroom, the folded shape of which resembles small hills (or, again, to such a screen decorated with a pattern of small hills). Fourth, it may refer to combs worn in women's hair for decoration. The third explanation is adopted in the following modern Chinese translation.
4. 重叠   adj. overlapping.   5. 金   n. gold. Here it refers to morning light (*chén guāng* 晨光).
6. 灭 (滅)   v. (of a light, fire, etc.) to go out. See also P30 note 5.
7. 度   v. to cross, pass. See also P48 note 9.   8. 腮   n. cheek. 香腮 the lady's beautiful cheek.
9. 雪   n. snow. Here it indicates the lady's snow-white (*bái xī* 白皙) skin.
10. 懒(懶)   adj. lazy; sluggish. 👉他懒懒的，不愿意动 He feels sluggish and does not want to move at all. Cf. 倦 in P68 note 7.
11. 蛾   n. moth. 蛾眉 means "moth-shaped brows."
12. 弄妆   v. to apply makeup. MdnC: 打扮 (*dǎ bàn*). 👉她打扮得很漂亮 She made herself up in a pretty way.
13. 梳   v. to comb one's hair 👉她正在梳头 She is combing her hair. See also P99 note 14.

14. 花 n. flower. Here it means the flowers woven into her hair.

15. 镜 (鏡) n. mirror. 前后镜 two mirrors placed in front and behind (here, to see the flowers).

16. 交相 adv. each other. MdnC: 互相 (*hù xiāng*). 17. 映 v. to reflect. See also P22 note 4.

18. 帖 v. to paste, stick to. MdnC: 贴 (*tiē*). ☞窗上贴了报纸 Newspaper was pasted over windows.

19. 绣 (繡) v. to embroider. ☞她在裙子上绣了朵花 She embroidered a flower on a skirt.

20. 襦 n. jacket. MdnC: 短袄 (*duǎn ǎo*). 21. 鹧鸪 (鷓鴣) n. Chinese francolin, partridge.

现代文翻译 Modern Chinese Translation

晨光⁵照在重叠的屏风上，光影一闪一灭⁶(惊醒了睡着的女子。她微微一动），鬓发像云一样横过她白皙⁹的脸庞。(之后)她懒懒¹⁰地起床，然后开始画眉，慢慢地梳¹³洗打扮¹²自己。

照照插在头上的花，看了前镜，又看看后镜，花和美丽的容颜互相¹⁶映衬着。 穿上绣¹⁹花的丝制短袄，²⁰上面贴¹⁸了新花样，是一对对金鹧鸪。

评论与提问 Comment and Question

This lyric song is famous for its ornate diction and images. The poet presents a female figure's morning routine through detailed descriptions of a series of images. Are these images purely descriptive or do they also function to convey emotions? ☞*HTRCP*, pp. 253−254 for discussion of this poem.

练习 EXERCISES

一 填空 Fill in blanks

A. 诗词填字: 打 咽 教 畔 争 懒 道 灭 荡 郁 苦 薄 牵 汲 守 灰 皎 梳 残 度 盈

1. 金蟾____锁烧香入，玉虎____丝____井回。 2. ____起画蛾眉，弄妆____洗迟。

3. 青青河____草，____ ____园中柳 。 4. ____起黄莺儿，莫____枝上啼。

5. 小山重叠金明____，鬓云欲____香腮雪。 6. 眉翠____，鬓云____。

7. ____ ____楼上女，____ ____当窗牖。 8. 不____离情正____。

9. 春心莫共花____发，一寸相思一寸____。 10. ____子行不归，空床难独____。

B. 现代文填词: 郁郁 偏偏 窥视 打扮 惊醒 在乎 争 牵 贴 滴

1. 山中的松树____ ____葱葱。 2. 窗上____了报纸。

3. 一声巨响把她____ ____ 。 4. 汗水从脸上____ 下来。

5. 一个可疑的人正向房间内____ ____ 。 6. 他____着马往前走。

7. 她____ ____得很漂亮。 8. 他不____ ____个人安危，冲进火中救人。

9. 事情的发展____ ____跟他的希望相反。 10. 大家都____着发言。

二 形近字辨析 Distinguish easily confused characters

1. 玉虎牵丝＿＿井回　a. 及　b. 极　c. 汲　　2. ＿＿起画蛾眉　a. 懒　b. 赖　c. 籁
3. ＿＿＿＿当窗牖　a. 较　b. 皎　c. 胶　　4. 新＿＿绣罗襦　a. 贴　b. 帖　c. 粘
5. 一寸相思一寸＿＿　a. 灭　b. 灰　c. 火　　6. 弄妆＿＿洗迟　a. 疏　b. 流　c. 梳
7. 空阶＿＿到明　a. 滴　b. 摘　c. 嘀　　8. 照花前后＿＿　a. 镜　b. 竟　c. 境

三 连句 Match the first part with the second

1. 娥娥红粉妆( )　2. 贾氏窥廉韩掾少( )　3. 小山重叠金明灭( )　4. 春心莫共花争发( )
5. 青青河畔草( )　6. 梧桐树，三更雨( )　7. 飒飒东风细雨来( )　8. 啼时惊妾梦( )
9. 眉翠薄，鬓云残( )　10. 懒起画蛾眉( )

a. 芙蓉塘外有轻雷　b. 不道离情正苦　　c. 郁郁园中柳　　d. 不得到辽西
e. 弄妆梳洗迟　　f. 一寸相思一寸灰　g. 夜长衾枕寒　　h. 宓妃留枕魏王才
i. 纤纤出素手　　k. 鬓云欲度香腮雪

四 句读 Punctuate and translate the following excerpts from three or more poems

飒飒东风细雨来芙蓉塘外有轻雷一叶叶一声声空阶滴到明照花前后镜花面交相映昔为倡家女今为荡子妇荡子行不归空床难独守啼时惊妾梦不得到辽西

五 听写 Dictation

1. ＿＿ 心 ＿＿ ＿＿ ＿＿ ＿＿ ＿＿，一 ＿＿ ＿＿ ＿＿ 一 ＿＿ ＿＿。
2. ＿＿ ＿＿ ＿＿，＿＿ ＿＿ ＿＿，＿＿ 长 ＿＿ ＿＿ ＿＿。
3. ＿＿ ＿＿ ＿＿ ＿＿ 明 ＿＿，＿＿ ＿＿ ＿＿ ＿＿ 香 ＿＿ ＿＿。
4. ＿＿ ＿＿ ＿＿ ＿＿ 草，＿＿ ＿＿ ＿＿ ＿＿ 中 ＿＿。
5. ＿＿ ＿＿ ＿＿ 上 ＿＿，＿＿ ＿＿ ＿＿ 当 ＿＿ ＿＿。
6. ＿＿ ＿＿ ＿＿，红 ＿＿ ＿＿，＿＿ ＿＿ ＿＿ ＿＿ 秋 ＿＿。
7. ＿＿ ＿＿ ＿＿ 风 ＿＿ ＿＿ ＿＿，＿＿ ＿＿ ＿＿ 外 ＿＿ ＿＿ ＿＿。
8. ＿＿ 时 ＿＿ ＿＿，＿＿ 得 ＿＿ ＿＿ ＿＿。

14

闺 怨

Plaints of Young Women (II)

P65

yè jīn mén
谒¹金 门²

To the Tune "Audience at Golden Gate"

[táng] wěi zhuāng
[唐] 韦 庄³

[Tang Dyn.] Wei Zhuang

kōng   xiāng   yì
空⁴   相   忆▲

Vain to remember him,

wú   jì   dé   chuán   xiāo   xī
无   计⁵   得   传⁶   消   息▲

No way to get news through.

tiān   shàng   cháng   é   rén   bù   shí
天   上   嫦   娥⁷   人   不   识▲

Chang'e in the heavens doesn't recognize me.

jì   shū   hé   chù   mì
寄⁸   书⁹   何   处   觅▲¹⁰

Where shall I seek him, to send him a letter?

xīn   shuì   jué   lái   wú   lì
新   睡   觉¹¹   来   无   力▲

Waking, languid, from new sleep.

bù   rěn   bǎ   yī   shū   jì
不   忍   把¹² 伊¹³ 书   迹▲¹⁴

Can't bear to take up the remains of his letter.

mǎn   yuàn   luò   huā   chūn   jì   jì
满   院   落   花   春   寂   寂▲

A courtyard full of fallen blossoms—spring is lonely, lonely—

duàn   cháng   fāng   cǎo   bì
断   肠¹⁵   芳   草   碧▲¹⁶

Heartbreaking, the fragrant grasses green.

[小令 short lyric song]

(Tr. Maija Bell Samei, *HTRCP*, p. 254)

字词释义 Vocabulary Notes

1. 谒 (謁) v. to visit. MdnC: 拜见(*bài jiàn*) to pay a formal visit.
2. 谒金门 (謁金門) "Audience at Golden Gate," title of a tune.
3. 韦庄(韋莊) (style 字, Duānjǐ 端己, 836–910), a famous *ci* poet in the late Tang. He and Wen Tingyun 温庭筠 are the leaders of the Huajian School (*huā jiān pài* 花间派). See Wen Tingyun's biographic note in P46 note 2.

4. 空 (*kōng*) adv. in vain, for nothing. MdnC: 徒劳 (*tú láo*). 🖙 和他争论是<u>徒劳</u>无益的 It is useless to argue with him.

5. 计 (計) n. strategy. See also P08 note 14.   6. 传 (傳 *chuán*) v. to spread. See also P52 note 6.

7. 嫦娥 Chang'e, originally known as Heng'e 姮娥, Chinese moon goddess. See also P73 note 1.

8. 寄 v. to send. See P08 note 9.   9. 书 (書) n. letter. MdnC: 书信 (*shū xìn*). See also P91 note 6.

10. 觅 (覓) v. to seek, search. MdnC: 找 (*zhǎo*). 🖙 他在<u>找</u>一本书 He is searching for a book.

11. 觉 (覺 *jué*) v. to wake up. MdnC: 睡醒 (*shuì xǐng*). See also P96 note 8. See P28 note 4 for a different meaning of the word.

12. 把 v. to hold. See also P12 note 12.   13. 伊 pron. a third person pronoun. MdnC: 他 (*tā*).

14. 书迹 (書跡) n. a specimen of a person's handwriting.   15. 断肠 (腸) adj. heartbroken.

16. 碧 adj. bluish green, blue. See also P40 note 10.

现代文翻译 Modern Chinese Translation

<u>徒劳</u>[4]地思念着他，没有办法告诉他(我的思念)。天上的嫦娥不认识我，想给他寄封<u>书信</u>[9]，可要到哪里去<u>找</u>[10]他呢？

刚刚<u>睡醒</u>，[11]感觉全身无力，心中已经悲苦，怎能再拿起他的书信来看？窗外，院子里满是落花，春天是这样的寂寞。草地芳香碧绿，而我的心中却只有悲伤。

评论与提问 Comment and Question

This poem is a soliloquy by a young woman yearning for her absent lover. Depictions of falling blossoms and the green grass of springtime abound in Chinese poetry. These two prominent images function as "objective correlates" (T. S. Eliot's word) to a broad range of emotions. In P27 and P28, for instance, falling blossoms evoke different kinds of emotions. Does the depiction of falling blossoms bring forth yet a different kind of emotional response here? 🖙 *HTRCP*, pp. 254–255 for a discussion of this poem.

P66

wū yè tí
乌 夜 啼[1]

[nán táng] lǐ yù
[南唐] 李 煜[2]

To the Tune "Crows Call at Night"

[Southern Tang] Li Yu

wú yán dú shàng xī lóu
无 言 独 上 西 楼 △[a]

Without a word, alone I climb the West Pavilion.

yuè rú gōu
月 如 钩 △[a] [3]

The moon is like a hook.

jì mò wú tóng shēn yuàn suǒ shēn qiū
寂 寞 梧 桐[4] 深 院 锁[5] 深 秋 △[a]

In the lonely inner garden of *wutong* trees is locked late autumn.

jiǎn	*bú*	*duàn*						
剪⁶	不	断▲ᵇ						

Cut, it doesn't break,

lǐ	*huán*	*luàn*
理⁷	还	乱▲ᵇ

Tidied, a mess again—

shì	*lí*	*chóu*
是	离	愁Δᵃ

This separation grief.

bié	*shì*	*yì*	*bān*	*zī*	*wèi*	*zài*	*xīn*	*tóu*
别	是	一	般⁸	滋	味⁹	在	心	头Δᵃ

It's altogether a different kind of flavor in the heart.

[小令 short lyric song]

(Tr. Maija Bell Samei, *HTRCP*, pp. 246–247)

字词释义 Vocabulary Notes

1. 乌 (烏) 夜啼 "Crows Call at Night," title of a tune. This poem is also entitled "Pleasure at Meeting" ("Xiāng jiàn huān" 相见欢) in some collections.

2. 李煜 (style 字，Chóngguāng 重光, 937–978), a great *ci* poet and the last emperor of the Southern Tang, one of the small kingdoms that arose during the Five Dynasties period (906–960). He is known for broadening the thematic range of *ci* poetry to include themes such as the downfall of the country and the transience of life.

3. 钩 (鈎) n. hook.   4. 梧桐 n. Chinese parasol tree. See also P63 note 14.

5. 锁 (鎖) v. to lock up. 📖 他锁门了 He locked the door. See also P82 note 4, P87 note 12, and P88 note 9. See P62 note 9 for a different meaning of the word.

6. 剪 v. to cut (with scissors). See also P59 note 6.

7. 理 v. to put in order, tidy up. 📖 他要把事情理出个头绪 He wants to get things into shape.

8. 一般 a sort, a kind.   9. 滋味 n. taste, flavor.

10. 笼罩 (*lǒng zhào*) v. to envelop, shroud.

现代文翻译 Modern Chinese Translation

　　我独自走上西楼，抬头望，月亮象一个弯钩挂在天边，低下头，院子里寂寞的梧桐树被秋意深深地笼罩¹⁰着。

　　心中的离愁，想剪，却剪不断，想理⁷清楚，却还是乱的，这真是不一样的滋味啊！

评论与提问 Comment and Question

Ci poetry has been called "long and short lines" (*cháng duǎn jù* 长短句) since its lines are often of uneven length. 👉 *HTRCP*, p. 247 for an analysis of the line configuration of this particular tune and *HTRCP*, pp. 245–246, 392–395 for a discussion of the generic features of *ci* poetry in general. After reading this discussion, can you compare this poem with a *shi* poem on a similar theme and identify the essential differences between the two in rhythm, syntax, and structure?

P67

<table>
<tr><td>dié</td><td>liàn</td><td>huā</td></tr>
<tr><td>蝶</td><td>恋</td><td>花¹</td></tr>
</table>

To the Tune "Butterflies Lingering Over Flowers"

[běi sòng] ōu yáng xiū

[北宋] 欧阳修²

[Nothern Song Dyn.] Ouyang Xiu

tíng	yuàn	shēn	shēn	shēn	jǐ	xǔ
庭	院	深	深	深	几	许▲³

Deep in the walled garden, deep—how deep?

yáng	liǔ	duī	yān
杨	柳⁴	堆⁵	烟

Mist stacks on willows,

lián	mù	wú	chóng	shù
帘	幕⁶	无	重⁷	数▲

Uncountable layers of screens and blinds.

yù	lè	diāo	ān	yóu	yě	chù
玉	勒⁸	雕⁹	鞍¹⁰	游	冶¹¹	处▲

The jade bridle and ornate saddle are in the brothel district—

lóu	gāo	bú	jiàn	zhāng	tái	lù
楼	高	不	见	章	台¹²	路▲

Though the tower is tall, one can't see Zhangtai Road.

yǔ	hèng	fēng	kuáng	sān	yuè	mù
雨	横¹³	风	狂	三	月	暮▲¹⁴

A driving rain, a mad wind, late in the third month.

mén	yǎn	huáng	hūn
门	掩¹⁵	黄	昏

A door keeps out the twilight,

wú	jì	liú	chūn	zhù
无	计	留	春	住▲

But there's no way to keep spring from going.

lèi	yǎn	wèn	huā	huā	bù	yǔ
泪	眼	问	花	花	不	语▲

With tear-filled eyes I ask the blossoms, but the blossoms do not answer—

luàn	hóng	fēi	rù	qiū	qiān	qù
乱¹⁶	红¹⁷	飞	入	秋	千¹⁹	去▲

In a swirl of red they fly into the swings.

(Tr. Maija Bell Samei, *HTRCP*, p. 257)

[小令 short lyric song]

字词释义 Vocabulary Notes

1. 蝶恋 (戀) 花 "Butterflies Lingering Over Flowers," title of a tune. This poem is also attributed to Feng Yansi 冯延巳 (903−960), under the tune title "Magpie Perching on a Branch" ("Què tà zhī" 鹊踏枝) in some collections.

2. 欧阳修 (歐陽脩) (style 字, Yǒngshū 永叔; literary name 号, Liùyī jūshì 六一居士, 1007–1072), one of the dominant figures of Northern Song literature and politics. He is known as a master of writing in a variety of genres and is one of the "Eight Masters of the Tang and Song Prose" (*Táng Sòng bādàjiā* 唐宋八大家). He is also famous for having compiled *The New History of the Tang Dynasty* (*Xīn táng shū* 新唐书).

3. 许 (許) somewhat, a little. See also P17 note 15 for a different meaning of the word.

4. 杨 (楊) 柳 n. poplar and willow. See also P39 note 8.

5. 堆 v. to pile up, stack. 👉桌上堆满了书 The desk is piled with books.

6. 帘幕 (簾幕) n. hanging curtains.

7. 重 (*chóng*) n. layers. See P17 note 6. 无重数 many layers.

8. 勒 v. to tighten; used here as a noun meaning "bridle."

9. 雕 v. to carve, engrave. See also P97 note 8.

10. 鞍 n. saddle. 玉勒雕鞍 refers to the husband who is seeking pleasure outside.

11. 冶 v. to. smelt (metal). 游冶 means "to go out to seek pleasure" (*xún huān zuò lè* 寻欢作乐).

12. 章台 (臺) a street name in Han Dynasty Chang'an, where many brothels were located. Later on, it became a euphemism for the brothel district. (Samei; *HTRCP*, p. 260)

13. 横 (*hèng*) adj. harsh and unreasonable, perverse. Here it means that the rain is fierce (*měng liè* 猛烈).

14. 暮 adj. late. MdnC: 末 (*mò*). See P18 note 13 for a different meaning of the word.

15. 掩 v. to cover, close. MdnC: 关 (*guān*). 👉请关门 Please close the door.

16. 乱 adj. in a mess, in disorder. MdnC: 凌乱 (*líng luàn*). 👉屋内很凌乱 The room is a mess. See also P88 note 12.

17. 红 (紅) adj. red. Here it refers to flowers.

18. 秋千 n. swing.

现代文翻译 Modern Chinese Translation

庭院深深，有多深呢？园中的杨柳被烟雾笼罩着，院中的帘幕非常多。 (丈夫)骑着马去寻欢作乐[11]的地方，即使登上院中的高楼，也还是看不到！

雨下得很猛烈，[13]伴着狂风。这是三月末[14]了。把黄昏关[15]在门内，却无法留住春天。眼中含着泪水，去问春花，春花却不回答，凌乱[16]的落花飞到秋千[18]那里去了。

评论与提问 Comment and Question

This poem begins with a powerful question "Deep in the walled garden, deep—how deep?" The repetition of the character "deep" three times also reveals how deep a sigh comes from the lady's heart. The piling up of images that block her view and a reference to her pleasure-seeking husband (玉勒雕鞍) make clear the reason for the lady's deep sigh: she is cloistered in a lonesome house while her husband is frolicking in the brothels. How is the lady's despondence skillfully projected onto the world of nature in the second stanza? 👉*HTRCP*, p. 258 for a discussion of this poem.

P68

wǔ	líng	chūn
武	陵[1]	春[2]

[sòng] lǐ qīng zhào

[宋] 李 清 照[3]

Spring at Wuling

[Song Dyn.] Li Qingzhao

fēng	zhù	chén	xiāng	huā	yǐ	jìn
风	住[4]	尘[5]	香	花	已	尽[6]

The wind stopped, the flowers have all gone, and the fragrance remains in the earth.

rì	wǎn	juàn	shū	tóu
日	晚	倦[7]	梳	头△

It is late, but I still weary of combing my hair.

wù	shì	rén	fēi	shì	shì	xiū
物	是	人	非	事	事	休△[8]

Things are still the same, but he is no more; everything goes to the end.

yù	yǔ	lèi	xiān	liú
欲	语	泪	先	流△

Before I speak, tears run down.

wén	shuō	shuāng	xī	chūn	shàng	hǎo
闻	说	双	溪[9]	春	尚	好

I heard Twin Brooks is still beautiful.

yě	nǐ	fàn	qīng	zhōu
也	拟[10]	泛[11]	轻	舟△

I also plan to go boating.

zhǐ	kǒng	shuāng	xī	zé	měng	zhōu
只	恐[12]	双	溪	舴	艋[13]	舟△

I only fear that grasshopper-like boat at Twin Brooks

zài	bú	dòng	xǔ	duō	chóu
载[14]	不	动	许	多	愁△

is not able to carry so much grief.

[小令 short lyric song]

(Tr. Jie Cui)

字词释义 Vocabulary Notes

1. 武陵　Wuling, a place name from "The Peach Blossom Spring" ("Táo huā yuán jì"桃花源记) written by the great Jin poet Tao Qian 陶潜. It is in present-day Changde 常德, Hunan Province. See Tao Qian's biographic note in P10 note 1.

2. 武陵春　"Spring at Wuling," title of a tune. This poem was written in 1135, six years after Li Qingzhao's husband died. At that time, she lived in Jinhua 金华, Zhejiang province as a temporary refuge from the Jurchen invasion.

3. See the biographic note in P08 note 2.　　4. 住　v. to stop. See also P35 note 8.

5. 尘　n. dust, dirt. See also P39 note 6.　　6. 尽 (盡)　v. to exhaust. See also P03 note 11.

7. 倦　adj. weary, tired. See also P94 note 1. Cf. 懒 in P64 note 10.

8. 休　v. to stop, cease. See also P07 note 13.

9. 双 (雙) 溪　Twin Brooks, name of a river in Jinhua, Zhejiang province.

10. 拟 (擬)　v. to intend, plan. MdnC: 计划 (*jì huà*). 👉他计划下个月去北京 He plans to go to Beijing next month.

11. 泛　v. to float [formal]. 👉泛舟西湖 to go boating on the West Lake. See P78 note 4 for a different meaning of the word.

12. 恐　v. to dread, worry. See also P42 note 8.

13. 舴艋　n. small boat, whose shape looks like a grasshopper (*zhà měng* 蚱蜢).

14. 载 (載 *zài*)　v. to carry, hold. 👉卡车上载满了沙子 The truck was fully loaded with sand. See also P96 note 4. See P18 note 5 for a different meaning of the word.

现代文翻译 Modern Chinese Translation

　　风停⁴了，花都谢了，尘土中满是花香。天晚了，我却懒得去梳头。 景物还是原来的景物，人却已不在，一切都不同了。 想要开口，泪却先流下来。

　　听说双溪的春色还好，也计划¹⁰泛¹¹舟前往。只是担心蚱蜢¹³一样的小船，载¹⁴不动我许多的哀愁。

评论与提问 Comment and Question

This lyric is about the poetess' deep sorrow over the loss of her beloved, even though she does not explicitly mention her loss. The bereft poetess chooses to convey her grief indirectly by depicting how she was torn between a desire to appreciate the spring splendor and a fear of being overwhelmed by sorrow when seeing scenes of past happiness.

　　In this lyric, the last two lines describe how deep the sorrow inside is in a rather refreshing way. Sorrow cannot be measured, but here it has weight. Even a boat cannot manage to carry it. It is thus clear that the sorrow inside is too heavy to bear! Compare these two lines with the last line in Li Yu's "To the Tune 'Beautiful Lady Yu'" (P97). Describe the similarities and differences between the ways the two poets describe sorrow.

练习　EXERCISES

一 填空 Fill in blanks

A. 诗词填字: 寞 觉 锁 流 章 断 般 识 忆 恐 掩 把 滋 理 觅 寂 传 冶 味 载 休 剪 计

1. 玉勒雕鞍游＿＿处，楼高不见＿＿台路。　　2. ＿＿ ＿＿梧桐深院＿＿深秋。

3. 新睡＿＿来无力，不忍＿＿伊书迹。　　　　4. ＿＿ 不＿＿，＿＿还乱。

5. 物是人非事事＿＿，欲语泪先＿＿。　　　　6. 门＿＿黄昏，无＿＿留春住。

7. 只＿＿双溪舴艋舟，＿＿不动许多愁。　　　8. 别是一＿＿ ＿＿ ＿＿在心头。

9. 天上嫦娥应不＿＿，寄书何处＿＿。　　　　10. 空相＿＿，无＿＿ 得＿＿消息。

B. 现代文填词: 徒劳 堆 凌乱 锁 理 计划 载

1. 他＿＿ ＿＿下个月去上海?　　　　2. 屋内很＿＿ ＿＿。

3. 请把门＿＿上。　　　　　　　　　　　4. 他要把事情＿＿出个头绪来。

5. 桌子上＿＿满了书。　　　　　　　　　6. 卡车满＿＿着沙子回来了。

7. 跟他们争论是＿＿＿＿无益的。

二 形近字辨析 Distinguish easily confused characters

1. 寄书何处＿＿　　　　a. 觉　b. 觅　c. 览　　2. 月如＿＿　　　a. 购　b. 钩　c. 构

3. 雨横风狂三月 ＿＿　a. 幕　b. 墓　c. 暮　　4. 也＿＿泛轻舟　a. 拟　b. 似　c. 以

5. 玉勒雕鞍游＿＿处　a. 冶　b. 治　c. 台　　6. 日晚＿＿梳头　a. 卷　b. 圈　c. 倦

7. 物是人非事事＿＿　a. 体　b. 休　c. 沐　　8. 杨柳＿＿烟　　a. 谁　b. 推　c. 堆

三 连句 Match the first part with the second

1. 杨柳堆烟( )　　2. 满院乱花春寂寂( )　　3. 物是人非事事休( )　　4. 天上嫦娥人不识( )

5. 门掩黄昏( )　　6. 风住尘香花已尽( )　　7. 泪眼问花花不语( )　　8. 新睡觉来无力( )

9. 只恐双溪舴艋舟( )　　10. 无言独上西楼( )

a. 不忍把伊书迹　　b. 月如钩　　　　c. 日晚倦梳头　　d. 乱红飞过秋千去

e. 寄书何处觅　　　f. 无计留春住　　g. 断肠芳草碧　　h. 载不动许多愁

i. 欲语泪先流　　　k. 帘幕无重数

四 句读 Punctuate and translate the following excerpts from three or more poems

剪 不 断 理 还 乱 是 离 愁 别 是 一 般 滋 味 在 心 头 风 住 尘 香 花 已 尽 日 晚 倦 梳 头 满
院 乱 花 春 寂 寂 断 肠 芳 草 碧 雨 横 风 狂 三 月 暮 门 掩 黄 昏 无 计 留 春 住 泪 眼 问 花
花 不 语 乱 红 飞 过 秋 千 去

五 听写 Dictation

1. ＿＿ 是 ＿＿＿ ＿＿＿ ＿＿＿， ＿＿ ＿＿ 先 ＿＿。

2. ＿＿ 不＿＿， ＿＿＿ ＿＿＿， 是 ＿＿ ＿＿， 别是一 ＿＿ ＿＿ ＿＿在心＿＿。

3. 天上 ＿＿ ＿＿ ＿＿ ＿＿＿， ＿＿ ＿＿ ＿＿＿ ＿＿。

4. 满＿＿ ＿＿＿ 春 ＿＿ ＿＿， ＿＿＿＿ ＿＿＿。

5. ＿＿ ＿＿ 三 ＿＿ ＿＿， 门 ＿＿ ＿＿， 无＿＿ ＿＿ 春 ＿＿。

6. 只＿＿ ＿＿ ＿＿ ＿＿， ＿＿ 不 ＿＿＿ ＿＿。

7. ＿＿ ＿＿＿ ＿＿＿ 处， ＿＿ ＿＿ 不 ＿＿＿ 路。

15

宫 怨

Plaints of Palace Ladies

yù   jiē   yuàn
玉 阶¹ 怨²

[nán cháo]   xiè tiǎo
[南朝] 谢 脁³

Jade Stairs Resentment

[Southern Dyn.] Xie Tiao

xī	*diàn*	*xià*	*zhū*	*lián*	
夕⁴	殿	下	珠	帘	In the evening hall, the bead curtain is lowered;
liú	*yíng*	*fēi*	*fù*	*xī*	
流	萤⁵	飞	复	息△⁶	Drifting glowworms fly, then rest.
cháng	*yè*	*féng*	*luó*	*yī*	
长	夜	缝⁷	罗	衣	Through the long night, sewing a gossamer dress:
sī	*jūn*	*cǐ*	*hé*	*jí*	
思	君	此	何	极△⁸	This longing for you—when will it ever cease?

[五言古绝 pentasyllabic ancient quatrain]

(Tr. Xiaofei Tian, *HTRCP,* p. 143)

字词释义 Vocabulary Notes

1. 阶 (階) n. stairs. See also P63 note 17. 玉阶 refers to stairs in the palace.
2. 玉阶 (階) 怨 "Jade Stairs Resentment," title of a *yuefu* song, classified under "Lyrics for Accompanied Songs" (*xiànghè gēcí* 相和歌辞) in Guo Maoqian's 郭茂倩 (1041−1099) *Collection of Yuefu Poetry* (*Yuèfǔ shījí* 乐府诗集).
3. See the biographic note in P14 note 2.   4. 夕 n. evening. MdnC: 傍晚 (*bàng wǎn*).
5. 萤 (螢) n. firefly. MdnC: 萤火虫 (*yíng huǒ chóng*). 流萤 flying fireflies.
6. 息 v. to stop, rest. MdnC: 停 (*tíng*).   7. 缝 (縫) v. to stitch, sew. See also P42 note 7.
8. 极 (極) n. the utmost, extreme. 📧 为了达到目的，他真是无所不用其极 He would go to any extreme in order to achieve his goal.

现代文翻译 Modern Chinese Translation

　　傍晚⁴宫殿里的珠帘已经放下了，萤火虫⁵飞来飞去，直到夜深了才停⁶下来。漫漫长夜，她(无心入睡)缝着丝衣，心中的思念哪有尽头啊！

评论与提问 Comment and Question

This poem is a quatrain (*juéjù* 绝句) bearing a *yuefu* title. It describes a palace lady who yearned for her beloved. The poet avoids direct expression of the lady's resentment, but every image implies her deep loneliness. Can you explain how each image imparts a sense of sorrow? 👈 *HTRCP*, p. 144 for a detailed analysis of the images in this poem and pp. 143–144 for a discussion of the development of the quatrain in the Southern Dynasties.

P70

yù   jiē   yuàn

玉 阶¹ 怨

[*táng*] *lǐ bái*

[唐] 李 白²

Lament of the Jade Stairs

[Tang Dyn.] Li Bai

On jade stairs, the rising white dew

Through the long night pierces silken hose

Retreating inside, she lowers crystal shades

And stares at the glimmering autumn moon

(Tr. Charles Egan, *HTRCP*, p. 212)

[五言古绝 pentasyllabic ancient quatrain]

字词释义 Vocabulary Notes

1. 玉阶 (階) 怨 See P69 note 2.   2. See the biographic note in P19 note 3.
3. 侵 v. to invade, infiltrate. See also P94 note 3. Here it means "to wet" (*jìn shī* 浸湿).
4. 袜 n. socks, hose.
5. 却 (卻) conj. but, yet. See also P08 note 17.   6. 水晶 n. crystal.
7. 玲珑 (瓏) adj. (of things) ingeniously and delicately wrought, exquisite. 👈这座玉石雕刻真
   是玲珑剔透 This jade carving is really exquisitely wrought.

现代文翻译 Modern Chinese Translation

　　玉石台阶上生了露水。夜里站久了，露水浸湿³了丝袜。回到房间里，放下水晶帘，(却不想去睡觉，隔着帘子) 望着玲珑⁷的秋月。

评论与提问 Comment and Question

Xie Tiao is one of the Six Dynasties poets whom Li Bai admired most. His poems have some direct influence on Li Bai's writing, as is the case with this poem. 👉 *HTRCP*, p. 212 for a comment on this influence. Compare P69 and P70 and describe the similarity of these two poems in theme, image, and language. Which of these two poems is more implicit in expressing a palace lady's resentment?

P71

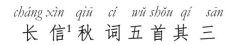

cháng xìn qiū cí wǔ shǒu qí sān
长 信¹ 秋 词 五 首 其 三

[táng] wáng chāng líng
[唐] 王 昌 龄²

Five Songs of the Autumn of the Abiding Faith Hall, No. 3

[Tang Dyn.] Wang Changling

fēng	*zhǒu*	*píng*	*míng*	*jīn*	*diàn*	*kāi*
奉³	帚⁴	平	明⁵	金	殿	开△

Clutching a broom at daybreak, she opens the golden hall

qiě	*jiāng*	*tuán*	*shàn*	*zàn*	*péi*	*huí*
且	将	团	扇⁶	暂⁷	裴	回△⁸

Then, clasping her round moon fan, she wanders for a while

yù	*yán*	*bù*	*jí*	*hán*	*yā*	*sè*
玉	颜⁹	不	及	寒	鸦¹⁰	色

Her jade face can't compare with the brightness of cold crows

yóu	*dài*	*zhāo*	*yáng*	*rì*	*yǐng*	*lái*
犹¹¹	带	昭	阳¹²	日	影	来△

Which still carry reflections of the sun at Zhaoyang Palace

[七言律绝 heptasyllabic regulated quatrain, tonal pattern IIa, see *HTRCP*, p. 171]

(Tr. Charles Egan, *HTRCP*, p. 214)

字词释义 Vocabulary Notes

1. 长 (長) 信 or 长信宫 the Abiding Faith Hall, built in the Han dynasty.
2. See the biographic note in P49 note 2.
3. 奉　v. to give or present with respect. 👉他把新书双手奉上 He respectfully presented the new books with both hands.
4. 帚　n. broom. MdnC: 扫把 (*sào bǎ*).　　　　5. 平明　n. dawn.
6. 团 (團) 扇　n. a round fan with a handle. It was often used in the palace, and thus was also called a "palace fan" (*gōng shàn* 宫扇).
7. 暂 (暫)　adv. for the time being, for the moment. MdnC: 暂且 (*zàn qiě*). 👉讨论暂且告一段落 The discussion ended for the time being.
8. 裴回　or 徘徊 (*pái huái*)　v. to hang around, pace up and down. See also P37 note 6.

9. 颜 (顔) n. face, countenance. MdnC: 容颜 (*róng yán*) [formal]. ☞她美丽的容颜渐渐老去
   Her beautiful face ages gradually. See also P97 note 12.
10. 寒鸦 (鴉) n. crows in the cold weather of late fall . See also P33 note 6.
11. 犹 (猶) adv. still. See also P44 note 10.
12. 昭阳 (陽) or 昭阳殿 the Palace of Luminous Sunshine, where the imperial concubines lived in
    the Han Dynasty.

现代文翻译 Modern Chinese Translation

天刚亮，金殿门一开，(我)就拿着扫把⁴开始打扫。(做完之后) 暂且⁸拿着团扇走来走去。(我)美丽的容颜¹⁰还比不上乌鸦的颜色，它刚从昭阳殿飞过，还带着太阳的光彩啊！

评论与提问 Comment and Question

This poem is the third of a series of five poems that depict the cloistered life of Lady Ban of the Han Dynasty in the Abiding Faith Hall. ☞ *HTRCP*, pp. 214−215. A crow is generally regarded as an ugly, inauspicious bird, but its color is considered here better-looking than the complexion of the palace lady. Through this comparison, what has the poet told us about her physical and emotional condition?

P72

qiū xī
秋 夕

Autumn Evening

[*táng*] *dù mù*
[唐] 杜 牧¹

[Tang Dyn.] Du Mu

hóng	*zhú*	*qiū*	*guāng*	*lěng*	*huà*	*píng*
红	烛	秋	光	冷	画	屏△²

Red candles, autumnal light
    and a cold painted screen,

qīng	*luó*	*xiǎo*	*shàn*	*pū*	*liú*	*yíng*
轻³	罗	小	扇	扑⁴	流	萤△

A light, silky little fan
    swings to swat a firefly.

tiān	*jiē*	*yè*	*sè*	*liáng*	*rú*	*shuǐ*
天	阶⁵	夜	色	凉	如	水

Up the heavenly stairs, the evening skies
    are as cool as water,

zuò	*kàn*	*qiān*	*niú*	*zhī*	*nǚ*	*xīng*
坐	看	牵	牛⁶	织	女⁷	星△

She sits there gazing at the Cowboy
    and the Weaving Girl.

[七言律绝 heptasyllabic regulated quatrain, tonal pattern IIa, see *HTRCP*, p. 171]

(Tr. Zong-qi Cai)

字词释义 Vocabulary Notes

1. See the biographic note in P22 note 2.　　2. 屏　n. screen.

3. 轻 (輕)　adj. light. MdnC: 轻巧 (qīng qiǎo) light and handy. 👉这款手机很轻巧 This type of cell phone is pretty handy.

4. 扑 (撲)　v. to throw oneself on. Here it means "to swat" (pū dǎ 扑打).

5. 天阶 (階)　n. stairs in heaven. It refers to the heavenly palace.

6. 牵牛　牵牛星, or 牛郎星, the Star of the Cowherd, the Second Star of the Drum at the River, or more literally, Riverdrum II. 牛郎(Niú láng) and 织女(Zhī nǚ) are names from ancient Chinese legend. 牛郎 , a farmer on the earth, and 织女 granddaughter of the Queen Mother of the West (Xīwángmǔ西王母), met on the earth and became a loving couple. However, their love was forbidden by heaven's ruler, and thus they were forced to be separate later and live on opposite sides of the Milky Way. The only time they were permitted to meet each year was on the seventh day of the seventh month of the Chinese Lunar Calendar (qī xī 七夕). On that day, magpies made a bridge (què qiáo 鹊桥) so that the separated couple could be together again for a brief time.

7. 织 (織) 女星　Star of the Weaving Girl, the star .

现代文翻译 Modern Chinese Translation

　　秋天的夜晚，红色的烛光照着冰冷的画屏，我拿着轻巧³的丝质小扇，扑打⁴着飞来飞去的萤火虫。天上的夜色冰凉得像水一样，我坐在这里，看着天上的牛郎织女星。

评论与提问 Comment and Question

All but one poems of this unit feature a motif of insomnia. This motif entails a familiar series of activities for a palace lady: sitting in a courtyard, watching the night sky, catching fireflies, feeling the chill of an autumn night, despondently retiring into her bedchamber, and so on. Each poet seeks to depict these activities in a way that best reveals the inner world of a palace lady—her loneliness, her ennui, and her despair over an inexorable wasting of her beauty and life. Compare this poem with Xie Tiao's and Li Bai's (P69, P70) and describe how differently Du Mu handles the insomnia motif from his predecessors. Which of these poems is most aesthetically appealing to you?

P73

cháng　é
嫦　娥¹　　　　　　　　　　　　　　Chang'e

[táng] lǐ shāng yǐn
[唐] 李 商 隐²　　　　　　　　　　　[Tang Dyn.] Li Shangyin

yún　mǔ　píng　fēng　zhú　yǐng　shēn
云　母³　屏　风⁴　烛　影　深△　　　Behind the mica screen, candles cast deep shadows

cháng	hé⁵	jiàn	luò	xiǎo⁶	xīng	chén
长	河⁵	渐	落	晓⁶	星	沉△⁷

The Great River slowly sinks, and dawn stars are drowned

cháng	é	yīng	huǐ⁸	tōu	líng	yào⁹
嫦	娥	应	悔⁸	偷	灵	药⁹

Chang-e must regret stealing the elixir—

bì	hǎi	qīng	tiān	yè	yè	xīn
碧	海	青	天	夜	夜	心△

Over blue sea, in dark sky, thinking night after night

(Tr. Charles Egan, *HTRCP,* p. 219)

[七言律绝 heptasyllabic regulated quatrain, tonal pattern IIa, see *HTRCP*, p. 171]

字词释义 Vocabulary Notes

1. 嫦娥 see P65 note 7.
2. See the biographic note in P03 note 2.
3. 云 (雲) 母 n. mica.
4. 屏风 (風) n. screen.
5. 长 (長) 河 long river, used here to indicate the Milky Way.
6. 晓 (曉) n. dawn. See also P03 note 15.
7. 沉 v. to sink. 👉船沉了 The boat has sunk.
8. 悔 v. to regret. MdnC: 后悔 (*hòu huǐ*). 👉他后悔今天没穿件厚外套 He regretted not having worn a thick coat.
9. 灵药 (靈藥) n. elixir or "immortal pill." The story from *The Work of Master Huainan* (*Huái nán zǐ* 淮南子) tells that Houyi 后羿, Chang'e's husband, got an immortal pill from the Queen Mother of the West. Each person only needs half of the pill to become immortal. Chang'e did not know the instruction of immortal pills. She stole it from Houyi and swallowed the entire pill. Then she started to float into the sky due to the overdose. At last she landed on the moon and had to live there lonely from then on.

现代文翻译 Modern Chinese Translation

云母屏风上有蜡烛深深的影子，银河渐渐落下了，拂晓的星星也沉⁷下去了。嫦娥应该后悔⁸当初偷了不死的灵药，现在只好每天每夜孤独地面对碧蓝的大海和青天。

评论与提问 Comment and Question

This poem is entitled "Chang'e," but is actually a subtle expression of the poet's own loneliness. 👉 *HTRCP,* p. 219 for an annotation on the Chang'e story.

练习 EXERCISES

一 填空 Fill in blanks

A. 诗词填字: 深 殿 扑 息 沉 奉 阶 冷 颜 缝 侵 将 渐 轻 极 却 犹 暂 望 影

1.玉＿＿生白露，夜久＿＿罗袜。 2.云母屏风烛影＿＿，长河＿＿落晓星＿＿。

3. ____ 下水晶帘，玲珑 ____ 秋月。　4. ____ 帚平明金殿开，且 ____ 团扇 ____ 裴回。
5. 夕 ____ 下珠帘，流萤飞复 ____ 。　6. 玉 ____ 不及寒鸦色，____ 带昭阳日 ____ 来。
7. 长夜 ____ 罗衣，思君此何 ____ 。　8. 红烛秋光 ____ 画屏，____ 罗小扇 ____ 流萤。

B. 现代文填词: 玲珑 极 后悔 沉 容颜 暂且 奉 轻巧
1. 她美丽的 ____ ____ 渐渐老去。　　2. 讨论 ____ ____ 告一段落。
3. 船 ____ 了。　　　　　　　　4. 我很 ____ ____ 没穿件厚外套。
5. 我双手 ____ 上一杯茶。　　　　6. 这款手机很 ____ ____ 。
7. 这座玉石雕刻真是 ____ ____ 剔透。　8. 为了达到目的，他真是无所不用其 ____ 。

二 形近字辨析 Distinguish easily confused characters

1. 夜久 ____ 罗袜　　a. 侵　b. 浸　c. 寝　2. 长河 ____ 落晓星沉　a. 浙　b. 渐　c. 斩
3. 嫦娥应悔 ____ 灵药　a. 愉　b. 输　c. 偷　4. 红烛秋光 ____ 画屏　a. 玲　b. 冷　c. 拎
5. ____ 帚平明金殿开　a. 春　b. 奉　c. 捧　6. 轻罗小扇 ____ 流萤　a. 扑　b. 朴　c. 仆

三 连句 Match the first part with the second

1. 长夜缝罗衣( )　2. 玉颜不及寒鸦色( )　3. 云母屏风烛影深( )　4. 天阶夜色凉如水( )
5. 却下水晶帘( )　6. 奉帚平明金殿开( )　7. 嫦娥应悔偷灵药( )　8. 夕殿下珠帘( )

a. 且将团扇暂裴回　b. 玲珑望秋月　　c. 流萤飞复息　d. 碧海青天夜夜心
e. 坐看牛郎织女星　f. 犹带昭阳日影来　g. 思君此何极　h. 长河渐落晓星沉

四 句读 Punctuate and translate the following excerpts from three or more poems

玉阶生白露夜久侵罗袜长夜缝罗衣思君此何极却下水晶帘玲珑望秋月红烛秋光冷画屏轻罗小扇扑流萤玉颜不及寒鸦色犹带昭阳日影来嫦娥应悔偷灵药碧海青天夜夜心

五 听写 Dictation

1. 云____ ____ ____ ____ ，长____ ____ ____ ____ ____ 。
2. ____ ____ 平____ ____ ____ ____ ，且 ____ ____ ____ ____ ____ ____ 。
3. 长 ____ ____ ____ ____ ，____ ____ ____ ____ 何 ____ 。
4. ____ ____ ____ ____ 色，____ ____ ____ ____ 日 ____ ____ 。
5. ____ 下 ____ ____ ____ ，____ ____ ____ ____ 月。
6. 红____ ____ ____ ____ ____ ，____ ____ 小 ____ ____ ____ 。

16

咏 物

Depiction of Things: Sensuous, Allegorical, and Personified

P74

yǒng chí shàng lí huā shī
咏 池 上 梨 花 诗
[*nán cháo*] *wáng róng*
[南 朝] 王 融[1]

In Praise of Pear Blossoms on the Pond

[Southern Dyn.] Wang Rong

fān	*jiē*	*mò*	*xì*	*cǎo*
翻[2]	阶	没[3]	细	草

On ruined steps they cover the fine grass

jí	*shuǐ*	*jiàn*	*shū*	*píng*
集[4]	水	间[5]	疏[6]	萍△[7]

In pooled water they scatter among the duckweed

fāng	*chūn*	*zhào*	*liú*	*xuě*
芳	春	照	流	雪

Fragrant spring shines on flowing snow

shēn	*xī*	*yìng*	*fán*	*xīng*
深	夕	映[9]	繁	星△

Deep night reflects myriad stars

[五言古绝 pentasyllabic ancient quatrain]

(Tr. Charles Egan, *HTRCP*, p. 202)

字词释义 Vocabulary Notes

1. 王融 (style 字, Lètiān 元长，468–494), a famous poet in the Southern Qi. He is one of the "Eight Friends of the Prince of Jingling" (*Jìng líng bā yǒu* 竟陵八友).
2. 翻 v. to to turn over. 翻阶 means "ruined steps."
3. 没 (*mò*) v. to cover, submerge. MdnC: 埋没 (*mái mò*). 📖泥石流埋没了整个小镇 The mudslide submerged the whole town.
4. 集 v. to collect, gather. 集水 water accumulated in the pool.
5. 间 (間 *jiàn*) v. to separate. MdnC: 间隔 (*jiàn gé*). 📖房子之间间隔二十米 There is a space of twenty meters between each two houses.
6. 疏 adj. sparse, scattered. MdnC: 稀疏 (*xī shū*). 📖他的头发很稀疏 His hair is sparse. See also P76 note 7.
7. 萍 n. duckweed. See also P53 note 14.   8. 映 v. to reflect. See also P22 note 4.

现代文翻译 Modern Chinese Translation

　　梨花落在台阶上，埋没[3]了细小的青草，落入池水中，间隔[5]开了稀疏[6]的浮萍。在美好的春天里，梨花像流动的白雪一般美丽。在深夜中，映衬着天上的繁星。

评论与提问 Comment and Question

This poem is an ancient-style poem. The poet deliberately avoids using the grammatical function words (*xū zì* 虚字), but chooses content words (*shí zì* 实字). For instance, the third character of every line is a verb: *mò* 没, *jiàn* 间, *zhào* 照, *yìng* 映. How would you describe the aesthetic effect these verbs yield in the poem? ☞ *HTRCP*, pp. 202−203 about the use of content words in this and other Six Dynasties poems.

P75

jǐn   sè
锦 瑟²

[*táng*] *lǐ shāng yǐn*
[唐] 李 商 隐²

Brocade Zither

[Tang Dyn.] Li Shangyin

jǐn	*sè*	*wú*	*duān*	*wǔ*	*shí*	*xián*
锦	瑟	无	端³	五	十	弦△⁴

The brocade zither without reason has fifty strings;

yì	*xián*	*yí*	*zhù*	*sī*	*huá*	*nián*
一	弦	一	柱⁵	思	华⁶	年△

each string has its bridge; one longs for the flowering years.

zhuāng	*shēng*	*xiǎo*	*mèng*	*mí*	*hú*	*dié*
庄	生⁷	晓⁸	梦	迷⁹	蝴	蝶¹⁰

Master Zhuang, in dawn dream, is lost in a butterfly;

wàng	*dì*	*chūn*	*xīn*	*tuō*	*dù*	*juān*
望	帝¹¹	春	心	托¹²	杜	鹃△¹³

Emperor Wang's springtime heart is entrusted to the cuckoo.

cāng	*hǎi*	*yuè*	*míng*	*zhū*	*yǒu*	*lèi*
苍¹⁴	海	月	明¹⁵	珠	有	泪¹⁶

On the grey sea, the moon shines bright, and the pearl has tears;

lán	*tián*	*rì*	*nuǎn*	*yù*	*shēng*	*yān*
蓝	田¹⁷	日	暖	玉	生	烟△¹⁸

At Indigo Field, the sun is warm, and jade gives off smoke.

cǐ	*qíng*	*kě*	*dài*	*chéng*	*zhuī*	*yì*
此	情	可	待	成	追	忆¹⁹

This feeling, one can wait for it to become a recollection;

zhǐ	*shì*	*dāng*	*shí*	*yǐ*	*wǎng*	*rán*
只	是	当	时	已	惘	然△²⁰

only at the time it was already bewildering.

(Tr. Robert Ashmore, *HTRCP*, p. 195)

[七言律诗 heptasyllabic regulated verse, tonal pattern IIa, see *HTRCP*, p. 172]

字词释义 Vocabulary Notes

1. 瑟　n. See P01 note 25. 锦瑟, "brocade zither."　2. See the biographic note in P03 note 2.

3. 无 (無) 端　See P58 note 8.　4. 弦　n. the string of a musical instrument.

5. 柱　n. pillar, column. Here it refers to the bridge of a Chinese string instrument

6. 华 (華)　n. flowery, prosperous, flourishing. 华年, glorious time of youth. See P83 note 27 for a different meaning of the word.

7. 庄 (莊) 生　or 庄子 (given name 名, Zhōu 周, ca. 369–ca. 286 B.C.E.) a leading Daoist philosopher living in the State of the Song during the Warring States Period. He and Lao zi 老子 are the most influential Daoist philosophers in Chinese history. They are often mentioned together as "Lao-Zhuang" (Lǎo Zhuāng 老庄). His work *Zhuangzi* (*Zhuāng zǐ* 庄子 is famous for his profound philosophical thoughts, his marvelous imagination, and his beautiful prose style.

8. 晓 (曉)　n. dawn. See also P03 note 15.　9. 迷　v. to be lost. 👉他迷路了 He's lost his way.

10. "庄生"句　an story from "Talks on Equality of All Substances" ("Qí wù lùn" 齐物论) in *Zhuangzi*. In this story, "Zhuangzi dreamed he was a butterfly—so vividly that, on waking, he could not longer feel sure whether he was really Zhuangzi or a butterfly." (Ashmore; *HTRCP*, p. 196).

11. 望帝　Emperor Wang (Name, Dù Yǔ 杜宇) According to "Records of Shu" ("Shǔ zhì" 蜀志) in *The History of the State of Huayang* (*Huá yáng guó zhì* 华阳国志) by Chang Qu 常璩 in the Jin Dynasty, Du Yu came to the throne in Shu (present-day Sichuan province) at the end of the Warring States Period. He successfully controlled the water there. Later he retired from his throne and lived in West Mountain 西山. Unfortunately, Shu fell, and Du Yu died. His spirit became a cuckoo and cried with blood in the spring. The cuckoo has been called Du Yu since then.

12. 讬 (託)　v. to entrust. MdnC: 托付 (*tuō fù*). 👉我把这个孩子托付给他了 I have entrusted him with this child.

13. 杜鹃 (鵑)　n. cuckoo.　14. 苍 (蒼)　adj. blue, green. 苍海 means "sea."

15. 月明　an allusion to a legend that pearls wax and wane along with the moon.

16. 珠有泪 (淚)　an allusion to a story told in *A Comprehensive Accounts of Things* (*Bó wù zhì* 博物志) by Zhang Hua 张华 (232–300). The story goes that shark people (*jiāo rén* 鲛人), who lived outside the Southern Sea, weep pearl tears.

17. 蓝田　in the present-day Xi'an area, Shaanxi province. It is a place famous for its jade.

18. 玉生烟 (煙)　There are disagreements about what this line alludes to. Some scholars believe it alludes to the love story of Ziyu and Han Zhong told in *Seeking the Spirits* (*Sōu shén jì* 搜神记) written by Gan Bao 干宝 (?–336). The story goes that Princess Ziyu 紫玉 of the State of Wu in the Spring and Autumn Period fell in love with Han Zhong 韩重. Han went to ask Ziyu's father, King Fuchai 夫差 (r. 495–473 B.C.E.), for his permission to marry his daughter, but his request was rejected. After he left on an extended trip, Ziyu pined for Han so much that she soon died. When Han returned, he went to Ziyu's grave to tell her of his earnest grief. Ziyu appeared before him in spirit and gave him a pearl. When Ziyu's mother rushed forward to embrace her, she dissolved like smoke. Another text often cited as a possible point of reference is the comment by Dai Shulun 戴叔伦 (732–789)

that the scenes of poetry are like the mist that rises from the fine jade of Lantian in the warmth of the sun. (Ashmore; *HTRCP*, p. 197).

19. 追忆 (憶)   v. to recall, recollect [formal].

20. 惘然   adj. lost, frustrated, disappointed [formal]. 👆他感到惘然若失 He felt lost.

现代文翻译 Modern Chinese Translation

　　锦瑟啊， 为什么有五十根弦呢！ 每一弦每一柱弹出的音节都让我想起曾经的青春年华。 庄子清晨梦见自己化身成了蝴蝶，望帝将自己对故国的思念托付[12]给了杜鹃。当大海上月光明亮时，鲛人[16]的眼泪变为珍珠；当太阳光暖暖地照在蓝田时，美丽的玉石生出了朦胧的烟雾。 这过去的感情会成为美好的追忆，[19]只是当时却让人感到惘然[20]若失。

评论与提问 Comment and Question

This poem epitomizes Li Shangyin's poetic art. If his "Untitled" (P62) contains "local" ambiguities about the speaker's gender and her/his reasoning process, this poem features a "global" ambiguity about the poem's subject itself, though the title identifies an object of depiction (hence the poem's placement in this unit).

What is this poem about? Ever since the poem was written, this question has fascinated readers and inspired them to come up with new interpretations. The poem has been taken to be: 1) a reminiscence of a secret lover named or nicknamed "Brocade Zither," 2) a metaphorical depiction of a flute performance, 3) mourning for the poet's deceased wife, 4) a general reflection on love, 5) a self-pitying lament, 6) an account of the creative process, and 7) a lament over the decline of the Tang. Each of these seven well-known views finds something in the poem that supports it, but none has garnered enough evidence on literal and allusive levels to make it conclusive and close up the horizon for new interpretations.

This undecidability of the poem's subject is the result of Li's radical fragmentation of the *lüshi* structure. In this poem, we cannot perceive the customary topic+comment structure, let alone an orderly four-stage progression (*qǐchéng zhuǎnhé* 起承转合). While each couplet itself is clear and coherent, the relationship of the four couplets is absolutely not. It does not even suggest a coherent mental process. The poem amounts to nothing more than a clustering of four descriptive or reflective fragments.

In view of his fondness of ambiguities, there is reason to believe that Li intentionally breaks up the *lüshi* structure to entertain the reader with inexhaustible interpretive possibilities. Indeed, this play of indeterminacy is the poem's very source of aesthetic pleasure. The more the reader's interpretive expectation is frustrated, the more he is inspired to create a new meaning out of the poem's enigmatic, enchanting images and allusions. This is the reason why this incomprehensible poem has become one of the best-loved poems among Chinese literati. 👉 *HTRCP,* pp. 195–197, for a close reading of this poem.

P76

shān yuán xiǎo méi
山 园 小 梅

Small Plum Tree in a Garden in the Hills, No. 1

[bĕi sòng] lín bū
[北宋] 林逋¹

[Northern Song Dyn.] Lin Bu

zhòng	fāng	yáo	luò	dú	xuān	yán
众	芳²	摇	落	独	暄³	妍⁴

When all other flowers have fallen, it alone shows warmth and beauty

zhàn	jìn	fēng	qíng	xiàng	xiǎo	yuán
占⁵	尽	风	情⁶	向	小	园△

Taking charge of all romantic feeling in the small garden.

shū	yǐng	héng	xié	shuǐ	qīng	qiǎn
疏⁷	影	横	斜	水	清	浅

Spare shadows slant across waters that are clear and shallow,

àn	xiāng	fú	dòng	yuè	huáng	hūn
暗	香	浮	动⁸	月	黄	昏△⁹

Hidden fragrance hangs and drifts under a moon hazy and dim.

shuāng	qín	yù	xià	xiān	tōu	yǎn
霜¹⁰	禽¹¹	欲	下	先	偷	眼¹²

The frosty bird wants to alight but steals a glance at it first,

fĕn	dié	rú	zhī	hé	duàn	hún
粉	蝶	如	知	合¹³	断	魂△¹⁴

If powder-dabbed butterflies knew of it, their hearts would break.

xìng	yǒu	wēi	yín	kě	xiāng	xiá
幸	有	微¹⁵	吟¹⁶	可	相	狎¹⁷

Luckily, chanting poetic lines softly I'm able to befriend it,

bù	xū	tán	bǎn	gòng	jīn	zūn
不	须	檀	板¹⁸	共	金	樽△¹⁹

No need for the singing girl's clappers or a golden goblet of wine.

(Tr. Ronald Egan, *HTRCP,* p. 309)

[七言律诗 heptasyllabic regulated verse, tonal pattern I, see *HTRCP*, p. 171]

字词释义 Vocabulary Notes

1. 林逋   (style 字, Jūnfù 君复，967–1028), a reclusive poet and artist in the Northern Song. He is famous for his love of plum and crane. He remained unmarried throughout his life, and called "plum as his wife and crane as his children" (*qī méi hè zǐ* 妻梅鹤子). This poem has been long regarded as a masterpiece on the plum blossom.

2. 芳   adj. fragrant, used here as a noun, meaning "flowers."

3. 暄   adj. warm. MdnC: 温暖 (*wēn nuǎn*).   4. 妍   adj. beautiful. MdnC: 美丽 (*měi lì*).

5. 占   v. to occupy. ☞这个项目占用了他不少时间 This project took up much of his time.

6. 风(風) 情   n. amorous feelings.   7. 疏   adj. sparse. See also P74 note 6.

8. 浮动 (動)   v. to float, drift. ☞树叶在水上浮动 Leaves floated on the water.

9. 黄昏   n. dusk. Here it means "yellowish" (*hūn huáng* 昏黄).

10. 霜   n. frost. Here it means "white."   11. 禽   n. bird.   12. 偷眼   v. to steal a glance.

13. 合   adv. should. See P09 note 8 and P12 note 7 for different meanings of the word.

14. 魂　n. soul. See also P80 note 18 and P95 note 15. 断魂, overwhelmed with joy or sorrow.

15. 微　adj. small, trivial. Here it means "softly, in a soft voice." (*dī shēng* 低声).

16. 吟　v. to chant, recite. See also P03 note 20.　　17. 狎　v. to be (improperly) intimate with.

18. 檀板　n. hardwood clappers. 19. 樽　n. wine goblet. MdnC: 酒杯 (*jiǔ bēi*). See also P83 note 29.

20. 风光 (*fēng guāng*)　n. scene, view.　　　　21. 倾倒 (*qīng dǎo*)　v. to greatly admire.

现代文翻译 Modern Chinese Translation

　　百花都被寒风吹落了，只有梅花独自开放，美丽[4]的景色把整个小园的风光[20]都占[5]尽了。梅花稀疏的影子或横或斜地映在清浅的水中。花香浮动[8]在昏黄[9]的月光之下。白鸟想飞下来，先偷看梅花一眼。蝴蝶如果知道梅花的美丽，应该会为之倾倒。[21] 幸好我可以低声[15]地吟唱，来亲近梅花，不用敲着檀板，拿着金色的酒杯[19]来欣赏它。

评论与提问 Comment and Question

To Chinese literati, the plum blossom is a symbol of three lofty ideals. Its white color represents moral purity, its defiance of cold winter symbolizes moral courage and integrity, and its subtle fragrance signifies an elegant noble aloofness from all things vulgar or glamorous. The symbolic significance of the plum blossom is so well known that few poets explicitly dwell upon it. Instead, they focus their attention on its sensuous appeal: its color, its "untimeliness," and its fragrance.

　　In depicting the plum blossom, the greatest challenge is to find a novel and effective way to capture and dramatize its impact on our senses. Lin Bu has met this challenge brilliantly. The sight of plum blossoms is easily captured in words but difficult to make poetic because it is too familiar to us. So, to defamiliarize our visual perception of them, Lin directs our attention from their plain whiteness to their graceful reflection on a pond, tinged by the moonlight, from our normal perspective to a bird's sight of them. The sparse shadows of plum blossoms also evoke our sense of touch as they make the wintry barrenness more keenly felt. The fragrance is perhaps the most intangible of our sense impressions to be captured in words, but Lin Bu has come up with a most ingenious solution: to depict butterflies being attracted to the fragrance of plum blossoms and let us imagine our own response to it. This dramatization of the sensuous appeal of the plum blossom is unrivalled and has earned Lin Bu everlasting fame. ☞ *HTRCP*, pp. 309–311 for an introduction to the subgenre "depiction of things" and for a close reading of this poem.

P77

méi huā
梅花

[*běi sòng*] *wáng ān shí*
[北宋] 王 安 石[1]

qiáng	*jiǎo*	*shù*	*zhī*	*méi*
墙	角	数	枝	梅

Plum Blossom

[Northern Song Dyn.] Wang Anshi

In the wall corner

a cluster of plum flowers

líng	*hán*	*dú*	*zì*	*kāi*
凌²	寒	独	自	开△

Defying the winter cold
        put forth their solitary blossoms.

yáo	*zhī*	*bú*	*shì*	*xuě*
遥³	知	不	是	雪

From a distance one can tell
        it isn't the show of a snow shower

wèi	*yǒu*	*àn*	*xiāng*	*lái*
为	有	暗	香	来△

Only because from there
        wafts their subtle fragrance.
          (Tr. Zong-qi Cai)

[五言律绝 pentasyllabic regulated quatrain, tonal pattern Ia, see *HTRCP*, p. 171]

字词释义 Vocabulary Notes

1. See the biographic note in P13 note 3.
2. 凌 prep. approach. ☞火车于明天凌晨一点到达 The train will arrive at 1 a.m. tomorrow.
3. 遥 (遙) adj. distant, remote. See also P19 note 6.

现代文翻译 Modern Chinese Translation

    墙角有几枝梅花，冒着严寒独自开放了。从远处就可知道(那是开放的梅花而)不是雪，因为有香气暗暗传来。

评论与提问 Comment and Question

Pentasyllabic quatrain, the shortest form of *shi* poetry, is considered best suited for capturing a heightened moment of perception. The heightened moment depicted by Wang Anshi is that of a pleasant recognition: the white patches on the walls' corner are plum blossoms, not snow as they seem. This recognition—an avoidance of perceptual error—is made possible by the poet's smelling of the fragrant plum blossom. So this single act of recognition captures and in some ways dramatizes the impact of plum blossoms on our senses of sight, touch, and smell.

P78

hǎi	*táng*
海	棠¹

Crabapple

[*běi sòng*] *sū shì*
[北宋] 苏 轼²

[Northern Song Dyn.] Su Shi

dōng	*fēng*	*niǎo*	*niǎo*	*fàn*	*chóng*	*guāng*
东	风	袅	袅³	泛⁴	崇⁵	光△

The east wind blows gently,
        suffused in their pleasant glow,

xiāng	*wù*	*kōng*	*méng*	*yuè*	*zhuǎn*	*láng*
香	雾	空	濛⁶	月	转⁷	廊△⁸

Through a mist of their fragrance
        the moon passes the corridor

zhǐ	*kǒng*[9]	*yè*	*shēn*	*huā*	*shuì*	*qù*
只	恐	夜	深	花	睡	去

gù	*shāo*	*gāo*	*zhú*	*zhào*	*hóng*	*zhuāng*
故	烧	高	烛	照	红	妆△[10]

In the depth of night I fear
the flowers may go to sleep,
So high up I lit candles
to shine upon their red finery.
(Tr. Zong-qi Cai)

[七言律绝 heptasyllabic regulated quatrain, tonal pattern Ia, see *HTRCP,* p. 171]

字词释义 Vocabulary Notes

1. 海棠 n. Chinese flowering crabapple.   2. See the biographic note in P31 note 2.
3. 袅袅 (裊裊) adv. wafting in the wind.
4. 泛 v. to be suffused with. 👉她的脸上泛着红光 Her face is suffused with blushes. See P68 note 11 for a different meaning of the word.
5. 崇 adj. high, lofty, sublime. 崇光 radiance.   6. 空濛 adj. hazy. See also P31 note 5.
7. 转 (轉 *zhuǎn*) v. See P16 note 12.   8. 廊 n. corridor. MdnC: 回廊 (*huí láng*) winding corridor.
9. 恐 v. to dread, fear. See also P42 note 8.
10. 红 (紅) 妆 n. red makeup. See also P04 note 20. Here it refers to the beautiful appearance of the flowering crabapple.
11. 光泽 (*guāng zé*) n. shiny gloss, sheen.

现代文翻译 Modern Chinese Translation

东风轻轻地吹着，海棠泛[4]着美丽的光泽。[11]花香弥漫在雾中，月亮转[7]过回廊[8](照不到海棠)。(我)只担心夜深了，海棠就这样睡着了，于是点着高高的烛火来照亮美丽的海棠。

评论与提问 Comment and Question

Pathetic fallacy is a rhetorical figure that "signifies any description of inanimate natural objects that ascribes to them human capabilities, sensations, and emotions"(John Ruskin's words). If Yang Wangli's "A Small Pond" (P32) features two lines of pathetic fallacy, this poem is a pathetic fallacy throughout. In fact, if we substitute the word "beauty" (*jiārén* 佳人) for the title "Crabapple" 海棠 and for the word "flower" 花 in line 3 (making the line read: 只恐夜深佳人睡), the poem will be a straightforward depiction of a beautiful woman. As such, the poem would of course be a banal one. But as a description of crabapple trees, the poem is a rare example of complete pathetic fallacy in Chinese poetry. While Western poets (especially the Romantics) use pathetic fallacy profusely, only a limited number of Chinese poets show an abiding interest in this rhetorical figure.

P79

méi huā jué jù
梅花绝句

A Quatrain on Plum Blossoms

[*nán sòng*] *lù yóu*
[南宋] 陆 游[1]

[Southern Song Dyn.] Lu You

wén	*dào*	*méi*	*huā*	*chè*	*xiǎo*	*fēng*
闻	道[2]	梅	花	坼[3]	晓[4]	风△

I hear that plum blossoms
     have braved the chilly wind at dawn,

xuě	*duī*	*biàn*	*mǎn*	*sì*	*shān*	*zhōng*
雪	堆	遍	满	四	山	中△

Piles and piles of snow have covered
     the mountains all around.

hé	*fāng*	*kě*	*huà*	*shēn*	*qiān*	*yì*
何	方	可	化[5]	身	千	亿

By what can I be transformed
     into zillions of me

yí	*shù*	*méi*	*huā*	*yí*	*fàng*	*wēng*
一	树	梅	花	一	放	翁△

So that each blossoming plum tree
     has one of me?
     (Tr. Zong-qi Cai)

[七言律绝 heptasyllabic regulated quatrain, tonal
pattern IIa, see *HTRCP,* p. 171]

字词释义 Vocabulary Notes

1. See the biographic note in P17 note 1.   2. 闻 (聞) 道 v. to be told. MdnC: 听说 (*tīng shuō*).
3. 坼 v. to tear. MdnC: 分开 (*fēn kāi*).   4. 晓 (曉) See P03 note 15.   5. 化 v. to turn into.

现代文翻译 Modern Chinese Translation

听说[2]梅花迎着清晨的寒风(开放了。我去看时，梅花)象雪堆一样，满山遍野，到处都
是。用什么方法可把我变成千万个，这样每株梅花下面就有个我在那里观赏！

评论与提问 Comment and Question

Topic+comment is the most typical structure of regulated quatrains, especially heptasyllabic ones.
In each of the four quatrains in this unit, the first couplet gives a direct depiction of the thing named
in the title, and the second couplet expresses the poet's emotive-reflective response to the thing.

More often than not, it is the extraordinariness of this emotive-reflective response, not the
finesse of external description, that earns fame for a quatrain. So it is no wonder that an absolute
majority of oft-quoted quatrain lines are the second couplet of a poem. A cursory look at the famous
quatrain lines shaded in grey in this workbook leaves no doubt about this point.

To render their emotive-reflective responses extraordinary, quatrain poets employ a broad
array of rhetorical and structural devices, including "pathetic fallacy" (P13, P78, P79), hyperbole
(P19), question (P28, P59, P79), question and answer (P37), condition and result (P39), supposition
and inference (P34, P87), a negative statement and explanation (P36), and so on.

The second couplet of this poem uses pathetic fallacy in the form of a question. Is this
instance of pathetic fallacy identical to that of the previous poem? Which of the two indicates a
higher degree of empathy between the observer and the observed? Please note that the wording of
the last line allows for different takes on the poet's desired relationship with the plum blossoms.

练习 EXERCISES

一 填空 Fill in blanks

A. 诗词填字：遥 讬 泛 没 暗 迷 间 凌 疏 角 浮 坼 转 映 堆 照
1. 庄生晓梦____蝴蝶，望帝春心____杜鹃。 2. 芳春____流雪，深夕____繁星。
3. ____影横斜水清浅，暗香____动月黄昏。 4. ____知不是雪，为有____香来。
5. 东风袅袅____崇光，香雾空濛月____廊。 6. 墙____数枝梅，____寒独自开。
7. 闻道梅花____晓风，雪____遍满四山中。 8. 翻阶____细草，集水____疏萍。

B. 现代文填词：间隔 稀疏 埋没 浮动 惘然 托付
1. 泥石流____ ____了整个村子。 2. 他感到____ ____若失。 3. 他的头发很____ ____。
4. 每两排树间____ ____三米。 5. 他把孩子____ ____给我。 6. 树叶在水面上____ ____。

二 形近字辨析 Distinguish easily confused characters

1. 望帝春心____杜鹃 a. 托 b. 讬 c. 拖 2. 众芳摇落独____妍 a. 喧 b. 暄 c. 渲
3. 蓝田日____玉生烟 a. 暖 b. 缓 c. 暖 4. 闻道梅花____晓风 a. 析 b. 折 c. 坼
5. 香雾空濛月____廊 a. 转 b. 砖 c. 传 6. ____寒独自开 a. 陵 b. 棱 c. 凌

三 连句 Match the first part with the second

1. 遥知不是雪( )   2. 苍海月明珠有泪( )   3. 疏影横斜水清浅( )   4. 只恐夜深花睡去( )
5. 芳春照流雪( )   6. 庄生晓梦迷蝴蝶( )   7. 何方可化身千亿( )   8. 霜禽欲下先偷眼( )

a. 故烧高烛照红妆   b. 深夕映繁星   c. 望帝春心托杜鹃   d. 一树梅花一放翁
e. 蓝田日暖玉生烟   f. 为有暗香来   g. 粉蝶如知合断魂   h. 暗香浮动月黄昏

四 句读 Punctuate and translate the following passage

翻阶没细草集水间疏萍遥知不是雪为有暗香来庄生晓梦迷蝴蝶望帝春心讬杜鹃闻道梅花坼晓风雪堆遍满四山中只恐夜深花睡去故烧高烛照红妆

五 听写 Dictation

1. ____ ____ ____ ____ ____ 水____ ____ ，____ ____ ____ ____ ____ 月 ____ ____ 。
2. ____ ____ 月 ____ ____ ____ ，____ ____ 日 ____ ____ ____ 。
3. ____ 生 ____ ____ ____ ，____ ____ 春 ____ ____ ____ 。
4. ____ ____ ____ 花 ____ ____ ____ ，____ ____ ____ ____ ____ 中 。

17

咏史：名人

Meditation on History: Famous People

P80

yǒng huái gǔ jì   qí sān
咏怀¹古迹², 其三

[táng] dù fǔ
[唐] 杜甫³

Meditation on Ancient Ruins, No. 3

[Tang Dyn.] Du Fu

qún	*shān*	*wàn*	*hè*	*fù*	*jīng*	*mén*
群	山	万	壑⁴	赴⁵	荆	门ᐃ⁶

Myriads of mountains and valleys
　　　　　　hurry toward Jingmen

shēng	*zhǎng*	*míng*	*fēi*	*shàng*	*yǒu*	*cūn*
生	长	明	妃⁷	尚	有	村ᐃ⁸

Where Consort Luminous grew up
　　　　　　there's still a village.

yí	*qù*	*zǐ*	*tái*	*lián*	*shuò*	*mò*
一	去⁹	紫	台¹⁰	连	朔¹¹	漠¹²

The Purple Palace—once she's gone—
　　　　　　links itself with barren deserts,

dú	*liú*	*qīng*	*zhǒng*	*xiàng*	*huáng*	*hūn*
独	留	青	冢¹³	向	黄	昏ᐃ

A green tomb—that alone remains—
　　　　　　faces the bleak dusk.

huà	*tú*	*xǐng*	*shí*	*chūn*	*fēng*	*miàn*
画	图¹⁴	省¹⁵	识	春	风	面¹⁶

A portrait painter, through him how could the
emperor have recognized
　　　　　　a face so charming like spring breeze?

huán	*pèi*	*kōng*	*guī*	*yuè*	*yè*	*hún*
环	珮¹⁷	空	归	月	夜	魂ᐃ¹⁸

Her jade bracelets return in vain—
　　　　　　a phantom in a moonlit night.

qiān	*zǎi*	*pí*	*pá*	*zuò*	*hú*	*yǔ*
千	载¹⁹	琵	琶²⁰	作	胡²¹	语

For a thousand years her *pipa* tunes
　　　　　　echo the tones of the Huns,

fēn	*míng*	*yuàn*	*hèn*	*qǔ*	*zhōng*	*lùn*
分	明	怨	恨	曲	中	论ᐃ

Clearly her woes and lament are
　　　　　　expressed in the tunes.
　　　　　　　　　(Tr. Zong-qi Cai)

[七言律诗 heptasyllabic regulated verse, tonal pattern Ia,
see *HTRCP*, p. 172]

字词释义 Vocabulary Notes

1. 咏怀 (詠懷) v. to sing one's feelings.　　2. 古迹 (跡) n. place of historical interest.

3. See the biographic note in P20 note 1.　　4. 壑 n. valley. See also P15 note 12.

5. 赴 v. to go to. MdnC: 奔赴 (*bēn fù*). 👉战士们奔赴前线 The solders hurried to the front.

6. 荆门 (門) or 荆门山 Jingmen Mountains, in present-day Jingmen 荆门, Hubei Province.

7. 明妃 王昭君 (name 名，Qiáng 嫱；style 字，Zhāojūn 昭君，52 B.C.E?-?) one of the "Four Beautiful Women" (*sìdà měirén* 四大美人) in ancient China. In 36 B.C., she entered the harem of the Emperor Yuan of the Han 汉元帝 (r. 48-33B.C.E.). Because she refused to bribe the imperial painter, her portrait was poorly done to the effect that her beauty eluded the attention of Emperor Yuan. As a result she was never visited by the emperor. In 33 B.C., Xiongnu's 匈奴 ruler Huhanye 呼韩邪 visited Chang'an on a homage trip. There he asked to marry a princess of the Han. According to the *History of the Latter Han* (*Hòu Hàn shū* 后汉书), Wang Zhaojun volunteered to join the Huhanye. When summoned to court, her beauty dazzled the emperor and made him regret his decision to send her to Xiongnu. Later, she became the consort of Huhanye and gave birth to two sons.

8. 村 n. village. Here it refers to the village where Wang Zhaojun was born. It is in present-day Zigui 秭归, Hubei province.

9. 去 v. to leave, be away from. MdnC: 离开 (*lí kāi*). 👉他离开我们有三年了 He has been away from us for three years. See P38 note 3 for a different meaning of the word.

10. 紫台 (臺) or 紫宫 the Purple Palace, where the emperors lived in the Han.

11. 朔 n. north. MdnC: 北方 (*běi fāng*).　　12. 漠 n. desert. MdnC: 沙漠 (*shā mò*).

13. 冢 n. burial mound. MdnC: 坟墓(*fén mù*).

14. 画图 (畫圖) to draw a picture. Here it refers to Wang Zhaojun's portrait.

15. 省 (*xǐng*) v. to be aware. 省识 means "to get to know"(*rèn shi* 认识).

16. 春风 (風) 面 refers to Wang Zhaojun's beautiful face.

17. 珮 n. jade ornament. See also P21 note 9. 环佩 "jade ornament," used as a metonym for Wang Zhaojun.

18. 魂 n. soul, spirit. See also P76 note 14.　　19. 载 (載 *zǎi*) n. year. See also P18 note 5.

20. 琵琶 n. a plucked string instrument with a fretted fingerboard. See also P51 note 5.

21. 胡 it refers to the ethnic groups in the north and west of ancient China. See also P38 note 8.

22. 山脉 (*shān mài*) n. mountain range.

23. 满腔悲愤 (*mǎn qiāng bēi fèn*) full of grief and indignation.

现代文翻译 Modern Chinese Translation

　　连绵的山脉²²(随着长江)，奔赴⁵荆门山。这里还留有王昭君出生成长的山村。(王昭君)一人离开⁹皇宫，从此一生都和北方¹¹的沙漠¹²连在一起，最后只留下一座青色的坟墓¹³，独自面对黄昏。凭着画像，汉元帝怎能认识¹⁵到王昭君的美貌？(结果昭君死在匈奴，)只有在月夜时她的灵魂才能回到故乡。昭君所作胡人音调的琵琶曲千年留传，曲中诉说的分明是<u>满腔悲愤</u>[23]啊！

评论与提问 Comment and Question

Meditation on history is a very complex mental process, in which a poet freely moves between past, present, and future. In thinking about a historical event or figure, he tends to dwell upon the causes of success or failure, the impact on the present, and the lessons to be heeded for the future. If he uses the regulated form of *shi* or *ci* poetry, a poet faces the added challenge of turning its fixed formal rules from constraints into devices that aid the spatial-temporal thrusts of his meditation. This poem shows how ingeniously Du Fu adapts the *lüshi* form to advance his meditation on the tragic life of Consort Luminous.

First, he utilizes the required couplet use to blend the highlights of her past life with the present traces of her. Each couplet is a vignette encapsulating a past-present comparison: her childhood set against her home village today (first couplet); her journey of exile juxtaposed with a present sight of her tomb (second couplet); the fateful distortion of her portrait coupled with her present nightly return as a ghost (third couplet); and her self-made *pipa* tunes being performed and appreciated today (fourth couplet).

Second, Du consciously exploits the *lüshi* structural rule—be it the topic+comment or the four-stage progression—to reveal his deepening reflective process. The first two couplets sketch Consort Luminous' life as a topic for reflection, while the next two couplets offer the poet's doleful reflection about the cause of her tragic exile and its heavy toll on her inner life before and after her death.

Third, Du exploits the rule of required parallelism to achieve a maximum "imagistization" of narration and reflection in the two middle couplets. Consider his truncation of the consort's life and death into a series of images: the Purple Palace...the barren deserts/the green tomb...bleak dusk. If these images are milestones of the consort's life and death, then the verbs (一去, 连; 独留, 向) linking up these images indicate how she passed through these milestones physically and emotionally.

The composition of the next parallel couplet is no less impressive. This couplet employs four metonyms in a row (画图 for the painter, 春风面 for the youthful consort, 环佩 and 月下魂 for the returning consort), spanning from the consort's early days in court to her afterlife. More importantly, it reveals a great leap in the poet's reflective process. While he dwells upon the cause of the consort's exile in line 5, the poet abruptly turns to the consequence of this exile on her afterlife in the next line.

In many ways, Du Fu's construction of these two parallel couplets seems to anticipate the montage technique in modern cinema. Like the latter, it effects a radical truncation of narration, an abrupt leap in thought, and a dramatic collage of colors.

P81

bā zhèn tú
八 阵 图[1]   The Diagram of Eight Formations

[táng] dù fǔ
[唐] 杜 甫²

[Tang Dyn.] Du Fu

gōng	*gài*	*sān*	*fēn*	*guó*
功³	盖⁴	三	分	国⁵

His accomplishment towers over
　　　the split of Three Kingdoms,

míng	*chéng*	*bā*	*zhèn*	*tú*
名⁶	成	八	阵	图△

His fame is achieved with
　　　the Diagram of Eight Formations.

jiāng	*liú*	*shí*	*bú*	*zhuàn*
江	流	石	不	转⁷

The river was rushing past
　　　but the formation rocks didn't move.

yí	*hèn*	*shī*	*tūn*	*wú*
遗	恨⁸	失⁹	吞¹⁰	吴△¹¹

An eternal regret he bore—
　　　that ill-conceived annexation of Wu.
(Tr. Zong-qi Cai)

[五言古绝 pentasyllabic ancient quatrain]

字词释义 Vocabulary Notes

1. 八阵图 (八陣圖)　the Diagram of Eight Battle Formations, made by Zhuge Liang 诸葛亮 (style 字, Kǒngmíng 孔明，181−234). Zhuge Liang was prime minister of the Shu 蜀 (221−263) during the Three Kingdoms Period. He is often regardedd as the greatest strategist of his time.

2. See the biographic note in P20 note 1.

3. 功　n. merits and achievements, contributions. MdnC: 功绩 (*gōng jì*). ☞这位将军功绩卓著 This general has distinguished achievements.

4. 盖　v. to surpass. MdnC: 盖过 (*gài guò*). ☞他的成绩盖过了其他选手 His scores surpassed all the other contestants'.

5. 三分国 (國)　refers to the split of the Han into three kingdoms.

6. 名　n. name, fame. MdnC: 名声 (*míng shēng*) reputation. ☞他的名声很坏 He had a poor reputation.

7. 转 (轉 *zhuàn*)　v. to turn, revolve, rotate. ☞地球绕着太阳转 The earth revolves round the sun. 石不转 here indicates that the rocks in the Diagram of Eight Formations don't budge at all when the river flows.

8. 恨　n. regret. MdnC: 遗憾 (*yí hàn*). See also P93 note 13. 遗恨 enduring regret. See P07 note 10 for a different meaning of the word.

9. 失　n. mistake. MdnC: 失策 (*shī cè*) unwise. ☞这样非常失策 This was a very unwise move.

10. 吞　v. to swallow. MdnC: 吞并 (*tūn bìng*) to swallow up. ☞这个小公司被吞并了 This small company was swallowed up.

11. 吴 (吳)　or 东吴　the Wu Kingdom during the Three Kingdoms Period. 失吞吴 refers to the unwise, failed attempt by Liu Bei 刘备 (style 字, Xuándé 玄德, 161−223), the Emperor of the Shu, to swallow up the Wu.

12. 卓著 (*zhuō zhù*)　adj. distinguished, outstanding.

现代文翻译 Modern Chinese Translation

诸葛亮的功绩[3]盖过[4]了三分天下，八阵图使他名声[6]卓著![12]江水流动，但是八阵中的石头却不转动。可惜刘备失策[9]要吞并[10]东吴，（破坏了计划，）使诸葛亮遗憾[8]终生。

评论与提问 Comment and Question

This poem is quite well known and frequently included in poetry anthologies. In our opinion, however, it is famous because of the poet, not its own artistic merits. Indeed, it is not hard to see that this poem is artistically inferior to most of the quatrains you have read. The four lines of the poem are all generalized statements about the accomplishments or failures of Zhuge Liang, arranged in a straight order.

Many scholars hold that the quatrain is the only major poetic form in which Du Fu does not excel. There seems a simple reason for his lackluster performance: the shortness of the pentasyllabic quatrain form. Given only 20 characters in a quatrain, he simply does not have enough space to pursue his signature syntactic and structural maneuvers, as he consistently does in a regulated verse (see the previous poem). Can you think of any other reason for his less than perfect use of the quatrain form?

P82

suí gōng
隋 宫[1]

Sui Palace

[táng] lǐ shāng yǐn
[唐] 李 商 隐[2]

[Tang Dyn.] Li Shangyin

zǐ quán gōng diàn suǒ yān xiá
紫 泉[3] 宫 殿 锁[4] 烟 霞[5]

Purple Spring's palace halls
    lay locked in the twilight mist;

yù qǔ wú chéng zuò dì jiā
欲 取 芜 城[6] 作 帝 家△

He wished to make the Overgrown City
    a home of emperors.

yù xǐ bù yuán guī rì jiǎo
玉 玺[7] 不 缘[8] 归 日 角[9]

The jade seal, if it had not somehow
    become the Sun-horn's,

jǐn fān yīng shì dào tiān yá
锦 帆[10] 应 是 到 天 涯△[11]

Brocade sails, then, would have reached
    heaven's end.

yú jīn fǔ cǎo wú yíng huǒ
于 今 腐[12] 草 无 萤 火

To this day the rotten grass is
    without the glimmer of fireflies,

zhōng gǔ chuí yáng yǒu mù yā
终[13] 古 垂[14] 杨 有 暮[15] 鸦△

From antiquity the drooping willows endure,
    with the sunset crows.

dì	*xià*[16]	*ruò*	*féng*	*chén*	*hòu*	*zhǔ*[17]	
地	下	若	逢	陈	后	主	Beneath the earth, if he would run into
							the Latter Lord of Chen,
qǐ	*yí*[18]	*chóng*	*wèn*	*hòu*	*tíng*	*huā*△[19]	
岂	宜	重	问	后	庭	花	How could it be fitting to ask about
							"Rear Courtyard Flowers"?
							(Tr. Zong-qi Cai)

[七言律诗 heptasyllabic regulated verse, tonal pattern Ia, see *HTRCP*, p. 172]

字词释义 Vocabulary Notes

1. 隋宫   Sui Palace. Here it refers to elaborate palace compounds Emperor Yang of the Sui Dynasty 隋炀帝 (r. 605–617) ordered built in Guangling 广陵 (present-day Yangzhou 扬州, Jiangsu province) as a temporary capital during his southern sojourns.
2. See the biographic note in P03 note 2.
3. 紫泉   Purple Spring, a river in the Chang'an area (in present-day Xi'an area, Shaanxi province). 紫泉宫殿 refers to the Sui palace at Chang'an (the capital of the Sui Dynasty).
4. 锁 (鎖)   v. to lock. See also P66 note 5.   5. 霞   n. rosy clouds. See also P33 note 5.
6. 芜 (蕪) 城   overgrown city, an allusion to the essay "*Fu* on Overgrown City" ("wú chéng fù" 芜城赋) written by the Southern Dynasties poet Bao Zhao 鲍照 (414–466). In this essay, Bao Zhao described the rise and decline of Guangling.
7. 玉玺 (璽)   n. jade seal, the symbol of imperial authority.   8. 缘 (緣)   See P36 note 9.
9. 日角   sun horn, a physiognomic term for hornlike protuberances on the forehead of someone destined to become emperor. Here it stands for Li Yuan 李渊 (Emperor Gaozu of the Tang 唐高祖, r. 618–626), the first Tang emperor. (Ashmore; *HTRCP*, p. 197).
10. 帆   n. sail.   See also P40 note 9. 锦帆, brocade sails, used as a synecdoche for the boats Emperor Yang rode in his southern excursions.
11. 天涯   n. the end of the world. See also P47 note 8.
12. 腐   adj. rotten. MdnC: 腐烂 (*fǔ làn*). 📖 这些肉已经腐烂了 These meats have rotted. See P44 note 6 for a different meaning of the word.
13. 终 (終)   adj. whole, all, entire. 终古 means "through all ages" (*cóng gǔ zhì jīn* 从古至今).
14. 垂   v. to droop. See also P04 note 21.   15. 暮   n. dusk, evening. See also P18 note 13.
16. "地下" 句   an anecdote from the *Remaining Records of the Sui Dynasty* (*Suí yí lù* 隋遗录) , telling that Emperor Yang of the Sui visited Chen Shubao, the last emperor of the Southern Dynasties, and asked to hear Chen's favorite song "Flowers in the Rear Courtyard."
17. 陈后主 (陳後主)   or 陈叔宝 (r. 582–589), the last Emperor of the Chen of the Southern Dynasties. Chen Shubao indulged himself in women and literature and neglected state affairs. In 589, he was taken prisoner by the Sui army and the Chen fell.
18. 宜   adj. suitable, appropriate. See also P31 note 9.
19. 后 (後) 庭花   "Rear Courtyard Flowers," a famous song written by Chen Shubao to praise the beauty of his favorite concubine Zhang Lihua 张丽华. The complete name of this song is "Jade Trees and Flowers in the Rear Courtyard" ("Yù shù hòu tíng huā" 玉树后庭花).
20. 天命 (*tiān mìng*)   n. destiny, fate.   21. 绝迹 (*jué jì*)   v. to disappear, vanish.

现代文翻译 Modern Chinese Translation

　　长安城中的紫泉宫被锁在了烟雾和云霞中，(而隋炀帝)却还想把遥远的广陵作为帝王之家。如不是因(天命 [20] 所归，)玉玺属于有日角之相的李渊，可能隋炀帝的龙船早已开到天边了！如今腐烂 [12] 的草中，萤火虫早已绝迹；[21] 当年河边的杨树，现在也只有乌鸦在上面鸣叫了。亡国之君的隋炀帝死后，如果遇到同样是亡国之君的陈后主，怎敢又问起那首《后庭花》！

评论与提问 Comment and Question

To fully appreciate the beauty of this great poem, read the commentaries on its use of historical allusions and its syntactic innovations in *HTRCP*, pp. 191−193, 388−390. By comparing this poem with Du Fu's "Spring Scene" (P91), can you explain the benefit of an increased use of function words in heptasyllabic regulated verse?

P83

niàn nú jiāo   chì bì huái gǔ
念奴娇[1] 赤壁[2]怀古[3]

[běi sòng] sū shì
[北宋] 苏 轼[4]

To the Tune "The Charm of Niannu":
Meditation on the Past at Red Cliff

[Northern Song Dyn.] Su Shi

dà	*jiāng*	*dōng*	*qù*						
大	江[5]	东	去						

The Great Yangtze runs east,

làng	*táo*	*jìn*		*qiān*	*gǔ*	*fēng*	*liú*	*rén*	*wù*
浪	淘[6]	尽	、	千	古	风	流[7]	人	物▲

Its waves have swept away heroes of past ages.

gù	*lěi*	*xī*	*biān*	*rén*	*dào*	*shì*
故	垒[8]	西	边	人	道	是、

Lying to the west of the old fort, it is said,

sān	*guó*	*zhōu*	*láng*	*chì*	*bì*
三	国[9]	周	郎[10]	赤	壁▲

Is the Red Cliff, known because of Zhou Yu of the Three Kingdoms.

luàn	*shí*	*chuān*	*kōng*
乱	石	穿	空

Rugged stone walls pierce the sky.

jīng	*tāo*	*pāi*	*àn*
惊	涛[11]	拍	岸

Angry waves beat the banks,

juǎn	*qǐ*	*qiān*	*duī*	*xuě*
卷[12]	起	千	堆	雪▲

Churning up water like piles of frosty snow.

jiāng	*shān*	*rú*	*huà*
江	山	如	画

The mountains and the River look like a painting,

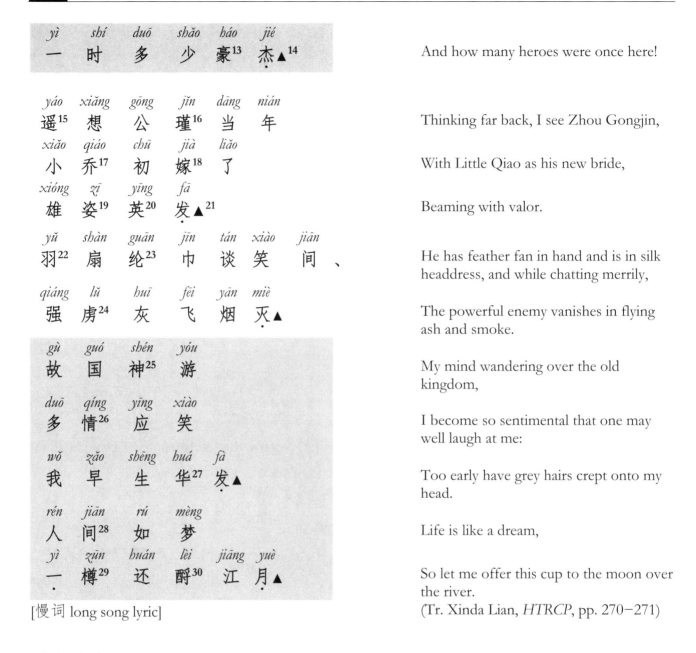

yì	shí	duō	shǎo	háo	jié	
一	时	多	少	豪[13]	杰▲[14]	

And how many heroes were once here!

yáo	xiǎng	gōng	jǐn	dāng	nián
遥[15]	想	公	瑾[16]	当	年

Thinking far back, I see Zhou Gongjin,

xiǎo	qiáo	chū	jià	liǎo
小	乔[17]	初	嫁[18]	了

With Little Qiao as his new bride,

xióng	zī	yīng	fā
雄	姿[19]	英[20]	发▲[21]

Beaming with valor.

yǔ	shàn	guān	jīn	tán	xiào	jiān
羽[22]	扇	纶[23]	巾	谈	笑	间、

He has feather fan in hand and is in silk headdress, and while chatting merrily,

qiáng	lǔ	huī	fēi	yān	miè
强	虏[24]	灰	飞	烟	灭▲

The powerful enemy vanishes in flying ash and smoke.

gù	guó	shén	yóu
故	国	神[25]	游

My mind wandering over the old kingdom,

duō	qíng	yīng	xiào
多	情[26]	应	笑

I become so sentimental that one may well laugh at me:

wǒ	zǎo	shēng	huá	fā
我	早	生	华[27]	发▲

Too early have grey hairs crept onto my head.

rén	jiān	rú	mèng
人	间[28]	如	梦

Life is like a dream,

yì	zūn	huán	lèi	jiāng	yuè
一	樽[29]	还	酹[30]	江	月▲

So let me offer this cup to the moon over the river.
(Tr. Xinda Lian, *HTRCP*, pp. 270−271)

[慢词 long song lyric]

字词释义 Vocabulary Notes

1. 念奴娇 (嬌)　"The Charm of Niannu ," title of a tune.
2. 赤壁　Red Cliff, in present-day Chibi 赤壁, Hubei province, is the site of the "Battle of Red Cliffs" (*Chìbì zhī zhàn* 赤壁之战) at the very end of the Han Dynasty. In this battle, Zhou Yu 周瑜 (style 字, Gōngjǐn 公瑾, 175−210), the commander of the army of the Wu Kingdom 吴 (222−280), successfully frustrated the effort by the northern warlord Cao Cao 曹操 (style 字, Mèngdé 孟德, 155−220) to conquer the areas south of the Yangtze River. This decisive battle prevented Wei 魏 (220−265) from annexing Wu and another kingdom, Shu 蜀 and ushered in the Three Kingdoms Period (220−280). (Lian; *HTRCP*, p. 272).

3. 怀 (懷) 古   meditation on the past. This poem was written by Su Shi on a visit to what he thought was the site of the Battle of Red Cliffs. However, most modern scholars agree that this Red Cliffs is not the famous battlefield, but a different place in present-day Huanggang 黄冈, Hubei province.

4. See the biographic note in P31 note 2.   5. 江   refers to the Yangtze River. See also P44 note 1.

6. 淘   v. to wash in a basket, sift out.

7. 风 (風) 流   adj. distinguished and admirable.

8. 垒 (壘)   n. rampart. MdnC: 营垒 (*yíng lěi*) barracks and enclosing walls.

9. 三国 (國)   Three Kingdoms, namely Wei 魏, Shu 蜀, and Wu 吴.

10. 周郎   or 周瑜, see Zhou Yu's biographic note in note 2. 郎 is an appellation of a young man.

11. 涛 (濤)   n. huge waves. MdnC: 波涛 (*bō tāo*). 👉大海波涛汹涌 The huge waves of the sea rage on. See also P89 note 7.

12. 卷   v. to roll up. See also P52 note 13.

13. 豪   n. a person of extraordinary power or endowment. 👉文豪 A literary giant.

14. 杰 (傑)   adj. outstanding, prominent. MdnC: 杰出 (*jié chū*). 👉他是一位杰出的科学家 He is an outstanding scientist. 豪杰 means "a person of exceptional ability, a hero."

15. 遥   adv. from a distance. See also P19 note 6.   16. 公瑾   Zhou Yu's style name.

17. 小乔 (喬)   Little Qiao, Zhou Yu's wife. She was the younger daughter of Qiao Xuan 乔玄 (109－183), a famous minister at the end of the Han. See 二乔 in P87 note 13.

18. 嫁   v. (of a woman) to get married.   19. 姿   n. posture, carriage. 雄姿 heroic posture.

20. 英   n. hero, outstanding person. MdnC: 英俊 (*yīng jùn*) handsome and spirited.

21. 发 (發 *fā*)   v. to send out. MdnC: 焕发 (*huàn fā*) to shine, glow. 👉她容光焕发 Her face is glowing with health. See P62 note 24 for a different meaning of the word.

22. 羽   n. feather. MdnC: 羽毛 (*yǔ máo*). 羽扇 a fan made from birds' feathers.

23. 纶 (綸)   n. green silk thread. 纶巾 black silk ribbon scarf.

24. 虏   v. to seize, capture; n. enemy (*dí rén* 敌人).   25. 神   n. spirit. 神游 to visit a place mentally.

26. 多情   adj. full of tenderness or affection.

27. 华 (華)   adj. (of hair) grey. See P75 note 6 for a different meaning of the word.

28. 人间 (間)   n. the world. Here it means "life" (*rén shēng* 人生).

29. 樽   n. wine goblet. See also P76 note 19.   30. 酹   v. to pour out a libation.

31. 灰烬 (*huī jìn*)   n. ashes.   32. 多愁善感 (*duō chóu shàn gǎn*) adj. sentimental.

现代文翻译 Modern Chinese Translation

　　长江向东流去，千年来的英雄人物都被浪花冲洗尽了！那旧营垒[8]的西边，就是人们所说的三国时周瑜大败曹操的赤壁。陡峭的石头穿入了天空，惊人的波涛[8]拍打着河岸，卷起的浪花像千堆雪一样。江山壮美如画一样，那时有多少的英雄豪杰啊！

　　回想当年，小乔刚嫁给周瑜时，周瑜英俊[20]焕发，[21]手拿羽毛[22]扇，头戴青丝头巾。谈笑之间，敌人[24]的船队已被烧成灰烬。[31]神游[25]三国战场，该笑我太多愁善感[32]了，以致过早生出了白头发。 人生就像梦一样，还是敬一杯酒给江上的明月吧！

评论与提问 Comments and Questions

1. Su Shi's song lyrics are famous for his style of "heroic abandon" (*háofàng* 豪放). "Heroic" refers to a grand vision while "abandon" means freedom from any restriction. This lyric is a good example of this style. The broad strokes of a grand view in the first stanza mark a sharp contrast with his portrayal of minute details in P64 and P67. ☞ *HTRCP*, pp. 272–273 for a close reading of this lyric song.

2. Su Shi has been long criticized or praised for his practice of "treating *ci* as *shi*" (*yǐ shī wéi cí* 以诗为词). Compare this poem with the *shi* poems on similar themes (for instance, P81, P87) and determine if Su does write this lyric song in the style of a *shi* poem.

P84

nán xiāng zǐ *dēng jīng kǒu* *běi gù* *tíng yǒu huái*
南 乡 子¹ 登 京 口² 北 固 亭³ 有 怀⁴

[nán sòng] *xīn qì jí*
[南宋] 辛弃疾⁵

To the Tune of "South Village":
Meditation on the Past on the Beigu
Pavilion

[Southern Song Dyn.] Xin Qiji

hé *chù* *wàng* *shén* *zhōu*
何 处 望 神 州△⁶

Where to look for the Divine State?

mǎn *yǎn* *fēng* *guāng* *běi* *gù* *lóu*
满 眼 风 光⁷ 北 固 楼△

A boundless scene meets the eye
here in the Beigu Tower.

qiān *gǔ* *xīng* *wáng* *duō* *shǎo* *shì*
千 古 兴⁸ 亡⁹ 多 少 事

Of all the rise and fall since antiquity,
how many stories can be told?

yōu *yōu*
悠 悠△¹⁰

Boundless and endless,

bú *jìn* *cháng* *jiāng* *gǔn* *gǔn* *liú*
不 尽¹¹ 长 江 滚 滚¹² 流△

The unending Yangtze surges forward,
waves upon waves.

nián *shào* *wàn* *dōu* *móu*
年 少¹³ 万 兜 鍪△¹⁴

At a young age he commanded
an army of ten thousand helmets;

zuò *duàn* *dōng* *nán* *zhàn* *wèi* *xiū*
坐 断¹⁵ 东 南 战 未 休△¹⁶

Occupying the Southeast
he never stopped fighting his enemies.

tiān *xià* *yīng* *xióng* *shuí* *dí* *shǒu*
天 下 英 雄 谁 敌 手¹⁷

Of the great heroes in the world,
who were his adversaries?

cáo *liú*
曹¹⁸ 刘△¹⁹

Cao and Liu.

shēng	zǐ	dāng	rú	sūn	zhòng	móu
生	子	当	如	孙	仲	谋△[20]

If one is to have a son,
he should be like Sun Zhongmou!
(Tr. Zong-qi Cai)

[小令 short lyric song]

字词释义 Vocabulary Notes

1. 南乡 (鄉)子 "South Village," title of a tune.
2. 京口 present-day Zhenjiang 镇江, Jiangsu province.
3. 北固亭 or 北固楼, North Bulwark Pavilion built on the North Bulwark Mountain 北固山 (in the northeast of present-day Zhenjiang, 镇江, Jiangsu province), facing the Yangtze River.
4. 怀 (懷) n. meditation on the past.
5. See the biographic note in P16 note 3.
6. 神州 China. According to "Zou Yan's Biography"("Zōu yǎn zhuàn" 邹衍传) in *The Records of the Grand Scribe (Shǐ jì* 史记), China was called "Red County and Divine State"(*Chìxiàn Shénzhōu* 赤县神州). 神州 now means China.
7. 风 (風) 光 n. view, sight, scene. 👉三月风光正好 The views in March are just great.
8. 兴 (興) v. to rise, thrive. MdnC: 兴盛 (*xīng shèng*) prosperous, thriving, flourishing. 👉国家强大兴盛 The nation is strong and prosperous. See also P89 note 13. See P85 note 1 for a different meaning of the word.
9. 亡 n. death. MdnC: 灭亡 (*miè wáng*) to fall. 👉秦朝灭亡了 The Qin fell. See also P89 note 14.
10. 悠悠 adv. long. See also P07 note 9.
11. "不尽"句 this line was rewritten from the fouth line of Du Fu's "Climbing high" (*dēng gāo* 登高). See P93.
12. 滚 (滾) v. to turn. 滚滚 means "billowing, rolling." See also P93 note 9.
13. 年少 young age. It refers to Sun Quan 孙权 (style 字, Zhòngmóu 仲谋, 182−252), who became the King of Wu in 222 and declared himself Emperor of the Wu Dynasty in 229.
14. 兜鍪 n. ancient helmet. 万兜鍪 ten thousand helmets, referring to the Wu army.
15. 坐断 v. to occupy, hold. MdnC: 占据 (*zhàn jù*). 👉他们占据了有利地位 They occupied a better position.
16. 休 v. to stop. See also P07 note 13.
17. 敌手 n. opponent, adversary.
18. 曹 曹操. See his biographic note in P83 note 2.
19. 刘 (劉) 刘备. See his biographic note in P81 note 11.
20. 孙仲谋 (孫仲謀) 孙权. According to Pei Songzhi's 裴松之 (372−451) note on *The Chronicles of the Three Kingdoms (Sān guó zhì* 三国志), Cao Cao attacked Sun Quan at Ruxu 濡须 (in present-day Chao County 巢县, Anhui province) in 213, but failed and had to withdraw his army. Before he left, he saw Sun Quan's army, and sighed, "If one is to have a son, he should be like Sun Zhongmou."
21. 指挥 (*zhǐ huī*) v. to command.

现代文翻译 Modern Chinese Translation

哪里才能望到中原！在北固亭上，满眼都是美丽的风光[7](却看不到中原大地)。千百年来，多少国家兴盛[8]灭亡,[9]这些都过去了，只有长江水，一直向东奔流而去。

孙权年少时，就指挥[21]军队，占据[15]东南边，不停地与敌人作战。天下的英雄谁能成为他的敌手呢？只有曹操和刘备。难怪曹操会说，"生儿子就应该生像孙权这样的！"

评论与提问 Comment and Question

This tune inevitably invites a comparison with the regulated verse form. It has exactly the same number of characters as a heptasyllabic regulated verse: 56 in total. Like a heptasyllabic regulated verse, it features an alternation of 2+2+3 and 4+3 rhythms as well as a level-tone rhyme. Its stanzaic division also harks back to the bipartite division of natural and human scenes prevalent in regulated verses. All these similarities lend credence to a widely accepted view that many tunes in short *ci* poetry are derived by refashioning the regulated verse form.

Of the many tunes adapted from the regulated verse form, this tune stands out for its conspicuous use of a two-character line in each stanza. This two-character line may be seen to have resulted from a re-placement of the two characters shorn off the first line of each stanza. The resulting pattern of 5-, 7-, 7-, 2-, and 7-character lines generates a sustained rhythm of contraction and expansion. This new rhythm, in turn, undergirds a new poetic process radically different from the four-stage progression in a regulated verse.

The poetic process pursued by Xin Qiji here is that of topic and comment, both within and between the stanzas. Each stanza is a twin topic+comment stanza, knit together by the pivotal third line. In the first stanza, the third line 千古兴亡多少事 functions simultaneously as the comment on the two preceding lines and as the topic of the next two lines. The third line in the second stanza does exactly the same. The relationship between the two stanzas, too, may be understood in terms of topic+comment. Does this interlocking of topic+comment constructions enable the poet to meditate on history in a new mode? Distinguish this reflective mode from Du Fu's (e.g. P91).

练习 EXERCISES

一 填空 Fill in blanks

A. 诗词填字: 连 转 垂 冢 省 缘 梦 锁 吞 鳌 帆 休 涛 魂 兜 取 卷 腐 醉 断

1. 画图____识春风面，环佩空归月夜____。　2. 江流石不____，疑恨失____吴。

3. 于今____草无萤火，终古____杨有暮鸦。　4. 惊____拍岸，____起千堆雪。

5. 紫泉宫殿____烟霞，欲____芜城作帝家。　6. 人间如____，一樽还____江月。

7. 玉玺不____归日角，锦____应是到天涯。　8. 年少万____ ____ ____。

9. 一去紫台____朔漠，独留青____向黄昏　10. 坐____东南战未____。

B. 现代文填词: 占据 焕发 灭亡 兴盛 杰出 腐烂 吞并 失策 功绩 波涛

1. 她看起来容光＿＿＿ ＿＿＿ 。   2. 这么做非常＿＿＿ ＿＿＿ 。

3. 这个小公司被＿＿＿ ＿＿＿ 了。   4. 他们＿＿＿ ＿＿＿ 了有利地位。

5. 大海＿＿＿ ＿＿＿汹涌。   6. 秦朝＿＿＿ ＿＿＿ 了。

7. 他＿＿＿ ＿＿＿卓著。   8. 国家＿＿＿ ＿＿＿繁荣。

9. 这些肉已经＿＿＿ ＿＿＿ 了。   10. 他是一位＿＿＿ ＿＿＿ 的科学家。

二 形近字辨析 Distinguish easily confused characters

1. 羽扇＿＿＿巾谈笑间　a. 轮　b. 纶　c. 论　　2. 雄＿＿＿英发　　　　a. 资　b. 咨　c. 姿

3. 群山万壑＿＿＿荆门　a. 赴　b. 赶　c. 赳　　4. 一去紫台连朔＿＿＿　a. 摸　b. 漠　c. 模

5. 强＿＿＿灰飞烟灭　a. 虏　b. 虑　c. 虎　　6. 大江东去浪＿＿＿尽　a. 掏　b. 淘　c. 陶

7. 三国周＿＿＿赤壁　a. 朗　b. 浪　c. 郎　　8. 功＿＿＿三分国　　a. 盖　b. 益　c. 盉

三 连句 Match the first part with the second

1. 江流石不转( )　　2. 地下若逢陈后主( )　　3. 千载琵琶作胡语( )　　4. 故垒西边人道是 ( )

5. 乱石穿空( )　　　6. 紫泉宫殿锁烟霞( )　　7. 千古兴亡多少事( )　　8. 江山如画( )

9. 年少万兜鍪( ) 10. 画图省识春风面( )

a. 分明怨恨曲中论　b. 惊涛拍岸　　　c. 欲取芜城作帝家　d. 坐断东南战未休

e. 三国周郎赤壁　　f. 遗恨失吞吴　g. 岂宜重问后庭花　h. 环佩空归月夜魂

i. 悠悠，不尽长江滚滚流　j. 一时多少豪杰

四 句读 Punctuate and translate the following passage

群 山 万 壑 赴 荆 门 生 长 明 妃 尚 有 村 如 今 腐 草 无 萤 火 终 古 垂 杨 有 暮 鸦 遥 想 公 瑾 当 年 小 乔 初 嫁 了 雄 姿 英 发 羽 扇 纶 巾 谈 笑 间 强 虏 灰 飞 烟 灭 天 下 英 雄 谁 敌 手 曹 刘 生 子 当 如 孙 仲 谋

五 听写 Dictation

1. ＿＿＿ ＿＿＿ ＿＿＿ ＿＿＿作＿＿＿ ＿＿＿，＿＿＿ ＿＿＿ ＿＿＿ ＿＿＿ ＿＿＿中 ＿＿＿。

2. ＿＿＿ ＿＿＿ ＿＿＿ ＿＿＿无 ＿＿＿ ＿＿＿，＿＿＿ ＿＿＿ ＿＿＿有 ＿＿＿ ＿＿＿。

3. ＿＿＿ ＿＿＿三＿＿＿ ＿＿＿，＿＿＿ ＿＿＿八＿＿＿ ＿＿＿。

4. ＿＿＿石＿＿＿ ＿＿＿，＿＿＿ ＿＿＿ ＿＿＿ ＿＿＿，＿＿＿起＿＿＿ ＿＿＿ 。

5. ＿＿＿ ＿＿＿ ＿＿＿多少＿＿＿，＿＿＿ ＿＿＿，不＿＿＿ ＿＿＿ ＿＿＿ ＿＿＿ ＿＿＿。

6. 一 ＿＿＿ ＿＿＿ ＿＿＿ ＿＿＿ ＿＿＿，＿＿＿ ＿＿＿向 ＿＿＿ ＿＿＿。

7. ＿＿＿ ＿＿＿ ＿＿＿ ＿＿＿ ＿＿＿ ＿＿＿，＿＿＿ ＿＿＿ ＿＿＿作＿＿＿家。

18

咏史：王朝兴衰

Meditation on History: Rise and Fall of Dynasties

P85

qiū xīng qí bā
秋兴¹ 其八

[táng] dù fǔ
[唐] 杜 甫⁴

Autumn Meditations, No. 8

[Tang Dyn.] Du Fu

kūn	*wú*	*yù*	*sù*	*zì*	*wēi*	*yí*
昆	吾³	御	宿⁴	自	逶	迤⁵

Kunwu park and Yusu lodge are out there in the remote distances;

zǐ	*gé*	*fēng*	*yīn*	*rù*	*měi*	*bēi*
紫	阁	峰⁶	阴⁷	入	渼	陂△⁸

the shadow of Purple Tower peak enters Meibei lake.

xiāng	*dào*	*zhuó*	*yú*	*yīng*	*wǔ*	*lì*
香	稻⁹	啄¹⁰	余	鹦	鹉¹¹	粒¹²

Fragrant rice: leftovers from pecking, parrots' grains;

bì	*wú*	*qī*	*lǎo*	*fèng*	*huáng*	*zhī*
碧¹³	梧¹⁴	栖¹⁵	老	凤	凰¹⁶	枝△

emerald *wutong* trees: till old age perched, phoenixes' branches.

jiā	*rén*	*shí*	*cuì*	*chūn*	*xiāng*	*wèn*
佳	人	拾¹⁷	翠¹⁸	春	相	问¹⁹

Lovely ones gathered kingfisher feathers to give as springtime gifts;

xiān	*lǚ*	*tóng*	*zhōu*	*wǎn*	*gèng*	*yí*
仙	侣²⁰	同	舟	晚	更	移△

transcendent companions shared a boat, moving off again toward evening.

cǎi	*bǐ*	*xī*	*céng*	*gān*	*qì*	*xiàng*
彩	笔²¹	昔²²	曾	干²³	气	象²⁴

My many-colored writing brush once strove with the climate;

bái	*tóu*	*yín*	*wàng*	*kǔ*	*dī*	*chuí*
白	头	吟²⁵	望	苦	低	垂△

now my white head, chanting and gazing, in despondency droops.

[七言律诗 heptasyllabic regulated verse, tonal pattern I, see *HTRCP*, p. 171]

(Tr. Robert Ashmore, *HTRCP*, p. 186)

字词释义 Vocabulary Notes

1. 兴 (興) n. meditation. See P84 note 8 for a different meaning of the word.

2. See the biographic note in P20 note 1.

3. 昆吾   a place in Shanglin Park (*shàng lín yuàn* 上林苑) of the Han Dynasty, It is in the west of present-day Lantian 蓝田, Shaanxi province.

4. 御宿   Yusu Lodge, an imperial lodge for Emperor Wu of the Han 汉武帝 (r. 140−87 B.C.E.) in the south of the capital Chang'an. This ancient capital lies in the south of present-day Chang'an County 长安县, Shaanxi province. 御 means "imperial."

5. 逶迤   adj. winding; meandering [formal].

6. 紫阁 (閣) 峰   Purple Tower Peak, a peak on the Zhongnan Mountains 终南山, in the southeast of present-day Hu County 户县, Shaanxi province.

7. 阴 (陰)   n. an area north of a hill or south of a river. See P15 note 10 for a different meaning of the word.

8. 渼陂   Lake Meibei, in the west of present-day Hu County 户县, Shaanxi province. It was a famous scenic spot in the Tang Dynasty.

9. 稻   n. rice. See also P16 note 7. 10. 啄   v. to peck. 👉小鸡啄米 The chicken pecks at the rice.

11. 鹦鹉 (鸚鵡)   n. parrot.   12. 粒   n. grain.   13. 碧   adj. emerald. See also P40 note 10.

14. 梧   or 梧桐   n. Chinese parasol tree. See also P63 note 14.

15. 栖 (棲)   v. (for birds) to perch. MdnC: 栖息 (*qī xī*). 👉水鸟在岛上栖息 Water fowls are perched on the island.

16. 凤 (鳳) 凰   n. phoenix.

17. 拾   v. to pick up, collect. 👉小孩子拾到了一个钱包 The child picked up a wallet.

18. 翠   adj. emerald green. See also P20 note 3. Here it refers to kingfisher feathers.

19. 相问 (問)   v. to give gifts to each other.

20. 侣   n. companion. MdnC: 伴侣 (*bàn lǚ*). 仙侣   means "a great companion."

21. 彩笔 (綵筆)   n. colored writing, an allusion to "The Biography of Jiang Yan"("Jiāng Yān zhuàn"江淹传) in the *History of the Southern Dynasties* (*Nán shǐ* 南史). The story goes that the Southern Dynasties poet Jiang Yan 江淹 (444−505) met the Jin Dynasty writer Guo Pu 郭璞 (276−324) in a dream. Guo Pu asked him to return the multicolored writing brush that Guo Pu had lent him long before. After he woke up, Jiang Yan found that his literary talent had gone. Here 彩笔 refers to a great talent for writing. (Ashmore; *HTRCP*, pp. 187−188).

22. 昔   n. the past. See also P18 note 3.

23. 干 (*gān*)   v. to have something to do with. MdnC: 干预 (*gān yù*) to intervene, interfere. 👉我不便干预你们内部的事情 It is not appropriate for me to interfere in your internal affairs.

24. 气 (氣) 象   n. climate. "干气象" refers to the story that Du Fu's essay "Three Great Presents" ("Sān dà lǐ" 三大礼) once gained appreciation from Emperor Xuan of the Tang唐玄宗 (r. 712−756).

25. 吟   v. to recite. See also P03 note 20.   26. 倒映 (*dào yìng*)   v. to be reflected in water.

27. 赏识 (*shǎng shì*)   v. to recognize the worth of.

现代文翻译 Modern Chinese Translation

　　昆吾和御宿曲曲折折地延伸着，紫阁峰倒映²⁶在渼陂中。 鹦鹉啄¹⁰着剩下的香稻粒，凤凰栖息¹⁵在美丽的梧桐树枝上。美人拾¹⁷起翠鸟的羽毛，作为春天的礼物送给我们，同船的伴侣到了晚上仍继续一同游览。 高超的文才过去曾受过皇帝的赏识，²⁷ 现在头发白了，只能望着长安，低下头来苦苦地吟唱。

评论与提问 Comments and Questions

1. This poem is the last one of "Autumn Mediations"秋兴, a set of eight poems which arguably represents the highest achievement in the *qilü* form in Tang poetry. ☞*HTRCP*, pp. 185–188 for a brief introduction to this set of eight poems and a detailed analysis of this poem.

2. The second couplet in this poem is very well known for its deliberately mangled syntax: rice does not peck while *wutong* tree does not perch. ☞*HTRCP*, pp. 187 and try to explain the purposes of this syntactic experiment.

P86

wū   yī   xiàng
乌 衣 巷¹

Black Clothes Alley

[táng]   liú   yǔ   xī
[唐] 刘 禹 锡²

[Tang Dyn.] Liu Yuxi

zhū	*què*	*qiáo*	*biān*	*yě*	*cǎo*	*huā*
朱	雀³	桥⁴	边	野	草	花

By the Red Sparrow Bridge
        wild grass and flowers grow,

wū	*yī*	*xiàng*	*kǒu*	*xī*	*yáng*	*xié*
乌	衣	巷	口	夕	阳	斜△

On the entrance of Black Clothes Alley
        the evening sun casts its slanting glow.

jiù	*shí*	*wáng*	*xiè*	*táng*	*qián*	*yàn*
旧	时	王⁵	谢⁶	堂⁷	前	燕⁸

The swallows who made their abode
        in the Wang and Xie mansions of old

fēi	*rù*	*xún*	*cháng*	*bǎi*	*xìng*	*jiā*
飞	入	寻	常⁹	百	姓¹⁰	家△

Now fly in and out of the homes
        of ordinary, common folk.
          (Tr. Zong-qi Cai)

[七言律绝 heptasyllabic regulated quatrain, tonal pattern IIa, see *HTRCP*, p. 171]

字词释义 Vocabulary Notes

1. 乌衣巷 Black Clothes Alley, on the southern bank of the Qianhuai River 秦淮河 (in present-day Nanjing 南京, Jiangsu Province). During the Three Kingdoms Peroid, the Wu army was stationed here, and all the soldiers were dressed in black. From then on, it has been called "Black Clothes Alley."

2. See the biographic note in P02 note 2.   3. 雀 n. sparrow.

4. 朱雀桥 (橋) Red Sparrow Bridge, by the side of Black Clothes Alley, in present-day Nanjing 南京, Jiangsu province.

5. 王　王导　(style, Màohóng 茂弘, 276–339), a famous minister in the beginning of the Eastern Jin Dynasty. His residence was in Black Clothes Alley.

6. 谢 (謝)　谢安　(style, ānshí 安石; literary name, Dōngshān 东山, 320–385) a famous politician and strategist in the Jin. His prominent family also lived in Black Clothes Alley.

7. 堂　n. the main room of a house. See also P10 note 21.　　　8. 燕　n. swallow.

9. 寻 (尋)常　adj. ordinary, common. 👈今天的面试非比寻常 The interview today was unusual. See also P92 note 7.

10. 百姓　n. the common people.　　　11. 豪门望族 (*háo mén wàng zú*)　n. prominent family.

12. 衰败 (*shuāi bài*)　v. to decline.

现代文翻译 Modern Chinese Translation

朱雀桥边长满了杂草和野花，夕阳的余光斜照在乌衣巷口。过去的 (豪门望族¹¹)现在都已衰败¹²了，连常停在)王导谢安两家的燕子，也飞到寻常老百姓的家里了。

评论与提问 Comment and Question

This poem is probably the least intrusive case of historical meditation ever recorded in a quatrain. There is no trace of a reflective poet raising questions and making comments. On the surface, this poem is just a simple description of an ordinary urban quarter. To an informed reader, however, this description is packed with contrastive references to the past. Two proper names—"Red Sparrow Bridge" and "Black Clothes Alley"—evoke the bygone grandeur of this place, but only to be superimposed by the sight of its present desolation. Next, the mention of the Wangs and Xies, the two most powerful clans of the Eastern Jin, brings up similar memories of a glorious past, but again to be overlaid with the sight of the present lowly occupants of their residences. This blending of past and present is rendered seamless by the depiction of swallows returning to the same houses but different homes. Like a touching understatement, this seemingly simple poem conveys a deep pathos over the evanescence of all dynastic glories. Compare this poem with P89. Would you call the latter an opposite overstatement of the same theme?

P87

chì　*bì*
赤　壁¹

[*táng*]　*dù*　*mù*
[唐] 杜 牧²

Red Cliff

[Tang Dyn.] Du Mu

zhé　*jǐ*　*chén*　*shā*　*tiě*　*wèi*　*xiāo*
折　戟³　沉　沙　铁⁴　未　销_△⁵

A broken spear buried in the sand—
　　　　the iron not yet gone,

zì　*jiāng*　*mó*　*xǐ*　*rèn*　*qián*　*cháo*
自　将　磨⁶　洗　认　前　朝_△⁷

Grinding and washing it,
　　　　I fell to picturing a bygone age.

dōng	*fēng*	*bù*	*yǔ*	*zhōu*	*láng*	*biàn*
东	风⁸	不	与	周	郎⁹	便¹⁰
tóng	*què*	*chūn*	*shēn*	*suǒ*	*èr*	*qiáo*
铜	雀¹¹	春	深	锁¹²	二	乔△¹³

If east wind had not done
young Master Zhou a favor,

Bronze Bird Tower, come deep spring,
would have locked up the Qiao girls.
(Tr. Zong-qi Cai)

[七言律绝 heptasyllabic regulated quatrain, tonal pattern IIa, see *HTRCP,* p. 171]

字词释义 Vocabulary Notes

1. 赤壁   Red Cliff, see also P83 note 2.   2. See the biographic note in P22 note 2.
3. 戟   n. spear.   4. 铁 (鐵) n. iron.   5. 销 (銷)   v. to smelt (metal).
6. 磨   v. to rub, grind, polish. 他要磨剪子 He is going to sharpen the scissors.
7. 朝 (*cháo*)   n. dynasty. MdnC: 朝代 (*cháo dài*). 前朝 previous dynasties. See P92 note 3 for a different meaning of the word.
8. "东风"句   In the Battle of Red Cliffs (*Chìbì zhī zhàn* 赤壁之战), by taking advatange of a fortunate change in the direction of the wind, Zhou Yu 周瑜 defeated Cao Cao's million-strong troops.
9. 周郎   or 周瑜, see Zhou Yu's biographic note in P83 note 2.   10. 便   adj. convenient, easy.
11. 铜 (銅) 雀   or 铜雀台   Bronze Bird Tower, Cao Cao's pleasure palace in present-day Linzhang 临漳, Hebei province.
12. 锁 (鎖)   v. to lock up. See also P66 note 5.
13. 二乔 (喬)   the Two Qiaos. They are two daughters of the Han official Qiao Xuan 乔玄 (109–183). Both of them were famous beauties in the Three Kingdoms Period. The elder Qiao married Sun Ce 孙策 (175–200), Sun Qian's 孙权 elder brother, and the younger Qiao was Zhou Yu's 周瑜 wife. Cao Cao once claimed that to get the two Qiaos was one of the reasons he wanted to conquer the southern land of the Yangtze. See 小乔 in P83 note 17.
14. 掳 (*lǔ*)   v. to carry off, capture.

现代文翻译 Modern Chinese Translation

折断的战戟埋在泥沙中，没被毁坏。拾起来自己磨洗一下，还可认出是以前朝代⁷用过的。如果东风没有帮助周瑜取得赤 壁之战的胜利，那么大乔和小乔 (就会被曹操掳¹⁴ 走)，锁在铜雀台了！

评论与提问 Comment and Question

If Master Zhou is presented as a larger-than-life hero in Su Shi's poem (P83), he is here brought down to earth as an ordinary human being subjected to the whims or, to be more pertinent to his case, winds of fate. In the eyes of the poet, Zhou's defeat of the million-strong Wei invaders was due to good luck more than anything else. Had he not had the east wind to aid his strategy of a fire attack, Master Zhou would have suffered a defeat even more humiliating than Cao Cao's, no matter how great his military talent was. His wife and the wife of his sovereign would have been held captive in the Bronze Bird Tower built by Cao Cao expressly for his enjoyment of these two beauties.

In depicting a historical event, a historian is not supposed to entertain a subjunctive question like "what would have become of a nation, a people, or an individual if something had not happened." But for a poet, to raise such a question is highly desirable because it enables him to lead the reader beyond history to some broader truths about life. Has Du Mu's subjunctive question provoked you into pondering over any of these broad issues: the unpredictability of the course of history, the value of hero worship, the transience of successes and failures, the whims of fate, and the ultimate limit to human endeavor?

P88

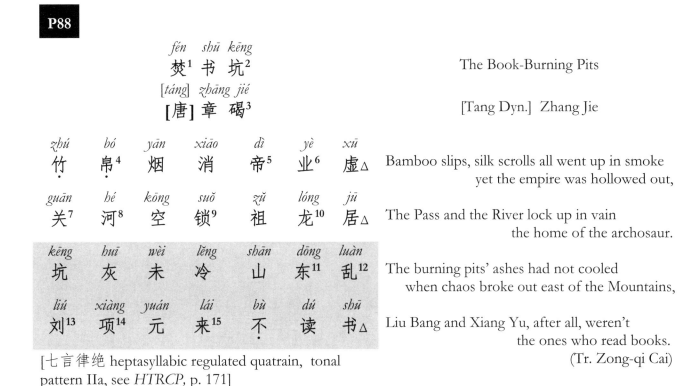

The Book-Burning Pits

[Tang Dyn.] Zhang Jie

fén shū kēng
焚¹ 书 坑²

[táng] zhāng jié
[唐] 章 碣³

zhú bó yān xiāo dì yè xū
竹 帛⁴ 烟 消 帝⁵ 业⁶ 虚△

Bamboo slips, silk scrolls all went up in smoke
                yet the empire was hollowed out,

guān hé kōng suǒ zǔ lóng jū
关⁷ 河⁸ 空 锁⁹ 祖 龙¹⁰ 居△

The Pass and the River lock up in vain
                the home of the archosaur.

kēng huī wèi lěng shān dōng luàn
坑 灰 未 冷 山 东¹¹ 乱¹²

The burning pits' ashes had not cooled
                when chaos broke out east of the Mountains,

liú xiàng yuán lái bù dú shū
刘¹³ 项¹⁴ 元 来¹⁵ 不 读 书△

Liu Bang and Xiang Yu, after all, weren't
                the ones who read books.
                (Tr. Zong-qi Cai)

[七言律绝 heptasyllabic regulated quatrain, tonal pattern IIa, see *HTRCP,* p. 171]

字词释义 Vocabulary Notes

1. 焚   v. to burn. 焚书, the burning of the books, a notorious event in the Qin Dynasty. In order to unify all thought and political opinion, the first Qin emperor 秦始皇 (r. 247−210 B.C.E.) took his primary minister Li Si's 李斯 (ca. 280−208 B.C.E.) suggestion of suppressing freedom of speech, and ordered all copies of the Confucian classics and most historical works burned.

2. 坑   n. hole, pit. 焚书坑 a pit for burning books in the Qin, located in Li Mountain 骊山, in the southeast of present-day Lintong 临潼, Shaanxi province.

3. 章碣 (style 字, Lìshān 丽山，836−905), a late Tang poet. This poem has earned him fame.

4. 竹帛　n. bamboo and silk. Before the Han Dynasty, people wrote on bamboo and silk since there was no paper. Later on, 竹帛 was used to refer to books or works.

5. 帝　n. emperor. Here it refers to the first Qin Emperor 秦始皇.

6. 业 (業)　n. enterprise, business. MdnC: 基业 (*jī yè*) foundation, imperial enterprise.

7. 关 (關)　or 函谷关, Hangu Pass, a strategic pass in present-day Lingbao 灵宝, Henan province. It was built just south of the Yellow River 黄河 by the State of Qin 秦国 in 361 B.C. as its eastern gate.

8. 河　or 黄河　Yellow River.　　9. 锁 (鎖)　v. to lock up. See also P66 note 5.

10. 祖龙 (龍)　archosaur, referring to the first Qin emperor 秦始皇.

11. 山东 (東)　the east of Xiao Mountains 崤山 (in the north of present-day Luoning 洛宁, Henan province) and Hangu Pass 函谷关 in the Warring States Period.

12. 乱 (亂)　adj. in disorder. See also P67 note 16. Here it means "rebellion" (*pàn luàn* 叛乱).

13. 刘 (劉)　or 刘邦　(style 字, Jì 季, 256−195 B.C.E.), the first emperor of the Han (r. 202−195 B.C.E.). Liu Bang was not well educated in his early life.

14. 项 (項)　or 项籍　(style 字, Yǔ 羽, 232−202 B.C.E.) a famous military leader from the late Qin period. In 209, Xiang's army defeated the Qin army in Julu 巨鹿 (present-day Xingtai 邢台, Hebei province), and after the Qin fell, he claimed himself "The Overlord of West Chu" (*Xīchǔ bà wáng* 西楚霸王). After a long struggle for power with Liu Bang, he was defeated and committed suicide by the Wu River 乌江 (present-day He County 和县, Anhui province). Xiang Yu preferred learning military strategy to reading books in his early life, according to "The Biography of Xiang Yu" ("Xiàng Yǔ běnjì" 项羽本纪) in *The Records of the Grand Scribe* (*Shǐ jì* 史记).

15. 元来　adv. originally.　　16. 险固 (*xiǎn gù*)　adj. strategically located and difficult access.

17. 冷却 (*lěng què*)　v. to cool down.

现代文翻译 Modern Chinese Translation

竹帛化为灰烟消失了，而秦始皇的基业[6]也空虚了。函谷关和黄河虽然险固，[16] 也只能锁住秦始皇的皇宫(却阻挡不了秦朝的灭亡)。焚书坑中的灰烟还没有冷却，[17] 崤山和函谷关以东的地方已出现了叛乱。[12] 让秦朝灭亡的刘邦和项羽原来都是不读书的人！

评论与提问 Comment and Question

This poem is a masterful play of irony at the expense of the first emperor of China. Each line introduces one ironic fact about his book burning. The burning of books, a move of thought control intended by him to enhance the empire, serves only to weaken it (line 1). With the country so weakened, the Hangu Pass and the Yellow River prove meaningless and useless—nothing left to defend except an empty capital (line 2). The ironic facts introduced by the next two lines are ever more detailed and startling: first, the book-burning had hardly ended when rebellions broke out in eastern China, and then, to crown it all, the rebel leaders did not read books at all. Can you find in any other poetic tradtion a play of irony as intricate as this one?

P89

[zhōng lǚ] *shān pō yáng* *tóng guān huái gǔ*
【中呂¹】 山坡羊² 潼关³ 怀古

To the Tune "Sheep on Mountain Slope" [*Zhonglü* key]: Meditation on the Past at Tong Pass

[yuán] *zhāng yǎng hào*
[元] 张 养 浩⁴

[Yuan Dyn.] Zhang Yanghao

fēng *luán* *rú* *jù*
峰 峦⁵ 如 聚▲⁶

Peaks and ridges press together,

bō *tāo* *rú* *nù*
波 涛⁷ 如 怒▲

Waves and torrents rage,

shān *hé* *biǎo* *lǐ* *tóng* *guān* *lù*
山 河 表 里⁸ 潼 关 路▲

Zigzagging between the mountains and the river runs the road through Tong Pass.

wàng *xī* *dū*
望 西 都△⁹

I look to the Western Capital,

yì *chóu* *chú*
意 踌 躇△¹⁰

My thoughts linger.

shāng *xīn* *qín* *hàn* *jīng* *xíng* *chù*
伤 心 秦 汉 经¹¹ 行 处▲

It breaks my heart to come to the old place of the Qin and the Han.

gōng *què* *wàn* *jiān* *dōu* *zuò* *liǎo* *tǔ*
宫 阙¹² 万 间 都 作 了 土▲

Now palaces and terraces have all turned to dust.

xīng
兴¹³

Dynasties rise,

bǎi *xìng* *kǔ*
百 姓 苦▲

The common folk suffer;

wáng
亡¹⁴

Dynasties fall,

bǎi *xìng* *kǔ*
百 姓 苦▲

The common folk suffer.

(Tr. Xinda Lian, *HTRCP*, pp. 335–336)

[小令 solo song poem]

字词释义 Vocabulary Notes

1. 中呂 *Zhong lü* Key, one of the *Gongdiao* keys (*gōng diào* 宫调). See *Gongdiao* keys in P09 note 1.

2. 山坡羊 "Sheep on Mountain Slope," title of a tune.

3. 潼关 (關) Tong Pass, in present-day Tongguan County 潼关县, Shaanxi province. North of Tong Pass is the Yellow River, and to the south of it mountains. This pass was first built in 196 and soon became an important strategic point.

4. 张养浩 (張養浩) (style 字, Xīmèng 希孟; literary name 号, Yúnzhuāng 云庄, 1269−1329), a famous Yuan poet. This poem has earned him great fame.

5. 峦 (巒) n. mountains in a range, [formal]. MdnC: 山峦 (*shān luán*).

6. 聚 v. to gather, get together. MdnC: 聚集 (*jù jí*). ☞广场上聚集了上千人 Thousands of people gathered in the square.

7. 波涛 (濤) n. large waves. See also P83 note 11.

8. 表里 n. the outside and inside. Here it refers to the Yellow River and Hua Mountain 华山 which are on either side of Tong Pass.

9. 西都 the Western Capital, namely Chang'an 长安 (present-day Xi'an 西安, Shaanxi province) in the Han Dynasty.

10. 蹰躇 (躊躇) v. to hesitate. Here it means that the poet has no peace of mind.

11. 经 (經) v. to pass through, undergo. MdnC: 经过 (*jīng guò*). ☞这汽车经过博物馆吗 Does the bus pass the museum? See P53 note 5 for a different meaning of the word.

12. 阙 (闕) n. watch tower, palace. 宫阙 means "imperial palace" (*gōng diàn* 宫殿).

13. 兴 (興) v. to rise, thrive. See also P84 note 8. 14. 亡 n. death, fall. See also P84 note 9.

15. 气势 (*qì shì*) n. momentum. 16. 磅礴 (*páng bó*) adj. boundless, majestic.

现代文翻译 Modern Chinese Translation

　　山峰山峦⁵好像都在这里聚集，⁶ 如同愤怒的波涛一样气势¹⁵磅礴，¹⁶ 外有黄河，内有华山，潼关就在这里。望向长安，心中难以平静。

　　经过秦汉旧址，心中伤感， 宫殿¹⁴都已化成尘土。朝代兴起，百姓受苦；朝代灭亡，百姓也受苦！

评论与提问 Comment and Question

Like P33, this solo song poem exemplifies an attempt by Yuan literati poets to turn a new genre of vulgar origin into a powerful device for emotional expression. What makes this poem particularly poignant is its juxtaposition of dynastic rise and fall with common people's perpetual suffering. Such a juxataposition is rarely seen in earlier poems on history. ☞*HTRCP*, pp. 336–337 for a close reading of this poem.

练习 EXERCISES

一 填空 Fill in blanks

A. 诗词填字: 啄 翠 阙 雀 寻 怒 望 吟 消 栖 蹰 磨 燕 聚 锁 移 折 躇 作 垂

1. 竹帛烟____帝业居，关河空____祖龙居。　2. 峰峦如____ ，波涛如____。

3. 香稻____余鹦鹉粒，碧梧____老凤凰枝。　4. ____西都，意____ ____。

5. ____戟沉沙铁未销，自将____洗认前朝。　6. 白头____ ____苦低____。

7. 旧时王谢堂前____，飞入____常百姓家。　8. 宫____万间都____了土。

9. 佳人拾＿＿＿春相问，仙侣同舟晚更＿＿＿＿。10. 铜＿＿＿＿春深＿＿＿＿二乔。

B. 现代文填词：经过 啄 聚集 拾 寻常 磨 干预 栖息
1. 广场上＿＿＿ ＿＿＿ 了几千人。　2. 他在＿＿＿＿ 剪刀。　　3. 许多水鸟＿＿＿ ＿＿＿在这座岛上。
4. 小鸟＿＿＿ 着地上的米粒。　　5. 他＿＿＿ 到了一个钱包。　6. 汽车＿＿＿ ＿＿＿图书馆吗？
7. 我们不能＿＿＿ ＿＿＿你们的内部事务。　8. 今天的面试非比＿＿＿ ＿＿＿。

二 形近字辨析 Distinguish easily confused characters

1. 波＿＿＿＿如怒　　　　a. 蹲 b. 涛 c. 寿　　2. ＿＿＿＿灰未冷山东乱　a. 抗 b. 杭 c. 坑
3. 佳人＿＿＿＿翠春相问　a. 恰 b. 拾 c. 抬　　4. 折戟沉沙铁未＿＿＿　a. 销 b. 稍 c. 悄
5. 自将＿＿＿＿洗认前朝　a. 磨 b. 摩 c. 糜　　6. 碧梧＿＿＿＿老凤凰枝　a. 晒 b. 洒 c. 栖

三 连句 Match the first part with the second

1. 昆吾御宿自逶迤( )　2. 朱雀桥边野草花( )　3. 坑灰未冷山东乱( )　4. 峰峦如聚 ( )
5. 东风不与周郎便( )　6. 彩笔昔曾干气象( )　7. 伤心秦汉经行处( )　8. 望西都( )
9. 香稻啄余鹦鹉粒( )　10. 折戟沉沙铁未销( )

a. 乌衣巷口夕阳斜　b. 意踌躇　　c. 铜雀春深锁二乔　d. 自将磨洗认前朝
e. 刘项元来不读书　f. 波涛如怒　g. 紫阁峰阴入渼陂　h. 碧梧栖老凤凰枝
i. 白头吟望苦低垂　j. 宫阙万间都作了土

四 句读 Punctuate and translate the following passage

朱 雀 桥 边 野 草 花 乌 衣 巷 口 夕 阳 斜 佳 人 拾 翠 春 相 问 仙 侣 同 舟 晚 更 移 彩 笔 昔 曾 干 气 象 白 头 吟 望 苦 低 垂 竹 帛 烟 消 帝 业 虚 关 河 空 锁 祖 龙 居 东 风 不 与 周 郎 便 铜 雀 春 深 锁 二 乔

五 听写 Dictation

1. ＿＿＿ ＿＿＿ ＿＿＿ 余 ＿＿＿ ＿＿＿ ＿＿＿，＿＿＿ ＿＿＿ ＿＿＿ 老 ＿＿＿ ＿＿＿ ＿＿＿。
2. ＿＿＿ ＿＿＿ ＿＿＿ ＿＿＿ 春 ＿＿＿ ＿＿＿，＿＿＿ ＿＿＿ ＿＿＿ ＿＿＿ 更 ＿＿＿。
3. ＿＿＿ ＿＿＿ 如＿＿＿，＿＿＿ ＿＿＿ 如 ＿＿＿，＿＿＿ ＿＿＿ ＿＿＿ ＿＿＿ ＿＿＿ ＿＿＿ 路。
4. ＿＿＿ ＿＿＿ ＿＿＿ ＿＿＿ 前＿＿＿，＿＿＿ ＿＿＿ ＿＿＿ ＿＿＿ ＿＿＿ 家。
5. ＿＿＿ ＿＿＿ ＿＿＿ 未＿＿＿，＿＿＿ ＿＿＿ ＿＿＿ ＿＿＿ 前 ＿＿＿。
6. ＿＿＿ ＿＿＿ ＿＿＿ ＿＿＿，＿＿＿ 空 ＿＿＿ ＿＿＿ ＿＿＿ ＿＿＿。

19

咏怀：感物而发

Reflection: In Response to Scenes and Events

P90

dēng yōu zhōu tái gē
登 幽 州¹ 台 歌

[táng] chén zǐ áng
[唐] 陈子昂²

A Song on Ascending Youzhou Terrace

[Tang Dyn.] Chen Zi'ang

qián	*bú*	*jiàn*	*gǔ*	*rén*	
前	不	见	古	人³	
hòu	*bú*	*jiàn*	*lái*	*zhě*	
后	不	见	来	者	
niàn	*tiān*	*dì*	*zhī*	*yōu*	*yōu*
念⁴	天	地	之	悠	悠⁵
dú	*chuàng*	*rán*	*ér*	*tì*	*xià*
独	怆⁶	然	而	涕⁷	下

I do not see the ancients before me,

Behind, I do not see those yet to come.

I think of the mournful breadth of heaven and earth,

Alone, grieving—tears fall.

[乐府 *yuefu* verse]

(Tr. Paula Varsano, *HTRCP*, p. 230)

字词释义 Vocabulary Notes

1. 幽州　the state of You, one of the twelve provinces in the era of the legendary sage King Shun, located in the north of present-day Hebei Province. During the Warring States Period, it was part of the state of Yan. 幽州台 (Youzhou Terrace) refers to the Golden Terrace 黄金台 built by King Zhao of the Yan 燕昭王 (r. 312 −279 B.C.E.) during the Warring States Period as a place where he recruited talented people into his service.
2. 陈 (陳) 子昂　(style 字, Bóyù　伯玉, 661−702), an outspoken critic of some of the harsh political policies implemented during Empress Wu's (627?−705) reign, and a strong advocate of a return to the ancient-style poetry of moral and social import. His poetical collection, entitled *Stirred by My Encounters* (*gǎn yù* 感遇) and from which this short *yuefu* song is taken, earned him the admiration of later poets like Du Fu and Han Yu.
3. 古人　ancient people. Here it refers to King Zhao of the Yan State or emperors who were courteous to the wise and learned.
4. 念　v. to think of.　　5. 悠悠　adv. long (time and space). See also P07 note 9.
6. 怆 (愴) adj. sorrowful. 7. 涕　n. tear. See also P52 note 8.　8. 贤明 (*xián míng*)　adj. wise.
9. 礼贤 (禮賢) 下士 (*lǐ xián xià shì*)　to be courteous to the wise and respectful toward the learned.

现代文翻译 Modern Chinese Translation

见不到以前贤明[8]的君王，也看不到以后能礼贤下士[9]的明君。感慨天地的广阔，独自站在幽州台上，心中感伤，禁不住泪流满面。

评论与提问 Comments and Questions

1. This poem is recognizable as a *yuefu* song because of both its title and its variation in line length. It was probably written late in the poet's life, during the period of time when he was being persecuted for his outspoken criticism of the government; this persecution would ultimately result in his death.

2. The theme of "climbing high and looking afar" is an ancient one, with roots that extend back to both the *Shijing* and the *Chuci*. As early as the Western Han, poets began climbing high and writing, not necessarily about what they saw, but about what they would have liked to see but could not.

3. As is often the case in very short poems, the most powerful mode of expression is silence. What is Chen Zi'ang not saying? How, specifically, does the poem manage to convey these unspoken thoughts and feelings?

P91

chūn   wàng
春 望
[táng] dù fǔ
[唐] 杜 甫[1]

Spring Scene

[Tang Dyn.] Du Fu

guó	*pò*	*shān*	*hé*	*zài*	
国	破	山	河	在	The country is broken, but mountains and rivers remain,
chéng	*chūn*	*cǎo*	*mù*	*shēn*	
城	春	草	木	深△	The city enters spring, grass and trees have grown thick.
gǎn	*shí*	*huā*	*jiàn*	*lèi*	
感	时	花	溅[2]	泪	Feeling the time, flowers shed tears,
hèn	*bié*	*niǎo*	*jīng*	*xīn*	
恨	别	鸟	惊	心△	Hating separation, a bird startles the heart.
fēng	*huǒ*	*lián*	*sān*	*yuè*	
烽	火[3]	连[4]	三	月[5]	Beacon fires span over three months,
jiā	*shū*	*dǐ*	*wàn*	*jīn*	
家	书[6]	抵[7]	万	金△	A family letter equals ten thousand taels of gold.
bái	*tóu*	*sāo*	*gèng*	*duǎn*	
白	头	搔[8]	更	短	My white hairs, as I scratch them, grow more sparse,

hún   *yù*   *bú*   *shèng*   *zān*

浑⁹   欲   不   胜¹⁰   簪_△¹¹   Simply becoming unable to hold hairpins.

[五言律诗 pentasyllabic regulated verse,   (Tr. Zong-qi Cai, *HTRCP*, p. 162)
   tonal pattern I, see *HTRCP*, p. 171]

字词释义 Vocabulary Notes

1. See the biographic note in P20 note 1.
2. 溅 (濺)   v. to splash, spatter. 刚刚被溅了一身水 I was spattered with water.
3. 烽火   n. beacon-fire. See also P49 note 3. Here It refers to war (*zhàn zhēng* 战争).
4. 连 (連)   v. to connect. MdnC: 持续 (*chí xù*) to continue. 两国间的文化交流已持续很久 Cultural interchanges between the two countries has gone on for awhile.
5. 三月   three months. Here it refers to a long time.
6. 书 (書)   n. letter. See also P65 note 9. 家书 means "family letter."
7. 抵   v. to be equal to. 干活他一个能抵我们两个 He can do the work of two of us.
8. 搔   v. to scratch. MdnC: 挠 (*náo*). 他挠挠头 He scratched his head.
9. 浑 (渾)   adv. simply. MdnC: 简直 (*jiǎn zhí*). See P17 note 4 for a different meaning of the word.
10. 胜 (勝)   n. victory. Here it means "to be able to hold."   11. 簪   n. hairpin.

现代文翻译 Modern Chinese Translation

    国家残破，只有山河依旧。长安城又是春 天，却已无人，只有茂密繁盛的花草树木。(我)感伤时局， 看到美丽的花朵禁不住流下眼泪。不愿离别，听到鸟叫声都感到心惊。战争³已持续⁴很久， (没有家人的消息，这时) 一封家书可以抵得上万两黄金般珍贵。忧伤烦恼让我头上的头发越来越少，简直⁹连发簪都插不住了。

评论与提问 Comment and Question

This poem is the example used for explaining the semantic, syntactic, structural, prosodic rules, and aesthetic ideals of regulated verse in *HTRCP*, pp. 162–174. Review those formal rules and compare them with the rules of Western sonnets (Petrarchan and Shakespearean). Which of the two forms do you think is more technically challenging?

P92

qǔ jiāng qí èr

曲江¹其二   The Qu River, No. 2

[táng] dù fǔ

[唐] 杜 甫²   [Tang Dyn.] Du Fu

cháo	*huí*	*rì*	*rì*	*diǎn*	*chūn*	*yī*
朝³	回	日	日	典⁴	春	衣△

Returning from court, day after day I pawn my spring robes;

měi	*rì*	*jiāng*	*tóu*	*jìn*	*zuì*	*guī*
每	日	江	头	尽	醉⁵	归△

each day by the lakeside I drink my limit, and only then go home.

jiǔ	*zhài*	*xún*	*cháng*	*xíng*	*chù*	*yǒu*
酒	债⁶	寻	常⁷	行	处	有

Wine debts, everywhere I go, are common;

rén	*shēng*	*qī*	*shí*	*gǔ*	*lái*	*xī*
人	生	七	十	古	来	稀△⁸

life spans reaching seventy, from ancient times, are few.

chuān	*huā*	*jiá*	*dié*	*shēn*	*shēn*	*xiàn*
穿⁹	花	蛱	蝶¹⁰	深	深	见¹¹

A flower-weaving butterfly, deep within, appears;

diǎn	*shuǐ*	*qīng*	*tíng*	*kuǎn*	*kuǎn*	*fēi*
点¹²	水	蜻	蜓¹³	款	款¹⁴	飞△

a water-dabbling dragonfly, slow and placid, flies.

chuán	*yǔ*	*fēng*	*guāng*	*gòng*	*liú*	*zhuǎn*
传¹⁵	语	风	光	共	流	转¹⁶

Pass word to these fine scenes, to linger and roam together:

zàn	*shí*	*xiāng*	*shǎng*	*mò*	*xiāng*	*wéi*
暂	时	相	赏¹⁷	莫	相	违△¹⁸

"Let's enjoy each other for a short while, and not part company."

[七言律诗 heptasyllabic regulated verse, tonal pattern Ia, see *HTRCP*, p. 172]

(Tr. Robert Ashmore, *HTRCP*, p. 182)

字词释义 Vocabulary Notes

1. 曲江 or 曲江池, the Qu River Pond, in the southern suburb of present-day Xi'an, Shaanxi province, was first built in the Han Dynasty. In the period of the Xuan Emperor of the Tang 唐玄宗 (r. 712–756), it was enlarged and rebuilt and became a famous scenic spot.

2. See the biographic note in P20 note 1.

3. 朝 (*cháo*) n. court. MdnC: 朝廷 (*cháo tíng*). See P87 note 7 for a different meaning of the word.

4. 典 v. to pawn. MdnC: 典当 (*diǎn dàng*). ☞他典当了自己的衣服 He pawned his clothes.

5. 醉 adj. drunk, tipsy. See also P51 note 7.

6. 债 (債) n. debt, loan. 酒债 means "debts owed to wineshops for the wine consumed."

7. 寻 (尋)常 adj. ordinary, common. See also P86 note 9.

8. 稀 adj. few, rare. MdnC: 稀少 (*xī shǎo*). ☞街上行人稀少 There were few people in the street. See also P94 note 9.

9. 穿 v. to cross. See also P52 note 22.   10. 蛱蝶 n. butterfly. MdnC: 蝴蝶 (*hú dié*).

11. 见 v. to see; used here in the sense of "现" (*xiàn*), which means "to appear." See also P16 note 14.

12. 点 (點) v. to touch on very briefly, skim. ☞蜻蜓点水 Dragonflies skimmed over the water.

13. 蜻蜓 n. dragonfly.   14. 款 adj. sincerely, leisurely , slowly. 款款 means "slowly"

15. 传 (傳 *chuán*) v. to pass. See also P52 note 6.　16. 流转 (轉) v. to wander about, roam.

17. 赏 (賞) v. to enjoy. MdnC: 欣赏(*xīn shǎng*). 👉他在欣赏音乐 He is enjoying music.

18. 违 (違) v. to be apart from, violate. MdnC: 违背 (*wéi bèi*). 👉不要违背自己的诺言 Don't go back on your words!

现代文翻译 Modern Chinese Translation

　　每天从朝廷³回来，(我)都去典当⁴春天穿的衣服，(用换来的钱)到江边买了酒，直到喝醉才回家。我到处买酒欠债，这都是平常小事。人能活到七十岁，自古以来就比较少。蝴蝶¹⁰在花丛中穿来飞去，时隐时现，蜻蜓在水面上点一下，慢慢飞着。传句话给这美丽的风光，"请你同美丽的蝴蝶和点水的蜻蜓一起流转，让我来欣赏 ¹⁷吧！哪怕只是暂时的；可不要连我这么点心愿也违背¹⁸啊！"

评论与提问 Comment and Question

This poem is a masterful display of techniques of the *qilü* form. The second couplet is a typical borrowed parallelism (*jièduì* 借对), in which the poet treats terms as parallel through wordplay on secondary meanings (寻常 in this case). In the third couplet, the verbs are deliberately delayed to the very last position in each line. 👉 *HTRCP,* pp. 182−183 for a detailed analysis of this poem. Think about the third couplet in this poem and the second couplet in P85, how do you evaluate the delicate artfulness in these two couplets? Why?

P93

<table>
<tr><td colspan="7" align="center">*dēng*　*gāo*
登　高¹
[*táng*]　*dù fǔ*
[唐] 杜 甫²</td><td>Climbing High

[Tang Dyn.] Du Fu</td></tr>
<tr><td>*fēng*
风</td><td>*jí*
急</td><td>*tiān*
天</td><td>*gāo*
高</td><td>*yuán*
猿³</td><td>*xiào*
啸⁴</td><td>*āi*
哀⁵</td><td>The wind is swift, the sky is high, and the gibbons cry sadly.</td></tr>
<tr><td>*zhǔ*
渚⁶</td><td>*qīng*
清</td><td>*shā*
沙</td><td>*bái*
白</td><td>*niǎo*
鸟</td><td>*fēi*
飞</td><td>*huí*
回△</td><td>The isle is clear, the sand is pale, and the birds fly back.</td></tr>
<tr><td>*wú*
无</td><td>*biān*
边</td><td>*luò*
落</td><td>*mù*
木⁷</td><td>*xiāo*
萧</td><td>*xiāo*
萧⁸</td><td>*xià*
下</td><td>Rustlingly, fall down the leaves of the boundless trees.</td></tr>
<tr><td>*bú*
不</td><td>*jìn*
尽</td><td>*cháng*
长</td><td>*jiāng*
江</td><td>*gǔn*
衮</td><td>*gǔn*
衮⁹</td><td>*lái*
来△</td><td>Roaringly, comes the endless Yangtze River.</td></tr>
<tr><td>*wàn*
万</td><td>*lǐ*
里</td><td>*bēi*
悲¹⁰</td><td>*qiū*
秋</td><td>*cháng*
常</td><td>*zuò*
作</td><td>*kè*
客</td><td>As a guest who is frequently thousands of *li* away from home, I lament the autumn.</td></tr>
</table>

bǎi	*nián*[11]	*duō*	*bìng*	*dú*	*dēng*	*tái*
百	年	多	病	独	登	台△

Being sick all the time in this life, I climb up the terrace alone.

jiān	*nán*	*kǔ*	*hèn*	*fán*	*shuāng*	*bìn*
艰	难	苦[12]	恨[13]	繁[14]	双	鬓[15]

The hardship and the extreme regret have greyed my temples.

liáo	*dǎo*	*xīn*	*tíng*	*zhuó*	*jiǔ*	*bēi*
潦	倒[16]	新[17]	停	浊[18]	酒	杯△

Being infirm in health, I just stopped drinking the cloudy wine from the cups.

(Tr. Li E)

[七言律诗 heptasyllabic regulated verse, tonal pattern IIa, see *HTRCP*, p. 172]

字词释义 Vocabulary Notes

1. 登高 to climb high, a favorite activity for the the Double Ninth Festival (*chóng yáng* 重阳). See also P12 note 14.

2. See the biographic note in P20 note 1.   3. 猿 n. ape. See also P35 note 7.

4. 啸 (嘯) v. to whistle. See also P26 note 6. Here it means "to cry."

5. 哀 n. grief. MdnC: 悲伤 (*bēi shāng*) sorrowful. ☞他感到很悲伤 He felt very sorrowful.

6. 渚 n. islet. See also P43 note 5.   7. 落木 n. fallen leaves. MdnC: 落叶 (*luò yè*).

8. 萧萧 a soughing of wind.   9. 衮衮 or 滚滚 adv. See P84 note 12.

10. 悲 adj. sad, sorrowful. 悲秋 means "to feel melancholic in the autumn time"

11. 百年 one hundred years. Here it refers to Du Fu's life.

12. 苦 adj. bitter, hard. Here it means "extreme" (*jí* 极). 13. 恨 n. regret. See also P81 note 8.

14. 繁 adj. complicated, numerous; used as a verb meaning "to increase."

15. 鬓 (鬢) n. hair on the temples. See also P03 note 18.

16. 潦倒 adj. frustrated. ☞他现在真是穷困潦倒 Now he is penniless and frustrated.

17. 新 adj. new, fresh; used as an adverb, meaning "newly, just"

18. 浊(濁) adj. muddy, dirty. 浊酒 means "unfiltered wine."

现代文翻译 Modern Chinese Translation

风吹得很急，天很高远，猿猴的叫声十分悲伤;[5]清冷的河中小洲，白色的沙岸，鸟儿飞来飞去。无边无际的落叶[7]飘落着；奔流不尽的长江滚滚而来。 我漂泊万里，常在异乡作客，看到这样的秋景，更感伤悲。一生多病，今天我独自走上高台。历经生活的艰难，很多的遗憾，两鬓已满是白发。 生活穷困潦倒，[16](只好喝酒消愁，可酒到嘴边，身体已承受不住，只好)停住了。

评论与提问 Comments and Questions

1. This poem is a heptasyllabic poem and each line has a 4+3 rhythm. The first segment of each line is a description that sets the tone of the poem; the second segment of each line strengthens the description in the first part by providing further related images or other information. Does a

4+3 rhythmic structure differ from a 2+2+3 structure in syntax and aesthetic effect? If yes, what are the aesthetic effects of using the 4+3 rhythm in this particular poem? ☞ *HTRCP*, pp. 387–392.

2. This poem is often singled out by critics for its extended use of parallelism. In most regulated verse, beginning and closing couplets are non-parallel, but they are quasi- parallel here. Discuss the pros and cons of making all the couplets parallel? ☞ *HTRCP*, pp. 173–174.

P94

juàn yè
倦[1] 夜

[táng] dù fǔ
[唐] 杜 甫[2]

A Weary Night

[Tang Dyn.] Du Fu

zhú	*liáng*	*qīn*	*wò*	*nèi*
竹	凉	侵[3]	卧[4]	内

The cold air from the bamboo grove
　　crept into the bedchamber,

yě	*yuè*	*mǎn*	*tíng*	*yú*
野	月	满	庭[5]	隅△[6]

The wilderness moonlight
　　flooded the yard and all corners.

zhòng	*lù*	*chéng*	*juān*	*dī*
重	露[7]	成	涓[8]	滴

Heavy was the dew
　　Dripping and dropping,

xī	*xīng*	*zhà*	*yǒu*	*wú*
稀[9]	星	乍[10]	有	无△

Sparse were the stars
　　appearing and disappearing.

àn	*fēi*	*yíng*	*zì*	*zhào*
暗	飞	萤	自	照

Flying in darkness
　　fireflies illumined for themselves,

shuǐ	*sù*	*niǎo*	*xiāng*	*hū*
水	宿[11]	鸟	相	呼△

Perching by water
　　birds called to each other.

wàn	*shì*	*gān*	*gē*	*lǐ*
万	事	干	戈[12]	里

Ten thousand things were
　　reduced to shields and dagger-axes,

kōng	*bēi*	*qīng*	*yè*	*cú*
空	悲	清	夜	徂△[13]

In vain I lamented
　　as the clear night ended.
(Tr. Zong-qi Cai)

[五言律诗 pentasyllabic regulated verse,
tonal pattern II, see *HTRCP*, p. 171]

字词释义 Vocabulary Notes

1. 倦　adj. weary, tired. See also P68 note 7.
2. See the biographic note in P20 note 1.
3. 侵　v. to invade, intrude into. See P70 note 3.
4. 卧内　n. bedroom. MdnC: 卧室 (*wò shì*).

5. 庭   n. front yard. See also P10 note 30.   6. 隅   n. border. See also P15 note 5.

7. 露 (*lù*)   n. dew.   See also P21 note 6. 重露 means "the dew became heavy."

8. 涓   n. brook. 涓滴 means "dripping of water."   9. 稀   adj. few, rare. See also P92 note 8.

10. 乍   adv. for the first time. ☞这幅画乍一看还不错 This painting is not bad at first glance.

11. 宿   v. to lodge for the night, stay overnight. See also P15 note 15.

12. 干戈   n. shield and dagger-ax, used as a metonym for war (*zhàn shì* 战事). See also P53 note 6.

13. 徂   v. to go. MdnC: 逝去 (*shì qù*) to pass.   ☞美好的时光逝去了 The beautiful time has gone.

现代文翻译 Modern Chinese Translation

竹林中的凉气侵入到卧室⁴里，月光照在庭院的每个角落。 竹叶上的露水越来越重，变成了小水珠儿，滴落下来；天上的星星稀少，乍¹⁰一看好像若有若无。

(月亮西沉)黑夜里飞来飞去的萤火虫，照亮了自己。 水中栖息的鸟儿互相呼唤着对方。这一夜想到的事情，都和战事¹²有关啊！(可自己却什么都不能做)只能慨叹这清凉的夜晚就这样逝去¹³了。

评论与提问 Comment and Question

If you compare this poem with the previous one, you shall notice a bold move by the poet: a flattening or simply dispensation of the customary "turning" in the third couplet. In most regulated verses, the third couplet effects a pivotal turning from nature to the human world, from description to reflection. But in this poem, natural description continues through the third couplet and manifests only a subtle change from a moonlit scene to a scene of pre-dawn darkness. Consequently, the poem displays a distinct sequential structure instead of topic+comment.

The extended description of this poem also reveals a unique mode of observation. Its succession of images is not what is seen by someone on the move as in Wen Tingyun's "An Early Morning Journey in the Shang Mountains" (P46). Nor does it even suggest a change of fields of vision as does Meng Haoran's "Visiting My Old Friend's Farmstead" (P12). Instead, it is a record of changing scenes within an unchanged field of vision from inside a bedroom. These changing scenes are observed at different times of a long night: early moonlit evening (first couplet), midnight when the moonlight fades (the second couplet), pre-dawn dark hours when fireflies are seen and birds begin to call (third couplet), and finally the end of the night (the final line).

At the poet's mention of the war, it dawns on us that the extended description is not to be taken at face value. Instead, it should be seen as revealing a prolonged process of reflection by the insomniac poet. In other words, this outwardly descriptive poem is in fact a profoundly reflective one. Apart from the mode of observation, can you see any other formal differences between this poem and Wen's or Meng's?

P95

qiū   lái
秋 來   The Advent of Autumn

[táng] lǐ hè
[唐] 李贺[1]

[Tang Dyn.] Li He

tóng	*fēng*	*jīng*	*xīn*	*zhuàng*	*shì*	*kǔ*
桐[2]	风	惊	心	壮	士[3]	苦

The wind from the parasol trees startling his heart
        a heroic man feels the pain,

shuāi	*dēng*	*luò*	*wěi*	*tí*	*hán*	*sù*
衰[4]	灯	络	纬[5]	啼	寒	素 ▲[6]

In the faint light cicadas
        cry aloud for winter clothes.

shuí	*kàn*	*qīng*	*jiǎn*	*yì*	*biān*	*shū*
谁	看	青	简[7]	一	编[8]	书

Who will read those bamboo slips
        bound as a book

bù	*qiǎn*	*huā*	*chóng*	*fěn*	*kōng*	*dù*
不	遣[9]	花	虫[10]	粉[11]	空	蠹 ▲[12]

And prevent flower moths
        eating and turning them into powder?

sī	*qiān*	*jīn*	*yè*	*cháng*	*yīng*	*zhí*
思	牵[13]	今	夜	肠[14]	应	直

Longing and worrying this night
        my guts ought to become straight,

yǔ	*lěng*	*xiāng*	*hún*	*diào*	*shū*	*kè*
雨	冷	香	魂[15]	吊[16]	书	客 ▲[17]

In cold rain the scented soul
        consoles this scholar.

qiū	*fén*	*guǐ*	*chàng*	*bào*	*jiā*	*shī*
秋	坟[18]	鬼	唱	鲍[19]	家	诗

Amidst the autumn tombs ghosts are singing
        the poems of Bao Zhao.

hèn	*xuě*	*qiān*	*nián*	*tǔ*	*zhōng*	*bì*
恨	血[20]	千	年	土	中	碧 ▲

The blood of the wronged after a thousand years
        has turned into jade in the earth.
        (Tr. Zong-qi Cai)

[古诗 ancient-style poem]

字词释义 Vocabulary Notes

1. See the biographic note in P21 note 1.

2. 桐　n. Chinese parasol tree. MdnC: 梧桐 (*wú tóng*).

3. 壮士　n. heroic man; vigorous man.

4. 衰　v. to decline. See also P54 note 6. 衰灯 means that "the light is faint."

5. 络纬 (絡緯)　n. mecopoda elongate which often cries at night in summer and fall.

6. 素　adj. white, simple. See also P60 note 10. 寒素 refers to clothes for cold weather.

7. 简 (簡)　n. bamboo slips for writing on. 青简 refers to the poems the poet had written.

8. 编 (編)　v. to weave, plait. 一编书 refers to the poet's works.

9. 遣　v. to send, dispatch. MdnC: 派 (*pài*). 📖他会派人来帮忙 He will send a person to help. See P96 note 1 for a different meaning of the word.

10. 花虫　or 蠹鱼　silverfish, fish moth.　　　11. 粉　n. powder.

12. 蠹   adj. moth-eaten.   13. 牵 (牽)   v. to pull. See also P62 note 11
14. 肠 (腸)   n. intestines. See also P47 note 7.   15. 魂   n. soul, spirit. See also P76 note 14.
16. 吊   v. to comfort. MdnC: 慰问 (*wèi wèn*).   17. 书 (書) 客   n. intellectual, scholar.
18. 坟   n. tomb. See also P99 note 8.
19. 鲍 (鮑) 鲍照 (style 字, Míng yuǎn 明远; 414–466), a famous poet in the Song of the Southern
    Dynasties. He and Xie Tiao 谢朓 are two favorite poets of Li Bai. See Xie Tiao's and Li Bai's
    biographic notes in P14 note 2 and P19 note 3. 鲍家诗 refers to Bao Zhao's poems.
20. "恨血"句   an allusion to the story of Chang Hong 苌弘 (?–492 B.C.E.) in *Zhuangzi* 庄子.
    Chang Hong was a famous scholar in the Zhou Dynasty. He was exiled to Shu 蜀 by King
    Jing of the Zhou 周敬王 (r. 519–476 B.C.E.) because of a false accusation. After he died,
    the Shu people kept his blood in a small box. Three years later, his blood became jade.
21. 蛀 (*zhù*)   v. (of moths, etc.) to eat.   22. 纠结 (*jiū jié*)   v. to entangle, snarl.

现代文翻译 Modern Chinese Translation

　　秋风吹动着梧桐²树叶，听得我又是心惊又是痛苦，(时光就这样飞快的逝去了)。微弱的灯光照着，络纬叫着，像是在说冬天要来了。我写下的这些诗篇，又有谁来欣赏，好不让它白白地被蠹鱼给蛀²¹成粉？ 今夜，愁思让我不能入眠，连纠结²²的心肠也被牵直了。在这阴冷的雨夜，鬼魂似乎也来慰问¹⁶我。隐隐约约听到坟墓中的鬼魂，在唱着鲍照写的诗，他的遗恨就像苌弘的碧血一样让人难忘！

评论与提问 Comments and Questions

1. With its eight 7-character lines, this poem has the familiar look of a heptasyllabic regulated verse.
    But is it really a regulated verse? To answer this question, you need to find out whether the poem
    observes or violates the semantic, syntactic, structural, and prosodic rules of regulated verse as
    explained in *HTRCP,* pp. 162–174.

2. Li He is known as the "ghost-poet" (*shīguǐ* 诗鬼) for his obsession with death and the
    underworld. This poem features his signature indulgence in morbid imagination. Are there any
    images or statements you personally find rather uncanny or eerie?

3. This poem exhibits a distinct aggregate structure. Its opening line explicitly tells us of the
    emotions to be meditated on (shock 惊 and sorrow 苦), while the ensuing lines each illuminate
    these emotions from a fresh perspective. As shown in this poem, an aggregate structure is one in
    which parts of a poem do not cohere as a linear process of description, narration, or reflection,
    but function as corresponding but loosely connected manifestations of certain emotion(s).
    Typically, this structure reveals the leaps and bounds by which an introspective poet meditates
    on his emotions or, in the words of the Chinese, "sings of his heart" (*yǒnghuái* 咏怀). It is used
    most extensively in the *ci* poetry (see, for instance, P68, P97, P99).

练习 EXERCISES

一 填空 Fill in blanks

A. 诗词填字: 隅 念 宿 债 登 抵 惊 侵 照 简 怆 溅 稀 悲 烽 遣

1. 酒____寻常行处有，人生七十古来____。　　2. 竹凉____卧内，野月满庭____。
3. 万里____秋常作客，百年多病独____台。　　4. ____火连三月，家书____万金。
5. 谁看青____一编书，不____花虫粉空蠹。　　6. 感时花____泪，恨别鸟____心。
7. ____天地之悠悠，独____然而涕下。　　8. 暗飞萤自____，水____鸟相呼。

B. 现代文填词: 持续 典当 潦倒 违背 稀少 悲伤

1.他____ ____了自己的衣服。　2. 不要____ ____自己的诺言。　3. 街上行人____ ____。
4. 他现在穷困____ ____。　5. 两国的文化交流____ ____很久了。6. 她感到很____ ____。

二 形近字辨析 Distinguish easily confused characters

1. 空悲清夜____　　　　a. 阻　b. 祖　c. 徂　　2. 独____然而涕下 a. 沧　b. 苍　c. 怆
3. ____倒新停浊酒杯　a. 缭　b. 撩　c. 潦　　4. 重露成____滴　　a. 捐　b. 涓　c. 绢
5. ____灯络纬啼寒素　a. 衰　b. 哀　c. 衷　　6. 家书____万金　　a. 抵　b. 低　c. 纸

三 连句 Match the first part with the second

1. 无边落木萧萧下( )　2. 穿花蛱蝶深深见( )　3. 桐风惊心壮士苦( )　4. 国破山河在( )
5. 酒债寻常行处有( )　6. 风急天高猿啸哀( )　7. 念天地之悠悠( )　　8. 万事干戈里( )

a. 衰灯络纬啼寒素　　b. 人生七十古来稀　c. 空悲清夜徂　　　d. 渚清沙白鸟飞回
e. 城春草木深　　　　f. 独怆然而涕下　　　g. 点水蜻蜓款款飞　h. 不尽长江衮衮来

四 句读 Punctuate and translate the following passage

前不见古人后不见来者烽火连三月家书抵万金万事干戈里空悲清夜徂万
里悲秋常作客百年多病独登台传语风光共流转暂时相赏莫相违

五 听写 Dictation

1. ____ ____ ____之 ____ ____，____ ____ ____而____ ____。
2. ____ ____花 ____ ____，____ ____ ____ ____ ____心。
3. ____ ____ ____ ____ ____ ____有，____ ____ ____ ____古____ ____。
4. ____ ____ ____ ____ ____ ____下，____ ____ ____ ____ ____ ____来。
5. ____ ____成 ____ ____，____ ____ ____有 ____。
6. ____ ____ ____唱 ____ ____，____ ____ ____ ____中____。

20

咏怀：往事回忆

Reflection: Remembering Things Past

qiǎn huái
遣¹ 怀

[táng] dù mù
[唐] 杜 牧²

Dispelling Sorrow

[Tang Dyn.] Du Mu

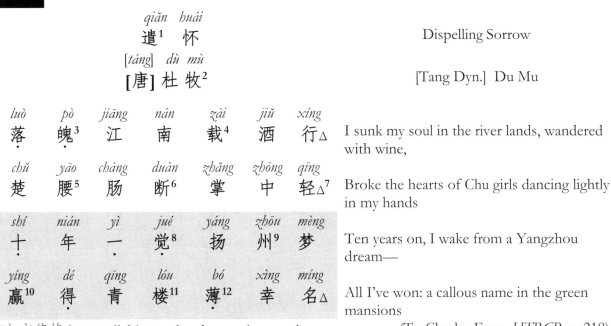

luò pò jiāng nán zài jiǔ xíng
落³ 魄 江 南 载⁴ 酒 行△

I sunk my soul in the river lands, wandered with wine,

chǔ yāo cháng duàn zhǎng zhōng qīng
楚 腰⁵ 肠 断⁶ 掌 中 轻△⁷

Broke the hearts of Chu girls dancing lightly in my hands

shí nián yì jué yáng zhōu mèng
十 年 一 觉⁸ 扬 州⁹ 梦

Ten years on, I wake from a Yangzhou dream—

yíng dé qīng lóu bó xìng míng
赢¹⁰ 得 青 楼¹¹ 薄¹² 幸 名△

All I've won: a callous name in the green mansions

(Tr. Charles Egan, *HTRCP*, p. 218)

[七言律绝 heptasyllabic regulated quatrain, tonal pattern IIa, see *HTRCP*, p. 171]

字词释义 Vocabulary Notes

1. 遣 v. to dispel. MdnC: 发泄 (*fā xiè*) to let off. 他在发泄个人情绪 He is giving vent to his personal feelings. 遣怀 to dispel sorrow. See P95 note 9 for a different meaning of the word.

2. See the biographic note in P22 note 2.

3. 落魄 adj. in dire straits, down and out [formal]. 他现在很落魄 He is in dire straits now. Here 落魄 means "to wander" (*piāo bó* 漂泊).

4. 载 (載 *zài*) v. to carry, hold. See also P68 note 14.

5. 楚腰 Chu girls, an allusion to "The Biography of Ma Liao"("Mǎ Liào zhuàn"马廖传) in the *History of the Han (Hàn shū* 汉书). The story goes that the King of the Chu State loved girls who had slim waists. Later on, 腰 became a synecdoche for slim girls. 楚腰 here refers to dancing girls.

6. 肠 (腸) 断 or 断肠 adj. heartbroken. See also P99 note 19.

7. 掌中轻 (輕) "dancing lightly in my hand," an allusion to the Han beauty Zhao Feiyan 赵飞燕 (32−1 B.C.E.), who was said to be so light that she could dance on the emperor's palm. (Egan; *HTRCP*, pp. 218−219).

8. 觉 (覺 *jué*) v. to wake up. See also P65 note 11.　9. 扬 (揚) 州　See P40 note 3.

10. 赢 (贏) v. to win, gain. 👉他赢了比赛 He won the game.

11. 青楼 (樓) green mansions, a euphemism for the dwellings of the courtesans.

12. 薄 adj. weak, light. See also P63 note 9. 薄幸 means "fickle, inconstant in love" (*bó qíng* 薄情).

13. 舞姿 (*wǔ zī*) n. a dancer's posture and movements.

14. 轻盈 (*qīng yíng*) adj. slim and graceful.　　15. 优美 (*yōu měi*) adj. graceful.

现代文翻译 Modern Chinese Translation

　　漂泊³江南，日夜与酒为伴；纤细女子，美丽到令人断肠，舞姿¹³轻盈¹⁴优美。¹⁵十年过去了，回头看，扬州的往事仿佛是大梦一场，只在青楼美女间赢¹⁰得了薄情¹²的名声！

评论与提问 Comment and Question

This poem is the poet's remembrance of his life of pleasure in Yangzhou. The images of wine and beautiful girls in the first couplet tell us the dissipated life the poet once lived in Yangzhou. However, "落魄" in the beginning reveals that the poet does not feel happy but sorry for this memory. The second couplet is the poet's self-ridicule. The ten-year experience is just like a dream. The poet has not gained anything but a callous name. The poet here expresses his regret with a rather humorous tone.

P97

yú měi rén
虞美人¹

[*nán táng*]　*lǐ yù*
[南唐] 李煜²

chūn	*huā*	*qiū*	*yuè*	*hé*	*shí*	*liǎo*
春	花	秋	月	何	时	了▲³
wǎng	*shì*	*zhī*	*duō*	*shǎo*		
往	事⁴	知	多	少▲		

Spring flowers, autumn moon—when will they end?

Past affairs—who knows how many?

xiǎo	*lóu*	*zuó*	*yè*	*yòu*	*dōng*	*fēng*
小	楼	昨	夜	又	东	风△

Last night in the small pavilion the east wind came again.

gù	*guó*	*bù*	*kān*	*huí*	*shǒu*	*yuè*	*míng*	*zhōng*
故	国⁵	不	堪⁶	回	首⁷	月	明	中△

I dare not turn my head toward my homeland in the moonlight.

diāo	*lán*	*yù*	*qì*	*yīng*	*yóu*	*zài*
雕⁸	栏⁹	玉	砌¹⁰	应	犹¹¹	在▲

To the Tune "Beautiful Lady Yu"

[Southern Tang Dyn.] Li Yu

The inlaid balustrade and jade stairs must still be there—

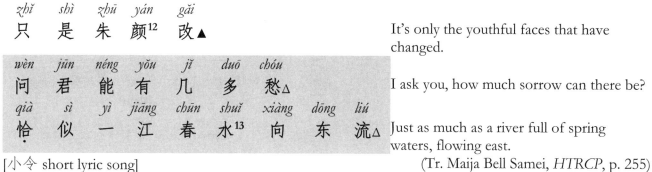

zhǐ	*shì*	*zhū*	*yán*	*gǎi*			
只	是	朱	颜¹²	改▲			

It's only the youthful faces that have changed.

wèn	*jūn*	*néng*	*yǒu*	*jǐ*	*duō*	*chóu*	
问	君	能	有	几	多	愁△	

I ask you, how much sorrow can there be?

qià	*sì*	*yì*	*jiāng*	*chūn*	*shuǐ*	*xiàng*	*dōng*	*liú*
恰	似	一	江	春	水¹³	向	东	流△

Just as much as a river full of spring waters, flowing east.

[小令 short lyric song]   (Tr. Maija Bell Samei, *HTRCP*, p. 255)

字词释义 Vocabulary Notes

1. 虞美人 "Beautiful Lady Yu," title of a tune.   2. See the biographic note in P66 note 2.

3. 了 (*liǎo*) v. to end. MdnC: 结束 (*jié shù*). ☞会议五点结束 The meeting will end at 5pm.

4. 往事 n. past events. ☞往事历历在目 The past events come clearly into view.

5. 故国 (國) homeland. Here it refers to the poet's Southern Tang dynasty.

6. 堪 v. to endure, can, may. ☞往事不堪回首 It is unbearable to recall the events of the past.

7. 回首 v. to look back, recall [formal].   8. 雕 v. to carve, engrave. See also P67 note 9.

9. 栏 (欄) n. balustrade. MdnC: 栏杆 (*lán gān*). 10. 砌 v. to build by laying bricks or stones.

11. 犹 (猶) adv. still. See also P44 note 10.

12. 颜 (顏) n. face, countenance. See also P71 note 9. 朱颜 means "flushed faces."

13. 春水 n. springtime water; a river swollen with spring snowmelt.

现代文翻译 Modern Chinese Translation

　　春天花开，中秋月圆，岁月交替，什么时候才结束³呢？ 往事⁴有多少啊！昨夜小楼又吹起了东风，站在月光下，想起故国，真是不堪⁶回首⁷啊！

　　雕花的栏杆⁹和玉砌的台阶应该还在，可是宫中美丽的容颜已经改变了。 问您能有多少愁怨呢？ 就好像是春天里向东流的江水，无穷无尽啊！

评论与提问 Comments and Questions

1. How does the opening pair of images create an opposition, and how is that opposed to or parallel with the "past affairs" of the second line?

2. In keeping with the character of the genre, this lyric song contains many colloquial elements. Among these are three interrogatives, of which only one receives an answer. Why do you think this final question and answer have been so prized? What makes the image of the last line work?

3. Do you envision a male or a female speaker for this poem? Why? How does your reading of the poet's biography influence your interpretation? ☞ *HTRCP*, pp. 255–257 for an analysis of this lyric song.

P98

<table>
<tr><td colspan="7" align="center">*huàn xī shā*
浣溪沙[1]</td><td align="center">To the Tune "Sand in Silk-Washing Stream"</td></tr>
<tr><td colspan="7" align="center">[*běi sòng*] *yàn shū*
[北宋] 晏 殊[2]</td><td align="center">[Northern Song Dyn.] Yan Shu</td></tr>
<tr>
<td>*yì*
一·</td><td>*qǔ*
曲</td><td>*xīn*
新</td><td>*cí*
词</td><td>*jiǔ*
酒</td><td>*yì*
一·</td><td>*bēi*
杯△</td>
<td>A new song, a cup of wine;</td>
</tr>
<tr>
<td>*qù*
去</td><td>*nián*
年</td><td>*tiān*
天</td><td>*qì*
气</td><td>*jiù*
旧</td><td>*chí*
池</td><td>*tái*
台</td>
<td>Last year's weather at the old pond terrace.</td>
</tr>
<tr>
<td>*xī*
夕·</td><td>*yáng*
阳</td><td>*xī*
西</td><td>*xià*
下</td><td>*jǐ*
几</td><td>*shí*
时</td><td>*huí*
回△</td>
<td>The setting sun sinks in the west—when to return?</td>
</tr>
<tr>
<td>*wú*
无</td><td>*kě*
可</td><td>*nài*
奈</td><td>*hé*
何[3]</td><td>*huā*
花</td><td>*luò*
落·</td><td>*qù*
去</td>
<td>Do what one may, blossoms will fall;</td>
</tr>
<tr>
<td>*sì*
似</td><td>*céng*
曾</td><td>*xiāng*
相</td><td>*shí*
识·</td><td>*yàn*
燕</td><td>*guī*
归</td><td>*lái*
来△</td>
<td>As if we knew each other, the swallows come back.</td>
</tr>
<tr>
<td>*xiǎo*
小</td><td>*yuán*
园</td><td>*xiāng*
香</td><td>*jìng*
径·[4]</td><td>*dú*
独</td><td>*pái*
徘</td><td>*huái*
徊△[5]</td>
<td>In the little garden I pace a fragrant path alone.</td>
</tr>
</table>

[小令 short lyric song]

(Tr. Maija Bell Samei, *HTRCP*, pp. 258−259)

字词释义 Vocabulary Notes

1. 浣溪沙　"Sand in Silk-Washing Stream," title of a tune.
2. 晏殊　(style 字, Tóngshū 同叔，991−1055), a famous poet in the early Northern Song. He is regarded as a leader of the "School of the Delicate and Restrained" (*wǎnyuēpài* 婉约派) in the *ci* poety of the early Northern Song.
3. 无可奈何　to have no way out, have no alternative. 👉面对这样的问题我们真是无可奈何 We have no way out when facing such a problem.
4. 径　n. path. See also P23 note 6.　　5. 徘徊　v. to hang around. See also P37 note 6.

现代文翻译 Modern Chinese Translation

　　听一曲新写的词，喝一杯酒。去年这时候的天气，池塘和亭台都还在，不过夕阳西下了，不知什么时候再回来啊！

　　眼前的花就这样落下来，我无可奈何；燕子飞回来了，我好像曾经见过它们。在小院飘着花香的小路上，我独自徘徊着。

评论与提问 Comment and Question

This lyric song presents a simple picture: a figure with a cup of wine in hand paces a path in the garden alone, seeing the old pond terrace, fallen blossoms, and swallows. However, the emotion expressed is ambiguous: is the subject missing an old friend with whom he was together a year ago? Is he sighing for the loss of the beautiful spring blossoms (and thus, time's inexorable passing)? How do the various images differently reflect on the passage of time? How do the parallelisms and contrasts in the poem function? ☞HTRCP, pp. 258–259 for an analysis of this lyric song and explain what you think is the subject of the poet's gentle lament.

P99

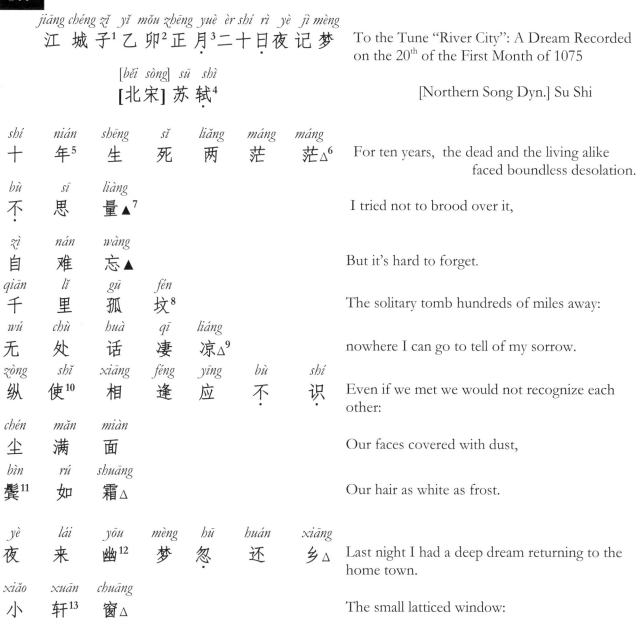

jiāng chéng zǐ yǐ mǒu zhēng yuè èr shí rì yè jì mèng
江 城 子¹ 乙 卯² 正 月³ 二 十 日 夜 记 梦

[běi sòng] sū shì
[北宋] 苏 轼⁴

To the Tune "River City": A Dream Recorded on the 20ᵗʰ of the First Month of 1075

[Northern Song Dyn.] Su Shi

shí   nián   shēng   sǐ   liǎng   máng   máng
十 年⁵ 生 死 两 茫 茫△⁶

For ten years, the dead and the living alike faced boundless desolation.

bù   sī   liàng
不 思 量▲⁷

I tried not to brood over it,

zì   nán   wàng
自 难 忘▲

But it's hard to forget.

qiān   lǐ   gū   fén
千 里 孤 坟⁸

The solitary tomb hundreds of miles away:

wú   chù   huà   qī   liáng
无 处 话 凄 凉△⁹

nowhere I can go to tell of my sorrow.

zòng   shǐ   xiāng   féng   yīng   bù   shí
纵 使¹⁰ 相 逢 应 不 识

Even if we met we would not recognize each other:

chén   mǎn   miàn
尘 满 面

Our faces covered with dust,

bìn   rú   shuāng
鬓¹¹ 如 霜△

Our hair as white as frost.

yè   lái   yōu   mèng   hū   huán   xiāng
夜 来 幽¹² 梦 忽 还 乡△

Last night I had a deep dream returning to the home town.

xiǎo   xuān   chuāng
小 轩¹³ 窗△

The small latticed window:

zhèng	*shū*	*zhuāng*				
正	梳[14]	妆△[15]				She's putting on her make-up.
xiāng	*gù*	*wú*	*yán*			
相	顾[16]	无	言			Facing each other, we had no words
wéi	*yǒu*	*lèi*	*qiān*	*háng*		
惟[17]	有	泪	千	行△		but a thousand lines of tears.
liào	*dé*	*nián*	*nián*	*cháng*	*duàn*	*chù*
料[18]	得	年	年	肠	断[19]	处

I imagine the place that has broken my heart year after year:

míng	*yuè*	*yè*
明	月	夜

A moonlit night,

duǎn	*sōng*	*gāng*
短	松	冈△[20]

The Low Pine Hills.

[慢词 long song lyric]

(Tr. Zong-qi Cai)

字词释义 Vocabulary Notes

1. 江城子 "River Town," title of a tune.
2. 乙卯 (年) the year of 1075. The traditional Chinese calendrical system is composed of Stems (*gān* 干) and Branches (*zhī* 支). Stems include ten Heavenly Stems (*tiān gān* 天干), which 乙 belongs to; Branches include twelve Earthly Branches (*dì zhī* 地支), which 卯 belongs to. Stems and Branches is a cyclic numeral system of 60 combinations of the above two cycles. Su Shi's first wife passed away in 1065. Ten years later, Su Shi wrote this poem in memory of her.
3. 正 (*zhēng*) 月 first month in the Chinese lunar calendar.
4. See the biographic note in P31 note 2.
5. 十年 ten years, referring to the ten years since Su Shi's wife died.
6. 茫茫 adj. boundless and indistinct. 👉他感到前途茫茫 He felt his prospects were bleak.
7. 思量 v. to turn something over in one's mind, consider. 👉他思量了半天，决定还是不去了 He considered it for a while, and decided not to go.
8. 坟 n. tomb. See also P95 note 18.
9. 凄凉 adj. miserable. 👉他晚景凄凉 He led a miserable and dreary life in his old age.
10. 纵 (縱) 使 conj. even if, even though.
11. 鬓 (鬢) n. hair on the temples. See also P03 note 18.
12. 幽 adj. deep and remote. See also P23 note 7. 幽梦 dreamland.
13. 轩 (軒) n. windows. See also P12 note 9.
14. 梳 v. to comb one's hair. See also P64 note 13.
15. 妆 (妝) n. makeup. See also P04 note 20.
16. 顾 (顧) v. to look back, look at. See P38 note 17 for a different meaning of the word.
17. 惟 adv. only. MdnC: 只 (*zhǐ*). Cf. 唯 in P29 note 7.

18. 料 v. to expect, anticipate. MdnC: 料想 (*liào xiǎng*). 👉这真是<u>料想</u>不到的事情 Who would have thought this would happen!

19. 肠 (腸) 断 adj. heartbroken. See also P96 note 6.

20. 冈 (岡) n. ridge (of a hill). 短松冈, Low Pine Hills is the place where Su Shi's wife's tomb was.

现代文翻译 Modern Chinese Translation

十年了，(我和你)生死相隔，遥不可及！不去思量，[7]却难以忘怀。(你在)千里之外孤零零的坟墓里，我都没办法和你说说这些年凄凉[9]的生活。即使再相见，你也应该认不出我了，我如今已是尘土满面，两鬓斑白了！

夜里梦中，忽然回到家乡，见到小窗前，你正在梳妆打扮。(终于见到了，你我却)一直望着彼此，说不出来话，只[17]有眼泪，流个不停！料想[18]得到，每年让我伤心不已的地方，就在明月照耀的夜晚，那短松冈上啊！

评论与提问 Comment and Question

In logic, there are two opposite processes of reasoning: inductive and deductive. Inductive reasoning proceeds from individual instances to generalizations and deductive reasoning works the other way round.   In poetry, we can perceive two corresponding processes of emotional expression: internalization and externalization. Internalization is a process in which a certain external phenomenon (an object, a scene, an event, and so on) arouses emotional responses in a poet, followed by his attempt to reflect on and express his emotions. Externalization is a process in which the poet begins with general statements about his emotions and then presents their "objective correlatives" (T. S. Eliot's words), such as an object, a scene, an event, and so on, in an effort to make manifest his innermost emotions.

A sustained process of externalization is most evident in this poem. The poet begins the poem by stating what has made his yearning for his deceased wife so unbearable: the insurmountable invisible separation between the living and the dead, aggravated by a physical separation from her tomb. What follows is a series of two imagined scenes. Each imagined encounter with his wife presents a feeble attempt by the poet to overcome the separation through imagination. Each attempt is thwarted by the recognition of a new grief: the change of their faces beyond mutual recognition (lines 6–8), the loss of their ability to communicate with each other (lines 9–13), and the perpetuation of his sorrow in years to come (lines 14–16). Does this poem display a distinct aggregate structure? Read the comments on aggregate structure in P95 and formulate your answer.

P100

chāi tóu fēng
钗 头 凤[1]

[nán sòng] lù yóu
[南宋] 陆 游[2]

To the Tune "Phoenix Hairpin"

[Southern Song Dyn.] Lu You

hóng   sū   shǒu   huáng   téng   jiǔ
红 酥[3] 手▲ 、黄 滕 酒▲[4]

Her red and soft hands
and the Yellow Cane wine,

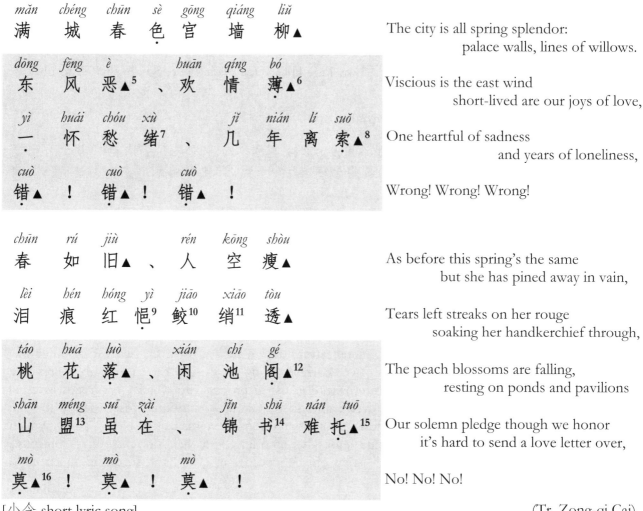

mǎn	chéng	chūn	sè	gōng	qiáng	liǔ
满	城	春	色	宫	墙	柳▲

The city is all spring splendor:
　　　　palace walls, lines of willows.

dōng	fēng	è		huān	qíng	bó
东	风	恶▲5	、	欢	情	薄▲6

Viscious is the east wind
　　　　short-lived are our joys of love,

yì	huái	chóu	xù		jǐ	nián	lí	suǒ
一	怀	愁	绪7	、	几	年	离	索▲8

One heartful of sadness
　　　　and years of loneliness,

cuò		cuò		cuò	
错▲	！	错▲！		错▲	！

Wrong! Wrong! Wrong!

chūn	rú	jiù		rén	kōng	shòu
春	如	旧▲	、	人	空	瘦▲

As before this spring's the same
　　　　but she has pined away in vain,

lèi	hén	hóng	yì	jiāo	xiāo	tòu
泪	痕	红	悒9	鲛10	绡11	透▲

Tears left streaks on her rouge
　　　　soaking her handkerchief through,

táo	huā	luò		xián	chí	gé
桃	花	落▲	、	闲	池	阁▲12

The peach blossoms are falling,
　　　　resting on ponds and pavilions

shān	méng	suī	zài		jǐn	shū	nán	tuō
山	盟13	虽	在	、	锦	书14	难	托▲15

Our solemn pledge though we honor
　　　　it's hard to send a love letter over,

mò		mò		mò	
莫▲16	！	莫▲	！	莫▲	！

No! No! No!

[小令 short lyric song]　　　　　　　　　　　　　　　　　　(Tr. Zong-qi Cai)

字词释义 Vocabulary Notes

1. 钗头凤 (釵頭鳳)　"Phoenix Hairpin," title of a tune. This poem tells a love story between Lu You and his first wife Tang Wan 唐琬. Both Lu You and Tang Wan were talented in poetry. They loved each other very much and got married. However, Lu You's mother disliked Tang Wan, and eventually forced Lu You to divorce her. Later Lu You and Tang Wan got married again respectively. In 1155, Lu You visited Shenyuan 沈园 and met Tang Wan by chance. Both of them were greatly saddened. Lu You thus wrote this poem on the wall. Tang Wan also wrote a poem to the same tune to answer Lu You's and express her sorrow.

2. See the biographic note in P17 note 1.

3. 酥　adj.　soft. MdnC: 柔软 (róu ruǎn). 📖垫子很柔软 This cushion is soft.

4. 黄滕酒　or 黄封酒　a wine made in the Song Dynasty.

5. 恶(惡 è)　v.　to dislike. MdnC: 可恶 (kě wù) detestable. 📖这些蚊子太可恶了 What a nuisance these mosquitos are!

6. 薄　adj.　weak. See also P63 note 9.

7. 绪 (緒) n. end of thread. 愁绪, "gloomy mood."

8. 索 n. large rope. Here it means "all alone, all by himself." MdnC: 离群索居 (*lí qún suǒ jū*) to live all alone [formal].

9. 悒 adj. sorrowful, depressed, unhappy. The character here is used in the sense of "浥" (*yì*), which means "to wet, moisten." 红浥 means "to wet her makeup."

10. 鲛 (鮫) n. shark. Here it refers to the shark people (*jiāo rén* 鲛人), who lived outside the Southern Sea. See also P75 note 16.

11. 绡 (綃) n. raw silk fabric. 鲛绡 refers to raw silk or "handkerchief"(*shǒu pà* 手帕), woven by the shark people.

12. 阁 (閣) n. pavilion (usu. two-storied). See also P14 note 10.

13. 盟 n. pledge. 山盟 means "a solemn pledge of love."

14. 锦书 (錦書) See P08 note 10.

15. 托 v. to ask, entrust. 👉这事就托给他吧 Let's entrust the matter to her.

16. 莫 v. let it be. MdnC: 罢了 (*bà le*). See P04 note 24 for a different meaning of the word.

现代文翻译 Modern Chinese Translation

　　红润柔软³的小手，捧着黄封酒，⁴ 满城春天的景色，宫墙外柳树绿了。(我们一同在柳树下饮酒，欣赏春天的景色。) 东风太可恶⁵了，(把欢乐吹走了，) 使我们的情感淡薄了。满心都是忧愁，几年的分离，让我非常孤独。回想起来，都是错啊！

　　又是春天了，美景还是一样的，可是 (她)人却瘦了很多。泪水不停，把脸上的红妆都洗掉了，手帕也湿透了。桃花落在寂寞的池塘亭台上，永远相爱的山盟还在，却没有办法托人给她送去情书，罢了！¹⁶

评论与提问 Comment and Question

Phoenix Hairpin" is a tune created by Lou You specially for expressing his extreme sorrow over his forced divorce with his beloved soul mate Tang Wan. Its prosodic, syntactic, and structural design is aimed at translating this sorrow into an outburst of sounds, images, and statements.

The rhyme is extremely dense: 18 of the 60 characters in this short poem are rhyming characters, all in short, explosive "departing tone" (*qùshēng* 去声) or "entering tone" (*rùshēng* 入声). Each stanza presents a forceful crescendo of trisyllabic segments: 3+3, 4+3, 3+3, 4+4, 3 (or 1+1+1). This march of trisyllabic segments gains momentum each time it is delayed by a tetrasyllabic block until it reaches a climatic ending in 1+1+1.

Each of the two stanzas is topic+comment: first, a snapshot of Tang Wan, and then Lou You's heartrending outcries. Two rhymes are used in each stanza, one for the topic section and the other for the comment section. As the two stanzas are strictly symmetrical in line configuration, thematic role, and rhyme use, the poem can be said to have a twin topic+comment structure.

Do you think the dynamics of this tune are sufficient for the poet to express his extreme sorrow?

练习　EXERCISES

一　填空 Fill in blank

A. 诗词填字：凄 魄 凉 奈 绪 首 盟 断 曲 赢 孤 托 曾 堪 觉 索 旧

1. 无可____何花落去，似____相识燕归来。　2. 千里____坟，无处话____ ____。
3. 十年一____扬州梦，____得青楼薄幸名。　4. 山____虽在，锦书难____。
5. 落____江南载酒行，楚腰肠____掌中轻。　6. 故国不____回____月明中。
7. 一____新词酒一杯，去年天气____池台。　8. 一怀愁____，几年离____。

B. 现代文填词：柔软 可恶 料想 思量 凄凉 茫茫 不堪 结束

1. 她晚景____ ____。　2. 他____ ____半天，决定不去了。　3. 往事____ ____回首。
4. 会议五点____ ____。　5. 这真是____ ____不到的事情。　6. 垫子很____ ____。
7. 他感到前途____ ____。　8. 蚊子真是太____ ____了。

二　形近字辨析 Distinguish easily confused characters

1. 雕栏玉____应犹在　a. 彻　b. 砌　c. 切　2. 短松____　a. 冈　b. 风　c. 岗
3. ____有泪千行　a. 维　b. 唯　c. 惟　4. 锦书难____　a. 拖　b. 托　c. 讬
5. 落____江南载酒行　a. 魄　b. 魂　c. 愧　6. 一怀愁____　a. 绪　b. 赌　c. 睹

三　连句 Match the first part with the second

1. 料得年年肠断处( )　2. 十年一觉扬州梦( )　3. 无可奈何花落去( )　4. 山盟虽在( )
5. 问君能有几多愁( )　6. 春花秋月何时了( )　7. 落魄江南载酒行( )　8. 一怀愁绪( )

a. 似曾相识燕归来　　b. 几年离索　　c. 明月夜，短松冈　　d. 楚腰肠断掌中轻
e. 往事知多少　　　　f. 锦书难托　　g. 赢得青楼薄幸名　　h. 恰似一江春水向东流

四　句读 Punctuate and translate the following passage

春花秋月何时了往事知多少东风恶欢情薄一怀愁绪几年离索夜来幽梦忽还乡小轩窗正梳妆无可奈何花落去似曾相识燕归来小园香径独徘徊

五　听写 Dictation

1. 小 ____ ____ ____又____ ____，____ ____不____ ____ ____ ____ ____中。
2. ____ ____ ____南____ ____ ____，____ ____ ____ ____ ____中____。
3. 问____ ____有____ ____ ____，____ 一____ ____向____。
4. ____ ____ ____花____，____ ____ ____ ____ ____来。
5. ____ ____ ____，人____，____。

<h1 style="text-align:center">文学议题列表</h1>
<h2 style="text-align:center">List of Literary Issues Discussed</h2>

1. 文体 Genres

1.1 古体诗 Ancient-Style Poetry

    1.1.1 四言诗 tetrasyllabic poem   P01 ☞ *HTRCP*, p. 382

    1.1.2 乐府 music bureau poems   P06, P90 ☞ *HTRCP*, pp. 84–85

    1.1.3 五言诗 pentasyllabic poems   P10, P11, P14, P38, P60, P69, P70 ☞ *HTRCP*, pp. 385–387

    1.1.4 古绝 ancient quatrains   P69, P70 ☞ *HTRCP*, pp. 143–144

    1.1.5 七言诗 heptasyllabic poems   P21, P95

1.2 近体诗 Recent-Style Poetry ☞ *HTRCP*, pp. 162–172, 199–200, 219–223

    1.2.1 五言律诗 pentasyllabic regulated verses   P12, P15, P23, P24 ☞ *HTRCP*, pp. 162–172

    1.2.2 七言律诗 heptasyllabic regulated verses   P03, P13, P17, P18 ☞ *HTRCP*, pp. 199–200

    1.2.3 五言律绝 pentasyllabic regulated quatrains P27, P29, P31 ☞ *HTRCP*, pp. 219–223

    1.2.4 七言律绝 heptasyllabic regulated quatrains P08, P19, P20, P22 ☞ *HTRCP*, pp. 219–223

1.3 词 Lyric

    1.3.1 小令 short lyric songs   P04, P05, P07, P66 ☞ *HTRCP*, pp. 245–246

    1.3.2 慢词 long lyric songs   P83, P99 ☞ *HTRCP*, pp. 262–263

1.4 曲 Song ☞ *HTRCP*, pp. 329–330

    1.4.1 小令 solo song poems   P09, P33, P47, P89 ☞ *HTRCP*, pp. 330–333

    1.4.2 散套 song suite ☞ *HTRCP*, pp. 330, 449–351

2. 韵律 Prosody

2.1 韵脚 Rhyme ☞ *HTRCP*, pp. 6–7

    2.1.1 rhyme in level tone   P02, P04

    2.1.2 rhyme in oblique tone   P14, P67

    2.1.3 rhyme in both level and oblique tones   P33

    2.1.4 multiple rhymes in a poem   P01, P06, P21, P63 ☞ *HTRCP*, pp. 245–247

2.2 节律 Rhythm ☞ *HTRCP*, pp. 7, 381–388

    2.2.1 2+3 rhythm of pentasyllabic poems P10, P38 ☞ *HTRCP*, pp. 103–105

    2.2.2 2+2+3 and 4+3 rhythms in heptasyllabic poems P53, P82, P94 ☞ *HTRCP*, pp. 391–392, 388-390

    2.2.3 five major semantic rhythms of hexasyllabic lines   P16

    2.2.4 varied rhythms in *ci* poetry P84, P100

2.3 平仄 Tonal Patterning

    2.3.1 four tonal patterns of the regulated quatrain ☞ *HTRCP*, 169–171

    2.3.2 four tonal patterns of the regulated verse ☞ *HTRCP*, 171–172

2.3.3 tonal patterning in *ci* poetry   ☞ *HTRCP*, 247–248

2.3.4 tonal patterning in *qu* poetry   ☞ *HTRCP*, 331–332

3. 句法 Syntax

3.1 主谓句 Subject + Predicate Sentence   ☞ *HTRCP*, pp. 7–9, 380–381

3.1.1 subject + predicate sentences in Wang Wei's "Calling Bird Brook"   P27

3.1.2 subject + predicate sentences in Du Fu's "Upon Hearing the Recapture of Henan and Hebei"   P52

3.1.3 mangled subject + predicate sentences in Du Fu''s "Autumn Meditation, No. 8"   P85

3.2 题评句 Topic + Comment Sentence   ☞ *HTRCP*, pp. 7–9, 382–396

3.2.1 topic + comment sentences in the *Shijing*   P01

3.2.2 successive use of topic + comment sentences in "Nineteen Old Poem, No. 2"   P60

3.2.3 successive use of topic + comment sentences in Du Fu's "The Jiang and Han Rivers"   P44   ☞ *HTRCP*, pp. 174–176

3.2.4 topic + comment sentences in Yang Wanli's "A Small Pond"   P32

3.3 对句 Parallel Couplet

3.3.1 definition of the parallel couplet   P13   ☞ *HTRCP*, p. 165

3.3.2 "parallel phrasing" in a prototype of regulated verse by Xie Tiao   P14

3.3.3 "flowing-water couplet"   P52

3.3.4 "borrowed parallelism"   P92   ☞ *HTRCP*, pp. 183, 185

3.4 倒装句法 Syntactic Inversion

3.4.1 multiple inversions in Wang Changling's "Following the Army"   P49

3.4.2 multiple inversions in Wang Wei's "Visiting the Xiangji Temple"   P24

4. 章节结构 Stanza Organization

4.1 诗的题评章节 Topic + Comment Stanzas in *Shi* Poetry   ☞ *HTRCP*, p. 382

4.1.1 topic + comment stanza in the *Shijing*   P01

4.1.2 *xing* and stanzaic organization   P01   ☞ *HTRCP*, pp. 14, 20, 25

4.2 词的题评章节 Topic + Comment Stanzas in *Ci* Poetry

4.2.1 Bai Juyi's "Prolonged Longing"   P07

4.2.2 interlocked topic + comment stanzas in Xin Qiji's "To the Tune of 'South Village'"   P84

4.2.3 Lu You's "To the Tune 'Phoenix Hairpin'"   P100

5. 诗篇结构 Poem Structure

5.1 题评结构 Topic + Comment Structure

5.1.1 topic + comment structure in pentasyllabic ancient-style *shi* poetry   P42, P60   ☞ *HTRCP*, pp. pp. 103–104, 112–113, 385–387

5.1.2 topic + comment structure and four-stage progression in a pentasyllabic regulated verse   P80   ☞ *HTRCP*, pp. 165–169

5.1.3 topic + comment structure of a heptasyllabic quatrain   P62   ☞ *HTRCP*, pp. 387–388

5.1.4 topic + comment structure of a heptasyllabic regulated verse   P53   ☞ *HTRCP*, pp. 387–392

5.2 起承转合 Four Stage Progression

5.2.1 four-stage progression of a regulated quatrain   P29

5.2.2 four-stage progression of a regulated verse   P12, 62   ☞ *HTRCP*, pp. 165–169

5.2.3 four-stage progression annulled in Li Shangyin's "Brocade Zither"   P75

5.3 聚集结构 Aggregate Structure

5.3.1 introspection and aggregate structure in Li He's "Advent of Autumn"   P95

5.3.2 radical fragmentation of the *lüshi* structure in Li Shangyin's "Brocade Zither"   P75

5.3.3 introspection and aggregate structure in Su Shi's "To the Tune 'River City'"   P99

6. 词藻 Diction

6.1 连绵字 Alliterative and Rhyming Binomes   ☞ *HTRCP*, pp. 382, 395-397

6.1.1 complete and partial reduplicatives used in *Shijing*   P01

6.1.2 successive use of reduplicatives in "Nineteen Old Poems, No 2"   P60

6.2 实字与虚字 Content and Empty Words

6.2.1 preponderance of content words in an ancient quatrain by Wang Rong   P74

6.2.2 preponderance of content words in regulated verses   P43, P74   ☞ *HTRCP*, pp. 163–164

6.2.3 preponderance of content words in Meng Haoran's quatrain "An Overnight Stay by the Jiande River"   P43

6.2.4 avoidance of "empty words" in a regulated verse   P43, 74   ☞ *HTRCP*, pp. 163–164

6.2.5 padding words used in a *sanqu* poem   P09   ☞ *HTRCP*, p. 333

6.3 典故 Allusion

6.3.1 conflicting historical allusions in Li Shangyin's "Untitled"   P62

6.3.2 hidden allusions in Wang Anshi's "Written on Master Huyin's Wall, No.1"   P13

7. 意象 Imagery

7.1 兴 (*Xing*) Affective Image

7.1.1 affective image in a topic+comment line in the *Shijing*   P01

7.1.2 *xing* and stanzaic organization   P01   ☞ *HTRCP*, pp. 14, 20, 25

7.1.3 images as "objective correlatives" to emotions   P99

7.2 比 Analogical Image

7.2.1 used in Meng Jiao's "Song of a Traveling Son"   P42

7.3 特殊视听效果 Special Visual and Aural Effects

7.3.1 play of elusive images and Chan vision   P23, P24, P25, P26, P27

7.3.2 optical illusion in Meng Haoran's "An Overnight Stay by the Jiande River"   P43

7.3.3 images used to evoke a perceptual process   P34, P94

7.3.4 noun-images used to suggest a temporal process   P46, P47

8. 修辞 Rhetorical Devices

8.1 拟人 Personification

    8.1.1 complete personification in Su Shi's "Crabapple" P78

    8.1.2 topic + comment lines and partial personification in Yang Wanli's "A Small Pond" P32

8.2 反讽 Irony

    8.2.1 masterful play of irony in Zhang Ye's "The Book-Burning Pits" P88

8.3 暗喻与代称 Metaphor and Metonym

    8.3.1 successive use of metonyms in Du Fu's "Meditations on Ancient Ruins, No. 3" P80

    8.3.2 metaphors in Li Shangyin's "Untitled" P03

8.4 重复 Repetition

    8.4.1 incremental repetition in the *Shijing* P01 ☞ *HTRCP*, pp. 19–20

    8.4.2 anadiplosis used in a *yuefu* poem P06 ☞ *HTRCP*, p. 23

8.5 时空巧构 Spatio-Temporal Maneuvering

    8.5.1 two kinds of human time in "Nineteen Old Poems, No. 1" P38 ☞ *HTRCP*, pp. 105–106

    8.5.2 spatial consciousness in frontier poems: China proper versus the land of nomads P39

    8.5.3 handling of time and space in poems on homesickness P54, P55

    8.5.4 strategies of temporal imagination in Wang Changling's "Setting Out for the Frontiers" P50

    8.5.5 abrupt shifts of viewing perspectives in Li Bai's "Watching the Waterfall of Mount Lu" P19

    8.5.6 velocity of movement captured in Li Bai's "Departing Baidi in the Morning" P35

    8.5.7 "see big within small": an aesthetic ideal of the quatrain form P51

    8.5.8 a feat of spatial maneuvering in Jiao Dao's "Crossing the Sanggan River" P58

    8.5.9 a feat of temporal maneuvering in Li Shangyin's "Night Rain: A Poem Sent to the North" P59

    8.5.10 moments of heightened perception in a quatrain by Wang Anshi P77

入声字列表

List of Entering-Tone Characters, with Phonetic Transcriptions

This list contains the entering-tone characters used in the recent-style *shi* poems and *ci* poems presented in his workbook. All entering-tone characters end with the unaspirated consonant *p*, *t*, or *k*. Prevalent though they were during Tang and Song times, entering tones no longer exist in modern standard Chinese, but they are preserved in many regional Chinese dialects like Cantonese and Hakka.

bā 八	peat	dú 独	duwk	jiá 荚	kep	pù 瀑	buwk
bái 白	baek[1]	dú 毒	dowk	jiǎo 角	kaewk	qiè 妾	tshjep
bǎi 百	paek	duó 铎	dak	jié 杰	gjet	qī 戚	tshek
běi 北	pok[2]	fā 发	pjot	jú 菊	kjuwk	qī 七	tshit
bì 必	pjit	fú 宓	mit	jué 觉	kaewk	qià 恰	kheap
bǐ 笔	pit	fù 复	pjuwk	jué 绝	dzjwet	qǔ 曲	khjowk
bì 壁	pek	gé 阁	kak	kè 客	khaek	què 却	khjak
bì 碧	pjaek	gé 隔	keak	là 腊	lap	què 雀	tsjak
bié 别	bjet	gè 各	kak	là 蜡	lap	rì 日	nyit
bó 薄	bak	guō 郭	kwak	lè 乐	lak	rù 入	nyip
bó 柏	paek	guó 国	kwok	lì 力	lik	ruò 若	nyak
bó 泊	bak	hé 合	hop	lì 立	lip	sà 飒	sop
bó 帛	baek	hè 壑	hak	lì 历	lek	sè 瑟	srit
bù 不	pwot	hè 鹤	hak	lì 粒	lip	sè 色	srik
cè 侧	tsrik	hū 忽	xwot	lù 鹿	luwk	shī 失	syit
chā 插	tsrheap[3]	huó 活	hwat	lüè 略	ljak	shí 十	dzyip
chè 坼	trhaek	jī 积	tsjek	luò 落	lak	shí 拾	dzyip
chǐ 尺	tsyhek	jī 跡	tsjek	luò 洛	lak	shí 识	syik
chì 赤	tsyhek	jí 及	gip	lǜ 绿	ljowk	tà 踏	thop
chū 出	tsyhwit	jí 极	gik	miè 灭	mjiet	tà 闼	that
cuò 错	tshak	jí 即	tsik	mì 觅	mek	tiě 铁	thet
dé 得	tok	jí 集	dzip	mǒ 抹	mat	tuō 讬	thak
dī 滴	tek	jǐ 戟	kjaek	mò 莫	mak	tuō 托	thak
dí 笛	dek	jí 汲	kip	mò 漠	mak	wà 袜	mjot
dié 蝶	dep	jì 寂	dzek	mò 寞	mak	wù 物	mjut
mù 目	muwk	shí 实	zyit	yǐ 乙	'it	xī 息	sik
mù 木	muwk	shí 石	dzyek	yì 亿	'ik	xī 夕	zjek
mù 幕	mak	shì 轼	syik	yì 亦	yek	xī 惜	sjek
niè 啮	nget	shuō 说	sywet	yì 浥	'ip	xī 昔	sjek
pò 魄	phaek	shuò 朔	sraewk	yì 悒	'ip	xiá 狎	heap
pū 扑	phuwk	sù 宿	sjuwk	yì 驿	yek	xuě 雪	sjwet
pǔ 朴	phaewk	suǒ 索	sak	yì 忆	'ik	yào 药	Yak

yè 叶	yep[4]	yuè 月	ngjwot	zhú 竹	trjuwk	zú 足	tsjowk
yè 谒	'jot	yù 玉	ngjowk	zhú 烛	tsyowk	zuó 昨	dzak
yī 一	'jit	zhé 折	dzyet	zhuó 著	drjak	zuò 作	tsak
yù 欲	yowk	zhī 织	tsyik	zhuó 啄	traewk		
yuè 悦	ywet	zhí 直	drik	zhuó 浊	draewk		

Transcriber's Note:

This transcription is based on the "Early Middle Chinese" system of pronunciation as given in the *Qièyùn* 切韵 (literally, "Cutting rhymes"), an important Chinese dictionary of 601 CE, arranged according to rhyme, which indicates pronunciations in some detail. The transcription is philologically accurate in that it represents all the distinctions known from the *Qièyùn* and other Middle Chinese sources. Designed with nonspecialists in mind, it uses only the letters and symbols of the English keyboard. However, there were more sounds in Middle Chinese than we have letters, so some sounds are represented by two, three, or even four letters. Also, Middle Chinese had some sounds that modern English does not, and vice versa (as with any two languages). In order to represent Middle Chinese pronunciation, some arbitrary conventions are necessary. The following are the main ones (described more fully in William H. Baxter, *A Handbook of Old Chinese Phonology* [Berlin: Mouton de Gruyter, 1992], pp. 27–85).

— William H. Baxter

[1.] The cluster "ae" and "ea" represent single vowel sounds (probably like the vowels of "bat" and "bet" respectively).

[2.] The letter "o" is used to represent a sound which was probably like the short "u" of English "tug" (not like the usual English "o").

[3.] The letter "r" after a consonant indicates that it is pronounced with retroflexion—that is, with the tip of the tongue turned back to touch the hard palate. English does not use such sounds, but they are found in many other languages, including modern Mandarin (written *zh-*, *ch-*, *sh-* in pinyin) and the languages of the Indic family (such as Hindi). An "h" after a consonant indicates that it is aspirated (that is, pronounced with an audible puff of breath after it). So a combination like "tsrh-" represents a ch-like consonant which is retroflex (as indicated by the -r-) and aspirated (as indicated by the -h-) —more or less like the Mandarin sound written "ch" in pinyin romanization.

[4.] The letter *y* at the beginning of a word represents an ordinary *y* sound, but the combinations *sy* and *zy* present, respectively, sounds like *sh* and *zh* (the sound between the vowels in "pressure" and "pleasure," respectively). Similarly, *tsy* presents a *ch* sound (without aspiration; if it is aspirated, it is written *tsyh* [for example, *chi* 赤 *tsyhek*]). When a *y* sound appears after the initial consonant or at the end of the syllable, it is written as *j* (as is customary in linguistics).

所 用 字 列 表
Character List

A

 āi 哀 sorrow P93
　　👉悲伤(bēi shāng)
ǎi 霭(靄) mist P15
　　👉雾气(wù qì)
ài 嗳(嗳) instinct P14
　　嗳嗳 P10
ān 安 quiet P38
　　鞍 saddle P67
　　安禅 P24

B

bá 跋涉 to trudge P44
bǎ 把 to hold P12,65
　　👉握住(wò zhù)
bái 白草 white grass P33
　　白日 white sun P34,38,52
　　👉太阳(tài yang)
bǎi 百姓 P86
bān 斑白 P54
bǎn 板桥 P02,46
bàn 伴 companion P52
bǎo 保重 P38
bào 报 to report P42
　　👉报答(bào dá)
　　抱怨 to complain P48
bēi 悲 sad P93
bèi 倍 double P55
　　👉更加(gèng jiā)
bēn 奔流 P19
bì 壁 wall P13,36
　　蔽 to cover P38
　　👉遮蔽(zhē bì)
　　碧 bluish green P40,65,85
　　👉碧蓝(bì lán)
biān 编(編) to weave P95
biàn 遍 all over P55
　　便 convenient P87
biàn 辨 to distinguish P11
　　👉辨析(biàn xī)
biǎo 表里 P89
bié 别枝 P16
bìn 鬓(鬢) P03,54,63,93,99

bō 波涛 P89
bó 泊 to berth P20, 43
　　👉停泊(tíng bó) P45
　　薄 ①to approach P24
　　　②weak, light P63,96,100
　　👉淡(dàn)

C

cái 才 gift P62
　　👉才华(cái huá)
cǎi 采 to pick (v.) P01
　　彩云 P35
cán 残(殘) P03,08,33,63
　　👉谢(xiè) P03
　　👉乱(luàn) P63
cán 蚕(蠶) P03
cāng 苍(蒼) blue P75
cēn 参差 P01
chā 插 to stick in P55
chāi 钗(釵) hairpin P04
　　钗头凤 P100
chái 柴 firewood P25
　　👉柴火(cháihuo)
chán 蝉(蟬) cicada P16
　　蟾 toad P21
　　👉蟾蜍(chán chú)
　　禅(禪) P23
　　蝉鬓 P04
chāng 倡 singing girl P60
cháng 裳 skirt P08,52
　　👉裙(qún)
　　肠(腸) intestine P47, 95
　　长相思 P07
　　长途 P44
　　长河 P73
　　肠断 P96, 99
chǎng 场(場) ground P12
chàng 畅谈 P12
cháo 巢 nest P38
　　朝 ① dynasty P87
　　👉朝代(cháo dài)
　　　② court P92
　　👉朝廷(cháo tíng)
chè 坼 to tear P79
　　👉分开(fēn kāi).

chén 尘 dust P39, 68
　　👉尘土(chén tǔ)
chén 沉 to sink P73
　　晨风 P06
　　尘网 P10
　　沉吟 P04
　　沉醉东风 P09
chéng 乘① to take P17
　　👉趁(chèn)
　　　② to ride P18, 41
　　成合 P09
　　👉团聚(tuán jù)
chóng 重① layers P17,35,67
　　　② again P38
　　崇 high P78
　　重叠 P64
　　重阳 P12
chóu 愁① to worry P03
　　👉担忧(dān yōu)
　　　② distress P07
　　👉离愁(lí chóu)
　　踌躇 P89
chū 初 beginning P23
chǔ 楚腰 P96
chù 矗立 P48
chuān 川 river P18, 19
　　穿 to cross P52, 92
chuán 传(傳) to spread P52,65,92
chuàng 怆(愴) sad P90
chuí 垂 to droop P04, 82
　　垂钓 P30
chūn 春情 P09
　　春心 P62
　　春水 P97
　　春风面 P80
cí 辞(辭) to leave P35, 40
　　👉告别(gào bié)
　　慈 kind P42
　　👉慈祥(cí xiáng)
cōng 憁 happiness P14
　　👉欢乐(huān lè)
　　憁郁 P14
cóng 从军行 P49
cú 徂 to go P94
　　👉逝去(shì qù) to pass
cuī 摧 to destroy P06

	催 to urge	P51
cuì	翠 emerald green	P20,63,85
cūn	村 village	P80
cùn	寸草	P42

D

dǎ	打湿	P21
	打翻	P21
dài	带 sash	P04
	待 to wait	P09
	玳瑁	P06
dān	丹 red	P53
dàn	但 ① only.	P03
	☞只(zhǐ)	
	② as long as	P50
	☞只要 (zhǐ yào)	
dāng	当 (當) ① facing	P06
	② should	P06
	☞应当 (yīng dāng)	
dàng	荡漾 to wave	P31
	荡子	P60
dào	道 to speak	P38, 63
	☞说 (shuō)	P38
	☞在乎(zàihu)	P63
	稻 rice	P16,85
	倒映	P85
dé	得 to get	P01
	☞得到 (dé dào)	
dēng	登高	P55, 93
dī	滴 to drip	P63
dí	笛.bamboo flute	P48
	敌手	P84
dǐ	抵 to be equal to	P91
dì	帝 emperor	P88
diān	巅 (巓) peak	P10
diǎn	典 to mortgage	P92
	☞典当 (diǎn dàng)	
	点(點) to touch	P92
diàn	殿 hall	P04
diàn	簟 bamboo mat	P08
	☞竹席 (zhú xí)	
diāo	雕 to carve	P67, 97
	凋落	P08
diào	钓 (釣) to fish	P30
	吊 to comfort	P95
	☞慰问(wèi wèn)	
dié	蝶恋花	P67
dōu	兜鍪	P84
dǒu	陡峭	P24
dú	独 (獨) alone	P08, 26
	☞独自 (dú zì)	

	毒龙	P24
	☞欲念 (yù niàn)	
dù	度 to cross	P48, 50,64
	☞过 (guò)	
	蠹 moth-eaten	P95
	渡头	P07
	☞渡口 (dù kǒu)	
	杜鹃	P75
duàn	断肠	P65
dào	堆 to pile up	P67
duō	多才	P09
	多情	P83
	多才多艺	P09
	多愁善感	P83
duó	铎(鐸)	P46

E

é	娥娥	P60
	蛾眉	P64
è	恶(惡) to dislike	P100
	☞可恶(kě wù)	
ér	儿 (兒) child	P05
	☞小孩儿(xiǎo háir)	
ěr	尔 (爾) like this	P11
	☞这样 (zhè yàng)	

F

fā	发(發) ① to develop	P62
	② to send out	P83
	☞焕发(huàn fā)	
fān	帆 sail	P40, 82
	翻 to to turn over	P74
fán	樊 cage	P10
	繁 complicated	P93
	烦杂	P10
fǎn	反侧	P01
	反 back	P38
fàn	泛 ① to float	P68
	② to be suffused	P78
fāng	方 ① not until	P03,07
	☞才 (cái)	
	② rectangular	P10
	③ just	P31
	☞正 (zhèng)	
	芳 fragrant	P76
	方始	P07
fàng	放 to release	P52
fèi	吠 to cry	P06
	☞叫 (jiào)	
fēn	分明	P04

	纷(紛) various	P14
	纷乱	P14
	分野	P15
fén	焚 to burn	P88
	坟 tomb	P95, 99
fěn	粉 powder	P95
fēng	风 (風) Airs	P01
	丰 (豐) abundant	P16
	☞丰收 (fēng shōu)	
	峰 peak	P24, 36
	☞山峰 (shān fēng)	
	枫 (楓) maple	P45
	烽火	P49, 91
	枫树	P33
	风光	P76, 84
	风流	P83
féng	缝 (縫) to stitch	P42, 69
	逢 to meet	P55
fèng	缝 chink	P21
	奉 to give	P71
	凤凰	P85
fú	服 to miss	P01
	☞思念 (sī niàn)	
	浮 to float	P38
	☞飘浮 (piāo fú)	
	凫 (鳧) wild duck	P46
	☞野鸭(yě yā)	
	芙蓉 lotus	P62
	☞荷花 (hé huā).	
	浮动	P76
fǔ	腐 rotten	P44, 82
	☞迂腐 (yū fǔ)	P44
	☞腐烂 (fǔ làn)	P82
fù	复(複) again	P17
	☞重复 (chóng fù)	
	赴 to go to	P80
	☞奔赴(bēn fù)	
	覆盖	P30

G

gǎi	改 to change	P03
	☞改变 (gǎi biàn)	
gài	盖 to surpass	P81
	☞盖过(gài guò)	
gān	干 to disturb	P85
	☞干预 (gān yù)	
	干戈	P53, 94
gǎn	感 to feel	P37
	☞感想 (gǎn xiǎng)	
gāng	冈 (岡) ridge	P99
gāo	高 tall	P06

	高耸	P23
gé	阁(閣)pavilion	P14, 100
gè	个 (個)	P09
gēng	更①to change	P21
	📖更新 (gēng xīn)	
	② watch	P63
	更漏子	P63
gōng	功 merit	P81
	📖功绩(gōng jì)	
	攻破	P50
gòng	共 and	P04
	📖和 (hé)	
gōu	钩 hook	P65
gū	孤 alone	P29,40,44,48
	📖孤单 (gū dān)	
gǔ	鼓 drum	P01, 17
	股 strand	P05
	古迹	P80
	古人	P90
gù	顾(顧)①to think	P38
	📖考虑(kǎo lǜ)	
	② to look back	P99
	故人	P12,39,40
	故国	P97
guà	挂 to hang	P19
guān	冠 hat	P17
	📖帽(mào)	
	关 (關) pass	P50
	纶(綸)	P83
	关山月	P49
	关关	P01
	官场	P10
	官军	P52
guǎn	馆(館) house	P26
guāng	光泽	P78
guī	归(歸) to return	P07,42,
	📖归来 (guī lái)	44,58
	闺(閨) chamber	P49
guì	桂 cassia tree	P21
	桂花	P27
gǔn	滚(滾) to turn	P84, 93
guō	郭 outer wall	P12,14,22
guò	过(過) to visit	P12, 24
	📖拜访 (bài fǎng)	

H

hǎi	海 ocean	P49
	海棠	P78
hán	含 to keep in mouth	P20
	寒鸦	P33, 71
hàn	汗青	P53

háo	豪 a great person	P83
hǎo	好转	P44
hé	合①whole	P09
	② to surround	P12, 15
	📖环绕 (huán rào)	
	③ should	P76
	📖应该(yīng gāi)	
	荷 lotus	P14
	何用	P06
	📖为什么 (wèi shén me)	
hè	壑 valley	P15, 80
hén	痕 mark	P04
	📖痕迹 (hén jì)	
hèn	恨①to hate	P07
	📖怨恨(yuàn hèn)	
	② to regret	P81, 93
	📖遗憾 (yí hàn)	
héng	横 horizontal	P36
hèng	横 perverse	P67
hóng	泓 a deep pool	P21
	鸿(鴻)	P33
	📖大雁 (dà yàn)	
	红(紅) red	P67
	红粉	P60
	红妆	P78
hòu	后庭花	P82
hú	胡 ethnic group	P38,50,80
	槲 daimyo oak	P46
hù	户 door	P10
	护 to guard	P13
	📖保护(bǎo hù)	
huā	花 flower	P64
	花虫	P95
huá	划 to scratch	P05
	华 (華)①flowery	P75
	②grey	P83
huà	化①to melt	P20
	②to transform	P79
	📖变成 (biàn chéng)	
	画堂	P63
	画图	P80
huái	怀(懷) mediation	P84
	怀古	P83
huǎn	缓(緩) slow	P38
	📖松 (sōng)	
huàn	浣溪纱	P98
huāng	荒 wasteland	P10
	📖荒地(huāng dì)	
huáng	篁	P26
	黄沙	P16
	黄花	P33
	皇恐 (惶恐)	P53

	黄莺	P61
	黄昏	P76
huī	灰 ash	P03
	晖(暉) sunshine	P42
	灰烬	P83
huí	回 circle	P46
	回荡	P23
	回首	P97
huǐ	悔 to regret	P73
hūn	昏 dark	P47
	📖黄昏 (huáng hūn)	
hún	浑(渾)① murky	P17
	📖浑浊 (hún zhuó)	
	② simply	P91
	📖简直 (jiǎn zhí)	
	魂 soul	P76,80,95
huó	活水	P37

J

jī	羁(羈)	P10
	积雪	P20
jí	即 at once	P52
	📖立即 (lì jí)	
	汲 to draw	P62
	极(極) extreme	P69
	集 to collect	P74
jǐ	戟 balberd	P87
jì	寄 to mail	P08,59,65
	计(計) way	P08,65
	📖办法(bàn fǎ)	
	迹 mark	P46
	📖足迹 (zú jì)	
	际 (際) border	P10, 40
	寂静	P27
jiā	佳 good	P55
jiá	蛱蝶	P92
jià	嫁 to get married	P83
jiān	坚贞	P05
	间阔	P09
jiǎn	剪 to cut	P59, 66
	简(簡) bamboo slip	P95
jiàn	见 to see	P16, 92
	涧(澗) brook	P27
	鉴(鑒) mirror	P37
	📖镜子 (jìng zǐ)	
	间(間) to separate	P74
	📖间隔 (jiàn gé)	
	溅(濺) to splash	P91
jiāng	将 (將) to carry	P13
	📖携带 (xié dài)	

	江城子	P99
jiàng	将 general	P50
jiāo	鲛(鮫) shark	P100
	交相	P64
	📖互相(hù xiāng)	
jiǎo	角 angel	P32
	皎皎	P60
jiào	教 to allow	P50, 61
jiē	阶(階) steps	P63, 69
	📖台阶(tái jiē)	
jié	结(結) construct	P11
	📖建(jiàn)	
	杰 outstanding	P83
	📖杰出(jié chū)	
	节拍	P41
jīn	金 gold	P64
	金蟾	P62
jǐn	锦书	P08,100
	紧锁	P08
jìn	尽(盡)①to exhaust	P03,34,39, 40, 68
	②to the limit	P29
	进士	P53
jīng	经(經)①classics	P53
	② to pass	P89
	📖经过(jīng guò)	
	惊(驚) to shock	P61
	📖惊醒(jīng xǐng)	
	精致	P08
	精通	P53
jǐng	景 shadow	P25
jìng	境 place	P11
	径 path(n.)	P23,24, 30,98
	📖小路(xiǎo lù)	
	镜(鏡) mirror	P64
jiū	纠结	P95
	九天	P19
jiù	就 to draw near	P12
	📖靠近(kào jìn)	
jū	雎鸠	P01
jú	菊	P11
jǔ	举 to raise	P57
jù	具 to prepare	P12
	📖准备(zhǔn bèi)	
	聚 to gather	P89
	📖聚集(jù jí)	
juān	捐 to abandon	P38
	涓 brook	P94
	涓涓	P32
juǎn	卷 to roll over	P52, 83
juàn	倦 weary	P68, 94
jué	绝(絕)① to cut off	P06
	📖断绝(duàn jué)	

	②to the limits	P30
	觉① to sense	P28
	📖察觉(chá jué)	
	② to wake up	P65, 96
	📖睡醒(shuì xǐng)	
	绝迹	P82
jūn	君子	P01
	菌 mushroom	P14
	📖蘑菇(mó gū)	
	K	
kāi	开垦	P10
	开启	P62
kān	堪 to endure	P97
kē	科	P09
kè	客舍	P39, 58
kēng	坑 hole	P88
kōng	空 in vain	P65
	📖徒劳(tú láo)	
	空濛	P31,78
kǒng	恐 fear	P42,68, 78
	📖担心(dān xīn)	
kòng	空 to empty	P23
	📖涤荡(dí dàng)	
kòu	扣 to knock	P17
	📖敲(qiāo)	
kū	枯 withered	P47
	📖枯萎(kū wěi)	
kǔ	苦 bitter	P93
kuǎn	款 lesuirely	P92
	款待	P17
kuáng	狂 crazy	P52
kuàng	旷(曠) spacious	P43
	📖空旷(kōng kuàng)	
kuī	窥(窺) to spy	P62
	📖窥视(kuī shì)	
	L	
lā	拉 to pull	P06
	📖折断(zhé duàn)	
là	蜡(蠟) candle	P63
	腊(臘)	P17
	📖腊月(là yuè)	
	蜡(蠟) 炬	P03
	📖蜡烛(là zhú)	
lài	籁(籟) sound	P23
lán	兰舟	P08
	栏(欄) balustrade	P97
	📖栏杆(lán gān)	
lǎn	懒(懶) lazy	P64
láng	廊 porch	P78

	郎君	P05
lè	乐(樂) to please	P01
	📖取悦(qǔ yuè)	
	勒 to tight	P67
lěi	累 overlapping	P14
	📖重叠(chóng dié)	
	垒(壘) rampant	P83
	📖营垒(yíng lěi)	
lèi	酹 to pour out	P83
lěng	冷 cold	P24
	冷却	P88
lí	篱(籬) fence	P11
	📖篱笆(lí ba)	
	鹂(鸝) oriole	P20
	梨 pear	P74
lǐ	李 plum	P10
	理 to put into order	P66
	礼贤下士	P90
lì	历历	P18
	笠 a bamboo hat	P30
	📖斗笠(dǒu lì)	
	粒 grain	P85
lián	帘(簾) curtain	P04
	廉 curtain	P62
	📖帘子(lián zi)	
	连(連) to connect	P91
	📖持续(chí yù)	
	连绵	P36
	帘幕	P67
liàn	激滟	P31
liáng	凉州词	P48, 51
liáo	辽阔	P22
	潦倒	P93
liǎo	了 to end	P97
	📖结束(jié shù)	
liào	料 to expect	P99
	📖料想(liào xiǎng)	
liè	裂开	P21
lín	临 on the point of	P42
líng	凌 approach	P77
	铃铛	P46
	零丁	P53
	玲珑	P70
lǐng	岭 ridge	P36
liú	流 to flow	P01
	📖摘(zhāi)	
	流转	P92
liǔ	柳 willow	P02, 10
lǒng	笼罩	P66
lú	庐(廬) house	P11
	📖房屋(fáng wū)	
	炉(爐) burner	P63
lǔ	虏 to seize	P83

掳 to carry off　P87
lù　鹭 (鷺) egret　P20
　　露 dew　P21, 94
luán　鸾 (鸞)　P21
　　峦 mountain　P89
　　☞山峦 (shān luán)
luàn　乱 (亂) in a mess　P67, 88
　　☞凌乱 (líng luàn)
lún　轮 (輪) wheel　P21
　　轮廓　P21
luó　罗 (羅) ①silk　P04
　　　　②to line up　P10
　　☞罗列 (luó liè)
luò　落落　P53
　　☞稀稀落落 (xīxī luòluò)
　　落木　P93
　　☞落叶 (luò yè)
　　络纬　P95
　　落魄　P96
lǚ　侣 companion　P85
　　☞伴侣 (bàn lǚ)

M

má　麻 hemp　P12
mán　蛮 reckless　P05
　　☞莽撞 (mǎng zhuàng)
mǎn　满腔悲愤　P80
màn　漫 freely　P52
　　☞随意 (suí yì)
máng　茫茫　P99
máo　茅 (茆) thatch　P13,16,46
mào　芼 to pick　P01
　　☞摘 (zhāi)
　　茂密　P17
méi　眉 eyebrow　P08, 63
　　梅 plum tree　P56
　　眉头　P08
měi　美味　P17
mèi　寐 to be asleep　P01
　　☞睡着 (shuì zháo)
méng　盟 pledge　P100
　　蒙蒙　P15
měng　猛 suddenly　P09
mí　迷 to be lost　P75
　　迷离　P14
　　弥漫　P15
mì　觅 (覓) to seek　P65
　　☞找 (zhǎo)
　　密集　P14
mián　眠 sleep　P28, 45
　　☞睡觉 (shuì jiào)　P28
　　☞入眠 (rù mián)　P45

miàn　面 face　P04
　　☞脸 (liǎn)
　　面目　P36
miè　灭 (滅) to go out　P30, 64
míng　鸣 (鳴) to cry　P06
　　☞叫 (jiào)
　　明 bright　P46, 63
　　名 name　P81
　　☞名声 (míng shēng)
　　明艳　P17
mó　磨 to grind　P87
mǒ　抹 to apply　P31
mò　莫① don't　P04,17, 51
　　☞不要 (bú yào)
　　② let it be　P100
　　☞罢了 (bà le)
　　陌 a path　P21
　　☞小路 (xiǎo lù)
　　没 to cover　P74
　　☞埋没 (mái)
　　漠 desert　P80
　　☞沙漠 (shā mò)
　　漠漠　P14
mǔ　亩 measure word　P37
mù　暮① evening　P18,24,43,82
　　☞傍晚 (bàng wǎn)
　　② late　P67
　　☞末 (mò)
　　目 eye　P34

N

nǎ　那得 (哪得)　P37
nǎi　乃 to be　P06
　　☞是 (shì)
nán　难 (難) difficult　P03
　　南歌子　P04, 05
　　南乡子　P84
nǐ　拟 (擬) to plan　P68
　　☞计划 (jì huà)
nián　年少　P84
niàn　念 to think　P90
　　念奴娇　P83
niàng　酿 to brew　P17
niǎo　袅袅　P78
niè　啮 (嚙) to gnaw　P62
　　☞咬 (yǎo)
nòng　弄妆 to make up　P64
　　☞打扮 (dǎ bàn)

O

ǒu　藕 lotus root　P08

偶 by chance　P54

P

pái　排 to move　P13
　　☞推开 (tuī kāi)
　　徘徊　P37, 98
pán　蹒跚　P47
pàn　畔 bank　P60
　　☞边 (biān)
páng　磅礴　P89
pāo　抛 to throw　P53
péi　裴回　P71
pèi　珮 ornament　P21, 80
pí　琵琶　P51, 80
piān　偏① inclined to one side　P11
　　②contrary to expectation　P63
　　☞偏偏 (piān piān)
piāo　飘 to float　P21
　　飘零　P08
　　漂泊　P44
　　飘摇　P53
píng　萍 duckweed　P53, 74
　　☞浮萍 (fú píng)
　　屏 screen　P72
　　平明　P71
　　屏风　P73
pò　破碎　P53
pū　扑 (撲)　P72
pú　葡萄　P51
　　菩萨蛮　P64
pǔ　圃 garden　P12
　　朴 rustic　P17
pù　瀑布　P19

Q

qī　期 period of time　P59
　　☞日期 (rì qī)
　　栖 to perch　P85
　　☞栖息 (qī xī)
　　戚戚　P14
　　☞悲伤 (bēi shāng)
　　萋萋　P18
　　凄凉　P99
qí　畦 a piece of land　P13
　　旗 flag　P22
qǐ　起 to begin　P53
　　绮 (綺) beautiful　P56
qì　泣 weep　P21
　　☞哭泣 (kū qì)
　　砌　P97
　　气象　P85

	气势	P89
qiān	牵 (牽) to lead	P62, 95
	仟仟	P14
	☞茂盛 (mào shèng)	
qián	乾坤	P44
qiǎn	遣① to send	P95
	☞派 (pài)	
	②to dispel	P96
	☞发泄 (shū fǎ)	
qiāng	羌 ethic group	P48
	羌笛	P48, 49
qiāo	悄无声息	P32
qiáo	樵夫	P15
qiě	且 and	P38
	☞而且 (ér qiě)	
qiè	妾 concubine	P05, 61
qīn	亲 (親) close	P04
	☞亲密 (qīn mì)	
	衾 quilt	P63
	☞被子 (bèi zi)	
	侵 to invade	P70, 94
qín	琴 instrument	P01
	禽 bird	P76
qìn	磬 stone bell	P23
qīng	清 clear	P37,43
	☞清澈 (qīng chè)	
	轻 (輕) light	P72
	☞轻巧 (qīng qiǎo)	
	青鸟 (鳥)	P03
	清晰	P18
	蜻蜓	P32, 92
	青春	P52
	倾倒	P76
	青楼	P96
	轻盈	P96
qíng	晴 sunny	P15, 18
	情事	P04
	晴朗	P18
	情谊	P41
qióng	穷 (窮) poor	P34
	☞穷尽 (qióng jìn)	
qiū	秋千	P67
qiú	逑 spouse	P01
	☞配偶 (pèi ǒu)	
	求 to seek	P01
	☞追求 (zhuī qiú)	
qū	曲 curved	P02, 24
	☞曲折 (qū zhé)	
qú	渠 he/it	P37
qù	去① to go	P38
	☞距离 (jù lí)	
	② to leave	P80
	☞离开 (lí kāi)	
quán	泉 spring	P24
	☞泉水 (quán shuǐ)	
	泉眼	P32
què	却 (卻) ① yet	P08,59,70
	② to turn around	P52, 58
	☞回头 (huí tóu)	
	鹊 (鵲) magpie	P16
	☞喜鹊 (xǐ què)	
	雀 sparrow	P86
	阙 (闕) palace	P89
	R	
rán	燃烧 to burn	P03
rào	绕 (繞) to circle	P13
	☞围绕 (wéi rào)	
rén	人间 (間)	P83
rèn	仞 measure word	P48
rì	日夕	P11
	日角	P82
róu	柔 soft	P32
	☞柔和 (róu hé)	
rú	儒 Confucianism	P44
	襦 jacket	P64
	☞短袄 (duǎn ǎo)	
	如许	P37
rù	入 to enter	P15
	☞接近 (jiē jìn)	
ruò	弱 weak	P03
	若 if	P17
	☞如果 (rú guǒ)	
	若隐若现	P22
	S	
sà	飒飒	P62
sāi	腮 check	P64
sài	塞 frontier	P50
sān	三春	P42
sāng	桑 mulberry	P10
sāo	搔 to scratch	P91
	☞挠 (náo)	
sè	瑟 instrument	P01, 75
shā	沙场	P51
shān	山 mountain	P55
	山脉	P80
	山坡羊	P89
shǎng	赏 to enjoy	P92
	☞欣赏 (xīn shǎng).	
	赏识	P85
shào	少 young	P54,62
	☞年轻 (nián qīng)	
	绍缭	P06
shè	社	P16, 17
	☞土地庙 (tǔ dì miào)	
	舍 house	P39, 58
shēn	伸展	P12
	身世	P53
shén	神 spirit	P83
	神州	P84
shèn	甚 what	P04
	☞什么 (shénme)	
shēng	生to give birth to	P38
	☞活生生 (huó shēng shēng)	
	生烟mist	P14
	☞烟气 (yān qì)	
	生发 to arise	P19
shèng	胜 (勝) victory	P91
shī	失 mistake	P81
	☞失策 (shī cè)	
shí	时 (時) ① chance	P03
	☞时机 (shí jì)	
	② often	P27
	☞不时 (bù shí)	
	拾 to pick up	P85
shǐ	始 not until	P03
shì	适 (適) to adapt to	P10
	☞适应 (shì yìng)	
shōu	收 to collect	P52
	☞收复 (shōu fù)	
shǒu	守 to keep	P60
shū	淑 fair	P01
	殊 different	P15
	☞悬殊 (xuán shū)	
	梳 to comb	P64, 99
	书 (書) letter	P65,91,99
	☞书信 (shū xìn)	
	疏 sparse	P74, 76
	☞稀疏 (xī shū)	
	淑女	P01
	舒展	P08
	书迹	P65
	书客	P95
shǔ	黍 brown rice	P12
shuāi	衰 to decline	P54
	衰败	P86
shuāng	霜 frost	P45,58,76
	双调	P09
shuǐ	水调歌	P09
	水晶	P70
shuò	朔 north	P80
	☞北方 (běi fāng)	
sī	思 particle	P01
	丝 (絲) silk	P03,62
	飔 (颸)	P06
	思量	P99

sōng 松柏 P05
sōu 艘 measure word P30
sū 苏(蘇) to revive P44
　　酥 soft P100
　　☞柔软(róu ruǎn)
sú 俗 mundane P10
　　☞世俗(shì sú)
sù 宿 to lodge P15,43,94
　　素 white P60, 95
　　肃肃 P06
　　诉说 P16
suō 蓑 P30
suǒ 所 particle P06
　　锁(鎖)①lock P62
　　　②to lock up P66,82,87,88
　　索 large rope P100
　　☞离群索居(lí qún suǒ jū)

T

tà 踏 to stamp P04, 41
　　闼(闥) door P13
　　☞门(mén)
tái 苔 moss P13, 25
　　☞青苔(qīng tái)
tán 潭 deep pool P23, 24
　　檀板 P76
tàn 探看 P03
　　☞查看(chá kàn)
táng 堂 the hall P10, 86
　　塘 pool P37,46,62
　　☞池塘(chí táng)
tāo 涛 large wave P83, 89
　　☞波涛(bō tāo)
táo 桃 peach P10
　　淘 to weed out P83
téng 藤 vine P47
tī 梯 steps P02
　　☞台阶(tái jiē)
tí 题(題) to inscribe P35
tì 涕 tears P52
　　☞眼泪(yǎn lèi)
tiān 天都 P15
　　天阶(階) P72
　　天涯 P47,82
　　天淨沙 P33
tiě 铁(鐵) iron P87
tiè 帖 to paste P64
　　☞贴(tiē)
tíng 庭 front yard P10, 94
　　☞庭院(tíng yuàn)
tóng 桐 parasol tree. P95

同心 P04
tōu 偷眼 P76
　　☞偷看(tōu kàn)
tóu 投 to join P15
　　☞投宿(tóu sù)
tuán 团 a ball P21
　　团扇 P71
tūn 吞 to swallow P81
　　☞吞并(tūn bìng)
　　吞吞吐吐 P04
tún 豚 pig P17
tuō 托 to entrust P100
　　托(託)to entrust P75
　　☞托付(tuō fù)

W

wā 蛙 frog P16
　　☞青蛙(qīng wā)
wà 袜 sock P70
wǎn 绾 to tie P04
　　☞系(jì)
　　晚 late P38
wáng 亡 death P84,89
　　☞灭亡(miè wáng)
wǎng 惘然 P75
　　往事 P97
wēi 危 dangerous P24
　　☞陡(dǒu)
　　微 small P76
　　逶迤 P85
wéi 唯 only P29, 40
　　☞只 (zhǐ)
　　惟 only P99
　　☞只 (zhǐ)
　　违(違) to violate P92
　　☞违背(wéi bèi)
wèi 遗 to offer P06
　　☞赠送(zèng sòng)
　　未 not yet P56
　　☞没有(méi yǒu)
　　渭城曲 P39
wén 闻道 P79
　　☞听说(tīng shuō)
wèn 问 to ask P06
　　☞问候(wèn hòu)
wēng 翁 an old man P30
wò 卧 to lie P51
　　☞躺 (tǎng)
　　卧内 P94
　　☞卧室(wò shì)
wū 乌(烏) crow P45

乌夜啼 P66
wú 无力 P03
　　无题 P03, 62
　　无时 P17
　　☞随时(suí shí)
　　无那 P49
　　☞无奈(wú nài)
　　无端 P58,75
　　☞无缘无故(wú yuán wú gù)
　　梧桐 P63,66,85
　　无可奈何 P98
wǔ 武陵春 P68
wù 寤 to wake up P01
　　☞睡醒(shuì xǐng)
　　勿 don't P06, 38
　　误(誤) mistake P10
　　☞错误(cuò wù)

X

xī 昔 the past P18,60,85
　　惜 to cherish P32
　　☞爱惜(ài xī)
　　溪 brook P16
　　☞小溪(xiǎo xī)
　　夕 evening P69
　　☞傍晚(bàng wǎn)
　　息 to stop P69
　　☞停(tíng)
　　稀 few P92, 94
　　☞稀少(xī shǎo)
　　嬉戏 P14
　　西江月 P16
　　夕阳 P25
xì 细雨 P62
　　☞小雨(xiǎo yǔ)
xiá 霞 rosy cloud P33, 82
　　狎 P76
xiān 纤细 P60
　　纤纤 P60
　　仙 immortal P85
xián 闲(閒)①quiet P27
　　☞安静(ān jìng)
　　　②leisurely P29
　　☞悠闲(yōu xián)
　　弦 string P75
　　闲愁 P08
　　贤明 P90
xiǎn 险固 P88
xiàn 线(線) thread P42
xiāng 相与 P11
　　☞结伴(jié bàn)

	乡关	P18
	香炉	P19
	香料	P62
	相问	P85
xiàng	巷 alley	P10
	向往	P62
xiāo	箫(簫) floot	P17
	销(銷) to melt	P87
	绡(綃) silk fabric	P100
	消除	P08
	萧瑟	P47
	萧萧	P93
xiǎo	晓(曉) dawn	P03,28,73
	☞拂晓 (fú xiǎo)	75,79
	小荷	P32
	小山	P64
xiào	啸(嘯) to whistle	P26, 93
	☞呼啸 (hū xiào)	
	笑 to laugh	P51
	☞嘲笑 (cháo xiào)	
xié	携(攜) to take	P14
xiè	榭 pavilion	P14
	泻(瀉) to pour	P21
xīn	新 new	P93
	欣赏	P12
xīng	兴(興) ①to rise	P84, 89
	☞兴盛 (xīng shèng)	
	②mediation	P85
xǐng	省 to be aware	P80
xìng	荇菜	P01
xióng	雄伟	P15
xiū	休 to stop	P07,68,84
	☞停止 (tíng zhǐ)	
xiù	绣(繡)	P64
xū	须臾	P06
	☞很快 (hěn kuài)	
	墟里	P10
	☞村落 (cūn luò)	
xǔ	许(許) ①to allow	P17
	☞允许 (yǔn xǔ)	
	② somewhat	P67
xù	絮 bits of fluff	P53
	☞柳絮 (liǔ xù)	
	绪(緒)	P100
xuān	喧 noisy	P11
	☞喧闹 (xuān nào)	
	轩(軒) window	P12, P99
	暄 warm	P76
	☞温暖 (wēn nuǎn)	
xuě	雪 snow	P64
xún	寻常	P86, P92

	Y	
yā	鸦(鴉) crow	P33
yá	涯 shore	P38, 47
yà	轧(軋) to roll over	P21
yān	烟(煙) smoke	P10
	烟尘	P21
	烟花	P40
yán	檐(簷) eaves	P10, 13
	☞屋檐 (wū yán)	
	颜(顔) face	P71, 97
	☞容颜 (róng yán)	
	妍 beautiful	P76
	☞美丽 (měi lì)	
yǎn	掩 to cover	P67
	☞关 (guān)	
yàn	厌(厭) to satisfy	P29
	☞满足 (mǎn zú)	
	雁 wilde goose	P46
	燕 swallow	P86
	雁字	P08
yáng	扬(揚) to throw up	P06
	杨柳	P39,48,67
	杨柳枝	P02
yāo	邀 to invite	P12
	☞邀请 (yāo qǐng)	
yáo	遥 distant	P19,55,77,83
	☞遥远 (yáo yuǎn)	
yǎo	窈窕	P01
yě	冶 to smelt	P67
yè	咽 to choke	P24
	☞哽咽 (gěng yè)	
	谒(謁) to visit	P65
	☞拜见 (bài jiàn)	
	业(業) enterprise	P88
	☞基业 (jī yè)	
	夜光杯	P51
	谒金门	P65
yī	依 to rely on	P34
	☞依傍 (yī bàng)	P34
	☞依恋 (yī liàn)	P38
	伊 he	P65
	☞他 (tā)	
	依依	P10
	依稀	P10
	一自	P09
	☞自从 (zì cóng)	
	一剪梅	P08
	一般	P66
yí	疑 to doubt	P17,19,57
	☞怀疑 (huái yí)	
	宜 suitable	P31, 82
	☞适合 (shì hé)	

	遗憾	P81
yǐ	倚 to lean on	P07
	☞靠 (kào)	
yì	亦 also	P03
	☞也 (yě)	
	忆(憶) to recall	P04, 55
	☞思念 (sī niàn)	
	浥 to moisten	P39
	☞湿润 (shī rùn)	
	驿 post	P46
	☞驿站 (yì zhàn)	
	异(異) different	P55
	悒 sorrowful	P100
yīn	阴(陰) ① shaded	P15
	② north of a hill	P85
	音 sound	P54
	☞口音 (kǒu yīn)	
	殷勤	P03
yín	吟 to chant	P03,42,76, 85
	☞吟唱 (yín chàng)	
	银河	P19
yǐn	饮(飲) to drink	P31
yìn	隐(隱) to lean	P04
	☞靠 (kào)	
	荫(蔭) to shade	P10
	☞遮蔽 (zhē bì)	
yīng	英 hero	P83
	☞英俊 (yīng jùn)	
	莺(鶯) oriole	P22
	鹦鹉	P85
yíng	萤(螢) firefly	P69
	☞萤火虫 (yíng huǒ chóng)	
	赢 to win	P96
	迎合	P10
	盈盈	P60
yǐng	影 reflection	P23
	☞倒影 (dào yǐng)	
yìng	映 to reflect	P22,64,74
	☞映衬 (yìng chèn)	
yǒng	永 eternal	P44
	牖 window	P60
	☞窗户 (chuāng hu)	
	咏怀	P80
yōu	悠 longing for	P01
	幽 remote	P23,26,99
	☞幽深 (yōu shēn)	
	悠悠	P07,18,84,90
	悠然	P11
	幽会	P06
	优雅	P60
	优美	P96
	咏怀	P80
yóu	犹(猶) still	P44,71,97

	游子	P38, 42
	游荡	P60
yǒu	友 to befriend	P01
	📖亲近 (qīn jìn)	
	有所思	P06
yú	榆 elm	P10
	隅 border	P15, 94
	渔 fishing	P45
	余晖	P25
	虞美人	P97
yǔ	羽 feather	P83
	📖羽毛(yǔ máo)	
yù	郁郁	P60
	玉玺	P82
	玉阶怨	P69, 70
yuān	渊(淵) deep pool	P10
yuán	猿 ape	P35,93
	📖猿猴 (yuán hóu)	
	缘 because	P36,82
	源头	P37
	元来 (原来)	P88
yuàn	掾 an official	P62
yuè	悦 to please	P23
	📖取悦 (qǔ yuè)	
	越调	P33,47
yún	云母 mica	P73
yùn	韵(韻) rhythm	P10
	📖个性 (gè xìng)	
	Z	
zá	杂(雜)	P06
zāi	哉 particle	P01
	栽 to plant	P13
	📖种 (zhòng)	
zǎi	载(載) year	P18,80
zài	载(載) to carry	P68,96
zān	簪 hairpin	P06,91
zàn	暂(暫) shortly	P71
	📖暂且 (zàn qiě)	
zāo	遭逢	P53
zé	舴艋	P68
zhà	乍	P94
zhài	债 (債) debt	P92
zhǎn	辗转	P01
zhàn	占 to occupy	P76
zhǎng	涨(漲) to rise	P59
	📖拐杖 (guǎn zhàng)	
zhāo	朝 early morning	P35,39
	📖早晨 (zǎo chén)	
	招待	P17
zhào	照耀	P23
zhè	鹧鸪	P64
zhēn	斟 to pour	P51
zhěn	枕 headrest	P62
zhēng	征(徵) ① jouney	P46
	📖远行 (yuǎn xíng)	
	②expedation	P50,51
	争(爭) to contend	P63
zhī	之① particle	P01
	📖的(de)	
	②pron.	P01
	📖她 (tā)	
	枝 branches	P16
zhǐ	指 finger	P04
	📖手指 (shǒu zhǐ)	
	枳	P46
	指挥	P84
zhì	陟 to ascend	P14
	📖登(dēng)	
	制 to control	P24
	📖控制 (kòng zhì)	
	智慧	P44
zhōng	钟 (鐘) bell	P01
	终 whole	P82
zhǒng	冢 grand	P80
	📖坟墓(fén mù)	
zhōu	洲 an islet in river	P01
	周星	P53
zhǒu	帚 broom	P71
zhū	珠 pearl	P04
	朱 red	P05,86
	茱萸	P55
zhú	竹 bamboo	P23
	烛 candle	P59
	竹帛	P88
zhǔ	拄 to lean	P17
	渚 islet	P43, 93
zhù	住 to stop	P35, 68
	📖停止 (tíng zhǐ)	
	著 marked	P56
	柱 pillar	P75
	蛀 to eat	P95
zhuǎn	转 to turn	P16,78
	📖转弯 (zhuǎn wān)	
zhuàn	转(轉) to revolve	P81
zhuāng	妆 (妝) makeup	P04,60,99
	装饰	P62
zhuàng	壮 strong	P44
	📖壮志 (zhuàng zhì)	
	状 shape	P62
	壮士	P95
zhuī	追忆	P75
zhuō	拙 awkward	P10
	📖朴拙 (pǔ zhuō)	
	卓著	P81
zhuó	啄 to peck	P85
	浊(濁) muddy	P93
zī	姿 posture	P83
	滋味	P66
zǐ	子 child	P52
	📖孩子 (háizi)	
	紫 purple	P19
zōng	踪 track	P30
	📖踪迹 (zōng jì)	
zòng	纵(縱) to indulge	P52
	📖纵情 (zòng qíng)	
	纵使	P99
zǒu	走马	P21
zǔ	阻 to hinder	P38
	📖艰险 (jiān xiǎn)	
	祖龙	P88
zuì	醉 drunk	P51, 92
zūn	樽 goblet of wine	P76, 83
	📖酒杯(jiǔ bēi)	
zuò	坐断	P84
	📖占据(zhàn jù)	

练习答案

Answer Key to Unit Exercises

Unit 1 一 B. 1.吟唱 2.亲近 3.担忧 4.曲折 5.殷勤 6.思念 7.时机 8.痕迹
二 1. b. [a. 恨 P07 note10; c. 狠(hěn) adj. relentless] 　2. a. [b. 情(qíng) n. love; c. 晴 P15 note 11]
3. a. [b. 绕 P13 note 11; c. 饶(ráo) v. to forgive] 　4. a. [b. 琛(chēn) n. treasure; c. 深(shēn) adj. deep]
5. b. [a. 重 P17 note 6; c. 捶(chuí) v. to pound] 　6. c. [a. 载 P18 note 5; b. 栽 P13 note 8]

Unit 2 一 B. 1.莽撞 2.归来 3.问候 4.团聚 5.停止 6.缠绕 7.毁坏 8.断绝 9.赠送 10.办法
二 1. c. [a. 漂(piāo) v. to float; b. 瓢(piáo) n. dipper] 　2. a. [b. 份(fèn) n. share; c. 吩(fēn) v. to tell]
3. b. [a. 樵 P15 note 16; c. 焦(jiāo) adj. burnt] 　4. b. [a. 状 P62 note 28; c. 壮 P44 note 11]
5. b. [a. 清 P37 note 9; c. 请(qǐng) v. to invite] 　6. c. [a. 伯(bó) n. uncle; b. 泊 P20 note 7]
7. a. [b. 绵 P36 note 10; c. 棉(mián) n. cotton] 　8. b. [a. 杨 P39 note 8; c. 汤(tāng) n. soup]

Unit 3 一 B. 1.握住 2.拜访 3.结伴 4.辨析 5.建 6.世俗 7.准备 8.携带
二 1. c. [a. 镜(jìng) n. mirror; b. 竟(jìng) v. to finish] 　2. a. [b. 辩(biàn) v. to argue; c. 辫(biàn) n. braid]
3. a. [b. 缘 P36 note 9; c. 录(lù) v. to record] 　4. b. [a. 廷(tíng) n. court; c. 挺(tǐng) v. to erect]
5. c. [a. 饶(ráo) v. to forgive; b. 晓 P03 note 15] 　6. b. [a. 侍(shì) to serve; b. 寺(sì) n. temple]
7. b. [a. 载 P18 note 5; c. 哉 P01 note 20] 　8. a. [b. 圆(yuán) n. circle; c. 因(yīn) n. reason]

Unit 4 一 B. 1.随时 2.悲伤 3.允许 4.丰收 5.投宿 6.重叠 7.浑浊 8.悬殊
二 1. c. [a. 暖(nuǎn) adj. warm; b. 缓 P38 note 12] 　2. a. [b. 锋(fēng) n. sharp point; c. 缝 P42 note 7]
3. b. [a. 萧 P93 note 8; c. 肃(sù) adj. solemn] 　4. b. [a. 偶 P54 note 1; c. 遇(yù) v. to meet]
5. a. [b. 蜡 P03 note 12; b. 借(jiè) v. to borrow] 　6. c. [a. 综(zōng) v. to sum up; b. 踪 P30 note 4]
7. c., a. [b. 而(ér) conj. and] 　8. b. [a. 吩(fēn) v. to tell; c. 份(fèn) n. share]

Unit 5 一 B. 1.更新 2.停泊 3.历历 4.映衬 5.遥远 6.轧 7.泻 8.载
二 1. a. [b. 睛(jīng) n. eye; c. 清 P37 note 9] 　2. c. [a. 泱(yāng) adj. vast b. 央(yāng) v. to entreat]
3. b. [a. 伯(bó) n. uncle; c. 柏 P05 note 8] 　4. b. [a. 领(lǐng) v. to lead; c. 冷(lěng) adj. cold]
5. a. [b. 栽 P13 note 8; c. 哉 P01 note 20] 　6. c. [a. 佰(bǎi) n. hundred; b. 百(bǎi) n. hundred]
7. a. [b. 璧(bì) n. jade; c. 碧 P40 note 10] 　8. c. [a. 摇 P53 note 13; b. 谣(yáo) n. ballad]

Unit 6 一 B. 1.呼啸 2.山峰 3.控制 4.不时 5.安静 6.倒影 7.哽咽
二 1. b. [a. 净(jìng) adj. clean; c. 晴 P15 note 11] 　2. b. [a. 间 P74 note 5; c. 闭(bì) v. to close]
3. a. [b. 人(rén) n. person; c. 八(bā) n. eight] 　4. c. [a. 仲(zhòng) second; c. 种 P13 note 8]
5. a. [b. 凉(liáng) adj. cool; c. 晾(liàng) v. to air] 　6. b. [a. 税(shuì) n. tax; c. 说 P38 note 22]
7. b. [a. 赖(lài) v. to rely; c. 懒 P64 note 10] 　8. a. [b. 蝉 P16 note 6; b. 单(dān) adj. single]

Unit 7 一 B. 1.孤单 2.爱惜 3.悠闲 4.察觉 5.踪迹 6.柔和 7.适合 8.满足
二 1. b. [a. 昔 P18 note 3; c. 蜡 P03 note 12] 　2. b. [a. 鸭 P46 note 13; c. 鸿 P33 note 7]
3. a. [b. 晴 P15 note 11; c. 睛(jīng) n. eye] 　4. a. [b. 惊 P14 note 4; c. 综(zōng) v. to sum up]
5. c. [a. 朦(méng) adj. dim; b. 濛(méng) adj. misty] 　6. a. [b. 维(wéi) v. to keep; c. 惟 P99 note 17]
7. a. [b. 脓(nóng) n. pus; c. 侬(nóng) pron. I] 　8. c. [a. 狐(hú) n. fox; b. 瓜(guā) n. gourd]

Unit 8 一 B. 1.穷尽 2.停止 3.面目 4.告别 5.依傍 6.徘徊
二 1. b. [a. 原(yuán) adj. original; c. 愿(yuàn) n. will] 　2. a. [b. 搂(lǒu) v. to hug; c. 缕(lǚ) n. thread]
3. a. [b. 掾 P62 note 17; c. 绿(lǜ) n. green] 　4. b. [a. 监(jiān) v. to supervise; c. 临 P42 note 6]
5. c. [a. 采 P01 note 23; b. 踩(cǎi) v. to trample] 　6. b. [a. 纸(zhǐ) n. paper; c. 抵 P91 note 7]
7. b. [a. 凌 P77 note 2; c. 棱(léng) n. edge] 　8. c. [a. 经 P53 note 5; b. 径 P23 note 6]

Unit 9 一 B. 1.报答 2.飘浮 3.慈祥 4.尘土 5.艰险 6.距离 7.碧蓝 8.依恋
二 1. b. [a. 扬 P06 note 14; c. 汤(tāng) n. soup] 　2. a. [b. 逢 P53 note 3; c. 篷(péng) n. covering]
3. a. [b. 挑(tiāo) v. to select; c. 佻(tiāo) adj. giddy] 　4. b. [a. 暖(nuǎn) adj. warm; c. 暧 P10 note 22]
5. b. [a. 璧 P13 note 2; c. 璧(bì) n. jade] 　6. a. [a. 辉(huī) n. shine; b. 挥 P84 note 21]

Unit 10 一 B. 1.迂腐 2.足迹 3.空旷 4.枯萎
二 1. a. [b. 优 P60 note 15; c. 忧 P03 note 17] 　2. c. [a. 矿(kuàng) n. ore; b. 广(guǎng) adj. wide]
3. c. [a. 铎 P46 note 4; c. 译(yì) v. to translate] 　4. b. [a. 场 P12 note 10; c. 杨 P39 note 8]
5. c. [a. 民(mín) n. people; b. 抿(mǐn) v. to furl] 　6. a. [b. 霞 P33 note 5; c. 霖(lín) n. rain]
7. b. [a. 马(mǎ) n. horse; c. 鸟(niǎo) n. bird] 　8. c. [a. 濡(rú) v to moisten; b. 需(xū) n. need]

Unit 11　一　B. 1. 破碎　2. 身世　3. 嘲笑　4. 随意　5. 立即　6. 纵情　7. 无奈　8. 飘摇　9. 遭逢　10. 惶恐

二　1. b. [a. 峰 P24 note 4; c. 逢 P53 note 3]　　　2. c. [a. 侠(*xiá*) adj. chivalrous; b. 狭(*xiá*) adj. narrow]

3. c. [a. 慢(*màn*) adj slow; b. 谩(*màn*) adj. rude]　4. b. [a. 从(*cóng*) prep. from; c. 丛(*cóng*) n. grove]

5. a. [b. 昨(*zuó*) n. yesterday; c. 做(*zuò*) v. to do]　6. b. [a. 叫(*jiào*) v. to cry; c. 孝(*xiào*) adj. filial]

7. b. [a. 杨 P39 note 8; c. 扬 P06 note 14]　　　　8. a. [b. 梯 P02 note 5; c. 剃(*tì*) v. to shave]

Unit 12　一　B.　1. 逢　2. 涨　3. 遍　4. 插　5. 举　6. 剪　7. 口音　8. 偶然

二　1. c. [a. 煎(*jiān*) v. to fry; b. 前(*qián*) n. front]　2. c. [a. 欺(*qī*) v. to cheat; b. 其(*qí*) pron. he/she]

3. c. [a. 度 P48 note 9; b. 镀(*dù*) n. plating]　4. a. [b. 者(*zhě*) c. 着(zhe)]

5. a. [b. 他(*tā*) pron. he; c. 弛(*chí*) v. to relax]　6. b. [a. 培(*péi*) v. to train; c. 陪(*péi*) v. to accompany]

7. b. [a. 倚 P07 note 14; c. 椅(*yǐ*) n. chair]　　8. a. [b. 编 P95 note 8; c. 匾(*biǎn*) n. an inscribed board]

Unit 13　一　B. 1. 郁郁　2. 贴　3. 惊醒　4. 滴　5. 窥视　6. 牵　7. 打扮　8. 在乎　9. 偏偏　10. 争

二　1. c. [a. 及(*jí*) v. to reach; b. 极 P69 note 8]　2. a. [b. 赖(*lài*) v. to rely; c. 籁 P23 note 12]

3. b. [a. 较(*jiào*) v. to compare; c. 胶(*jiāo*) n. glue]　4. b. [a. 贴 P64 note 18; c. 粘(*zhān*)v. to paste]

5. b. [a. 灭 P64 note 6; c. 火(*huǒ*) n. fire]　　6. c. [a. 疏 P74 note 6; b. 流 P01 note 12]

7. a. [b. 摘 P01 note 12; c. 嘀(*dí*) v. to whisper]　8. a. [a. 竟(*jìng*) v. to finish; b. 境 P11 note 4]

Unit 14　一　B.　1. 计划　2. 凌乱　3. 锁　4. 理　5. 堆　6. 载　7. 徒劳

二　1. b. [a. 觉 P28 note 4; c. 览(*lǎn*) v. to view]　2. b. [a. 购(*gòu*) v. to buy; c. 构(*gòu*) v. to form]

3. c. [a. 幕 P67 note 6; c. 墓 P80 note 13]　4. a. [b. 似(*sì*) adj. similar; c. 以(*yǐ*) v. to use]

5. b. [a. 治(*zhì*) v. to rule; c. 台(*tái*) n. stage]　6. c. [a. 卷 P52 note 13; b. 圈(*quān*) n. circle]

7. b. [a. 体(*tǐ*) n. body; c. 沐(*mù*) v. to wash]　8. c. [a. 谁(*shuí*) who; b. 推 P13 note 12]

Unit 15　一　B.　1. 容颜　2. 暂且　3. 沉　4. 后悔　5. 奉　6. 轻巧　7. 玲珑　8. 极

二　1. a. [b. 浸 P70 note 3; c. 寝(*qǐn*) n. sleep]　2. b. [a. 浙(*zhè*) Zhejiang province; c. 斩(*zhǎn*) v. to cut]

3. c. [a. 愉(*yú*) adj. happy; b. 输(*shū*) adj. lost]　4. a. [a. 玲 P70 note 7; c. 拎(*līn*) v. to carry]

5. b. [a. 春(*chūn*) n. spring; c. 捧(*pěng*) v. to hold]　6. a. [b. 朴 P10 note12; c. 仆(*pú*) n. servant]

Unit 16　一　B. 1. 埋没　2. 惘然　3. 稀疏　4. 间隔　5. 托付　6. 浮动

二　1. b. [a. 托 P100 note 15; c. 拖(*tuō*) v. to pull]　2. b. [a. 喧 P11note 5; c. 渲(*xuàn*) v. to wash with color]

3. c. [a. 暧 P10 note 22; b. 缓 P38 note 12]　4. c. [a. 析 P11 note 13; c. 折 P02 note 3]

5. a. [b. 砖(*zhuān*) n. brick; c. 传 P52 note 6]　6. c. [a. 陵(*líng*) n.hill; b. 棱(*léng*) n. edge]

Unit 17　一　B. 1. 焕发　2. 失策　3. 吞并　4. 占据　5. 波涛　6. 灭亡　7. 功绩　8. 兴盛　9. 腐烂　10. 杰出

二　1. b. [a. 轮 P21 note 4; c. 论(*lùn*) v. to discuss]　2. c. [a. 资(*zī*) n. expense; b. 咨(*zī*) v. to consult]

3. a. [b. 赶(*gǎn*) v. to catch; c. 赳(*jiū*) adj. valiant]　4. b. [a. 摸(*mō*) v. to feel; c. 模(*mó*) n. model]

5. a. [a. 虑 P38 note 17; c. 虎(*hǔ*) n. tiger]　6. b. [a. 掏(*tāo*) v. to pull out; c. 陶(*táo*) n. pottery]

7. c. [a. 朗 P18 note 15; b. 浪(*làng*) n. wave]　8. a. [b. 益(*yì*) n. benefit; c. 盎(*àng*) adj. full]

Unit 18　一　B.　1. 聚集　2. 磨　3. 栖息　4. 啄　5. 拾　6. 经过　7. 干预　8. 寻常

二　1. b. [a. 蹲 P89 note 10; c. 寿(*shòu*) n. age]　2. c. [a. 抗(*kàng*) v. to resist; b. 杭(*háng*) surname]

3. b. [a. 恰(*qià*) adv. just; c. 抬(*tái*) v. to lift]　4. a. [b. 稍(*shāo*) adv. slightly; c. 悄 P32 note 9]

5. a. [b. 摩(*mó*) v. to rub; c. 糜(*mí*) adj. rotten]　6. c. [a. 晒(*shài*) v. to bask; b. 洒(*sǎ*) v. to sprinkle]

Unit 19　一　B.　1. 典当　2. 违背　3. 稀少　4. 潦倒　5. 持续　6. 悲伤

二　1. c. [a. 阻 P38 note 5; b. 祖(*zǔ*) n. ancestor]　2 c. [a. 沧(*cāng*) adj. dark blue; c. 苍 P75 note 14]

3. b. [a. 缭 P06 note 9; b. 撩(*liáo*) v. to tease]　4. b. [a. 捐 P38 note 20; c. 绢(*juàn*) n. thin silk]

5. a. [a. 哀 P93 note 5; c. 衷(*zhōng*) n. heart]　6. a. [b. 低(*dī*) adj. low; c. 纸(*zhǐ*) n. paper]

Unit 20　一　B.　1. 凄凉　2. 思量　3. 不堪　4. 结束　5. 料想　6. 柔软　7. 茫茫　8. 可恶

二　1. b. [a. 彻(*chè*) adj. thorough; c. 切(*qiè*) v.to cut]　2. a. [b. 风(*fēng*) n. wind; c. 岗(*gǎng*) n. mound]

3. c. [a. 维(*wéi*) v. to keep; b. 唯 P29 note 7]　4. b. [a. 拖(*tuō*) v. to pull; c. 讬 P75 note 12]

5. a. [b. 魂 P76 note 14; b. 愧(*kuì*) adj. ashamed]　6. a. [b. 赌(*dǔ*) v. to gamble; c. 睹(*dǔ*) v. to see]